£12-99

# Essential Social Psychology

4

First published in Great Britain 1996 by
Edward Arnold, a division of Hodder Headline PLC,
338 Euston Road, London NW1 3BH

Distributed in the USA by
Routledge, Chapman and Hall, Inc.
29 West 35th Street, New York, NY 10001

*British Library Cataloguing in Publication Data*
Pennington, Donald C.
Essential social psychology
1. Social psychology
I. Title
302    HM251

ISBN 0 7131 6442 5

9  10  11  12  13    94  95  96  97  98

Typeset in 10/11 Times Compugraphic by
Colset Private Ltd, Singapore
Printed and bound in Great Britain by Page Bros, Norwich

# Essential Social Psychology

**Donald C. Pennington**
Principal Lecturer and Section Leader, Psychology, Sunderland Polytechnic

Edward Arnold
A member of the Hodder Headline Group
LONDON   NEW YORK   MELBOURNE   AUCKLAND

# Contents

Preface                                                                    ix
Acknowledgements                                                            x

**1 Introduction**                                                          1
Social psychology and everyday life
The scope of social psychology
Assumptions about human behaviour
Social psychology as science
Methods of investigation
The social psychology of experiments
Ethical considerations
Organization of this book
Summary
Suggestions for further reading

**2 Socialization I: The early years**                                     18
Socialization – themes and perspectives
Conceptions of childhood
Biological underpinnings
Cultural and sub-cultural influences
The first relationship
Maternal deprivation
Early years and later life
Summary
Suggestions for further reading

**3 Socialization II: A life-long process**                                38
Two themes: Social relationships and morality
Erikson's theory of social development
Kohlberg's theory of moral development
Moral behaviour
Summary
Suggestions for further reading

**4 Attitudes and attitude change**                                        59
The significance of attitudes
What are attitudes?
Measuring attitudes
Attitude organization and change
Other approaches to attitude change
Attitudes and behaviour
Summary
Suggestions for further reading

**5 Prejudice and conflict**                                          81
The scope of the problem
Three social psychological approaches
The individual approach
The interpersonal approach
The intergroup approach
Cultural, institutional and economic considerations
Reducing prejudice and conflict
Summary
Suggestions for further reading

**6 Social cognition I: Perception of ourselves and others**         103
Introduction
Fundamentals of perception
Forming impressions of others
Self-perception
Perceptual processes
Accuracy in person perception
Summary
Suggestions for further reading

**7 Social cognition II: The attribution approach**                  127
Introduction
Fundamental concepts
Theories of attribution
Attributional biases
Personality differences
Attributions in a social context
Application – depression
Summary
Suggestions for further reading

**8 Interpersonal attraction**                                       147
Introduction
Need for other people
Formation of relationships
Development of relationships
Intimate relationships
Summary
Suggestions for further reading

**9 Non-verbal communication and interpersonal behaviour**           170
Introduction
Significance in animals
Cross-cultural consistencies
Channels of non-verbal communication
Methodological issues
Visual interaction
Non-verbal behaviour and conversation
Social skills
Summary
Suggestions for further reading

**10 Social influence** 196
Introduction
Compliance
Conformity
Group polarization
Obedience to authority
The influence of roles
Is there a conforming personality?
Minority influence
Summary
Suggestions for further reading

**11 Groups and group performance** 220
Introduction
Individuals and groups
Group composition
Group structure and influence
Analysing group processes
Leadership
Decision making
Summary
Suggestions for further reading

References 247
Subject index 265
Author index

For:
Kyla
Tom
Jed
Toby

# Preface

In this book I have attempted to provide a representative introduction to the empirical discipline of social psychology. The areas covered in each chapter are largely traditional ones but I have also provided accounts of what I regard as important new developments. In any book of this nature one is aware of omissions; I could not hope to cover all aspects of social psychology in this short text. Already I have half in mind what I would like to include should this text be revised.

I hope this book appeals to all students of social psychology encountering the discipline for the first time; I particularly hope it will prove useful to 'O' and 'A' level students, those taking social psychology outside their main discipline of study and the interested layperson.

In writing this book I have learned much about social psychology myself. More importantly this book would not have been possible without the support and encouragement of numerous colleagues and friends. In particular I would like to thank Derek Rutter, Raymond Cochrane and numerous undergraduate students for commenting on early drafts of the chapters. It is with pleasure I thank Isabel Ford for continual support and encouragement when motivation flagged and doubt increased. My thanks also to Geraldine Godwin for doing such an efficient job of typing the book, and Wendy Munday for producing such clear drawings even when my versions were less than clear.

Donald C. Pennington

# Acknowledgements

The author and publisher would like to thank the following for their permission to reproduce the following figures. Full citation is given in the bibliography.

Academic Press (figs. 8.1 and 10.5); American Institute of Physics (fig. 11.2); American Psychological Association (figs. 3.1, 3.3, 4.4, 4.7, 6.7, 7.2, 8.3); Cambridge University Press (fig. 4.9); Gordon Coster (fig. 2.2); P. Ekman and W. Friesen (fig. 6.8); W.H. Freeman and Company (figs. 10.1, 10.2); Gower Publishing Company Limited (figs. 4.2, 4.3); Holt, Rinehart & Winston (figs. 8.5, 11.1); S. Karger AG (fig. 3.2); Macmillan Publishing Company (fig. 11.6); Methuen & Co. (fig. 9.2); Mouton de Gruyter (figs. 9.6, 9.7); North-Holland Publishing Company (fig. 9.5); George Weidenfeld & Nicolson Ltd (fig. 9.3); John Wiley & Sons Ltd (figs. 7.1, 9.8); Yale University Press (fig. 4.6).

# 1

# Introduction

1.1    Social psychology and everyday life
1.2    The scope of social psychology
1.3    Assumptions about human behaviour
1.4    Social psychology as science
       *1.4.1 Scientific enquiry    1.4.2 Theory and research in social psychology*
1.5    Methods of investigation
       *1.5.1 Correlational research    1.5.2 The laboratory experiment*
       *1.5.3 Field research    1.5.4 Validity of experiments*
1.6    The social psychology of experiments
1.7    Ethical considerations
1.8    Organization of this book
1.9    Summary
1 10   Suggestions for further reading

## 1.1  Social psychology and everyday life

Our experience and enjoyment of life is strongly affected and determined by other people: how we think about ourselves and how others think about us often determines how we behave. Specific social situations also influence our behaviour: behaviour appropriate at a party would be largely inappropriate at an interview or our place of work, for example. Social behaviour, our actions in the presence of one or numerous other people is, then, governed both by perceptions and social norms. Much of the time we are unaware of these influences. The discipline of social psychology – the scientific study of social behaviour and thought – offers insight and understanding based upon sound empirical evidence.

In everyday life we depend upon, interact with, influence and are influenced by many people: the presence of others is comforting; brief encounters with strangers are common when, for example, we go shopping; relationships reveal a wide diversity from acquaintances, work-mates, friends through to lovers and marriage partners. Some people we interact with just once and never see again; others become well-known to us through work or social activities; a small number of people are very special to us, such as spouses and/or close friends, and are permanent features of our lives. As a baby and young child our dependence upon others is total: not only do parents or caretakers provide for our physical needs but they also socialize us, so then as we get older we are able to interact, with confidence and ease, with peers and adults. Inadequate socialization, as will be seen in the next two chapters, is regarded by many social psychologists as an important factor in social delinquency. In later life, as adults, we depend upon people for company (being alone for long periods of time is often a very distressing experience), for information (in the form of, for example, how we are expected to behave in a particular social situation) and for pleasure (simply talking to somebody we are close to is enjoyable in itself and, when worried, may relieve us of a mental burden).

Acting appropriately, assessing ourselves and others, knowing when to succumb to the influence of other people and when to attempt to influence others to our way of thinking, are all common features of everyday life. To function effectively in these ways means we are all social psychologists in a sense. Without intuition and common sense our understanding of our social world would be greatly impaired resulting in socially clumsy, ineffective and inappropriate actions. Social psychology, the scientific study of social behaviour and thought, assesses the soundness and validity of these common-sense notions. Sometimes, as we shall see in this book, social psychology research gives surprising results: empirical evidence occasionally overturns what we commonly believe to be the case.

The aims of both the layperson and professional social psychologist are the same: both to understand and predict the behaviour of others and ourselves in the diversity of social situations that can and do confront us. In the absence of a degree of prediction and understanding organized society, of any sort, would soon disintegrate and collapse. If we or others behaved randomly, without control or order, prediction and understanding would become impossible. We often make mistakes – misjudging people and how they will behave – common sense is often a good guide but one which lacks objective, rigorous empirical support: our experience of the world is inevitably biased and subjective. The scientific study of social behaviour and thought attempts to provide an unbiased and objective way of understanding and predicting human social behaviour. If social psychology can offer greater understanding and prediction it should then enable us to achieve greater control over our own lives.

## 1.2 The scope of social psychology

The best way to discover the scope of social psychology is to read the following 10 chapters of this book. To offer a precise definition of social psychology would be presumptuous since it would impose restrictions on what ought and ought not to be appropriate areas of enquiry and be of little use since few other social psychologists would agree with my definition. Nevertheless a general characterization of social psychology as the *scientific study of social behaviour and thought* provides three elements common to most, if not all, aspects of social psychology. First, this conceptualization firmly establishes the discipline as one proceeding by scientific enquiry. More will be said about this in the next section. Here it is sufficient to say that social psychology gains knowledge through the *empirical method* of testing and formulating theories. Throughout this book empirical studies, largely laboratory experiments, are described in some detail to demonstrate how they offer support or refutation of a theory. Second, as we noted earlier, social behaviour is an object of study for the purposes of understanding and prediction. Many social psychologists claim social psychology can only be about behaviour since this is all that can be directly observed: we cannot see what people think and feel. The highly influential *behaviourist* approach in psychology generally, and social psychology in particular, staunchly adheres to this principle. However, whilst much of our everyday lives is concerned with behaviour to ignore how people think and feel not only omits a vastly important aspect of our social lives but may prevent understanding of the *causes* of behaviour. Hence, the third aspect of the conceptualization of social psychology given above includes social thought. This may appear a clumsy term, it probably is, but it serves to represent both how we think about ourselves and how others think about us. 'Thought' here is used to refer to such things as attitudes, values, beliefs, self-esteem, social perception, etc.

Representing social psychology as the scientific study of social behaviour and thought avoids imposing boundaries on legitimate areas of enquiry. This is necessary since the interests of social psychologists range from detailed enquiries into thought processes (social cognition) through to broader considerations of the individual in a societal context (sociological social psychology). Uniting these widely different perspectives is the attempt to understand how people interact and influence each other.

Perusal of the chapter headings will give you some idea of the scope of social psychology. These chapters do not exhaust the areas of study but, in my view, represent the essential and fundamental areas of enquiry. To do justice adequately to the full range and scope of social psychology would require a volume many times this size. Specialist books, dealing with particular areas or topics can be more profitably read by the student once he or she has a general foundation in social psychology. It is hoped that this is provided by this book.

## 1.3 Assumptions about human behaviour

In general conversation we often say 'it is in his nature to behave like that' or 'being like that comes naturally to her'. In everyday usage the words 'nature' or 'naturally' are ill-defined and ambiguous. In psychology, however, such a characterization would be taken to mean the person's behaviour is biological in origin and results from inheritance of specific genes.

Two positions are possible, both representing long traditions in psychology and philosophy: first, behaviour and characteristics such as intelligence, personality, etc. are entirely a result of *genetic make-up*. Second, behaviour and human characteristics result entirely from our *experience* of the world, from birth onwards. Few, if any, psychologists would now argue solely for a nature or nurture (experience) position, most now agree that human behaviour and characteristics are a result of the *interaction* of the two influences. Controversy still rages, however, often in a bitter and emotional way, over the relative contribution of each in determining a person's intelligence. Apart from the problem of no adequate, agreed-upon definition of intelligence (cynics say IQ is simply the ability to do IQ tests) evidence for one viewpoint or another is less than clear (see Eysenck and Kamin, 1981, for a good but rather passionate examination of the evidence).

In social psychology the contemporary approach claiming biology to be important, by drawing upon Darwin's theory of evolution, is known as *sociobiology* (Wilson, 1975). The claim is a relatively simple one, but difficult to substantiate satisfactorily with respect to human social behaviour: if human beings are solely a product of evolution then many social behaviours will have evolved in a similar way. Parental behaviour, aggression and altruism are claimed by sociobiologists to be a product of evolution rather than environmental experiences. Such claims have been heavily criticized (Ruse, 1979); one of the fundamental problems is that human beings inherit not only their genetic make-up but a society and culture, which is continually evolving, as well. Perhaps with non-human primates and other animals it is easier to see the biological and evolutionary contribution since animal 'societies' do not progress and change in any way comparable to that of humans.

In the topics that are dealt with throughout this book the nature/nurture theme will arise many times. Mostly reference will be made to animal studies, however, relevance and applicability to human social behaviour will be provided as appropriate.

The view that social behaviour can be explained in biological and/or evolutionary terms is one that dates back to the beginnings of modern social psychology. McDougall (1908) attempted an explanation of *all* social behaviour in terms of instincts. Two logical flaws have resulted in the demise of this approach: first, the number of instincts could be extended indefinitely so that every social behaviour could have an instinct attached to it. Second, by saying people have an instinct to be altruistic, for example, does not explain the causes of altruistic behaviour, but simply renames the behaviour. What is not explained is why people have instincts and how so many instincts could have evolved. The discipline of ethology, which will be described in the next chapter, offers a more sensible and circumscribed approach to the role of instincts in animal – both human and non-human – social behaviour.

# 1.4  Social psychology as science

Earlier it was pointed out that to function effectively with other people and in different social situations we need to be what might be called 'intuitive' social psychologists. Our experiences of others and ourselves in different social situations supplies us with knowledge about why people behave as they do and expectations about future social behaviour. Unfortunately, this common-sense or intuitive approach has a major shortcoming: each of us has different experiences of people and social situations leading to personal knowledge becoming idiosyncratic. Different people may explain the same behaviour differently, have different expectations and make different predictions about likely future behaviour. Social psychology as science attempts to provide objective and verifiable knowledge about human social behaviour, and hence escapes the dangers of idiosyncratic personal knowledge.

## 1.4.1  Scientific enquiry

Controversy exists within the philosophy of science over how scientific enquiry proceeds (see Chalmers, 1978, for a useful introduction to different

schools of thought). However, few would disagree that science is char-
terized by theory, hypothesis and observation. How these are related will
considered below: it is worth noting from the outset that it is the relationsh
between these three elements that is often a source of dispute.

A theory is a generalization concerning how we or the theorist thinks the
world or some part of it is; a theory offers a way of imposing order and sense
on the world and does so by offering a set of rules or regulations to explain
number of facts or observations. For example, a theory might be propounded
claiming people who are prejudiced have and make friends with others who
are also prejudiced. Our first question of the propounder of this theory
would be to ask what supportive evidence exists, then we could decide
whether the theory is true or false.

Theories operate at a level of abstraction allowing many hypotheses or
empirically testable predictions to be derived. So, for example, we may derive
the hypothesis that men who are prejudiced against women will tend to have
male friends who are also sexist. Alternatively, we may derive the prediction
that people prejudiced towards blacks will have friends who are prejudiced
towards Chinese (this is permissable since our theory was very general - too
general perhaps!). To test the validity of one or both of these predictions we
would need, first, to devise some *reliable* measure of the specific type(s) of
prejudice, then see if the relationship between prejudiced people and their
friends was as we predicted. If so, this would count as evidence supporting
our theory, if not evidence against the theory would have been obtained.

Karl Popper, a highly influential philosopher of science, has shown that a
scientific theory cannot logically be proved true, but it can be refuted. In fact,
Popper claims that in order for a theory to be scientific it must, in principle,
be capable of empirical refutation. A theory can never be accepted as true
since there is no guarantee, logically, that the future will be the same as the
past. We all expect the sun to rise tomorrow, but there is no logical reason
why it should. When observations disconfirm a theory it has, logically
speaking, been refuted. Few scientists apply such stringent criteria; for a
theory to be refuted *numerous* counter-observations are required. Of course,
this does pose the problem of knowing how many counter-observations are
needed. No hard and fast rules exist, unfortunately. Evidence consistent with
a theory offers support for that theory but nothing more; it does not and
cannot prove a theory to be true. This may seem surprising: we are told
science provides objective, true knowledge. However, because of the relationship between theory, hypothesis and observations science may offer
objective knowledge but whether it is true (ultimately) or not is another
matter. Perhaps the best that can be claimed for science is it offers a way of
discovering what is false, not what is true. To pursue these matters further is
not appropriate here, arguments and issues rapildly become involved a
complex; some flavour of the issues, I hope, has been conveyed.

### 1.4.2 Theory and research in social psychology

Social psychology is an empirical discipline. This not only means,
above, that predictions are tested by observation but also that s

*replicated*. Provided the researcher can describe the hypothesis, how observations were made and data collected, it is possible for another researcher to conduct a similar study. Replication, provided replications produce consistent data, enables the researcher to have greater confidence in accepting the implications of the data for the theory.

Where do theories come from and how are they constructed in social psychology? Many introductory texts will tell you theories are constructed from observations and facts. The story goes something like this: numerous observations lead to a regularity or number of regularities being noticed, these regularities lead to a theory. Take our example earlier: on numerous occasions, suppose, people we regard as prejudiced have friends who are also prejudiced. The role of the social psychologist is to determine the extent to which this 'theory' holds. Such an account, stereotyped as it is, places the derivation of theories from observations and facts, making these observations and facts neutral, objective and free from theory in the first place. Unfortunately, matters are not so simple or clear cut, 'facts' are often determined by the theoretical perspective in the first place and theories often guide the researcher towards establishing what are and are not the facts. Thomas Kuhn, another important philosopher of science, has shown this to be the case in the 'pure' sciences, such as physics. There is no reason to think this does not apply to psychology generally and social psychology in particular.

Whilst the relationship between observation and theory is complex, both are necessary to the scientific discipline of social psychology. Throughout this book you will find different theories described and empirical evidence cited as either supporting or questioning the validity of the theory.

You may wonder, especially after reading this book, how it is there are so many different theories in social psychology. Generally speaking, the days when psychologists constructed 'grand' theories attempting to explain all human behaviour, as attempted by such people as Freud, Skinner and McDougall, have passed. This has been replaced by 'mini' theories, theories limited to a specific domain of human social behaviour. Hence there are theories about child development, prejudice, aggression, social influence, etc., etc. Grand theories presented problems of testability and general applicability; limited domain theories are more easily tested but have the drawback of segmenting social behaviour into discrete compartments. Such compartmentalization is an unrealistic representation of the interlinking and continuity that exists between different social behaviours.

This may seem less than satisfactory to someone encountering social psychology for the first time, however, a parallel may be drawn between this state of affairs and how the sciences of physics and astronomy were in their infancy. Historians of science argue that science progresses by the emergence of new theories which incorporate a number of other more limited theories. Gradually, theories come to explain more, becoming more 'grand' in their scale. Optimists among philosophers of psychology argue the same process is happening in psychology. As social psychology progresses new theories will emerge which combine numerous earlier theories, since social psychology as an empirical, scientific discipline is less than 100 years old it is too early to expect grand theories to exist.

Whilst some of these points may be hard to grasp, I hope two issues will be kept in mind: first, although social psychology may appear fragmented on first encounter there is more coherence there really. Second, empirical enquiry, especially in the form of experiments, is vital for assessing the validity of a theory. With these points in mind we will now consider the different empirical strategies used in social psychology.

## 1.5 Methods of investigation

Social psychology employs three main methods of scientific investigation: correlational research, laboratory experiments and field research. Other methods are used, most notably archival research and surveys, but will not be discussed further since most of the research described in this book uses the three main categories given above. It should be noted that no one of these three methods is better than another. Laboratory experiments offer a high degree of control of variables but findings are often difficult to generalize to what goes on in everyday life. By contrast, field experiments, as their name implies, are conducted in real-life settings and hence have obvious relevance to everyday life. However, the social psychologist has much less control over variables and, as a consequence, can never be as certain as with laboratory experiments that variables found to influence behaviour are indeed the ones that *do* influence behaviour. It may be that an extraneous or uncontrolled variable, not thought of by the social psychologist, is able to explain the observed behaviour.

### 1.5.1 Correlational research

Correlational research has two aims: to assess (a) whether two or more variables are related: and (b) the type of relationship existing between the variables. Consider again our example of prejudiced people having prejudiced friends, this could be investigated using correlational research as follows: first, a questionnaire measuring prejudice would be required Numerous have been developed. One, which is described in Chapter 5, is the 'F-scale' which measures authoritarianism (Adorno *et al.*, 1950). A high score on this questionnaire indicates the person to be authoritarian, which is closely associated with being prejudiced. To test our theory the F-scale could be administered, say, to 100 people and the 20 highest scorers selected as our pool of prejudiced people. These 20 people would then be asked to name a friend; the researcher would then administer the F-scale to these 20 friends. Support for our theory would be obtained if the 20 friends also scored high on the F-scale.

A statistical procedure, resulting in a *correlation coefficient* provides a means of assessing this. A correlation coefficient can take on any value between − 1.00 to + 1.00. A correlation of + 1.00 would tell us a perfect *positive* relationship exists between the two variables. With our example this would mean prejudiced peoples' scores on the F-scale are exactly the same as the scores of their friends. Rarely are correlations this high in social psychology: a correlation of + 0.75 would be taken to indicate support for the theory. A correlation of − 1.00, by contrast, would indicate a perfect *negative* relationship between two variables. This would mean, with our example, that people with high F-scale scores had friends who scored very *low* on this scale, i.e. were unprejudiced. Perfect negative correlations are also very rare, again a correlation of around $-0.75$ would be a good indication of such a negative relationship. A correlation coefficient around zero indicates *no* relationship exists between the two variables: knowing somebody was prejudiced would not allow us to predict if their friends were or were not prejudiced. A low correlation (around zero) may not, however, mean our theory is incorrect; it could be that the F-scale was an inappropriate measure or did not measure prejudice adequately

Correlational research has the advantage of being relatively straightforward and easy to carry out: as long as the people you want to administer the questionnaire to can be identified and you have some confidence in the questionnaire itself, little further planning or expenditure of time is required. This type of research does have a major drawback though: *it cannot provide evidence for cause and effect*. The problem is this: suppose we find a high positive correlation between prejudiced people and their friends, this allows us to say prejudiced people have prejudiced friends, but it does not tell us why. Do these people (cause) choose their friends (effect) because the latter are prejudiced, or did their friends (cause) choose them (effect)? Often it may seem intuitively obvious what is cause and what is effect, but the correlation coefficient can never provide evidence to support our intuitions. Evidence of cause and effect is best achieved through the use of laboratory experiments.

### 1.5.2 The laboratory experiment

The laboratory experiment offers the highest degree of control over variables, yet it is not intended to replicate real-life situations. The primary aim is to establish, as far as possible, the effect upon behaviour of manipulating a certain variable, or number of variables.

Supposing we wished to conduct a laboratory experiment to test our theory about prejudiced people and their friends. Many experiments could be devised, but let us consider the following: our theory would lead us to predict that prejudiced people get on better with, and hence like, other people who share the same or similar prejudices on first acquaintance. Specifically, prejudiced people will like and be attracted to similarly prejudiced rather than unprejudiced strangers. The following experiment would test this: 100 people complete the F-scale, the 30 highest and 30 lowest scores are selected. Splitting each group, randomly, into sub-groups of 10 we could arrange for prejudiced people to converse with another prejudiced person for, say, 15 minutes. We could also arrange pairs of people such that unprejudiced people talked to another unprejudiced person, and prejudiced talked to unprejudiced. There would be 10 pairs of subjects for each type of dyad, as shown in Figure 1.1; the experimenter is manipulating how dyads (groups of two people) are constituted: the variable manipulated by the experimenter is called the *independent* variable.

Some measure or measures of attraction and liking would have to be taken. We could, for example, measure the amount of eye-contact taking place within the differently constituted dyads. Since eye-contact is a good indicator of whether we like somebody or not (see Chapter 9) we would expect higher

| TYPE OF DYADS | NUMBER OF DYADS | CONSTITUTION OF DYADS |
|---|---|---|
| Prejudiced | 10 | Prejudiced person – Prejudiced person |
| Mixed | 10 | Prejudiced person – Unprejudiced person |
| Unprejudiced | 10 | Unprejudiced person – Unprejudiced person |

**Figure 1.1** Design of experiment showing type, number and constitution of dyads.

levels for prejudiced dyads than in the other two types of pairings. Another measure of liking would be to ask subjects, on a previously devised questionnaire, how much they enjoyed talking to their partner, would like to talk to the person again, etc. These measures of the variables of liking and attraction are called the *dependent* variables.

*Controlled* variables are another important class of variables the experimenter must consider. The experimenter may want to control for age (just use subjects in a given age-band), sex (all male, all female or mixed groups of subjects), skin colour or any other variable which may seem important. This can be crucial. Suppose we did find higher levels of eye-contact with the prejudiced dyads, we would take this as support for our theory. However, if prejudiced dyads were all females and unprejudiced dyads all males, doubt would be cast on our interpretation of the data since research has consistently shown females to engage in more eye-contact than males. With this design of experiment we would have what is known as a *confounding* variable: sex of dyad has been confounded with prejudice of each person in the dyad. It would be impossible to claim that eye-contact was high because subjects were prejudiced, it could be because the subjects were females.

Laboratory experiments allow cause–effect relationships to be established but only if the experiment is carefully designed to control for important variables, avoid confounding of the independent with another, uncontrolled, variable and if the dependent variables provide reliable and valid measures. As you can appreciate, laboratory experiments require a great deal of careful planning. Problems of laboratory experiments will be dealt with later in this section and the next sections of this chapter.

### 1.5.3 Field research

Field research is not conducted in a grassy field but in the field of a real-life social setting, i.e. anywhere in public where people are going about their normal day-to-day activities. There are *three* main types of field research: naturalistic observation, the natural experiment and the field experiment. The researcher has little or no control over events with the former two types, with the latter, the field experiment, control over some variables is possible but not as much as in the laboratory experiment. The main advantage of field research is that findings can be generalized to other social situations; the main drawback is lack of control which may bring dangers of confounding variables. Generalizability (see the next section) comes at the expense of loss of control and precision.

*Naturalistic observation* involves going into a social setting and simply observing the behaviours that take place, without attempting or intending to influence the situation or the behaviours in any way. An ethical code must be adhered to: public social behaviour is there for anybody to see; naturalistic observation must not intrude or violate the privacy people are entitled to. It is usually necessary for the observer to decide beforehand which behaviours to record and measure. It is impossible to observe and record everything that takes place, even between just two people in conversation – try it some time and you will very quickly realize this. Naturalistic observation is a useful technique for pilot studies, generating ideas for further research and understanding how people interact. This method is not very good for testing predictions derived from a theory since the researcher has no control over what takes place.

The *natural experiment* capitalizes on real-life social events which offer a test of a theory or hypothesis. The most famous example of this is reported in the book *When Prophecy Fails* by Festinger, Riecken and Schachter (1956). These researchers heard of a spiritual group, headed by a woman called Mrs Keech, who believed herself to be in contact with aliens from outer space, who expected the world to end on a particular date. Some of the researchers joined the group, becoming *participant observers*, to discover how the attitudes of the real members changed after the 'doomsday' date had passed and the world had not ended. Festinger predicted, from his theory of cognitive dissonance (see Chapter 4), that members should show greater belief and conviction in Mrs Keech *after* the date on which the world was supposed to end. By becoming members of the group the researchers were able to observe, at first hand, the behaviour and expressed attitudes both before and after the doomsday date. Results were consistent with the predictions of cognitive dissonance theory.

Using naturally occurring social events as social psychology experiments often requires the researchers to become participant observers. There is a penalty for this: researchers may, inadvertently or otherwise, influence the attitudes and behaviours of individuals in the group. Another problem is that it is difficult, if not impossible, to predict when an event suitable for social psychological research is going to take place. Often a researcher will only get very short notice and may be unprepared or less well prepared than he or she would like to be. The main advantages are that naturally occurring events provide social situations which could not practically or ethically be conducted in a laboratory or field experiment.

The *field experiment* amounts to conducting a laboratory experiment in a real-life social setting. All the planning and preparation of a laboratory experiment is required – manipulation of the independent variable, measures of dependent variables and deciding which variables to control for. In the field experiment the researcher is trying to influence how people behave, testing predictions derived from a theory. For example, a field experiment could be devised to answer the question: 'are people more willing to take risks when they see somebody else (a model) taking a risk than in the absence of another risk taker?' A field experiment could be conducted at a pedestrian crossing at traffic lights counting the numbers of pedestrians crossing when the light (for the pedestrian) is on red. In the *control* condition, researchers could simply observe the number who cross when they are not supposed to. In the experimental condition one of the researchers would act as a 'model' and cross the light at red. A second researcher would count the number of people who also crossed. If repeated many times, and at different traffic lights, and more were found to cross in the presence of a model we would conclude the data supported the above hypothesis.

Field experiments offer the advantage of a real-life setting but have less control over the situation than laboratory experiments. Variables like the weather, number of people in the street, time of day, day of the week, etc. may all influence behaviour and be potential confounding variables. Field experiments are very popular in social psychology, as you will see, but require more careful planning than you might at first think.

### 1.5.4 Validity of experiments

Since experiments are such powerful tools in the process of scientific enquiry we need to be sure they can stand up to certain questions asked of them – questions to do with validity. There are three types of validity – internal, external and ecological. Social psychology experiments are unlikely to be valid in all these three ways; however, without internal validity an experiment is meaningless (Campbell and Stanley, 1966).

An experiment has *internal validity* if the results (measures of the dependent variables) can be clearly and confidently related to the manipulations of the independent variable. A confounding variable, you will remember, is where both the independent variable and some other variable not controlled by the experimenter are capable of explaining the results. An experiment with a confounding variable has *low* internal validity. No experiment can be devised to control for all possible variables; *randomly* assigning subjects to different experimental conditions ensures variables such as age, sex, personality, etc. are equally distributed among each of the conditions. This avoids, as far as possible, confounding variables.

*External validity* refers to the generalizability of results from one specific experiment to other experiments, subjects and measures. The question asked is, 'Can different experiments, using different procedures, subjects and measuring instruments, produce results consistent with that of the original experiment?' If the answer is yes an experiment can be said to be externally valid. This type of validity is important since support for a theory from numerous different experiments gives us more confidence in the theory than if support comes from only one experiment. Internal and external validity may stand in opposition to one another: an internally valid experiment is where very high control over external variables is achieved. However, such very high control would make the experiment so unique as to prevent generalization to other situations.

*Ecological validity* refers to the generalizability of results from an experiment to the 'real' world. Laboratory experiments are conducted in artificial situations where many, if not most, aspects of everyday social life are absent or controlled for. A laboratory experiment has ecological validity if the results are relevant and apply to what goes on in everyday life. For example, we will see (in Chapter 9) that knowing the patterns of non-verbal behaviour occurring between two people in conversation has proved useful for both identifying how people fail socially and how they may be helped to be more socially skilled. Such knowledge has been obtained by analysing video-recordings of people interacting in a social psychology laboratory. When reading an experiment described in this book ask yourself whether it has relevance to your or other people's social lives. If you are able to see ways in which it is relevant it will, in all probability, be ecologically valid.

## 1.6  The social psychology of experiments

A physicist conducting an experiment does so on inanimate matter, an interaction between the physicist and the material he or she is working on is not thought to take place (although see Capra, 1975, for a controversial view). Things are very different in social psychology, since the subject matter is other people and these people do interact with the experimenter. In view of this the social psychology experiment is itself a social situation and one which has attracted much research in attempts to identify sources of error and bias. Three main sources have been indentified; demand characteristics, experimenter effects and subject effects.

*Demand characteristics* are aspects of any social situation providing tacit or implicit cues as to the behaviour expected. If you go to a party, for example, you would be expected to socialize with others, not sit in a corner quietly on your own getting drunk! According to Orne (1962) the main demand characteristic of social psychology experiments is that of being a good subject. This involves cooperating with the experimenter and providing him with the data he wants. This may seem innocuous but is not when subjects try to puzzle out for themselves what the experiment is about and then act in a way to confirm the hypothesis under test. If this happens the whole point of the experiment and validity of the data are destroyed. For an experiment to produce valid results subjects should respond to the specific experimental conditions in a natural and spontaneous way, ignoring or in ignorance of what the experiment is actually about. To avoid demand characteristics as much as possible, the researcher conducts pilot studies giving post-experimental interviews to subjects to discover if there are obvious cues being picked up which could be eradicated. In the final analysis there can be no guarantee that an experiment is without demand characteristics.

*Experimenter effects* occur when results are influenced or distorted, either intentionally or unintentionally, by the characteristics or behaviour of the experimenter (Rosenthal, 1969). These include influences both on the subjects taking part in the experiment and on the data themselves. Unintentional errors of observation, recording or computation may be made so as to provide results consistent with the hypothesis under test. In extreme and rare cases data may be faked – the Cyril Bart scandal (see Eysenck and Kamin, 1981) being an unfortunate case in point.

Rosenthal (1969) has suggested three types of experimenter effects: biosocial, psychological and situational.

*Biosocial* are aspects of the experimenter about which little can be done, for example, age, sex, race and physical appearance. An attractive female experimenter may obtain different responses from subjects than an unattractive male experimenter. The way round this is to have a number of experimenters, rather than just one, conducting the research. *Psychosocial* factors are to do with the general attitude and personality of the experimenter: is the experimenter friendly or cold when giving instructions to the subject?, does the experimenter have an introvert or extrovert personality? Again using numerous experimenters goes some way to overcoming this problem, in addition a prearranged strategy, rehearsed beforehand, on how to interact with the subjects should be devised.

The most important and extensively researched factor is the *situational* one, this revolves around the issue of knowing the hypothesis the experiment is designed to test. Rosenthal (1969) has found a tendency for experimenters to produce results consistent with an hypothesis when this should not happen. Such *experimenter expectancy* effects were demonstrated by Rosenthal and Fode (1963) in a study where students were asked to train rats to run a maze. Half the students were told they had 'maze-bright' rats (i.e. would learn a maze quickly) and the other half told they had 'maze-dull' rats (i.e. would only learn slowly). In fact, Rosenthal and Fode gave rats of equal capability, neither dull nor bright, to both groups of students. The researchers found students who believed they had maze-bright rats produced results showing better performance than students who believed they had maze-dull rats. To avoid expectancy effects experimenters should be 'blind' to the hypothesis under test, or if this is not possible, a number of experimenters should be used but not told which experimental condition they were running at any one time.

*Subject effects* are many and varied. We have already encountered the problem of the 'good' subject; subjects may come along with a negative or hostile attitude attempting to disrupt or act in opposite ways to normal. Perhaps the most widespread subject effect is that of *evaluation apprehension*. People who know little about scientific psychology or encounter it via participation in an experiment often believe a psychologist has immediate and deep insight into one's mind. Not only is this wrong but it may lead the subject to behave in ways he or she would not normally. Evaluation apprehension may result in the subject attempting to present him or herself in a good light – as likeable, happy and fully understanding the experimenter's instructions. Often, in my experience, subjects are afraid or embarrassed to ask questions when unclear about what they are being asked to do. The experimenter has a duty to make the person both feel at ease and clearly understand what the task requires of him or her.

## 1.7 Ethical considerations

Experiments using people as subjects, in psychology generally and social psychology in particular, have to conform to an ethical code. Guidelines, some of which are given in Figure 1.2, are provided by the British Psychological Society and the American Psychological Association. Some experiments, perhaps already known to you, have caused widespread controversy since some feel they were unethical and should never have been conducted. Milgram's (1965) experiments, where subjects believed they were giving increasingly dangerous levels of electric shocks to a 'learner', are widely cited

ETHICAL PRINCIPLES FOR RESEARCH WITH HUMAN SUBJECTS

Whenever possible the investigator should inform the subjects of the objectives, and, eventually, the results of the investigation.

In all circumstances the investigator must consider the ethical implications and the psychological consequences for his subjects of the research he is carrying out.

An investigator should seek the opinion of experienced and disinterested colleagues whenever his research requires or is likely to involve:
(a)  Deception concerning the purpose of the investigation or the subject's role in it.
(b)  Psychological or physiological stress.
(c)  Encroachment upon privacy.

Deception of subjects, or withholding of relevant information from them, should only occur when the investigator is satisfied that the aims and objects of his research or the welfare of his subjects cannot be achieved by other means.

Where deception has been substantial, the subject should be offered the option of withholding his data, in accordance with the principle of participation by informed consent.

Studies on non-volunteers, based upon observation or records (whether or not explicitly confidential) must respect the privacy and psychological well-being of the subjects.

**Figure 1.2**  Extracts from 'Ethical Principles for Research with Human Subjects' published by the British Psychological Society.

in this context. These experiments are described in some detail in Chapter 10; you can make up your own mind. However, the problem is not an easy one to resolve; does the pursuit of knowledge condone the means by which it is achieved? At what point do we say someone is suffering unjustifiable personal harm or mental distress from taking part in an experiment? Most experiments conducted in social psychology do not raise such fundamental problems. However, most experiments do involve deceiving subjects in one way or another.

Suppose, for the sake of argument, you wished to find to how people look at each other when in conversation. To measure looking and eye-contact it would be best to place two people in a laboratory equipped with closed-circuit television so you could take a video-recording and analyse looking behaviour at some later time. Your dilemma, as the researcher, is this: two people turn up, you take them into the laboratory, sit them down and instruct them to converse with each other for 15 minutes. One subject says, 'What's this all about?'. You say you are studying how two people get acquainted, this satisfies the inquirer and the two proceed to have a conversation. Now consider the other option open to you as the experimenter: the subject also asks, 'What's this all about?', you tell the truth and say it is an investigation concerned with looking behaviour between two people in conversation. Now the subjects know what the study is about, but how might this knowledge effect their behaviour? It is bound to make them conscious of how they look at the other person when in conversation and so make it difficult for them to act normally. Self-consciousness may result in subjects avoiding looking at each other altogether, looking at each other all the time or looking in 'abnormal' ways. Ideally the experimenter wants to observe and measure spontaneous looking behaviour, telling the truth seriously threatens this. Given the objectives of the experiments, therefore, it is better to deceive subjects so they are not sensitized to the behaviours being observed.

When deception is used it is important that the experimenter *debriefs* subjects at the end of the experiment. Debriefing involves telling subjects the true purpose of the experiment, explaining why they were deceived, answering any questions they may have and providing reassurance where and if necessary. By debriefing the experimenter does everything possible to ensure subjects leave the laboratory feeling more or less satisfied and in a positive frame of mind.

Is there a way in which research could be carried out without the use of deception? Kelman (1967) proposes subjects be asked to role play. Subjects would be told about the experiment and asked what they would do in such a situation. The trouble with such an 'as if' approach is that people often behave in ways different from how they say they would behave (see Chapter 4 on the relationship between attitudes and behaviour). Furthermore, people asked to act or think as if they were not in possession of a certain piece of knowledge find it difficult to ignore what they already know (Pennington, 1981). Kelman's suggestion is interesting but, unfortunately, it is difficult to find a real substitute for spontaneous behaviour.

Field experiments raise further ethical problems: first, people are not usually asked if they wish to take part in an experiment. The researcher stages some event in a public place and observes the responses of the passers-by. Second, unwitting subjects in a field experiment are not usually debriefed, it is usually accepted that it is best for the people to remain ignorant of the fact they have just taken part in an experiment. Field experiments pose, I think, more ethical problems for social psychology than do laboratory experiments. At the very least they must be ethically acceptable and not make fools of, or upset people in any serious way.

Many of the issues and arguments I have presented in this chapter, particularly in the sections dealing with 'social psychology as science' and 'methods of investigation' will, I am aware, be hard to grasp by some readers encountering social psychology for the first time. Do not worry unduly about this since many of these points will emerge as you read the subsequent chapters of this book. It would be a very good idea if, after reading much of what follows, you return to this chapter and read it again. Armed with some knowledge of social psychology you will be in a better position to appreciate more fully the controversies and problems presented here.

## 1.8 Organization of this book

I have attempted to provide coverage of most of the major areas in social psychology, in doing this both traditional and more recent areas and approaches have been included. The book is intended to serve as a general introduction and review to modern experimental social psychology. It does not specifically deal with social problems, neither is it intended as an introduction to applied social psychology. Examples are used, throughout the book, of different social problems to highlight theory or relevance of research. Other books exist which explicitly deal with social problems and the relevance of social psychology to both understanding and helping with them (Gale and Chapman, 1984). In the process of writing this book I have been constantly aware of the omissions, for example, little or no attempt has been made at covering areas such as the social psychology of language and social aspects of mental health. Any introductory book makes trade-offs, I only hope the ones I have made have been in the right direction.

The next two chapters deal with socialization; in Chapter 2 the importance of early experiences with others, especially the mother or caretaker of the child, is assessed, Chapter 3 looks at theory and research whereby socialization is viewed as a process continuing throughout our lives. The remaining chapters are all to do with the adult in the social world: Chapters 4 to 7 focus on the individual. This broadens to consider people interacting with, mostly, just one other person (Chapters 8 and 9). Chapter 10 considers ways in which we are influenced in our beliefs and behaviours by other people. The final chapter, Chapter 11, looks at groups of people and how groups perform compared to individuals.

At the start of each chapter you will find an outline of the contents provided. a cursory look at each of these will give you a good idea of the scope of social psychology. At the end of each chapter a summary of the main points of that chapter is given together with suggestions for further reading. I have made a few comments in these suggestions which may guide you in deciding which would be the most appropriate for you to pursue.

Finally, I have made liberal use of tables and figures throughout the book, this serves to highlight results of research or make clearer what a theory is actually trying to say. Experimental social psychology makes extensive use of statistics, I have avoided this as much as possible and the statistics you will come across have been described earlier in this chapter. No statistical knowledge beyond this is assumed.

## 1.9 Summary

○ Our interacting with other people in everyday life means we are all social psychologists. As lay social psychologists we develop and maintain intuitions about our own and other people's behaviour. Social psychology assesses the soundness of these common-sense views.

○ Social psychology is the scientific study of social thought and social behaviour. Its aims are the understanding, explanation and prediction of behaviour.

○ Social psychology uses empirical methods of enquiry both to test and construct theories about human social behaviour. The scope of the discipline ranges from enquiries into thought processes through to societal influences upon behaviour.

○ Human behaviour, including social behaviour, results from an interaction of biological inheritance and environmental experiences. Biological influences are less pronounced in humans than in other animals.

○ Science is characterized by theory, hypothesis and observation; how these are related is a source of controversy. Karl Popper claims a theory can never be proved true; for a theory to be scientific it must be capable, in principle, of being falsified.

○ Social psychology is a scientific discipline: experiments are used to test hypotheses, and are capable of replication by any other social psychologist. Social psychology has many theories concerned with specific aspects of social behaviour and thought.

○ Three main methods of investigation are used in social psychology: correlational research, laboratory experiments and field research. Correlational research cannot provide evidence for cause–effect relationships between variables. Laboratory experiments offer a high degree of control but are often difficult to generalize to real-life social situations. Field research is of three main types; naturalistic observation, natural experiments and field experiments.

O Internal, external and ecological validity can be assessed for experiments. Without internal validity an experiment is meaningless. There is a trade-off between internal and external validity: the former may be achieved at the expense of the latter.

O Social psychology experiments are themselves a special kind of social situation and because of this may suffer bias from demand characteristics, experimenter effects and subject effects.

O All empirical research in social psychology must conform to certain moral and ethical standards. Unfortunately, to obtain spontaneous behaviour from subjects taking part in an experiment demands a degree of deception. It is important to debrief subjects after an experiment, telling them the true purpose of the experiment and removing, as far as possible, anxieties they may have.

## 1.10 Suggestions for further reading

Chalmers, A.F. *What is this Thing Called Science?* (Milton Keynes, Open University Press, 1978).
A very useful and easy to read introduction to the major issues and schools of thought in the philosophy of science. Provides both an historical survey and account of most recent views.

Jung, J., *The Experimenter's Dilemma* (New York, Harper and Row, 1971).
Provides detailed coverage of the full range of problems associated with conducting experiments in psychology. Not a book for the beginner, of intermediate difficulty, to be read if you have pursued the issues in a little more depth beforehand.

Kennedy, G., *Invitation to Statistics* (Oxford, Martin Robertson, 1983).
A very readable introduction to statistical concepts, their history and why statistics are important. It does this by avoiding jargon and number crunching, you do not need a mathematical bent to understand what is being said.

Tedeschi, J.T. and Lindskold, S., *Social Psychology: Interdependence, Interaction and Influence* (New York: John Wiley and Sons, 1976).
Very thorough and extensive introduction to social psychology, at a higher and fuller level than achieved by this book. The first two chapters go into more detail about the issues raised here. Probably the best book to go to after reading this chapter.

# 2

# Socialization: The early years

2.1 Socialization – themes and perspectives
2.2 Conceptions of childhood
2.3 Biological underpinnings
2.4 Cultural and sub-cultural influences
2.5 The first relationship
    *2.5.1 Attachment in animals   2.5.2 Attachment in humans   2.5.3 Differences in human attachment*
2.6 Maternal deprivation
    *2.6.1 Consequences in animals   2.6.2 Consequences in humans   2.6.3 Assessment*
2.7 Early years and later life
2.8 Summary
2.9 Suggestions for further reading

## 2.1 Socialization – themes and perspectives

Since the inception of psychology as an empirical discipline psychologists have increasingly acknowledged the importance and significance of childhood, especially the early years, as a foundation for later adolescent and adult functioning. Children are no longer viewed as 'small adults', as they once were, but as beings that operate at *qualitatively* different intellectual, emotional and social levels to that of adults. Theorists such as Kohlberg and Erikson (to be considered in detail in the next chapter) have proposed that social development proceeds through a series of stages. Kohlberg and Erikson have developed the ideas of Piaget and Freud, respectively, to the social world and have gone on to show that socialization is a *life-long process*.

There are two important points characterizing the idea that children, from birth onwards, pass through a series of stages of development. First, that each stage is qualitatively different from the next. This means that the intellectual, social and emotional behaviour at one stage differs fundamentally from another stage, not in degree or quantity but in *quality*. Second, each stage is passed through in an orderly way. Individuals, it is claimed, may vary in the speed with which each stage is negotiated, but cannot vary the order or 'skip' one.

Within this 'ages and stages' approach there is much agreement that the early years of life (about the first two years) are of vital importance to understanding a person's personality, ability to form relationships, social behaviour generally, etc. as an adult. Simply put, one's early experiences determine how all future social situations are approached (although see Clarke and Clarke, 1976 for an opposing view). Consistent with this general conception many social psychologists regard the first relationship as a prototype (blueprint or model) for future relationships in that it determines the way a person approaches and behaves and interacts with other people. This being the case the focus of attention by social psychologists has been the relationship between mother (or caretaker) and child.

The nature of the relationship between mother and child* – and attachment shown by the child for the mother – has been studied with two questions in mind. First, how important is it for a child to be attached to its mother? Second, what consequences, if any, does failure to form, or the breaking of an attachment have? Following from the latter question is the issue of whether negative consequences of maternal deprivation can be compensated for by later positive experiences.

In looking at the nature and development of attachment and effects of maternal deprivation it is important to acknowledge the influence of both biological and environmental forces acting within and on the individual. Neither can, nor indeed ought to, be ignored when seeking to understand and explain social development.

Before plunging into these issues it will prove useful to examine how conceptions of childhood have changed over the past few hundred years and how psychologists go about the scientific study of child development.

## 2.2 Changing conceptions of childhood

Roughly prior and up to the end of the eighteenth century children were treated, so it would seem to us, very harshly. They were often beaten, had to stand in the presence of adults, were given opiates to subdue them and forced to leave home at six or seven to work as servants. Maccoby (1980) attributed child-rearing practices to three factors: (a) the Puritan influence, where it was believed that a child's will had to be broken to eradicate sin; (b) the high rate of infant mortality (before 1750 only 25 per cent of children in London reached the age of five years). This must have prevented parents from forming strong emotional attachments to their children; (c) misinformation: beliefs about children and how to raise them were largely a product of superstition, folklore and religious dogma. Generally, then, childhood was a brutal and unhappy time for the individual and was often remembered as such by adults.

Largely through the influence of two great philosophers – John Locke and Jean Jacques Rousseau – much of this changed. Locke, towards the end of the eighteenth century, fostered a more gentle, rational and educational approach. The views of each differed quite dramatically. Locke argued that all behaviour was a product of experience (a person is born a 'blank slate' upon which experience writes itself). Thus children were not to be regarded as innately sinful. Rousseau said children should grow as nature intended: he

---

*Throughout this and the next chapter the use of the word 'mother' is meant to signify either mother or caretaker. Where the person's natural mother is meant this will be indicated.

said they could not be expected to reason in a logical way until they were ready to develop such a capacity.

Whilst views and practices changed throughout the eighteenth century it was only with Darwin's publication of *The Origin of Species* that a scientific approach to the study of children started. Darwin had two important influences: (a) that any account of child development had to integrate biological forces generally, and instincts in particular, into an explanation; (b) a *comparative approach* became possible. Comparing humans with other animals (usually those high up the tree of evolutionary development) would shed light on human developmental processes. The latter influence formed an important basis for the Behaviourist school of psychology. Behaviourists – such as Watson and Skinner – viewed behaviour as the *sole product* of how a person had been reinforced or punished earlier in life.

Between the 1920s and 1950s research on social development, especially in America, was largely dominated by Behaviourism. Behaviourists viewed children as 'small adults' but this position became less tenable and in the 1960s views changed. Socialization was seen to fall into developmental stages where infants were predisposed to learn certain things at particular periods in their lives.

These changing views led to the focus of attention shifting from animal research to human social development. Three main research methods were refined to investigate this. First, experimental techniques using *longitudinal studies* and *group comparisons*. Longitudinal studies are where a group of children are observed and specified behaviours are *measured* over a number of occasions for a set period of time. Group comparisons use two or more groups of children of different ages to compare behaviours of interest to the researcher. Second, single-case studies. Here one person is intensely investigated for a significant period of time. Third, cultural influences upon behaviour. This is looked at both *cross-culturally* and *sub-culturally*. The former provides information about how differences *between* societies affect social behaviour; the latter about how different influences *within* society influence behaviour.

To summarize, changing conceptions of childhood in the past few hundred years have led not only to changes in child rearing practices but to the development of a scientific approach to the study of children. Contemporary views of human social development take account of three components: (a) biological forces; (b) cultural/subcultural influences; and (c) the experiences of the individual. In what follows the first two are dealt with briefly and the third in some detail.

## 2.3 Biological underpinnings

Few psychologists would attempt to assess the contributions of biological (nature) and environmental (nurture) forces separately. Instead theorists and researchers now talk about the *interaction* between the two. A study by Thomas, Chess and Birch (1970) provides a nice demonstration of how children differ in temperament from birth and how these differences interact with environmental influences.

Thomas, Chess and Birch studied 85 families (contributing a total of 141

**Table 2.1** Three temperament categories with examples of representative behaviour in each (Adapted from Thomas, Chess and Birch, 1970).

| TEMPERAMENT TYPE | BEHAVIOUR MEASURED | | | |
|---|---|---|---|---|
| | *Motor activity* | *Regularity* | *Response to new person or object* | *General mood* |
| | Active to inactive periods | Hunger, sleep, excretion, wakefulness | Approach or avoidance | Friendly as opposed to unfriendly |
| 'Easy' | Variable | Very regular | Positive approach | Positive |
| 'Slow to warm up' | Low to moderate | Variable | Initial withdrawal | Slightly negative |
| 'Difficult' | Variable | Irregular | Withdrawal | Negative |

children); the children were investigated from birth for 14 years. These researchers measured nine different behaviours (for example, motor activity, regularity of physical function, response to new persons or objects, general mood) in the first few months of life. Such measures led them to believe there were three general types of temperament into which the majority of the children fitted. The three types and some of the characteristics associated with them are summarized in Table 2.1.

It was found that 65 per cent of the children could be classified according to such a scheme. Babies in the 'EASY' category were found to be asleep by around 6.30 p.m. every night at six months of age, and at 10 years to sleep for consistent lengths of time. By contrast, 'DIFFICULT' babies were found to sleep for varying times at six months and to fall asleep at different times in the evenings at 10 years. 'Difficult' children were found to cry at the approach of strangers at two months and experience severe homesickness when at a summer camp at 10 years.

Whilst temperament was reasonably similar for the same child at different ages the research also highlighted how environmental influences could reduce or increase a particular temperament characteristic. However, the study further showed that some children exhibited different temperament types at different ages. The point is that this, and other, research demonstrates both how temperament may persist in life and also, within limits, how it may be modified by particular experiences and circumstances. Further discussion of biological underpinnings will be left until we look specifically at attachment in animals and the ethological approach.

## 2.4 Cultural and sub-cultural influences

Any account of how a child develops into a social being must take account of the social context in which the child is reared. By social context is usually meant such things as family structure, cultural history and political-economic organization. Evidence about how such factors affect development in general and socialization in particular may be obtained by comparing: (a) different societies; and (b) different subcultures within a society.

In considering the influence of society upon the individual certain regularities and common features need to be taken into account. At the same time it is important to be aware that any society is composed of numerous social environments. Generally, though; from birth to adolescence the individual is exposed to a number of different and often conflicting influences.

In most societies the family is the major source of influence on the child up to the age of approximately five years. All primary relationships are important, starting with the mother and then significant others (father, siblings, other relatives). From this relatively closed world of the family the child comes to interact more with the neighbourhood in which he or she lives. Particularly important is the influence of peers and peer groups on social behaviour. Such factors offer first-hand experience and develop awareness of such things as status differences, order and authority figures. In many ways the education system exerts similar influences but does so in a more formal way and provides a greater reflection of society's values. As the child moves into adolescence social structures such as religious, political, economic and legal systems all have profound effects. For example, relationships and their formalization through marriage involve many of these social structures. But how do differences in these various agencies of socialization actually affect behaviour?

Bronfenbrenner (1970) compared differences in how children were brought up in America and Russia and looked at behavioural consequences by assessing the concern children in each culture showed for people of another, older, generation. The major differences Bronfenbrenner found in child rearing resulted from the 'collective' ethos in Russia and the more 'individualistic' approach in America. In Russia children were encouraged to be more involved in family and domestic matters, and instilled with a sense of social responsibility earlier. Children in Russia were found to spend considerably more time interacting with parents, other adults and older children than their American counterparts. Bronfenbrenner conducted a series of experiments looking at the willingness of children to engage in antisocial behaviour when the children knew that either their peers, other adults or nobody would know what they had done. It was found, generally, that Soviet children were much less willing to do antisocial things than their American counterparts. Furthermore, it was found that American children were most inclined to be antisocial when they thought their peers would be informed; this was not the case for the Russian children. Bronfenbrenner comes to the rather depressing conclusion that the American style results in more delinquent, socially and morally irresponsible individuals than does the Russian approach. Whiting and Whiting (1975), in looking at altruistic behaviour in different societies, suggest three conditions foster helpfulness: (a) contributing to the welfare of the family; (b) knowing that the tasks *have* to be done; and (c) awareness by the child of the importance of the tasks to the family's welfare.

In moving from considering societal to *sub-cultural* influences the crucial point is that sub-cultures offer an individual a number of *reference groups*. Reference groups provide such things as values, moral codes of conduct, and

**Table 2.2** Selection of items from Self-Esteem Inventory of Coopersmith (1967). There are 58 items in all, for each the child has to say whether the statement is representative of him or her ('Like me') or unrepresentative ('Unlike me'). Positive self-evaluations lead to a high self-esteem score.

SELF-ESTEEM INVENTORY

| | Like me | Unlike me |
|---|---|---|
| I'm pretty sure of myself | | |
| I often wish I were someone else | | |
| I'm easy to like | | |
| I'm popular with kids of my own age | | |
| My parents understand me | | |
| Kids usually follow my ideas | | |

help mould a person's self-esteem (the extent to which a person sees him or herself in a positive or negative way). This was demonstrated in a study by Coopersmith (1967) who developed a self-esteem questionnaire and administered it to groups of children on a number of different occasions. The questionnaire (some items of which are shown in Table 2.2.) reflects a child's evaluation of him or herself with respect to peers, parents, school and hobbies. Coopersmith found a high degree of consistency of self-esteem in individuals over a five-week period. Children tested again after three years showed very similar levels of self-esteem. The relevance of such findings will become more apparent in Chapter 3 when dealing with Erikson's theory of socialization and identity. Central to this theory is the concept of 'identity', where an important part of a positive sense of identity is high self-esteem.

In summary, psychologists have found both societal and sub-cultural influences important for understanding how a child becomes socialized into behaving and functioning in a given social structure. This more 'sociological' perspective tends to ignore the individual's experiences: by looking at the 'first relationship' we can explore this aspect more fully.

## 2.5 The first relationship

Bowlby (1951) has claimed that 'mother love in infancy and childhood is as important for mental health as are vitamins and proteins for physical health'. A very strong claim about the necessity of a loving first relationship for the child and one which, at the time, lacked sufficient empirical support to be accepted without reservation. Since then numerous empirical studies have been carried out, on both humans and other animals, to assess the function and importance of the mother–child relationship.

Two main questions have been addressed by much of the research: (a) does the first relationship for the child have to be with the *natural* mother (as Bowlby would seem to indicate) or would anybody who provided a caring environment do? (b) what are the consequences, if any, of failure to form an early, first relationship and what may be the consequences, again if any, of the breaking down of a first relationship once it has been formed? The first question is dealt with under the heading '*attachment*', the second under '*maternal deprivation*'.

Before proceeding it is important to be clear about what social psychologists mean when talking about attachment with respect to mother–child relationship. Any bond or affectional tie between two people may be called an attachment. Attachment is characterized by a caring or loving and *enduring* relationship. Applying attachment to the mother–child relationship: the *bond* between mother and child may be defined as *'the tendency, during the first two years of life, to seek the proximity of particular people, to be receptive to receiving care from these people, secure in their presence'* (Maccoby, 1980).

### 2.5.1 Attachment in animals

Bowlby has put forward a theory in which it is claimed that there is a strong biological (genetic) component in attachment. Using evidence from ethology (a branch of biology that investigates unlearned, and hence inherited, patterns of animal behaviour) to substantiate his claims, Bowlby likens human attachment to that found in lower animals.

Many species of animals exhibit behaviour patterns that elicit caretaking behaviour from the adult. For example, newly hatched herring-gull chicks peck instinctively at red dots. The red dot is on the adult bird, the pecking releases food from the adult to the chick. Leon (1977) has shown that particular pheromones (odorous secretions influencing behaviour) secreted by the mother rat causes the infant to seek the parent's proximity. In monkeys touch is a very important behaviour between mother and infant: mutual grooming, clinging to the mother's fur and body contact generally are thought to strengthen the attachment. Attempts to separate infant and mother result in quite aggressive and violent responses on the part of the mother and great stress for the infant monkey if the separation attempt is successful.

These and many other examples demonstrate two things: first, attachment is *instinctive* in many species, second, attachment develops as a result of *reciprocity*. Both adult and infant behaviours are *matched* – instinctive behaviour on the part of the infant causes instinctive responses from the adult, and *vice versa*.

Research by ethologists has helped refine and clarify our ideas about what instinctive behaviour is and how the environment can modify such behaviours. Both Tinbergen (1951) and Lorenz (1957) showed how instinctive behaviour can be modified by experience. Lorenz, working with newly hatched graylag geese, found young goslings had an inborn tendency to follow the mother goose. Lorenz further discovered that this following tendency generalized to any moving, noisy object. Whatever noisy, moving object the gosling first followed was followed thereafter. Lorenz called this *imprinting*. Such a predisposition to learn received further support when it was found that there are *critical and sensitive periods* during which imprinting takes place most quickly and successfully. For example, it was found that if young goslings were not exposed to any noisy, moving object in the first few days of life they were much less likely to imprint later on. Research

**Table 2.3** Key terms used to explain instinctive behaviour in animals (comments refer to imprinting in goslings).

| TERM | BRIEF EXPLANATION | COMMENTS |
|---|---|---|
| Imprinting | Inborn tendency to attach to first noisy, moving object encountered. | Normally takes place in first few days of life. |
| Critical period | Imprinting can only take place during this period. If outside the critical period imprinting will not take place. | Normal time up to 10 days. Both periods can be extended depending on environmental circumstances. |
| Sensitive period | Period of time when animal is most likely to imprint. The most sensitive period is shorter than the critical period. | |

suggested, then, that if imprinting did not take place during the critical or sensitive period then it probably never would; if it did it was likely to be much weaker (Hess, 1959).

Guiton (1959) has shown nature not to be so inflexible by demonstrating that the critical and sensitive period for imprinting can be extended. For example, young chicks kept in total isolation were found to remain capable of imprinting longer than chicks reared in groups. Those reared in groups imprinted each other and had a shorter critical and sensitive period than chicks reared in natural conditions with the mother. Environmental conditions can either shorten or lengthen the period during which the animal is sensitive to imprinting.

The concept of critical and sensitive periods has been seen as important to explaining attachment in humans and sub-human primates. Whilst few psychologists would subscribe to the view that imprinting takes place in human babies, the issue of whether there are critical and sensitive periods (i.e. periods when a child is most receptive to the caring and responsiveness of another person) has attracted much attention. Bowlby claims that there are both critical and sensitive periods and that there is an innate bias for a child to attach to one person (known as monotropy).

### 2.5.2 Attachment in humans

To investigate empirically the mother–child bond social psychologists have had to develop reliable measures of attachment. Two measures have been widely used: (a) *fear of strangers*, this is the response of the infant to the arrival of a strange person in both the presence and absence of the mother; and (b) *separation anxiety*, which is the amount of distress shown by the child when separated from the mother and the degree of comfort and happiness shown by the infant on reunion. Strong attachment is assumed to exist when a child shows a strong negative reaction to a stranger (cries, seeks proximity and physical contact with mother, etc.) and great distress when separated from the mother and joy/relief when reunited. Generally, weak attachment or lack of attachment is shown by little or no reactions in the above situations.

Schaffer and Emerson (1964) used these measures to plot the course of the development of attachment during the first 18 months of a child's life. They observed 60 babies and mothers in their own homes at monthly periods. Generally, they found three phases in the development of attachment – the 'indiscriminate', 'specific' and 'multiple' phases. These are summarized in Table 2.4 below. Schaffer and Emerson found important deviations from these generalizations. For example, not all 60 babies formed primary attachments to the mother, sometimes it was the father (30 per cent of babies) and sometimes another significant person (15 per cent of babies). A small percentage showed no attachment either to the mother, father or other significant person (relative, close friend of the parents, etc.).

**Table 2.4** Stages of attachment found by Schaffer and Emerson (1964).

| STAGE OF ATTACHMENT | ROUGH AGE RANGE | CHARACTERISTICS |
|---|---|---|
| *Indiscriminate Attachment* | up to about six months | Does not matter who holds baby. Smiles at anybody. Protests when put down whoever holding him or her. |
| *Specific Attachment* | from about seven months to a year | Usually to mother. Shows fear of strangers and separation anxiety. Intense for three to four months. Wide range of onset – six months to one year. |
| *Multiple Attachment* | from about one year onwards | Begins about three months after start of specific attachment. Broadens – first to one other person, then a number of significant others. |

Strength of attachment has been found to be positively associated with maternal responsiveness, which is characterized as the ability and sensitivity of the mother to respond to the baby's vocal and non-verbal signals. Ainsworth (1973), for example, has shown attachment to be strong when mothers responded in a consistent, regular and quick way when their children cried.

We need to consider the behaviours, on the part of the mother and child, that contribute to the general course of development suggested by Schaffer and Emerson, and particularly with respect to the development of the first relationship. The behaviours in each of the phases, summarized in Table 2.4, will be discussed in this context.

The *indiscriminate attachment* phase may be seen as a period during which preparations are made, on the part of the mother and child, for the development of the intense relationship. The child slowly focuses on one individual: becoming accustomed to being soothed, touched and smiled at by one person, the smell of the mother may also become familiar. Looking, smiling and crying constitute what may be called the first truly social behaviours. Wolff (1969) has shown that infant cries can be categorized into three types – hunger, anger and pain. Appropriate responses by the mother to these different cries are the beginnings of attachment. Looking and eye-contact are also important. Looking at the mother (and/or significant others) in the region of the face generally and the eyes in particular serves as a familiarization process and the start of a communication system for the child. As the child moves into the second six months of life smiling becomes more and more reserved for and directed at the mother. Generally, then, over the first six months of life looking, smiling and crying increasingly become directed away from numerous people to become focused on just one person.

The *specific attachment* phase is not only regarded as a possible prototype for future relationships but also seen as functioning to soothe the child and provide emotional security. Ainsworth (1973) has found four patterns of behaviour shown by children to strange environments and people. (a) When in a strange room with only the mother, the child first stays with the mother and then begins to explore the room. (b) The child rushes back to the mother when a stranger enters. (c) After a short time the child responds cautiously to the stranger's attempts to engage in play. (d) When the mother leaves the room the child often cries and plays much less. This general pattern suggests the attached person is used as a base from which to explore the world.

Attachment, shown by strong protest and distress when the child is separated from the mother, is at its most intense during the early part of the child's second year of life. Kagan (1976) has shown this to be the case in both children who spend all their time at home and those who spend five full days at nursery. Kagan (1976) has also shown a high degree of cross-cultural similarity by finding similar reactions to separation from the mother in both Kungsan Bushmen of Botswana and urban western children.

The *multiple attachment* phase begins roughly three months after the start of specific attachment, i.e. around the age of 12 to 15 months. Multiple attachment is characterized by the child showing separation anxiety with a number of people and seeking the proximity of those people. Schaffer and Emerson (1964) found very few of their sample of 60 children to be attached to only one person at 18 months. Later attachments have, on the whole, been found to be less intense than those in the specific attachment phase.

The quality and intensity of attachment, as we have seen, has been looked at by psychologists by observing the child's reaction to separation and encounters with strangers. The question arises as to why, exactly, should separation and strangeness often result in such distress? Current thinking on this matter (Schaffer, 1971; Bower, 1977) has tended to emphasize the *reciprocal* nature of mother–child interaction. This has led to a *communication theory* of attachment being proposed.

The communication theory of attachment is concerned with the way non-verbal behaviours such as smiling and eye-contact develop into a particular communication system between the mother and child. Stern (1974) found mother and child to engage in complex patterns of looking and eye-contact – the mother is concerned to engage in eye-contact, once established she goes on looking, all the while monitoring where the child is looking. Rutter (1984) has shown that children by the end of the second year can use looking and eye-contact to initiate and structure interaction as well as obtain feedback on their performance. Such a pattern is similar to that found in adults (Rutter, 1984). Collis and Schaffer (1975) have shown children to initiate such social interaction through their looking behaviour.

This complex but orderly pattern of non-verbal behaviour leads, over time, to the mother and child developing and maintaining an individualistic and unique (for the baby) style of communication. Schaffer (1971) suggests that by the age of about 7 months baby and mother have established a complex set of non-verbal routines extemely specific to the two individuals involved. For the child it provides an important source of information about the world, and upon separation the baby, effectively, has no one to communicate with. Strangers do not, as it were, 'speak the same language'. Separation anxiety and fear of strangers result, then, from the child being left socially 'stranded' and isolated from communication with the outside world. With the onset of language, round about the age of two, the child is able to communicate with many people. Not surprisingly, then, separation anxiety is found to diminish with the onset of language, lending further support to the communication theory of attachment.

### 2.5.3  Differences in attachment

We saw in the previous section that Schaffer and Emerson (1964) found children to vary in the quality and object (mother, father, etc.) of their attachment. Also, whilst finding some consistency from month to month in the intensity of a child's attachment, long-term consistency was less in evidence. Ainsworth and her colleagues (Ainsworth, Bell and Stayton, 1974; Ainsworth and Wittig, 1969) investigated different reactions of children to strangers and suggested three categories of attachment behaviour – 'avoidant', 'secure' and 'resistant'. These and their associated characteristics are summarized in Table 2.5. Ainsworth found the 'avoidant' type to be relatively rare, with the secure being the most common.

Over relatively short periods of time the child remains in the same category. Sroufe and Waters (1977) had independent observers classify 50 12-month old children according to the above typology: 32 were classified as secure, nine as avoidant and nine as resistant. Six months later classification of the same 50 children resulted in 48 being assigned to the same category as they were at 12 months. Less is known about stability of attachment over longer periods of time though.

Why should different attachment behaviours develop and persist? Leaving aside the general issues of maternal deprivation and child abuse, we need to look at both the child's *and* mother's contribution.

With Thomas, Chess and Birch's (1970) longitudinal study of temperament in children (described earlier in this chapter) it seemed that some children are naturally more difficult to handle, play with, feed, etc. than others. It may be, then, that children showing insecure (resistant in Table 2.5) attachment may be those seen to be 'difficult' in Thomas *et al.*'s classification. Schaffer and Emerson (1964) found some babies to dislike and resist being touched. Schaffer (1971) showed these 'resisters' to be highly active children and slower to develop a specific attachment.

Apart from the child's temperament what effect does responsiveness or lack of it have on the type of attachment that develops? Ainsworth and Bell

**Table 2.5** Different types of attachment behaviours shown by child when separated from the mother and upon reunion. From Ainsworth, Bell and Stayton (1971).

| TYPE OF ATTACHMENT | CHARACTERISTICS |
| --- | --- |
| *Avoidant* | Before separation – exploring and playing, unaffected by location of mother<br>Reunion – child ignores the mother |
| *Secure* | Before separation – at ease when playing, positive with strangers, not physically close<br>Reunion – goes to mother, then plays |
| *Resistant* | Before separation – difficulty in using mother as a base. Fussy and worrying.<br>Reunion – both seeks and is resistant to contact. |

(1971) observed 26 mother–child pairs every three weeks for the first year of the child's life. They observed such things as feeding patterns, speed of mother's response to crying, etc. Independent observers rated the mothers on four dimensions of mothering, then related patterns of mothering to type of attachment. The four dimensions of mothering are summarized in Table 2.6. These four dimensions are not independent of each other since, for example, highly sensitive mothers are usually very accepting of the child and understand more fully what mothering entails.

Ainsworth and Bell (1971) found that children who showed 'secure' attachment had responsive mothers. Independent observers tended to rate mothers of securely attached children as sensitive, accepting, cooperative and

**Table 2.6** Four dimensions of mothering used by Ainsworth (1973) in trying to relate 'responsiveness' of the mother to the type of attachment formed.

| RESPONSIVENESS DIMENSION | DESCRIPTION OF THE DIMENSION | |
| --- | --- | --- |
| *Sensitivity-Insensitivity* | *Sensitive* – | correct interpretation of baby's needs, able to see things from the child's point of view. |
| | *Insensitive* – | wishes and moods of mother dominate interaction. Lack of response often. |
| *Acceptance-Rejection* | *Acceptance* – | accepting of ties and responsibilities. Enjoys being with baby, not badly affected by baby being difficult. |
| | *Rejection* – | anger and resentment at ties and responsibilities. |
| *Cooperation-Interference* | *Cooperation* – | encourages baby's independence, patient in trying to get baby to do things he/she wants to do. |
| | *Interference* – | mother imposes will on child without concern for child's state of mind. |
| *Accessibility-Ignoring* | *Accessibility* – | aware of baby's changing moods, and minute-by-minute signalling. |
| | *Ignoring* – | concerned with own thoughts and feelings, fails to notice child's signalling. |

accessible. By contrast, mothers of children who were classified as 'avoidant' in their attachment behaviour were rated as rejecting and insensitive. 'Resistant' attachment was found to be related to rejecting, interfering and ignoring behaviour on the part of the mother.

Caution must be used in both generalizing and applying these findings since much further research, both within and between different cultures, is needed before the findings described above can be regarded as both reliable and valid. Also, it is important to bear in mind that attachment, as described earlier, is the result of *reciprocal* interaction between the mother and child and not simply under the control of one of the individuals (except in fairly extreme circumstances such as neglect or child abuse).

## 2.6  Maternal deprivation

The highly emotive topic of maternal deprivation has been looked at by psychologists with two main questions in mind: (a) do 'bad' early experiences follow the person into later life? For example, maternal deprivation has been alleged to be the cause of criminal behaviour, mental illness and psychopathic personalities; and (b) are there critical and sensitive periods in the first year or so of a child's life such that failure to form a specific attachment during this period means that the individual will experience difficulty forming deep and enduring relationships as an older teenager and adult? Attempting to answer both questions is important for evaluating the claims of such people as Bowlby and Erikson (see Chapter 3) who regard early experience as vital for psychological health and well-being.

It is important to be aware of two general problems with the term 'maternal deprivation' from the outset. First, use of the words embodies many assumptions about correct/incorrect, right/wrong ways, etc. of how children *should* be brought up. Further, there is an implicit assumption that we know what is a 'healthy' or 'well-balanced' personality. Second, as a concept, maternal deprivation does not represent a unitary phenomenon. As Rutter (1981) shows, maternal deprivation is comprised of a diverse range of behaviours and experiences. Whilst many distinctions are possible two have guided much research: (a) where there is a failure, for whatever reason, for a bond to form in the first place; and (b) where a specific attachment is formed and then broken (either for a short time then re-established, or permanently).

With these problems in mind we will proceed to look at the consequences of maternal deprivation first in animals then in humans.

### 2.6.1  Consequences in animals

Harlow and Harlow (1959) found both dramatic and long-lasting effects to result from depriving infant monkeys of *any* social contact. The Harlows raised two groups of monkeys in the following way: each monkey was put, separately, in a cage which contained two 'imitation' mothers made of wire and shaped to look like adult mother monkeys. One of these wire imitations was padded with terry cloth, the other left bare. In one experimental condition the bare wire imitation contained a feeder nipple, in the other condition the padded terry cloth imitation held the feeder. The Harlows

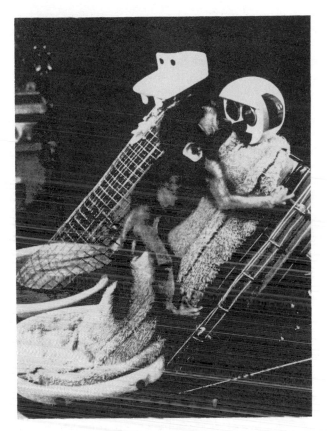

**Figure 2.1** The cloth and wire surrogate mothers used by Harlow (1959)

measured, among other things, the time spent clinging to the two surrogate mothers by the infant monkeys. Regardless of which conditions the monkeys were reared in it was found that infants clung most to the terry cloth 'mother'. Attachment, then, at least in sub-human primates is unlikely to derive from 'cupboard love' as people like Freud and Behaviourists such as Watson thought.

The monkeys lived in these conditions for the first six months of their lives. During this period they had no contact at all with other monkeys. The monkeys were put in cages with other monkeys and reared normally after the experiment. What consequences did this early deprivation have? At three years of age (adulthood) these monkeys were placed in individual breeding cages with a monkey of the opposite sex. The 'experimental' monkeys displayed quite abnormal social and sexual behaviour: monkeys of both sexes were found to be socially incompetent, sexual behaviour in females showed fear and aggression to the male, while male monkeys were found to be both fearful and clumsy in their sexual advances (Harlow and Harlow, 1959). Generally, these monkeys never behaved in a normal social way with other normally reared monkeys. This research demonstrates that monkeys, who have evolved as social animals, develop abnormally when deprived of early social experiences.

Kaufman and Rosenblum (1969) investigated maternal deprivation in monkeys where attachment was first allowed to develop, then the infant was separated from the mother for four weeks at the age of six months. Initial reaction to the separation was one of stress with displays of disruptive behaviour. This decreased over the four-week separation period, with infant monkeys behaving normally at the end. Upon reunion, above average levels of clinging and proximity seeking was shown by the infant for up to the next three months.

This and other similar research on monkeys and other animals tends to support the notion that there are critical and sensitive periods for attachment. Maternal deprivation in the sense of lack of opportunity to form *any* attachment has severe negative consequences for adult social functioning. Temporary separation, from the little evidence available, would appear not to result in such consequences.

### 2.6.2 Consequences in humans

Four 'syndromes' have been claimed to result from maternal deprivation – acute distress, conduct disorders, intellectual retardation and affectionless psychopathy (Rutter, 1981). Two main research strategies have been used to assess the validity of these claims: (a) when attachment has developed normally and is then disrupted. Disruption may be for a short time (often looked at in the context of infant hospitalization) or permanent (when children are taken into institutional care); (b) when the infant has not had an opportunity to develop an attachment to one person. This often occurs when a child is taken into care at a very early age since such children often experience a large number of 'caretakers' with no one person remaining a stable and enduring feature of their world.

Single case studies provide anecdotal information about the effects of severe deprivation in humans. For example, Curtiss (1977) reports the case of Genie, who experienced almost complete social deprivation for the first 13 years of life. When found, she could not walk, talk or keep herself clean and had a mental age of less than a five-year-old. After four years in a normal environment Genie was able to talk in short sentences and progressed to a mental age of 11. Clarke and Clarke (1976) give accounts of other known cases of 'total' deprivation. Freud and Dann (1951) report an intriguing but sad case of six Jewish children who lived together without their parents in a number of Nazi concentration camps during the Second World War. The children developed very strong attachments to each other and only at the age of three–four, when in England after the war, did they develop an attachment to an adult. These attachments were very intense and possessive on the part of the children. The study is of importance since it provides some evidence for *plasticity* of the child to move from one attachment figure to another. However, planned and controlled scientific studies are required so as objectively to evaluate consequences, if any, resulting from maternal deprivation. Each of the four syndromes mentioned earlier in this section will now be looked at.

On admission to hospital or residential care children have often been observed to show *acute distress*. Spitz and Wolf (1946) showed this reaction to be directly related to strength of the bond in the first place: the more intense the attachment the greater the *initial* distress reaction. Robertson and Robertson (1971) found less distress to be shown by the child when the new environment provided a 'family' type atmosphere. A 'family' environment was characterized by the child being looked after by a small group of people who were a relatively constant feature during the stay in hospital/residential nursery. Thus acute distress may result more from a strange environment than separation *per se*. Reactions upon returning home and reunion with the mother also seem to depend on the nature of the attachment before separation. Strong bonding before separation tends to result in initial rejection upon reunion swiftly followed by re-establishment of the relationship as it was before. In contrast, where the mother–child relationship was tense and difficult before, more enduring signs of disturbance were observed after reunion at home with the mother.

*Conduct disorders*, manifested by antisocial behaviour generally and sometimes delinquency, have been found to result more from discord and disharmony within the family than separation of the child from the mother. Rutter (1971), for example, showed divorce to be more associated with delinquency than death of a parent. Hetherington, Cox and Cox (1979) found that whilst conduct disorders may follow immediately after divorce, after two years much less disturbed behaviour was in evidence compared to children who lived in homes with continual marital disharmony.

Tizard and her colleagues (Tizard and Joseph, 1970; Tizard and Rees, 1974; Tizard and Hodges, 1978) have investigated the claim that *intellectual retardation* may result from maternal deprivation. Tizard has addressed two questions in this context: (a) to what extent, if any, do contemporary institutions retard development? and (b) to what extent can different institutional environments account for intellectual differences between children?

In one study Tizard compared two-year-olds living in residential nurseries with two-year-olds in working-class families. She found residential children to be excessively shy and clinging, due, she thought, to such children having only limited experience with adults and multiple caretaking due to rapid staff turnover. The question arises as to whether differences of this sort in the child's social world affect intellectual development.

In another study Tizard compared three groups of four and a half year olds who had spent between two and four years in residential care. Of the 65 children used in this study 24 had been adopted by the age of four and a half, 15 returned to their natural mothers and 26 were still in care. All children were found to have *at least* average intelligence, with the adopted children having the highest IQ of the three groups. Tizard found some evidence for retardation of linguistic ability at the age of two years but this was at least normal (if not better) by the time the children had reached the age of four and a half.

A further study by Tizard looked at the relationship between *type* of residential environment and development of language skills. Three types of

**Table 2.7** Residential environments compared by Tizard when looking for differences in linguistic abilities in residential children.

| RESIDENTIAL ENVIRONMENT | CHARACTERISTICS |
| --- | --- |
| *Highly centrally organized* | Matron 'ran' the nursery. Decision making centralized. Little scope for autonomy and initiative for nurses. |
| *Mixture of centrally and decentrally organized* | Centralized decision making with a degree of autonomy. Children could choose what to do up to a point. |
| *Highly decentralized* | Children in 'family' units. Children arranged own day. Staff made own decisions and worked autonomously. |

nurseries were compared (summarized in Table 2.7) and three types of data collected: (a) records and interviews with staff; (b) direct observations of interaction between children and staff; (c) psychological tests – vocal and non-verbal measures of intellectual abilities. It was found that whilst different environments did produce different abilities there was no evidence of retardation. Children in the 'highly decentralized' nursery achieved the highest test scores. In the decentralized setting verbal interaction between staff and children was found to be more informative, also greater time was spent by staff reading to and playing with the children.

To summarize, there appears to be little evidence of maternal deprivation resulting in intellectual retardation. Environments encouraging more contact, play, conversation, etc. and operating in small family groupings appear to produce above-average abilities. In short, a caring, intimate and stable environment seems to be more important than maternal care *per se* for intellectual development.

Rutter (1981) summarizes evidence (both anecdotal and experimental) for and against the claim that lack of an intense, stable and enduring attachment in early life may lead to personality disorders generally and *affectionless psychopathy* in particular. Evidence cited in favour tends to be of three types: (a) that psychiatric disorders as an adult often have roots in early childhood; (b) attempts to 'reverse' negative consequences of early extreme cases of deprivation are often less successful than when deprivation occurs in later childhood; (c) a greater relationship between early childhood and adult status has been observed than between adult status and later childhood. Evidence against comes from numerous studies showing how improvement in environment in middle and later childhood often leads to major positive changes in the child. For example, Skeels and Dye (1939) showed that orphaned children when transferred to an environment where there was more handling, play and permanency of others gained 32 IQ points when compared with a control group. Further, in a follow-up study 20 years later the experimental group was still found to be superior in intelligence.

Hard evidence about the effects of maternal deprivation on the ability of a person to form deep, enduring relationships later on in life is hard to come by. Tizard and Hodges (1978) found that late-adopted children (aged between four and eight years) developed deep relationships with their adopted parents. This was found even when the children showed no signs of attachment to a caretaker in an institution during their early years. However, late-adopted children after they had been adopted for two to three years showed similar social problems and attention-seeking behaviour as their institutional counterparts. Research shows, then, that 'it appears that although attachments can still develop for the first time after infancy, nevertheless fully normal social development may be dependent on early bonding' (Rutter, 1981, p. 190).

In summary, claims that deprivation of early attachment lead to 'affectionless psychopthy' have not been substantiated. Multiple caretaking *may* produce disruptive social behaviour but does *not* appear to affect the individual's ability to form and maintain a relationship with adopted parents. Further research is needed to see if this continues to be the case in adulthood.

### 2.6.3 Assessment

This section on maternal deprivation began by asking two questions: (a) whether 'bad' early experiences follow the person into later life; and (b) whether there is a critical and sensitive period in the first year or so of a child's life such that failure to form a specific attachment during this period would have negative social and intellectual consequences.

Both questions, as the research described here suggests, do not allow for simple answers. To answer the former question we first need to know whether the 'bad' experiences continue or not. If they do, the research on these four syndromes suggests difficulties may well be experienced in later childhood and adulthood. However, if circumstances 'improve', gains in intellectual ability, reduction of social problems, etc. can be expected. The second question, concerning a critical and sensitive period, also allows for no clear-cut answer: in extreme cases of deprivation, particularly in sub-human primates, later compensation has only limited effect. In less extreme cases of deprivation, either where no attachment has formed or one has formed and then been broken, no serious impairment to a person's ability to form relationships has been found. It seems that Bowlby overstated the case when he claimed that attachment *must* develop in the first years of life for an individual to engage in normal relationships later in life.

Much further research is needed before an adequate knowledge of the effects of different variables upon a child's social development is achieved. Much has been achieved in the past 30 years since the influential writings of Bowlby first appeared. However, it is now clear that the issues and problems are much more complex than they were once thought to be.

## 2.7 Early years and later life

Often, when reading texts on developmental psychology, one gets the impression, mistakenly, that by the time the child reaches the age of five or thereabouts personality, emotional responses and social behaviour generally are determined for life. As we have seen in the course of this chapter, the extent to which early childhood experiences predetermine later childhood, adolescence and adulthood is much less straightforward than psychologists once thought.

Socially, if socially is taken to refer both to relationships we form with other people and moral behaviour, much development takes place after the 'early years'. As will be shown in the next chapter, when dealing with the theories of Kohlberg and Erikson, social and moral development is thought not only to extend into late childhood and adolescence but *throughout* life. Kohlberg and Erikson take quite different views as to the significance of early experiences for later life. Erikson regards the early years as vital for instilling in the person a basic sense of trust concerning the world generally and other people in particular. Kohlberg, on the other hand, regards only the most extreme interpersonal traumas (such as total social deprivation) as of any significant consequence for later life. Both do agree, though, that social and moral development is a life-long process.

## 2.8 Summary

O Conceptions of childhood have changed dramatically over the past few hundred years. Children are no longer seen as 'small adults'.

O The scientific study of child development began in the wake of Charles Darwin. A comparative approach, comparing human and other animal development, became possible.

O In any account of child development both biological and cultural influences must be considered. Evidence for inheritance of temperament was described. Cultural influence was investigated by Bronfenbrenner by comparing Russian and American children's concern for other generations.

O Bowlby has been highly influential by using ethological research to suggest there is a critical and sensitive period in human social development.

O The first relationship, between mother and child, is called attachment. Strength of attachment is investigated by observing a child's reaction to strange environments/people and separation from the mother.

O Most children show an intense attachment from about seven months to a year. Psychologists have shown attachment to develop from reciprocity and suggested a 'communication theory'.

O Children show individual differences in attachment. Most can be classified as either 'avoidant', 'secure' or 'resistant'. Secure attachment tends to result from responsive mothers.

O Maternal deprivation takes many forms. The two main types researched are: (a) where no attachment develops; (b) where attachment forms and is then broken.

O Four syndromes have been claimed to result from maternal deprivation – acute distress, conduct disorders, intellectual retardation and affectionless psychopathy. Experimental research suggests: (a) early bad experiences can be compensated for later; (b) little relationship between maternal deprivation and intellectual retardation and personality disorders, except in extreme circumstances.

O More research is needed before it can be accepted that experiences in the early years have a fundamental and long-lasting effect on the individual. To date the case is not clearly shown.

## 2.9 Suggestions for further reading

Bowlby, J. *The Making and Breaking of Affectional Bonds* (London, Tavistock Publications, 1979).
Good introduction to Bowlby's views, very readable and providing a solid foundation before moving on to his more substantial books.

Maccoby, E. *Social Development: Psychological Growth and the Parent–Child Relationship* (New York, Harcourt Brace Jovanovich, 1980).
Comprehensive and well presented introduction to the area of social developments. Deals with the issues raised in this and the next chapter in detail.

Rutter, M. *Maternal Deprivation Reassessed* (2nd edn, Harmondsworth, Penquin, 1981).
Standard reading for anyone wanting an objective assessment of the evidence for and against the claimed effects of maternal deprivation. Get the second edition as this has important new chapters.

Schaffer, H.R. *The Growth of Sociability* (Harmondsworth, Penguin, 1971).
Useful introduction to research and theory on the development of the first relationship, between mother and child. Includes discussion of the relevance of other accomplishments (perceptual development) by the infant for the forming of the attachment bond.

# 3

# Socialization II: A life-long process

3.1    Two themes: social relationships and morality
3.2    Erikson's theory of social development
       *3.2.1 The 'eight stages of man'   3.2.2 Identity   3.2.3 Relationships in later life*
3.3    Kohlberg's theory of moral development
       *3.3.1 Three levels of moral reasoning   3.3.2 Measuring moral development*
       *3.3.3 Morality and ideology   3.3.4 Moral reasoning and moral behaviour*
3.4    *Moral behaviour*
       *3.4.1 The social learning theory approach   3.4.2 Television and moral behaviour*
3.5    Summary
3.6    Suggestions for further reading

## 3.1  Two themes: social relationships and morality

In Chapter 2 we looked at how the first relationship between child and mother may provide a 'blueprint' for the older individual to deal with the social world. We also looked at how failure to form an attachment or the disruption of an attachment may have negative effects on the ability of that person to form relationships later in life (as child, teenager or adult).

The general position advanced in what follows is that socialization is a continuous and life-long process. Whilst early experiences may be important they do not equip us to deal with social life as encountered by teenagers or adults. New experiences and new demands arise at different times in our lives. We have to change to deal with them and are changed in the process of dealing with them. Socialization then is a process that starts at birth and ends only with death. The former is considered by looking at Kohlberg's theory of *moral reasoning* and the Social Learning Theory approach to explaining *moral behaviour.* The latter is pursued by consideration of Erikson's eight-stage theory of pyschosocial development.

## 3.2  Erikson's theory of social development

Erik Erikson was strongly influenced by Freudian theory. However, unlike the Freudian approach which places heavy emphasis on *unconscious* mental processes, Erikson is more concerned with our day-to-day dealings with the social world. This is called *ego psychology* – since the ego (that part of our psychological structure we regard as the 'self') is thought to be that part of our personality which is largely conscious and in contact with the real world. (The unconscious part of our mind, according to psychoanalytic theory, has no awareness of the demands other people and society place upon us.) Erikson's ego psychology, then, is concerned to explain and understand how the individual copes with the everyday demands of social life, especially personal relationships and our attitude to society.

### 3.2.1 The 'eight stages of man'

Erikson (1950) proposes that the ego goes through eight stages of development: at each stage the individual has to negotiate a particular 'crisis' from which an *attitude* towards the self and other people develops. Crises may be negotiated in a positive or negative way: if positive the ego is *strengthened* and that attitude persists throughout a person's life, if negative the ego is weakened and the person goes into the next crisis without having resolved successfully the previous one.

The eight stages, shown in Table 3.1, are spread throughout a person's life with four occurring in childhood, one in adolescence and three in adulthood. The first stage is where the child learns a basic sense of *trust or mistrust* for the world in general and other people in particular. This takes place in the first year of life and the relationship between mother and child determines whether the person will feel secure and safe to explore the world. A satisfactory attachment, as characterized in Chapter 2, will allow the child to develop a sense of belonging or trust. The ego strength resulting from this is *hope*. Failure in the first relationship, such as through maternal deprivation, may lead to a sense of mistrust resulting in the person being fearful, lacking in confidence and perhaps being aggressive in achieving goals. This stage has attracted much attention from psychologists since it dovetails with work on attachment and maternal deprivation. It also supports the idea that early social experiences are important for later life.

The next three stages (*autonomy vs shame; initiative vs guilt;* and *industry vs inferiority*) are all concerned, in different ways, with the child learning to use and explore his or her own capabilities and potentials. Stage II is to do with self-confidence or self-esteem and is about feeling competent or not that one's objectives can be achieved. The negative aspect is self-doubt, shame in one's lack of abilities or poor abilities. Stage III, *initiative versus guilt*, centres around the development of a sense of responsibility for oneself with a sense of purpose emerging. During this stage sex and other role definitions (for example, social class) begin to take shape. Failure to develop a sense of purpose results in lack of independence and a persisting sense of guilt over this failure. Stage IV, *industry versus inferiority*, centres around the crisis of perceived self-competence at mastering tasks confronting the child. Initiative and purpose from the previous stage encourages the child to try all manner of new things; however, to risk trying new things is to risk failure. A realization of basic competence at tasks (in school and at play) results from success at attempting those tasks. In all these three stages Erikson is recognizing that the child is shifting from dependence on others (parents) to dependence on self. Self-determination in terms of self-will, purpose and competence (the ego strengths from these stages) has important implications for teenage and adult life. Career, hobbies, general social competence, etc. are all strongly

**Table 3.1** Eight stages of psychosocial development proposed by Erikson (1950). Table shows the 'crisis' at each stage, the successful outcome for the ego and the social relationships of prime importance at each stage.

| STAGE | ROUGH AGE | PSYCHOLOGICAL CRISIS | DESCRIPTION OF THE CRISIS | EGO STRENGTH | IMPORTANT RELATIONSHIPS |
|---|---|---|---|---|---|
| I | 0–1 yrs | Trust vs Mistrust | Learns to feel comfortable and trust parent's care; or develops distrust of the world. | Hope | Maternal person |
| II | 1–3 yrs | Autonomy vs Shame | Learns sense of competence by learning to feed oneself; play alone, use toilet; or feels ashamed and doubts own abilities. | Will | Parents |
| III | 3–5 yrs | Initiative vs Guilt | Learns to use own initiative in planning behaviour; or develops sense of guilt over misbehaviour. | Purpose | Basic family |
| IV | 5–11 yrs | Industry vs Inferiority | Learns to meet demands imposed by school and home responsibility; or comes to believe he or she is inferior to other people. | Competence | Family, neighbours, teachers |
| V | 11–18 yrs | Identity vs Identity Diffusion | Acquires sense of identity in terms of beliefs, vocation, etc.; or fails to achieve identity. | Fidelity | Peers, ingroups and outgroups |
| VI | 18–40 yrs | Intimacy vs Isolation | Engages in successful intimate relationship, joint identity with partner; or becomes isolated. | Love | Friends, lover |
| VII | 40–65 yrs | Generativity vs Stagnation | Helping others, allowing independence to children; or self-centred and stagnant. | Care | Spouse, children |
| VIII | 65–70 yrs | Integrity vs Despair | Reaps benefits of earlier stages, develops acceptance of temporary nature of life; or despairs over ever being able to find meaning in life. | Wisdom | Spouse, children, grandchildren |

influenced by one's sense of self-determination and self-esteem (Cooper-smith, 1967).

Adolescence is the period when most individuals go through an '*identity crisis*', this is Stage V in Erikson's scheme. The search for one's 'true self', or attempt to answer the question 'who am I?' are often seen to preoccupy teenagers. The positive outcome is a sense of identity which brings with it the ego strength of fidelity, one consequence of which is the ability to sustain loyal relationships with other people. The negative outcome is identity diffusion, where a person has been unable to establish a satisfactory identity for him or herself *and* has given up trying to achieve one. This may have grave consequences leading to depression and apathy, in extreme cases even suicide. The next section deals in more detail with this stage so further discussion will be left until then.

The next three stages all occur in adulthood, with the final one taking place only towards the end of one's life. Stage VI, *intimacy versus isolation*, concerns a crisis over whether the individual can give enough of him or herself to another, trust and reveal his or her inner self to another – does he or she develop an intimate (usually loving) relationship or become isolated? The ego strength of love is the positive result of being prepared to engage in a deep and intimate relationship. An inability to give in this sense may result in isolation and an absence of close, intimate relationships.

The stage of *generativity versus stagnation*, is concerned with helping others, especially the younger generation, to become responsible, self-determining individuals. In helping others Erikson means caring and giving without expectation of return: care is the ego strength. The negative aspect, stagnation, is where the person is unable to give freely and selflessly care; this results in the person becoming self-centred, preoccupied with his or her self and less willing to contribute to society.

The final stage, *integrity versus despair*, coincides by and large in the western world with the age of retirement from work. The crisis in this stage centres around the person being able or not to accept death. This stage also has a large retrospective element since the person looks back over life to assess whether ambitions have been achieved, goals attained, etc. Integrity, resulting in the ego strength of wisdom, results if the person regards life as having been and still being meaningful. Despair results from unfulfilled ambitions, frustrations and an inability to accept death since so little seems to have been achieved. This completes the cycle from birth to old age: Erikson says 'healthy children will not fear life if their elders have integrity enough not to fear death' (Erikson, 1950, p. 242).

### 3.2.2 Identity

In the course of a person's life it is perhaps in middle and late adolescence that dramatic and traumatic changes take place. The painful transition from childhood through adolescence to adulthood takes place, and at the heart of this process is the individual's search for *identity*. During Stages I to IV, according to Erikson, *identification* with others (parents, significant others) has been sufficient. However adolescence for Erikson is a time when the individual has to establish his or her own *unique* sense of identity. Two things happen in this search for one's own identity: (a) the adolescent rejects previous and existing identifications; (b) an identity crisis ensues. Evidence for the occurrence of (a) can be found simply by observation of the young in any generation. The desire not to conform to the values and standards of the older generation is shown, for example, by dressing and wearing hair differently. A crisis ensues because rejection of identifications leaves the teenager without an identity for a time. If this period should become extended the person may be unable to find an identity and identity diffusion, a negative state, may result. In identity diffusion the individual gives up attempting to establish a unique identity.

Matters are more complex than this since Erikson (1968) proposes four identity statuses that an individual may be in. These are described in Table 3.2. The status of identity achievement represents a successful resolution of the identity crisis, it results in the ego strength of fidelity – the ability to be able and want to offer commitment and loyalty to a job, political beliefs, and personal (intimate) relationships. By contrast, identity diffusion is a negative state where commitment and identity are lacking. Depression and apathy may set in and, in more extreme cases, if particularly negative, it may become self-perpetuating. The identity status of moratorium is a temporary one, it is positive because the individual is actively searching for an identity. This is achieved by suspending commitment, and trying out different styles of living and experimenting with relationships. Many societies provide the teenager with a means for doing this: in Britain, for example, 17/18 years olds have the opportunity to leave home and go into higher education. If a state of moratorium continues for too long it is likely to change into identity diffusion. The status of foreclosure is where the person has never experienced an identity crisis: identifications with parents/society have never been questioned. The individual has not arrived at a sense of identity by active, positive searching on his or her own part. Later in life people may experience quite traumatic and emotionally disturbing upheavals when foreclosure on identity does not give the individual a sufficient sense of self-identity. The identity crisis experienced by most people as teenagers may in some instances

**Table 3.2**  Four identity statuses and their description, from Erikson (1968).

| IDENTITY STATUS | DESCRIPTION |
| --- | --- |
| (a) Identity achievement | Person has gone through the identity crisis and achieved a sense of identity. This results in a firm commitment to such things as job, religion, moral values. |
| (b) Moratorium | Person in a state of identity crisis and actively seeking alternatives in an attempt to arrive at a commitment. A time of experimenting with different life styles. |
| (c) Foreclosure | Identity crisis has not been experienced. Parental values, societal values, etc. never been questioned. Accepts identification with parents/society as sufficient. |
| (d) Identity diffusion | Negative identity status. Individual shows little or no commitment to job, religion, values, etc. Not actively trying to make a commitment or seek an identity. |

only be experienced later in life (a few may never experience such a crisis at all). This highlights a very important aspect of Erikson's stages of psychosocial development – failures to resolve positively earlier crises have profound effects upon subsequent stages. This will be looked at explicitly in the next section on Relationships in Later Life.

Waterman and Waterman (1971) conducted a longitudinal study investigating changes in identity status in students during their first year at college. Two issues were looked at: (a) the pattern of changes in identity status; and (b) whether some statuses were more stable than others. Ninety-two first-year students were assessed for identity status at the beginning of their studies at college. This was done by semi-structured interviews in which each student was asked about intended occupation, religious beliefs and political views. Each interview was tape-recorded and played back to a number of judges who assigned the student to one of the four identity statuses. The same students were contacted a year later and assessed for identity status in a similar way.

Results provided support for Erikson's theory with respect to intended occupations but not for ideology (political and religious beliefs). Table 3.3 summarizes the findings, it shows that for occupational choice students moved into the moratorium status after the first year at college, also there was a decrease in the status of Identity diffusion after the first year. However, identity achievement decreased and identity diffusion increased after the first year with respect to political and religious beliefs, the reverse of what was predicted. Waterman and Waterman attributed this pattern of findings to the fact that they had used engineering students as subjects. They argued that vocation would be the primary consideration for such students, once this had been decided on they would move on to ideological (religious, political) issues. It might be expected that the reverse pattern from arts and social science students would be found, since social studies are far less career-specific than engineering.

Stark and Traxler (1974) provided evidence for the claim that late adolescence is characterized by an identity crisis by comparing the extent to which

**Table 3.3** Number of college students in each identity status for occupation and ideology when first joining college (first interview) and one year later (second interview). Adapted from Waterman and Waterman (1971).

| IDENTITY STATUS | FIRST INTERVIEW | SECOND INTERVIEW |
| --- | --- | --- |
| *Occupation* | | |
| Identity achievement | 11 | 12 |
| Moratorium | 11 | 22 |
| Foreclosure | 23 | 22 |
| Identity diffusion | 32 | 21 |
| *Ideology* | | |
| Identity achievement | 20 | 14 |
| Moratorium | 8 | 8 |
| Foreclosure | 38 | 31 |
| Identity diffusion | 14 | 27 |

**Table 3.4** Identity diffusion scores for males and females in two age groups. Higher scores indicates *less* identity diffusion. Adapted from Stark and Traxler (1974).

| AGE | SEX | MEAN IDENTITY DIFFUSION SCORE |
| --- | --- | --- |
| 17–20 | Males | 28.1 |
| 17–20 | Females | 30.6 |
| 17–20 | Males & females | 29.0 |
| 21–24 | Males | 32.1 |
| 21–24 | Females | 34.0 |
| 21–24 | Males & females | 33.8 |

identity diffusion existed in students in the 17–20 and 20–24 age range. Erikson's theory predicts that this status should occur less frequently in the older age range since a resolution of the crisis should have taken place. In this study the *degree* or intensity of identity diffusion was assessed, this was done by administering a questionnaire to over 500 subjects, the questionnaire gave a measure of identity diffusion. Table 3.4 depicts the findings, it shows two things: (a) identity diffusion decreases in the older age group as predicted; and (b) identity diffusion is less in females for both age groups. Stark and Traxler also showed that the status of identity diffusion is emotionally unpleasant: greater anxiety was shown by students in the 17–20 than 21–24 age range. Overall, then, both studies provide support for Erikson's theory about identity, but Waterman and Waterman (1971) show that matters are more complicated than the theory suggests.

### 3.2.3 Relationships in later life

A fundamental principle of Erikson's eight-stage approach to psychosocial development is that the outcome of a 'crisis' at one stage influences how the person approaches and proceeds through the next and subsequent stages. We do not have the space to explore this in its widest sense, instead we can address a specific aspect of this by asking how resolution of the identity crisis affects the intimacy versus isolation stage.

Orlofsky, Marcia and Lesser (1973) tested the hypothesis that identity achievement is more likely to lead to a positive outcome of the intimacy *vs* isolation crisis. College students were interviewed to determine: (a) their identity status; and (b) their intimacy status. Identity status was determined in a similar way to Waterman and Waterman (1971); intimacy status was determined by: (a) a half-hour semi-structured interview in which the existence of close, intimate relationships as assessed; and (b) a 20-item intimacy–isolation questionnaire. Three intimacy statuses – intimacy, stereotyped relationships and isolation – were found to exist and subjects were categorized into one of these. The stereotyped relationships status is where a person has a number of relationships but of a superficial nature, the other intimacy statuses are self-explanatory.

It was predicted that subjects with the identity status of identity achievement would be most likely to have close and intimate relationships, those in the diffusion status were more likely to fall into the intimacy status of

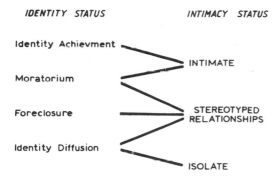

**Figure 3.1** Consequences of identity status for the Intimacy versus Isolation stage of psychosocial development. From Orlofsky and Lesser (1973).

'isolate'. The overall pattern of findings is depicted in Figure 3.1; from this it can be seen that the above predictions were confirmed. Also, the moratorium identity status may be seen as a positive one for the next stage, since such subjects were found to be as likely to engage in intimate as stereotyped relationships. The statuses of foreclosure and identity diffusion appear to prevent a person from a committed, intimate relationship.

We have seen in this and the previous section that Erikson's theory has received empirical support even though such support is not unequivocal. Much of what Erikson has to say though, especially with regard to the other stages, is in need of empirical investigation. Perhaps with the increased life expectancy in western society the later stages of generativity *vs* stagnation and wisdom *vs* despair will receive more attention from experimental social psychologists, with the hope that quality of life, from a social psychological point of view, may be improved.

## 3.3 Kohlberg's theory of moral development

We saw with Erikson's theory how 'crises' or crucial times occur throughout life, we also saw how personal relationships may be affected by how such crises are resolved. At one or two points we also saw that morality was centrally involved: for example, an intimate, enduring relationship requires trust of another as well as of oneself. Trust in a relationship will depend upon one's view of what is morally right and wrong. Kohlberg (1976) conceptualizes morality as *justice or fairness*, since moral situations or dilemmas are 'ones of conflict of perspectives or interest: justice principles are concepts for resolving these conflicts' (Kohlberg, 1976, p. 40). Justice for Kohlberg embodies the principles of *liberty*, *equality* and *reciprocity* and as such is fundamental to people thinking and acting in mature and responsible ways.

Kohlberg has proposed a theory of moral development which says that a person's moral *reasoning* passes through *three* developmental levels, with two *stages* in each level. It is important to bear in mind that Kohlberg is *not* explicitly concerned with moral *behaviour* but with people's moral *thinking and reasoning*. As we shall see later, this poses a problem for the theory since discrepancies often exist between a person's moral reasoning and that person's moral behaviour. In part this is because the theory is a *structural* one: it tells us the structure of people's moral reasoning not the content.

### 3.3.1 Three levels of moral reasoning

Kohlberg's work on the cognitive (thinking and reasoning) development of morality represents a specific adaptation and extension of Piaget's work on cognitive development in general. Piaget was interested to discover how the child comes to acquire knowledge about and understanding of the world in which he or she lives (for a good description and critique of Piaget's work see Boden, 1979). Piaget proposed that a child goes through three stages of intellectual development and that every child passes through these stages in an invariant order. Different children may pass through different stages at different speeds, some fast some slow, but each has to be gone through.

Kohlberg adhered to Piaget's basic principles and developed a theory proposing *three levels* of development in moral reasoning. Kohlberg further proposed that each level consisted of *two stages*. Table 3.5 states these six moral stages, provides a brief description of each and indicates the social consequences of each. The three levels are preconventional, conventional and post-conventional. *Conventional* means conforming to and upholding the rules, expectations and conventions of society and authority. At the *preconventional* level the rules are *external* to the self, the child here has no conception of right or wrong. At the conventional level rules of society or authority figures have been *internalized*, and understanding of right and wrong is in terms of conformity to social standards. At the *postconventional* level self-chosen principles dictate moral reasoning, i.e. rules of society or authority figures are only seen as right if they are consistent with the individual's right to liberty, equality and life.

Stages 1 and 2 are found predominantly in young children. Stage 1, punishment and obedience, is where right and wrong is based on the idea that good things are pleasurable and rewarding, bad things unpleasurable and punishing. Socially this is egocentric since the child is unable to recognize that other people have their interests and rights as well. Stage 2, instrumental purpose, is where right and wrong is the obeying of rules only if such behaviour furthers the interest of the individual. This stage is an advance over the previous one since other people's interests are recognized, but right and wrong is relative since what is right for one person (rewarding) may be wrong for another (punishing).

Stages 3 and 4, in the conventional level, mark a significant change since social conformity rather than individual gain forms the structure of moral reasoning. In Stage 3, interpersonal expectations and conformity, reasoning of right and wrong is based on expectations of others leading to gaining their approval. Morality is *conformity* to conventions, here *rules* are learned by children. Being a 'nice' person is behaving as others expect you to behave in your roles as brother, friend, male or female, etc. Stage 4, social system and conscience maintenance, is where morality is the *upholding* of conventions, societal rules and values: law and order as it exists in that society at the time is what is right. Doing one's duty is all-important, as is respect for authority.

**Table 3.5** The three levels of moral development, the two stages in each level with a description of each and the social perspective resulting from each. Adapted from Kohlberg (1976).

| STAGE | | DESCRIPTION OF STAGE | SOCIAL PERSPECTIVE |
|---|---|---|---|
| *Level I: Preconventional* | | | |
| STAGE 1: | Punishment and obedience | Whether something is good or bad depends on the consequence. The good is what the person wants and likes. | Egocentric, the views and interests of others are not considered. |
| STAGE 2: | Instrumental purpose | Follows rules to obtain self gratification of needs and wants. 'You scratch my back and I'll scratch yours'. | Right and wrong are relative, as everybody has their own interests and needs to pursue. |
| *Level II: Conventional* | | | |
| STAGE 3: | Interpersonal expectations and conformity | Right is what others expect of the person. Conform to rules and expectations as desire to be seen as a 'good person'. | Aware of other's feelings and interests. Able to put oneself in another's situation. |
| STAGE 4: | Social system and conscience | Right is upholding and maintaining rules and laws. Right is to do one's duty and respect authority. | Takes the point of view of the social system not other individuals. |
| *Level III: Postconventional* | | | |
| STAGE 5: | Social contract and individual rights | Rights of individuals to have their own values and opinions. Rules and laws for the benefit of community as a whole. | Considers people independently of social rules and laws. Prior to society perspective. |
| STAGE 6: | Universal ethical principles | Moral reasoning guided by ethical principles that should apply to all humanity. Laws only valid if reflect this. | Respect for moral principles in others when rational product of universal principles. |

The difference between Stages 3 and 4 is that in the latter there is an increased social perspective: from the right being what others expect of you to the right being the maintenance of law and order with an *awareness* of the need for this.

Stages 5 and 6, at the postconventional level, are the highest, most advanced and, according to Kohlberg, most desirable stages of moral development to attain. At this level, moral reasoning derives from what is regarded as *fair*, in terms of rights, values and laws, for any and all individuals living in society. Right and wrong is not to do with individual gain (preconventional) or conformity and maintenance of rules (conventional) but with *principled* reasoning, which may be against existing social standards and/or society's laws. Stage 5, social contract and individual rights, is where a person recognizes that moral rules/laws, social policies, etc. are attempts to promote the long-term welfare of the community. However, these rules and values can only be accepted if they also are regarded as being fair. Abiding by a social contract is for the moral reason that the greatest good for the greatest number of people is achieved. Stage 6, universal ethical principles, is the final and highest level of moral development. Here what is right or wrong is reasoned in terms of principles that transcend a particular society. At this stage a person is committed to principles of human conduct not laws and rules devised by any one society; occasionally people will step outside of the rules of their society since they see them as violating fundamental principles.

Kohlberg provides no strict guidelines as to the ages at which people are most likely to be in any one of these levels or stages. Rough guides are given though: the preconventional is usually considered to be in childhood and the conventional in adolescence. After adolescence it is less certain that an individual will continue to develop; Kohlberg claims that many people remain at a conventional level of moral reasoning, especially Stage 4, throughout their lives. Only a small percentage advance to Stage 5 and only very few to Stage 6. Furthermore, it may also be the case that some individuals never progress beyond Stage 2. For example, this might be due to impoverished social and educational experiences. It may even be that a whole society is at Stage 2 of moral development. However, such bold and sweeping claims are difficult, if not impossible, to substantiate.

Kohlberg does maintain that whilst not everybody may go through the six stages of development it is the case that a person at Stage 5, for example, *must* have passed through Stages 1–4 first. A person cannot skip a stage to reach a higher stage of moral reasoning. Kohlberg's theory also makes the controversial claim that Stages 5 and, especially, 6 represent the highest level of moral thinking for mankind. If everybody could attain principled moral reasoning war and violence might cease to exist. It might be argued, though, that Stage 6 is not the highest possible stage since an individual may feel above the law and not subject to the consequences of not abiding to it.

### 3.3.2 Measuring moral development

Kohlberg (1976) has developed a number of moral dilemmas which are given to a person to reason about. From this, Kohlberg claims, it is possible to assess the stage of moral reasoning a person is at. One commonly used moral dilemma, the 'Heinz dilemma', is as follows:

> In Europe a woman was near to death from a rare form of cancer. There was one drug that the doctors thought might save her, a form of radium that a druggist in the same town had recently discovered. The druggist was charging £2000, 10 times what the drug cost him to make. Heinz went to everybody he knew to borrow the money, but he could only get together about half of what the drug cost. He told the druggist that his wife was dying and asked him to sell it cheaper or let him pay later. But the druggist said, 'No'. So Heinz got desperate and broke into the man's store to steal the drug for his wife.
> *Should the husband have done that? Why?*

To assess stage of moral development a person would be told this story, then asked to state what the husband should have done and provide reasons for such a course of action. This dilemma focuses on the issues of the value of life and punishment (other dilemmas used by Kohlberg to deal with issues of property, conscience and personal relationships). Kohlberg then categorizes the reasons given justifying a certain course of action into one of the six stages of moral development. The following would be typical of a person at each stage:

*Stage 1* Heinz should not steal the drug. This is because he would be a thief and be punished by being sent to prison.

*Stage 2* Heinz should steal the medicine. This is because he needs his wife to look after him so it is important for him that she gets better.

*Stage 3* Heinz should steal the medicine. This is the right thing to do because others would think more highly of him and his wife would expect it of him.

*Stage 4* Heinz should not steal the medicine. This is so since if everone went around doing similar things there would be no law and order. It is one's duty to uphold the law.

*Stage 5* Heinz should steal the medicine. It is the druggist who is wrong to charge so much; the druggist was operating an unfair rule since the welfare of others suffers.

*Stage 6* Heinz should steal the medicine. Life is more important than property or money, people deserve the right to live wherever possible.

A thorough assessment of a person's stage of moral reasoning involves giving the person three different stories and looking at moral reasoning in each with respect to issues such as conscience, civil rights, truth, sex and sexual love (Kohlberg, 1976, has 11 categories of issues altogether). Assigning a person to a particular stage of moral development is not straightforward since it is found that an individual will give reasons justifying a course of action which exemplify numerous (often three or four) different moral stages. The strategy Kohlberg uses is to assign a person to the stage in which 50 per cent or more of his or her reasons are classified. This means that a person classified at, for

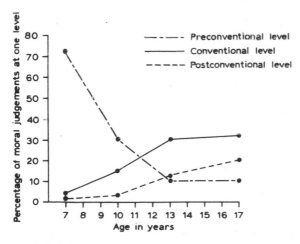

**Figure 3.2** Changes with age in the percentage of moral judgements at the three levels of moral development. Adapted from Kohlberg and Kramer (1969).

example, Stage 3 will also show evidence of being able to reason at higher (Stage 4) and lower (Stage 2) moral stages. Whether the person reasons *predominantly* at one of the stages is the criterion used for classification.

Kohlberg and Kramer (1969) used this method of measurement to demonstrate a progression in moral reasoning of children and adolescents from *lower to higher levels*. Figure 3.2 graphically displays the progression they found. It can be seen that, for example, a seven year old gives over 70 per cent of moral reasons at the preconventional level and less than five per cent at the higher two levels. By contrast a 13 year old gives just over 10 per cent at the preconventional level and 30 per cent at the conventional level. Generally, as children go from seven to 17 years they make fewer preconventional judgements and more conventional and, to a lesser extent, postconventional judgements. (The percentages for any one age group at the three levels do not total 100 per cent since some children could not be classified as predominantly at one level of moral development.) Whilst there are no strict guides to ages and stages/levels there is a general progression from middle childhood to late adolescence from lower to higher levels of moral reasoning.

### 3.3.3 Morality and ideology

How may the veracity of Kohlberg's six-stage theory of moral development be ascertained? Two approaches suggest themselves: (a) to see if there is a positive relationship between moral thought and moral behaviour; (b) to see if moral thought relates to ideological commitment and moral judgements of right and wrong concerning real rather than hypothetical situations. The former, moral thought and behaviour, will be dealt with in the next section since it represents a crucial problem for the theory. Here we will look at moral reasoning, ideology and real situations.

Candee (1976) attempted to relate stage of moral development of college students to judgements about the Watergate affair and the Lt Calley case. (The Watergate affair concerned attempts by President Nixon to cover up illegal break-ins at the Democratic Party headquarters; the Lt Calley case or the 'MyLai massacre' concerned the trial of Calley for the murder of 22 villagers during the Vietnam War). Subjects were asked a number of questions about each of these affairs, having to indicate whether they thought the behaviour was right or wrong, and why. In saying why, subjects had to indicate whether the reasons were to do with basic human rights or maintaining conventions and rules. Candee predicted that the higher the moral stage a person is at (assessed as described in the previous section) the more he or she would choose human rights as a justification for whether an action was right or wrong. Table 3.6 gives some of the questions used by Candee about these two affairs. The data show that the percentage of subjects choosing human rights as a justification increased with stage of development, as predicted. Some caution is needed in regarding these results as evidence for level of development and ideological commitment since media cover of these events may influence and determine how people reason.

Ideology relates, perhaps, most directly to political views. Fishkin *et al.* (1973) provided evidence that college students at the conventional level of moral reasoning were more likely to be conservative than those at the post-

**Table 3.6** Examples of questions put to subjects about Watergate and the My Lai massacre. Percentage of subjects in different stages of moral development giving the human rights alternative is shown. Adapted from Candee (1976).

| | HUMAN RIGHTS | MORAL STAGE | | | |
|---|---|---|---|---|---|
| QUESTION | ALTERNATIVE | 2 | 3 | 4 | 5 |
| (a) Do you approve or disapprove of Lt Calley being brought to trial? | Approve | 0% | 45% | 78% | 89% |
| (b) Should American officers be convicted for war crimes ordered by their superiors? | Should | 20 | 22 | 53 | 84 |
| (c) Howard Hunt sincerely believed he was helping his country. Was he right to participate in the Watergate affair? | No | 64 | 64 | 75 | 89 |
| (d) If impeachment alone were held today, based on what you know at this time would you be for or against impeachment? | For | 41 | 65 | 84 | 98 |

and preconventional levels. Those at the postconventional level tended to be more liberal or radical in their political views, i.e. more likely to be towards the left of the political spectrum. This research further showed that stage of moral development had clear consequences for moral behaviour. For example, over 40 per cent of students at Stage 5 had been arrested for participating in a Free Speech Movement sit-in at Berkeley University in 1964. By contrast only 13 and 9 per cent of students at Stages 3 and 4 respectively had been arrested for such activities.

More recent research, however, has pointed out that moral reasoning and political views may be one and the same thing. Emler *et al.* (1983) have shown that a person's stage of moral reasoning can change according to the perspective taken. Conservative subjects answering a moral reasoning questionnaire from their own perspective tend to be classified as in Stage 4 (conventional level of moral reasoning). However, when the same subjects were asked to answer the same questionnaire *as if* they were radicals (left-wingers) they tended to be classified as Stage 5 (postconventional moral reasoning). The point Emler *et al.* (1983) make is that political views may be more important for how a person reasons morally than level of development. The fact that conservatives reason mainly at the conventional level does not mean that they cannot reason at the postconventional level when required to do so. It is simply that they *prefer* to reason at one level rather than another.

### 3.3.4 Moral reasoning and moral behaviour

What consequences for behaviour, if any, are there for a person who reasons at predominantly a preconventional, conventional or postconventional level? The previous section resulted in conflicting answers to this question. Fishkin *et al.* (1973), as we saw, found moral behaviour in terms of participating in a sit-in to relate to Stages 5 and 6. However, Fishkin also found over

40 per cent of students at Stage 2 to have been involved in the sit-in as well. Emler *et al.* (1983) found conventional or postconventional level of moral reasoning with respect to political views to be a good indicator of the stage of moral reasoning that people could achieve. What emerges from these conflicting findings with respect to moral reasoning and behaviour is that the *context* may be important. The question we need to address, then, is how morality (in both thought and action) may be affected by particular social situations.

Bandura and McDonald (1963) conducted an experiment in which children of five to 11 years of age were given moral dilemmas to determine if they were preconventional or conventional in their moral reasoning. (Bandura and McDonald did not use the terms preconventional and conventional but 'objective' and 'subjective' modes of moral reasoning. *Objective* is where the child cited features of the moral dilemma that were *not* to do with the person – for example, where a child is judged naughtier because he has broken 15 rather than three cups. *Subjective* mode of reasoning is where the child cites such things as intentions and motives when saying if a behaviour was right or wrong. Objective corresponds to preconventional and subjective to conventional level.) Once the child's type or level of moral reasoning had been determined the child was put in a situation where an adult consistently spoke aloud either subjective or objective reasons in answer to moral dilemmas. After exposure to one of these types of 'models' the child was asked to state his or her preferred mode of moral reasoning. Later on children were tested again using a different set of moral dilemmas. Bandura and McDonald predicted that the social situation (behaviour of the model) would be highly influential on the way in which the child reasoned morally,

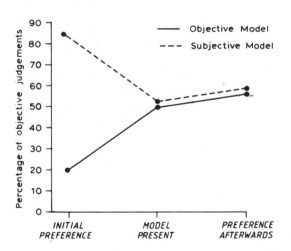

**Figure 3.3** Effect of 'objective' and 'subjective' models on children's moral judgements. Children initially preferring objective judgements show much less of a preference after exposure to a 'subjective' model. Children *not* initially preferring objective judgements show greater increase in such judgements when exposed to an 'objective' model. Adapted from Bandura and McDonald (1963).

regardless of the child's previously determined type or level of reasoning (pre-conventional or conventional).

Results confirmed these predictions: Figure 3.3 shows that children exposed to an 'objective' model preferred objective reasons and answers to moral dilemmas both immediately after and some time after exposure. Children exposed to a 'subjective' model preferred subjective answers and reasons. A control group of children, those exposed to no model, showed little change in their initial mode of moral reasoning over a similar period of time.

This experiment does show that one person's moral behaviour or reasoning can influence another's moral reasoning. The experiment does not, however, show there to be a relationship between how a person thinks and behaves morally. Bandura and McDonald's research suggests that perhaps the wrong question is being asked; perhaps it is simply enough to know the social situation (models a person has observed behaving) to predict moral behaviour. Moral reasoning and moral behaviour may not be strongly related: anecdotal evidence vividly demonstrates that people at the principled (postconventional) level of reasoning often engage in highly, by many people's standards, immoral behaviour. Moral behaviour may, then, be more a product of the social context than the way an individual thinks. This is the basic idea of social learning theory (Bandura, 1977), to which we now turn.

## 3.4 Moral behaviour

Kohlberg does not seriously address the issue of what people *actually do* – with respect to both thought and behaviour; he is primarily concerned with what people *can* do. This is an important distinction, made in many areas of psychology, between *competence* and *performance*. The fact that a person is competent to reason at a particular moral level does not mean the person will reason at this level (the Emler *et al.*, 1973 study, described earlier, demonstrated this). Similarly, the actions a person performs are not predictable from knowing a person's competence at moral reasoning. We can all think of people who in one context behave in a highly virtuous way (such as giving to charity) but in another context behave in a morally despicable way (steal from an employer, for example). Social learning theory (Bandura, 1977) suggests that moral behaviour results from *observational learning* where the most important factors to consider are not moral reasoning but 'the individual's specific expectancies about the consequences of different behavioural possibilities in that situation' (Mischel and Mischel, 1976, p. 89).

### 3.4.1 Social learning theory

Observational learning, the basis of social learning theory, is where behaviour is learned not by direct reward and punishment for behaving that way but by watching another behave and observing the *consequences* of that behaviour for the other person. Particularly in young children, but with adults as well, another person is a *model*, which the child identifies with and whose behaviour he or she imitates. The behaviour of the model provides the crucially important information about the consequences of behaving that way. If the consequences are seen to be rewarding for the model the observer will come to have the expectancy that he or she will be rewarded for behaving that way as well. Similarly, if the model is seen to be punished for a particular behaviour, the observer will expect also to be punished if he or she were to behave in that way. Consequences (rewards or punishments) expected from behaviour predict how people actually will behave. Observing the consequences of another's behaviour is said to be learning through *vicarious* reinforcement – vicarious since the person does not experience reinforcement him or herself but observes another experiencing or obtaining reinforcement (reward) or punishment for behaving that way. This formulation of observational learning allows for the person to have learned a behaviour without ever having performed it. Only when an appropriate situation arises will the learned behaviour actually be performed.

Much research on social learning theory has been on antisocial or morally undesirable behaviour. Bandura, Ross and Ross (1961) investigated the effects of exposure to aggressive and non-aggressive models where the model was not seen to obtain any rewards or punishments for behaving in that way. In this experiment half the subjects, who were children, were put into a room, one at a time, with an adult who behaved in an aggressive way. The adult was hitting and shouting abuse at a 'Bobo' doll (a Bobo doll is an adult-sized and adult-looking plastic inflatable):

> The model laid Bobo on its side, sat on it and punched it repeatedly on the nose. The adult model then raised the Bobo doll, picked up the mallet and struck the doll on the head. Following mallet aggression the model tossed the doll up in the air and kicked it about the room.

The other half of the subjects were put into a room, one at a time, with an adult model who spoke and acted in a subdued and non-aggressive manner. Half the children in each group (i.e. the aggressive and non-aggressive) were exposed to a male model and the other half to a female model.

After exposure to either the aggressive (male or female) or non-aggressive (male or female) model a child was put into another room in which there were 'aggressive'-type toys (Bobo doll, mallet) and 'non-aggressive'-type toys (tea set, crayons) to play with. Bandura *et al.* were interested in the extent to which children's play displayed aggression after being in one of the experimental conditions. This was measured by, amongst other things, counting the number of times a child hit the doll with a mallet or punched it. Table 3.7 summarizes the mean number of aggressive acts by male and female children who had been exposed to male or female aggressive or non-aggressive models. Aggressive behaviour was greater, for both measures of aggression, when the children had been in the room with the aggressive model. The table also shows boys to engage in more aggressive behaviour than girls, also boys punched the Bobo doll more if they had been exposed to a female rather than male model.

Further research by Bandura (1965), using a similar experimental paradigm with the Bobo doll, has shown how imitation of aggressive behaviour is affected by *consequences* experienced by the model. Children were found to be most aggressive when they observed an aggressive model

**Table 3.7** Mean number of aggressive acts by male and female subjects when exposed to either aggressive or non-aggressive male or female models. Adapted from Bandura, Ross and Ross (1961).

| MEASURE OF AGGRESSION | EXPERIMENTAL CONDITION | | | |
|---|---|---|---|---|
| | *Aggressive model* | | *Non-aggressive model* | |
| | Male | Female | Male | Female |
| (a) *Mallet aggression* | | | | |
| Male subjects | 28.8 | 25.5 | 6.7 | 18.7 |
| Female subjects | 18.7 | 17.2 | 0.5 | 0.5 |
| Males & Females | | 20.1 | | 6.6 |
| (b) *Punches Bobo doll* | | | | |
| Male subjects | 11.9 | 18.9 | 14.8 | 15.6 |
| Female subjects | 16.5 | 6.3 | 4.3 | 5.8 |
| Males & Females | | 13.4 | | 10.1 |

being rewarded for such behaviour. Second most aggressive behaviour resulted from children who had observed an aggressive model but where there were no consequences for such behaviour. Where the model was punished a low amount of aggression by children was found, but this was more than if the child had been exposed to no model at all. Bandura also found children who had initially observed an aggressive model being punished to imitate that behaviour when incentives (money, sweets) were offered by the experimenter. This demonstrates that the children learned the model's behaviour equally well regardless of consequences for the model. Different consequences for the model served either to *inhibit* or *facilitate* later performance of that behaviour. Similar effects of modelling have been shown to occur for pro-social behaviour (Bryan and Test, 1967).

Given that observational learning affects moral behaviour it is of interest to determine more precisely variables most likely to result in imitation of a model's behaviour. Three classes of variables have been investigated: (a) characteristics of the model; (b) characteristics of the observer; and (c) consequences for the model of that behaviour. The third we have already dealt with. With respect to (a), it has been found that imitation of behaviour is greater with people we perceive to be like ourselves. For example, models of the same sex and of similar age are more likely to be identified with and have greater influence over our behaviour. Models high in status and/or highly prestigious are also more likely to be influential. With respect to attributes of the observer the main variable affecting imitation seems to be self-esteem (especially in terms of self-confidence). People low in self-esteem are more likely to imitate a model's behaviour than people high in self-esteem.

In summary, social learning theory proposes that moral behaviour is learned from observation of models. Mere exposure may be sufficient, however consequences of the behaviour for the model determine whether the observer is likely to imitate that behaviour or not. Parents, other significant adults and peers serve as models for children, however television as a socializer of moral behaviour is increasingly considered to be an important influence.

### 3.4.2 Television and moral behaviour

Social psychologists are increasingly acknowledging the role of television as a powerful socializing force, especially for children and young teenagers. Many adventure programmes (such as *The 'A' Team*, *Dukes of Hazzard*) depict 'goodies' (upholders of societal standards) engaging in violence, aggression and/or illegal behaviour. Further, such acts are represented as having successful consequences and as being morally justified. Many people, including psychologists, have expressed concern that a diet of justified violence and aggression may have negative effects on those who watch such programmes – especially young children. The heroes in these programmes can be seen as being potential 'models' for young children – to this extent a social learning theory approach investigating the effects of television violence upon behaviour would seem appropriate.

Bandura, Ross and Ross (1963) investigated the impact of aggressive models presented to children either live, on film or on a cartoon strip. The greatest amount of imitated aggression resulted from children exposed to the 'live' model, followed by the film and then the cartoon. All three modes of presentation, however, resulted in more aggressive behaviour than a control group of children who were not exposed to an aggressive model. It would seem, then, that even such popular cartoons as *Tom and Jerry* may have undesirable influences. Experimental work has borne this out, for example, Ellis and Sekgra (1972) showed five year olds an aggressive or neutral cartoon that had appeared on television. Children who viewed the aggressive cartoon (in which incidents of hitting, kicking and tackling in a football match were displayed) behaved more aggressively when they were returned to the class-room than children who were shown the neutral cartoon (a song-and-dance musical). Steuer *et al.* (1971) showed aggressive cartoons to preschool children for 20 minutes a day, every day, for 11 days. These children became more aggressive to peers (kicking and pushing them) than a control group who had not seen the cartoons.

These, and many other studies, demonstrate an *immediate* effect of television violence and aggression, they do not show *lasting* effects though. Longitudinal studies, whereby a group of children are monitored over a number of years, are needed to see if there are lasting effects. Lefkowitz *et al.* (1972) did precisely this. They first assessed the amount of television violence watched by over 400 nine year olds, information about family background, aggressiveness of each child, etc. was also taken. The same children were contacted 10 years later, at 19 years of age, and assessed for aggressive behaviour. Among all the socialization variables recorded at nine years of age, the amount of television violence watched was found to be the best predictor of aggressive behaviour in late adolescence. More disturbing perhaps is research by Stein (1972) showing children, ranging in age from four to 11, to judge the morality (right or wrongness) of television violence on the basis of successful or unsuccessful outcomes *not* on the intentions of the characters. Behaviour is judged right if it is seen to lead to desired goals being achieved, a finding that fits in very well with Kohlberg's stages of moral development. Such reasoning is characteristic of Stage 2 (preconventional level) in Kohlberg's theory (see Table 3.5).

Research has also shown high exposure to television violence leading to people have a 'blunted' sensitivity to violence. Cline *et al.* (1972) found five to 12 year olds who watched a lot of television violence to show less emotional reactions (measured by heart rate, blood pressure and pulse amplitude changes) to a film containing violence than children of the same age who watched little television. Presumably, similar results would be found for people who watch many 'video nasties'. Insensitivity to violence may have the undesirable consequence of such people being prepared to *tolerate* more violence and aggression in others and in society as a whole.

In summary, television and, increasingly, home videos are recognized as important and powerful moral 'teachers'. Much of the research has sought to demonstrate how television violence may result in children and adults engaging in antisocial behaviour. By the same token, though, if television is such a powerful moral teacher *pro-social* behaviour may be encouraged by producing different types of television programmes.

## 3.5 Summary

○ Socialization is a process that starts at birth and continues throughout a person's life. Becoming a mature and socially responsible member of society is the major way in which socialization can be regarded as a life-long process.

○ Erikson proposes that there are eight stages or 'crises' that an individual goes through in his or her psychosocial development. Four of these stages are in childhood, one in adolescence and three in adulthood. The way in which one stage is passed through influences how the next and subsequent stages are negotiated.

○ Adolescence is marked by an 'identity crisis' – here the teenager throws off previous identifications and seeks his or her own unique sense of identity. Failure to achieve an identity results in 'identity diffusion' which may lead to apathy and depression.

○ Kohlberg's theory of moral development suggests there are three *levels* (preconventional, conventional and postconventional) of moral development with two stages in each level. Preconventional and conventional usually take place during childhood and adolescence respectively. Many people, according to Kohlberg, do not progress beyond Stage 4 (conventional level), very few individuals reach Stage 6.

○ The level and stage of moral development is measured by giving a person a moral dilemma (such as the Heinz dilemma) to reason about. A person who reasons about such issues as value of life, civil rights, conscience, etc. predominantly at one stage is classified as being at that stage of development.

○ Kohlberg's theory is a *structural* theory about moral reasoning it does not specify how people will actually reason in everyday life, nor does it predict behaviour from a knowledge of an individual's stage of moral development.

○ Social learning theory states that people learn by observing the consequences of behaviour of a 'model'. Reinforcement is not directly experienced but is said to be *vicarious*. A person may learn a behaviour but never actually behave in that way. However when an appropriate social context arises the learned behaviour will be enacted.

○ Much research in social learning theory has been on the effects of aggressive models (live or via the medium of television) on children's behaviour. Children are found to be more aggressive if they observe violence to further a person's attainment of objectives. Television is an important socializer, and may be just as powerful in influencing aggressive as well as pro-social behaviour.

## 3.6  Suggestions for further reading

Erikson, E. *Childhood and Society* (Triad/Paladin Paperback, 1950)
One of Erikson's most readable books, wide range of topics dealt with to highlight his theory; the book also shows how the 'ego' approach stems from aspects of Freudian theory.

Maccoby, E.E. *Social Development* (New York, Harcourt Brace Jovanovich, 1980)
Two chapters, 8 and 9, provide a substantial introduction to the range of theories and supporting empirical evidence. Good account of Kohlberg given; this is the source to read if you wish to follow up this chapter.

Stevens, R. *Erik Erikson: An Introduction* (Open University Press, 1983)
Clearly written introduction to the many aspects of Erikson's theory, the book is rather lacking in criticism and does not cite experimental evidence for and against the eight-stage approach.

Wright, D. *The Psychology of Moral Behaviour* (Harmondsworth, Penquin, 1971)
Good introduction and overview of theories and research dealing with moral behaviour; since behaviour is the focus little is said about Kohlberg. The book is good for providing an understanding of the behaviourist approach, of which Bandura was a successor.

# 4

# Attitudes and attitude change

4.1    The significance of attitudes
4.2    What are attitudes?
       *4.2.1 The structural approach   4.2.3 The functional approach*
4.3    Measuring attitudes
       *4.3.1 Indirect measures   4.3.2 Direct measures*
4.4    Attitude organization and change
       *4.4.1 Balance theory   4.4.2 Congruity principle   4.4.3 Cognitive dissonance*
4.5    Other approaches to attitude change
       *4.5.1 Self-perception theory   4.5.2 Impression management   4.5.3 Self-generated attitude change*
4.6    Attitudes and behaviour
       *4.6.1 Attitudes as causes of behaviour   4.6.2 Personality differences*
4.7    Summary
4.8    Suggestions for further reading

## 4.1  The significance of attitudes

The concept of attitude has been, and probably still is, regarded as central and fundamental to social psychology. Allport (1954), for example, viewed attitudes as 'the most distinctive and indispensable concept in social psychology'. It is not hard to see why. In virtually all aspects of our social life we are continually seeking out other people's attitudes, telling others of our views, and trying to change someone else's opinions. In the world of mass communications advertising campaigns are often aimed at instilling in us a positive attitude toward a particular product with the hope that this will result in us buying what they have to sell. Disagreements with others over what may be the appropriate or correct attitude to hold make us aware of their powerful emotional foundations. Attitudes, then, are important to understanding stereotyping, prejudice, voting intentions, consumer behaviour and interpersonal attraction to name but a few major areas in social psychology.

Attitudes are also important simply because people hold a very large number towards many objects and other people. How attitudes come to be formed is not something that will be dealt with explicitly here but 'societal mores' and cultural norms play an important role in determining the attitudes we hold, particularly with respect to highly emotive issues such as incest, rape, child battering, etc. Equally, attitudes towards minority groups (racial, ethnic, religious, for example) when strongly held and negative in character form the foundations of prejudice and discrimination. It is also important to remember that people differ markedly in their attitudes towards the same object or person. Social norms (implicit or explicit 'rules' of behaviour in one's peer group, social class, etc.) and/or cultural norms (more general codes of conduct and ethical standards of a society – again, these may be either explicit or implicit) may be responsible for a certain degree of uniformity, but individual experiences produce much diversity of opinion. For example, early childhood experiences (see Chapter 2), family background, level of educational attainment, sub-culture ethos all contribute to differences among people.

Two reasons for social psychologists directing so much attention to the study of attitudes are: (a) if we accept that the goals of social psychology are to both explain and predict behaviour then knowledge of people's attitudes should provide important insights; (b) attitudes are relatively enduring but also relatively easy to change (when considered in relation to beliefs and values) hence conditions and circumstances of change are important to discover. Beliefs and values may be distinguished as follows: *beliefs* are knowledge we have about the world (people and objects) and vary in how central or important they are for us. For example, a person who believed in the existence of God would hold a highly central belief affecting many other beliefs that he or she had about the world. By contrast, a person holding the belief that it is safer to wear sunglasses whilst driving in sunshine is unlikely to have many other beliefs influenced by this. Central beliefs influence and determine our whole cognitive structure, peripheral beliefs do not have wide-reaching influences upon how we think of the world (Rokeach, 1968). Furthermore, central beliefs are more resistant to change than peripheral beliefs. *Values* represent ethical codes, cultural and social norms. Just as people have beliefs about the world they also hold values about life, ways of living, conduct in relationships, etc. Values, like beliefs, can be central or peripheral, with central values being highly resistant to change. In a sense, although the distinction is not entirely clear-cut, beliefs represent what we *think* and know about the world and values represent how we *feel*, emotionally, about the world.

## 4.2  What are attitudes?

The problem of providing a good, clear and useful definition of attitudes is a product of at least two things: (a) the word 'attitude' is used in an extremely diverse and imprecise way in everyday language; (b) an attitude is a 'construct' that is used to refer to certain mental processes of a person. The latter presents a problem for scientific psychology. Physical scientists (chemists, physicists) can observe what they are experimenting on (even if this involves the use of, for example, electron microscopes); this is not the case for social psychologists investigating attitudes, since the presence of an attitude is only *inferred* from what people say and do. The term attitude is taken to characterize and summarize a collection of psychological phenomena; it also provides a neat shorthand way of summarizing simply something quite complex.

Social psychologists, in trying to be more analytic, scientific and go beyond everyday usage (see Chapter 1), have attempted to answer the question 'What are attitudes?' in two important but different ways. One approach has been to focus on the *structure* of attitudes; while another has looked at the different *functions* that attitudes serve for the person. Neither approach, on its own, offers a satisfactory answer to the question of 'what are attitudes?', taken together they may do so though.

### 4.2.1 The structural approach

The structural approach offers an understanding by looking at attitudes in relation to other key concepts; these being beliefs, values, intentions and behaviour (Fishbein and Ajzen, 1975). This reflects a traditional three-component analysis of affective, cognitive and conative components of attitudes (Katz, 1960). The *cognitive* component refers to beliefs (discussed earlier) about the attitude object; the *affective* component refers to the evaluation (good or bad) of the attitude object and hence reflects a person's values (see earlier); the *conative* component refers to behaviour with respect to the attitude object or person. Such an analysis allows a general definition of attitudes to be produced. Whilst there are many definitions, the following – suggested by Newcomb (1950) – captures the fundamental points: an attitude may be defined as 'a learned predisposition to respond in a consistently favourable or unfavourable manner with respect to a given object'. This definition incorporates four important aspects of attitudes relating to the structural approach: (a) attitudes are learned through experience; (b) they predispose people to behave (respond) in certain ways; (c) attitudes and behaviour conform to a principle of consistency – this will be dealt with in more detail later; (d) the unfavourable or favourable manner of behaving reflects the evaluative component of attitudes.

In the light of the above definition and structural analysis of the key components, Figure 4.1 shows how these all relate. Figure 4.1 shows that an attitude is formed from a confluence of a person's beliefs and values: the attitude, then, is a positive or negative evaluation about something or somebody (of course a person can also feel neutrally about something or someone as well). Figure 4.1 further shows that an attitude gives rise to an intention to behave in a certain way which in turn gives rise to the behaviour itself. An example will show better how this works.

**Figure 4.1** Structural analysis of attitudes showing the relationship between beliefs, values, intentions and behaviour.

Imagine a person called Isadore whose political attitudes we are trying to understand and predict the consequences of. It is known that Isadore has a positive attitude to the Labour Party. This results from certain beliefs about the Labour Party (for example, that it will spend more on housing the poor, take the lower paid out of the 'poverty trap', bring about unilateral nuclear disarmament, etc.). Since Isadore's attitude is positive these beliefs are associated with good values to her (that is, it is a good thing that the Labour Party will take the lower paid out of the poverty trap, etc.).

Having discovered how it is that Isadore has a positive attitude to the Labour Party we now want to explore the consequences. The positive attitude will give rise to intentions to behave in a positive way, for example, voting for the local Labour Party candidate, joining the Labour Party, etc. In short, we expect to find *consistency* between attitudes and intentions to behave. The final link in the chain, intentions to behave, again, is expected to conform to a principle of consistency. Knowledge of what Isadore intends to do should allow a high degree of confidence in predicting what she actually will do (vote Labour, be a member of the Labour Party, etc.). It is important to remember, though, that things other than attitudes and intentions determine behaviour. Habits, social norms, group pressure, etc. also exert powerful influences upon behaviour. It must be expected then that despite knowledge of beliefs, values, attitudes and intentions the expected behaviour will not always follow since people do not always do as they say they will do.

Fishbein and Ajzen (1975) proposed a more specific model than the one outlined above. In trying to explain the discrepancy between attitudes and behaviour (see later in this chapter) they say we must take attitudes towards *specific* behaviour and intentions to perform that specific behaviour into account. Hence, with the Isadore example Fishbein and Ajzen would not want to know her general attitude to the Labour Party to predict specific behaviours such as voting for the local Labour candidate. Instead, they would want to find out Isadore's *attitude* towards voting for the local candidate, her intention to vote for this person and also, her beliefs about the consequences of voting for the Labour candidate. Knowing this, together with Isadore's specific values about voting in this instance, leads, they argue, to a much more accurate prediction of behaviour. Subsequent research has provided good evidence for this (Ajzen and Fishbein, 1977).

The structural approach, then, allows us to see how attitudes relate to other concepts and gives some insight into how they might be used to predict behaviour. Whilst this approach tells us what attitudes are it does not tell us why people hold attitudes, i.e. what function they serve for the individual.

### 4.2.2 The functional approach

The functional approach (McGuire, 1969; Katz, 1960; Smith, Bruner and White, 1956) suggests that attitudes promote the well-being of an individual by serving, essentially, four functions. These are the adaptive function, the knowledge function, the self-expressive function and the ego-defensive function. The basic idea is that attitudes help a person to mediate between the inner demands of the self and the outside world (especially material, social and informational aspects).

The *adaptive* function concerns the extent to which attitudes enable a person to achieve a desired goal and avoid what is distasteful. Socially, an important process of identification takes place. A person develops similar attitudes to those people he or she likes and seeks out as friends those perceived to have similar attitudes. In short, this function is hedonistic in that it serves the purpose of increasing satisfaction or pleasure and avoiding punishment or pain.

The *knowledge* function concerns the information a person possesses about the physical and social world. This function allows the world to become a more familiar, predictable and less uncertain place since a certain structure is imposed or perceived. For example, stereotypes help simplify the social environment, because stereotypes determine what aspects of other people to attend to and what aspects to ignore. There is a cost of this though – a tendency to oversimplify and expect the social world to be a more predictable place than it actually is.

The *self-expressive* function acknowledges a need to tell others about oneself and to know one's own mind, i.e. be conscious of what we feel, believe and value. One aspect of this relates to the discussion of 'identity' in Chapter 2, where Erikson's view that a sense of identity is important for the well-being of a person was discussed, and how emotionally devastating loss or lack of identity can be for people.

The *ego-defensive* function suggests that attitudes can serve to protect people from themselves and other people. With respect to self-protection attitudes may serve to maintain self-image, for example, often there are times when we find it painful to think about how we have behaved. Probably most people, at some time, have experienced guilt and remorse upon waking in the morning after being rather the worse for drink at a party the night before where they did or said something embarrassing. Our attitude towards ourself as, essentially, a sensible, thoughtful and considerate person may help us not think about the embarrassing episode or dismiss it as unrepresentative of how we normally are. In short, positive attitudes about ourself help maintain a positive self-image. With respect to the ego-defensive function and other people, it is often the case that in dealing with threats to our ego (self-image, self-esteem) we project our own conflicts onto other people, as is sometimes the case with prejudice.

The functional approach has implications for how to go about changing attitudes: to attempt changing a person's attitude two things need to be known: (a) the attitude held; and (b) the function that attitude serves for the person. To effect attitude change the approach should match the function; for example, an attitude serving a knowledge function is most likely to be changed by exposing the person to new information. On the other hand, an attitude serving an ego-defensive function is unlikely to be changed by the presentation of new information.

This concludes an exploration of the issue of what attitudes are, showing that two approaches the structural and functional – offer different insights but complementary explanations.

## 4.3  Measuring attitudes

Two main reasons can be given for social psychologists attempting to measure attitudes: (a) often it is not enough to know that a person feels positively or negatively about an object or person, some indication of the extent or *strength* of positive or negative feelings is needed as well; (b) if the effectiveness of attempts to change attitudes is to be assessed an objective measure of a person's attitude *before* and *after* the attempt to change is needed.

Social psychologists have tried many ways of measuring attitudes, all with limited degrees of success. No one way has emerged as vastly superior to any other. In what follows a representative sample of different methods is described.

### 4.3.1 Indirect measures

Scientifically, the most objective methods for measuring attitudes would be those which people were either unaware of or unable consciously to affect. Indirect measures, where you do not ask the person about his or her attitude directly, have taken a number of forms: the three most common being physiological, unobtrusive and projective techniques.

Physiological techniques (such as galvanic skin response, heart rate, pupillary dilation) of measuring attitudes assume that the affective (emotional/evaluative) component of attitudes correlates with the activity of the autonomic nervous system (that part of the nervous system thought to be beyond our conscious control). Whilst little evidence exists showing correlation between physiological measures and attitudes Hess (1965) has shown a relationship with pupillary response. Hess found a relationship between the size of a person's pupil and his or her attitude: dilated pupils (i.e. increased pupil size) indicated a positive attitude, and pupil constriction (decrease in size) related to a negative attitude. These claims are not fully accepted by other psychologists. Generally, though, such an approach has met with only limited success. It may be possible to show a person holds an attitude strongly but not, except in the case of pupil size, whether it is positive or negative.

Unobtrusive measures rely on the assumption that behaviour is consistent with attitudes. So, for example, a measure of attitude towards religion may be frequency of church attendance. Or, to take another example, the extent to which two people like each other may be reflected in the amount of eye-contact they engage in (the more two people look at each other, the more they like each other). But as will be seen in a later section of this chapter, behaviour does not always provide a good guide to attitudes.

Projective techniques take advantage of the fact that people often project their own attitudes on to others. Hence asking someone to, for example, fill in the balloons in Figures 4.2 and 4.3 may provide us with knowledge of the person's attitude to authority. Depending on how these balloons were filled in it might be inferred that the person has a submissive or disrespectful attitude to authority.

There are both advantages and disadvantages associated with indirect techniques of attitude measurement. The advantages are that such techniques are less likely to produce socially desirable responses, the person is unlikely to know what attitude is being measured, and the attitude is unlikely to be affected by measurement. The disadvantages are that it is difficult to measure attitude strength; attitudes are inferred, and such measures are not as reliable as one would desire. Nevertheless, indirect measures often offer the only approach when investigating highly sensitive social topics.

**Figure 4.2 & 4.3** Examples of indirect, projective techniques for measuring a person's attitude. In Figure 4.2 you are required to give an explanation for why you are late; in Figure 4.3 you have to give an explanation for smoking. Adapted from Oppenheim (1966).

### 4.3.2 Direct measures

Direct measures (rating scales) of attitudes are, perhaps, those best known since they commonly appear in magazines, newspapers, etc. Two approaches will be described: the Likert scale and the Semantic Differential. These are the two most widely used in social psychology.

Likert (1932) developed a method of attitude measurement by summating responses to a considerable number of statements representative of the attitude in question. For example, if a social psychologist were interested in attitudes to euthanasia a list of, say, 30 statements relevant to the topic would be made. Half these would be favourable and half unfavourable. Subjects would rate each statement on a seven-point scale which would be drawn up as follows:

(1) It is the duty of doctors to keep people alive for as long as possible

| Strongly Agree | Agree | Agree Somewhat | Undecided | Disagree Somewhat | Disagree | Strongly Disagree |
|---|---|---|---|---|---|---|
| 1 | 2 | 3 | 4 | 5 | 6 | 7 |

(2) People suffering from a terminal illness should be helped to die if it is their wish

| Strongly Agree | Agree | Agree Somewhat | Undecided | Disagree | Disagree Somewhat | Strongly Disagree |
|---|---|---|---|---|---|---|
| 7 | 6 | 5 | 4 | 3 | 2 | 1 |

A person's attitude is simply the summed score from each question (notice in the above example that a high score indicates a favourable attitude to euthanasia, a low score an unfavourable attitude). This is the basis of the Likert method. However, a number of technical procedures are needed to ensure that response bias is not present, such as equal numbers of favourable and unfavourable items. The Likert method has the obvious advantage of being easy to construct and easy to administer.

The Semantic Differential, developed by Osgood, Suci and Tannenbaum (1957), provides both a measure of attitude strength and further information concerning the significance of the attitude to the individual.

The Semantic Differential entails the rating, on seven-point scales, of an attitude object (person or thing) on numerous bipolar adjective scales. For example, below is a number of bipolar adjectives related to attitudes to pornography:

PORNOGRAPHY

| | | | | | | | |
|---|---|---|---|---|---|---|---|
| Good | — | — | — | — | — | — | — Bad |
| Clean | — | — | — | — | — | — | — Dirty |
| Beautiful | — | — | — | — | — | — | — Ugly |
| Strong | — | — | — | — | — | — | — Weak |
| Active | — | — | — | — | — | — | — Passive |
| Cruel | — | — | — | — | — | — | — Kind |

Subjects would simply be asked to place a tick above one of the dashes corresponding to how they feel about pornography in relation to that bipolar adjective.

The Semantic Differential provides three types of information about the attitude object: evaluative, potency and activity information. The *evaluative* dimension (in the above example, good–bad, clean–dirty, beautiful–ugly) measures the favourableness or unfavourableness towards the attitude object. The *potency* dimension (strong–weak, cruel–kind) and the *activity* dimension (active–passive) provide additional information about the significance of that object or person to the individual whose attitude is being measured.

Generally, the evaluative dimension has been regarded as the most important of the three, as it is the dimension that measures the strength with which a person holds a particular attitude.

The direct methods used to measure attitudes are popular mainly because they are extremely easy to administer and construct, and provide reasonably valid and reliable measures. Considering both direct and indirect measures of attitudes it would be true to say that there is room for improvement and refinement of techniques to make attitude measurement both more reliable and accurate. Part of the problem social psychologists experience in predicting behaviour from attitudes, as we shall see later in this chapter, comes from poor measuring instruments.

## 4.4  Attitude organization and change

Social psychologists have accumulated a large amount of evidence showing attitudes to be both organized and changed according to the principle of *cognitive consistency*. Essentially the idea is that people strive to maintain consistency between: (a) beliefs, values and attitudes; (b) attitudes and behaviour; and (c) different attitudes. Organizing attitudes, beliefs and behaviour into internally consistent structures both underscores and presumes human rationality: rational behaviour may be seen as that consistent to both ourselves and other people.

Cognitive consistency is such a powerful force in our social lives that its absence or opposite (inconsistency) is experienced as extremely uncomfortable. Indeed, one theory (Bateson *et al.*, 1956) of schizophrenia claims that the disorder is caused by one person making two simultaneous but inconsistent communications to another, this inconsistent communication is called a 'double bind'. According to Bateson, schizophrenia is a psychological response by the person receiving these two inconsistent communications.

Whilst this is an extreme example of the uncomfortable nature of inconsistency, in more normal situations people are motivated to reduce or avoid inconsistency whenever possible. Research shows (see below) that the means of achieving consistency may deviate quite markedly from rational criteria: the desire to achieve consistency may be rational, but often the means of achieving it is not.

To look further at the idea of cognitive consistency and how it may be achieved three theories of cognitive consistency – Balance (Heider, 1958), Congruity (Osgood and Tannenbaum, 1955), and Dissonance (Festinger, 1957) – will be described. These are known as the 'family of consistency theories'.

### 4.4.1 Balance theory

Heider (1958) provided a simple system for describing the *subjective* environment of a person (the way the world is perceived). He conceptualized a person's environment to be made up of entities (people, ideas, events) and relations between entities and introduced two types of relations: (a) sentiment relations which are concerned with liking and disliking; and (b) unit relations which deal with belonging. The former relate to attitudes since they are affective/evaluative in nature.

Balance theory deals with *three* kinds of entities: (a) the person (P) whose subjective environment we are concerned with; (b) another person (O); and (c) an object (X), which may be a third person. Balance theory is concerned with how relations between the three entities are organized in terms of *P's cognitive structure*. With three entities (P, O and X) three sets of relations exist: between P and O, P and X, and O and X. Each relation can take one of two values, either like (represented by ' + ') or dislike (represented by ' – '). With three sets of relations and each taking on one of two values eight possible states of affairs exist. These are shown in Figure 4.4 below. According to Heider a balanced state exists 'if all three relations are positive in all respects, or if two relations are negative and one is positive'. The triads on the right in Figure 4.4 represent imbalanced or inconsistent states of affairs since they have either two positive or three negative relations. A person in one of these imbalanced states would be motivated to change his or her attitude (liking or disliking) to achieve a balanced state (one of the four triads on the left of Figure 4.4). Some examples will make this clearer.

Take triad (b) in Figure 4.4. This could be represented as follows: Polonius likes Ophelia (P ___+___ O); Polonius dislikes eating meat (P ___÷___ X); Polonius believes Ophelia to dislike eating meat (O ___–___X). Notice that it is what Polonius *believes* Ophelia's attitude to be, which may or may not

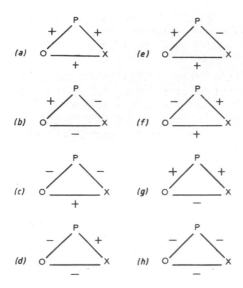

**Figure 4.4** The eight triads for three entities with positive or negative sentiment relations. The four triads on the left are balanced, the four on the right imbalanced. From Heider (1958).

correspond with what it actually is). This is a balanced or stable and harmonious state of affairs.

By contrast, using the same people and issues, triad (e) presents an uncomfortable state of affairs. Polonius likes Ophelia (P ___+___ O); Polonius dislikes eating meat (P ___−___ X); but this time Polonius believes Ophelia to like eating meat (O ___+___ X). Assuming (this is important for Balance theory) the issue of eating meat matters to Polonius, something has to change. A number of possible changes in attitudes can take place to achieve this balance, for example, Polonius could stop being a vegetarian and try to like meat, which would result in triad (a). Another possibility would be for Polonius to persuade Ophelia to dislike eating meat – resulting in triad (b). Or, more radically perhaps, Polonius could abandon his relationship with Ophelia – triad (c). Triad (d) is unlikely to result since all attitudes have to change.

To predict in advance which attitude is likely to change we would need to know more about the two people involved. With further information Rosenberg and Abelson (1960) maintain that attitude change takes place according to a principle of '*minimum effort*', which states that the attitude which requires the *least effort* to change will be the one that changes.

Balance theory accords quite well with our intuitions of harmony and disharmony between two people and significant things in their lives. However, in the special case where 'X' is a third person, the theory seems to break down. Take the 'eternal triangle': Polonius loves Ophelia; Polonius dislikes John (X); Polonius believes Ophelia to love John. This is triad (e) in Figure 4.4. The state of affairs is imbalanced (though not an uncommon one) but what can this change to? Surely not (a) where everybody likes/ loves each other, (c) seems the only sensible possibility. You work it out. Generally, balance theory runs into trouble when the third entity (X) is a person.

Balance theory suffers a number of other shortcomings: for example, relations between entities are only positive or negative, they do not admit degree of like or dislike. The theory deals with relations between a maximum of three entities. Multiple relations often exist between people and/or objects. Generally, balance theory oversimplifies, however, the approach is quite successful within this limited domain.

### 4.4.2 Congruity principle

Osgood and Tannenbaum's (1955) congruity principle is a special case of balance theory since it is concerned with how attitudes may change when a person is exposed to a *persuasive communication*. There are three elements, as with balance: the person (P); the source of the communication (S); and the message or communication itself (O). This captures the idea of a source making a statement about some issue (attitude object) which is then presented to the person (this could be verbally, or via newspapers/television).

As with balance, congruous (consistent) states are those where all three relations are positive or two are negative and one is positive, but congruity is different since it is concerned with how a communication by a source about an object affects the person's attitudes to *both* the source and the attitude object. One important difference between balance and congruity is that to reach a state of congruity from one of incongruity *both P's attitudes* – towards the source and towards the object – change.

Supposing Susan (the source) makes a positive statement about the deterrent effect of nuclear weapons (O). Further, suppose Paul (P) has a high regard for Susan, and has a negative attitude to nuclear weapons. Now, congruity also measures the *strength* with which attitudes are held on a scale ranging from + 3 (strongly positive), through 0 (neutral), to – 3 (strongly negative). With our example let us assume Paul to regard Susan highly ( + 3) and feel only slightly negative towards nuclear weapons ( – 1). This is represented in the left-hand triad in Figure 4.5. Congruity may be achieved by, for example, Paul slightly revising his opinion of Susan (to + 2) and changing his opinion of nuclear weapons to slightly positive ( + 1), this is represented in the right-hand triad of Figure 4.5. In predicting how congruity is achieved, Osgood and Tannenbaum say that the *strongest* held attitude changes *least*.

Congruity offers a model for looking at how a person is or may be influenced by persuasive communication generally, and within this framework social psychologists can investigate in more detail what makes effective and ineffective communications. Essentially, the question of 'who says what to whom with what effect' is addressed by this approach. The structure of the message, characteristics of the source (the communicator) and the person the message is aimed at (the target) have all been investigated.

Effects of communication and persuasion in attitudes was extensively researched by Janis and Hovland (1959) in the Yale Communication

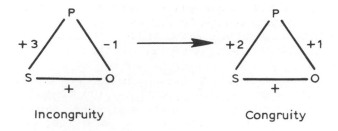

Incongruity                     Congruity

**Figure 4.5**  Moving from incongruity to congruity, notice that *both* P's attitudes change, the strongest held the least and the weakest held the most.

Research Programme. They investigated the independent variables of source, message and audience (target) factors and measured attitude change with respect to changes in opinions, perceptions, evaluations and behaviour. Janis and Hovland proposed that attitude change resulting from source factors occurred because such factors influenced the amount of *attention* paid to the communication; message factors influenced the comprehensibility of the message for the audience; and audience factors resulting in attitude change occurred because of acceptance by the audience of the communication. This, as well as the specific variables studied for each of the factors, is summarized in Figure 4.6.

Hovland, Janis and Kelley (1953) have shown that the source (the person making the communication) is more likely to be effective if that person is seen as, for example, trustworthy or an expert in the field. The motives of the source are also important – Walster, Aronson and Abrahams (1966)

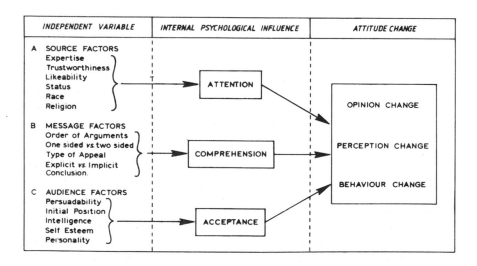

**Figure 4.6**  Diagram showing how different types of persuasive communication (independent variable) have psychological influence which results in attitude change. After Janis and Hovland (1959).

empirically demonstrated that a person who argued for a position against his own best interest was perceived as more credible (and hence more influential) than a person who argued for a position in his own best interests (resulting in little influence over others). If a murderer asks to be hanged you can believe he is telling the truth!

The message itself in a persuasive communication has been looked at in two main ways: first, fear appeals; second, organization of message. Are strong or weak fear appeals more effective in changing attitudes? It depends: for example, people high in self-esteem are more likely to be influenced a long time after the high fear appeal. Leventhal (1970) demonstrated that smokers shown a 'high fear' film on lung cancer were found to smoke less than smokers shown a 'low fear' film when contacted five months later.

The organization of the message has been looked at in two important ways: (a) one-sided or two-sided arguments; (b) order of the information presented. The latter is dealt with in some detail with respect to impression formation (Chapter 6). The effectiveness of one-sided or two-sided arguments depends on the nature of the audience (target of the communication). For example, it has been found that if the audience already believes in the position being argued for then a one-sided presentation is effective. However, if the audience is opposed to the position a two-sided, rather than a one-sided, argument is more likely to produce attitude change.

### 4.4.3 Cognitive dissonance

Festinger's (1957) theory of cognitive dissonance is the most widely researched cognitive consistency theory. There are two main reasons for this: first, it offers a general theory of human social motivation; and, secondly, it has a breadth of application far exceeding that of, say, balance and congruity.

Dissonance is defined by Festinger (1957) as 'a negative drive state which occurs whenever an individual holds two cognitions (ideas, beliefs, attitudes) which are psychologically inconsistent'. Dissonance theory, as with other 'consistency theories' starts from the assumption that a person's desired state is one of balance and harmony among beliefs, attitudes, etc. Dissonance theory enjoys such a wide range of application since it is concerned with any instance when two cognitions are psychologically inconsistent. Festinger's often quoted example of cigarette smoking and lung cancer demonstrates the point well.

For a person who smokes cigarettes the fact 'I smoke cigarettes' and the knowledge that cigarette smoking causes lung cancer should produce a state of dissonance (assuming, of course, that the person does not have a death-wish in the first place). Consonance (consistency) could be achieved in one of two ways: (a) the person could stop smoking; or (b) the person could ignore or refute the evidence linking smoking and lung cancer. The fact that many people continue to smoke in full knowledge of the harmful effects of smoking suggests that different people have different tolerance levels for dissonance. One problem for social psychologists, beyond the limit of this chapter, is to attempt to predict when and for whom dissonance provides motivation to change behaviour or attitudes.

As mentioned earlier the breadth of dissonance theory is its main strength, but no theory can be accepted without an examination of the empirical support for it. Three areas, in particular, have received considerable attention from dissonance theory researchers: decision-making, forced-compliance behaviour and effort.

## Decision making

Anyone who makes a decision in which each alternative considered has both positive and negative aspects is predicted to experience 'post-decisional dissonance'. The important point to note is that dissonance is experienced only *after* a decision has been taken; this is because the alternative taken will always embody both positive and negative aspects, and the alternatives rejected have positive features absent from the decision-maker's choice. Cognitive dissonance arises for the decision-maker since the cognitions of having selected an alternative with negative aspects and rejected others with positive aspects means a trade-off has been made. The decision-maker expects and hopes the trade-off will prove worthwhile, but does not really know this at the time. An example will help clarify the points being made.

Suppose you are trying to decide which car to buy and, for sake of simplicity, further suppose the choice is between a Ford and a British Leyland. One approach to assist decision-making would be to draw up a checklist of the important features you are looking for in a car and see how the two makes fare. Table 4.1 summarizes such an exercise. Assuming these seven features are the important ones for you and that they are equally weighted (of equal importance), the make with the greatest number of pluses, if we implement a simple decision rule, is the one to buy. So you go out and buy the British Leyland. It is now, having bought the car, that you will experience dissonance: this is because you have made a choice in which there are negative features (expensive, spares hard to get, etc.) and rejected a choice with some positive features (Ford is cheap, easy to get spares for, etc.).

Dissonance is reduced by *bolstering* the alternative decided on, this means that information will be selectively sought to make the choice taken seem even more attractive and the alternative rejected less attractive. Ehrlich *et al.* (1957) found that people who had just bought a new car looked at magazine

**Table 4.1** Balance sheet of features considered when buying a car and how Ford and British Leyland compare on these figures.

| FEATURE | FORD | VALUE | BRITISH LEYLAND | VALUE |
|---|---|---|---|---|
| Price | Relatively cheap | + | Expensive | − |
| Comfort | Hard & noisy | − | Smooth & quiet | + |
| Petrol | Not economical | − | Economical | + |
| Spares | Available & Cheap | + | Hard to get & expensive | − |
| Servicing | Infrequent & Cheap | + | Frequent & expensive | − |
| Image | Poor | − | Good | + |
| Reliability | Poor | − | Good | + |
| | TOTAL (+) = 3 | | TOTAL (+) = 4 | |

articles and advertisements which praised their choice of purchase, and, at the same time, ignored or read reports criticizing other alternatives considered but rejected.

Brehm (1956) further demonstrated that people downgrade the rejected alternative and upgrade the alternative taken. In this experiment a number of women were shown various household appliances, then asked to rate each appliance in terms of its attractiveness. Subsequently, each woman was given the choice of *one* of the two appliances she had rated most attractive. The women received the appliance of their choice and were asked to rate the two appliances again. Brehm found, as predicted by dissonance theory, that the appliance chosen was rated as more desirable and the rejected appliance as less desirable than before having made the choice.

Individual decision-making operates at so many levels in our lives – from deciding what car to buy, through organizational decisions up to international levels in politics – but at all levels the phenomenon of *post-decisional* dissonance applies. The point to emerge is that whilst pre-decisional behaviour may be rational, justification of the decision taken by cognitive bolstering (bolstering the chosen alternative and downgrading the merits of the rejected alternative) is *not* rational.

### Forced-compliance behaviour

The less a person is paid for doing something against his beliefs or attitudes the more he or she is likely to change those beliefs or attitudes. Conversely, the more a person is paid to do such a thing the less he or she has to justify it to him or herself, consequently, the less likely are his or her attitudes to change. This is perhaps one of the more surprising predictions of cognitive dissonance theory. The prediction derives from dissonance theory since a state of dissonance arises for a person when he or she is unable to justify his or her behaviour. Hence, doing something you do not agree with or arguing for a position opposite to your own views or attitudes where there is insufficient justification (external reward, for example) causes dissonance. The two cognitions, 'I am of such and such a view' and 'I am acting or arguing against my view' create dissonance. Dissonance can be reduced by changing one of the cognitions: the person has already done or said something against his or her view so this cannot change (unless he or she distorts the past). In consequence, it is most likely that the person's own views will change to be consonant (or less dissonant) with his or her behaviour. This was first investigated in a classic experiment by Festinger and Carlsmith (1959).

Festinger and Carlsmith had students perform a very dull and boring task (turning pegs in a peg-board) for one hour. The students were then asked to tell another subject, who was waiting to do the task, that the task was very interesting, worthwhile and good fun to do, i.e. they were asked to lie. There were two experimental conditions: students asked to lie about the task were paid either $20 or $1 to do so. Festinger and Carlsmith were interested in the students' attitude to the task *after* telling the waiting subjects that it was interesting. It was found that subjects who were paid $20 rated the task, after performing it, as boring and of little relevance, whilst subjects paid $1 rated the task, again after performing it, as interesting, relevant and enjoyable.

Such findings have been replicated in numerous experiments using such a 'forced compliance' paradigm. Often experimenters have asked subjects to write essays on a topic directly opposing their own views.

Findings from forced-compliance experiments are explained by dissonance theorists in terms of justification. The claim is that when there is sufficient *external* justification ($20 in the Festinger and Carlsmith experiment) subjects experience little, if any, dissonance and hence don't have to change their attitudes. However, when the external justification for telling a false-hood is insufficient ($1 payment) subjects experience cognitive dissonance. Since they cannot change their behaviour (they are forced or requested to comply with the experimenter's wishes), their attitudes change. The low reward condition ($1) offers insufficient external justification for the behaviour so *internal* justification is sought. The internal justification is that the task is actually interesting, hence dissonance is reduced or eliminated.

Two important modifications have been made to the basic propositions of dissonance theory. First Aronson (1969) suggests that we need to assume that people perceive themselves as decent and honest to experience dissonance in forced-compliance situations. This makes sense, since if you do not think lying to others is a bad thing then you will not need to justify your behaviour (either externally or internally). Second, Brehm and Cohen (1962) add the rider that dissonance can only be expected to exist when it is known that a person is committed in some way to the attitude. This highlights the point that if a person does not have very strong feelings about something disso-nance is hardly likely to be aroused since to speak here of counter-attitudinal behaviour does not really make sense.

## Effort

Before gaining acceptance to clubs, fraternities, groups, gangs, etc. there are often 'initiation rites' to go through. Dissonance theory shows that these 'rites of passage' serve a distinct social psychological function. The predic-tion is that the more effort a person puts into achieving a goal, the more attractive and worthwhile it is perceived to be when finally achieved. Dissonance theory is saying that *regardless* of how attractive, desirable, interesting, etc. the goal actually is, it is what a person goes through to achieve it that determines its worth. Why should a person experience dissonance here? If you gain membership to a club or society and have to go through 'hell and high water' to get this you are likely to be extremely upset if you subsequently discover the club or society to be boring and worthless to you. Dissonance arises since the cognition 'I have put a lot of time and effort into gaining entry to this club' and 'the club is dull and worthless' are dissonant, since people do not normally put a lot of time and effort into something useless. To reduce dissonance the person could leave the club or society he or she has just joined – this is unlikely since the person would have to acknowledge and accept that he or she had wasted time and effort. Festinger and Carlsmith predict the person will perceive the club or society to be interesting and worthwhile; this justifies the expenditure of time and effort.

Aronson and Mills (1959) devised an experiment to test this. They recruited women to join a group discussing the psychology of sex. However, before the women could join the discussion group they were told they had to go through a screening test (the screening test being the 'initiation'). Subjects were randomly allocated to one of three 'screening-test' conditions: (a) 'severe initiation' where the women had to recite aloud, in the presence of a male, obscene words and sexually explicit passages; (b) 'mild initiation' where women recited aloud sexual but not obscene words; (c) 'no initiation' where women were admitted to the discussion group without any screening.

After this the subjects in each condition listened to what they thought was a live discussion on the psychology of sex (in fact all subjects listened to the same tape recording of a discussion), which was deliberately made by the experimenters to be dull and boring. After listening to this boring discussion the subjects were asked how much they liked it, found it interesting and worthwhile, etc. Aronson and Mills found, consistent with the prediction of dissonance theory, outlined earlier, that subjects who had gone through the 'severe initiation' found the discussion interesting and worthwhile. Subjects admitted to the discussion without any initiation thought it dull and boring, whilst 'mild initiation' subjects found the discussion only slightly interesting and worthwhile.

On the basis of this, and other similar research, it can be seen that initiation rites in particular, or any situation in which a person struggles to gain acceptance, is likely to result in the goal when achieved being seen as desirable and worthwhile, regardless of whether it actually is or not!

### Summary

Cognitive dissonance theory has attracted a great deal of research because of its wide range of application. The dissonance arousing aspects of decision-making, forced-compliance behaviour and effort have all shown that whilst the desire to achieve harmony or consonance may be rational the means of achieving it often is not. Notice that in none of these experiments have social psychologists attempted to measure dissonance itself: it has been assumed to have been aroused by the experimental manipulations. That this is the case is less than obvious and explains why other theories have been advanced to explain the above phenomena and attitude change more generally.

## 4.5 Other approaches to attitude change

Up until now attitude change has been looked at from the point of view of the 'family of consistency theories'. Whilst the principle of cognitive consistency underlies attitude organization change and formation, there are other approaches which differ quite radically from that already described. Of these different approaches three will be described: self-perception theory, impression management and self-generated attitude change.

### 4.5.1 Self-perception theory

Bem (1967) pointed out that our actual behaviour often determines what we think, i.e. it is behaviour which determines the attitudes a person holds. So, to quote one of Bem's examples, 'since I eat brown bread then I must like brown bread'. Applying this logic to the Festinger and Carlsmith study described above, Bem would say that since the subjects are telling the other that the peg-board task is interesting then they find it to be so.

Self-perception theory states that a person *forms* his or her attitudes through self-observation of behaviour. In Bem's approach there is no need, as he says, 'to postulate an aversive motivational drive toward consistency' but it is important to ask how general an explanation of attitude formation and change this approach can offer. In cases where a person does *not* already possess an attitude or set of beliefs towards something, behaviour may be a good guide to attitudes. However, when a person already holds a strong attitude self-perception theory would seem less applicable. To understand *attitude formation* self-perception theory may be very useful, but in looking at *attitude change* the approach seems less productive.

### 4.5.2  Impression management

Tedeschi, Schlenker and Bonoma (1971) proposed that an individual is more concerned with *giving an impression* of consistency between attitudes and behaviour or attitudes and other attitudes than in actually maintaining *internal* consistency. The concern for the person is not in terms of maintaining consistency between his or her attitudes and behaviour but controlling or managing the impression that others form. Other people will assume that a certain behaviour reflects that person's attitudes and beliefs. This is what is wanted since it gives the individual control over how others will react to him or her. (Goffman (1959) discusses a very similar idea in his highly readable book *The Presentation of Self in Everyday Life*.)

The importance of and extent to which people try to control, manipulate and maintain particular impressions of themselves is obviously a powerful factor in explaining why people act as they do. Nevertheless, with such an approach one could never be sure when a person was acting from belief and conviction or when trying to cultivate the appropriate impression. In order to use the assumption that people behave in ways consistent with their attitudes means that people must do so much of the time: impression management seems to cause more problems than it solves.

### 4.5.3  Self-generated attitude change

Quite often thinking about something intensely and deeply for a significant period of time tends to crystallize one's attitudes. Tesser (1978) has suggested that thinking about one's own attitude serves to make that attitude more extreme, the attitude is said to 'polarize'.

Tesser and Conlee (1975) asked subjects' attitudes to topics such as prostitution, social revolution and political revolution. They were then asked to think about one of these issues for a period of time. Later their attitude to the issue they thought about was measured again. The independent variable was the amount of time subjects thought about the issue – they were asked to think about it for either 30, 60, 90 or 180 seconds. Tesser and Conlee found that the longer subjects had to think about the issue the more extreme the

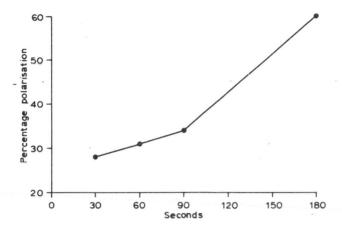

**Figure 4.7** Percentage polarization (extent to which attitudes become more extreme) after subjects were allowed to think about a topic for either 30, 60, 90 or 180 seconds. Adapted from Tesser and Conlee (1975).

attitude became. This is summarized in Figure 4.7. The figure shows that attitudes became much more extreme when subjects had been allowed a full three minutes to think about the topic.

Self-generated attitude change provides an alternative explanation for dissonance phenomena. Take, for example, a person who is asked to write an essay about the effectiveness of hanging as a deterrent for murder when the person initially believes the opposite to be the case – the task of writing the counter-attitudinal essay will make the person think of facts, arguments, etc. consistent with the position. This may be sufficient to change the person's attitude: 'seeing' something from another point of view often serves to make us more sympathetic to that point of view.

## 4.6 Attitudes and behaviour

Much of what has been said in this chapter is predicated upon the assumption that attitudes and behaviour go together in a consistent manner. Indeed, the definition of attitudes offered earlier reflects this. Generally, most theories (self-perception being the exception) assume that attitudes *cause* behaviour in some way. These assumptions have been, and still are, strongly held by many social psychologists. As will be shown, however, such matters are neither straightforward nor strongly supported by empirical data. Generally, research has shown a poor relationship between attitudes and behaviour (Wicker, 1969a).

### 4.6.1 Attitudes as causes of behaviour

The relationship between attitudes and behaviour was investigated in a famous study by La Piere (1934). La Piere travelled around America with a Chinese student and his wife. La Piere recorded how the two Chinese were treated in the numerous hotels and restaurants they visited. On only one occasion were they treated inhospitably. Six months later La Piere sent a letter to all the places he had visited asking if they would accept Chinese clientele. The surprising result was that over 90 per cent of the replies to La Piere's letter were negative: Chinese would *not* be welcome.

The dilemma of people saying one thing and doing another has continued to plague attitude–behaviour research. Why should this discrepancy exist? One possibility is that social psychologists have not devised sensitive or accurate enough tools with which to measure attitudes. Another reason is that, as with the La Piere study and many others, an attempt is made to relate *general* attitudes (attitudes to the Chinese) to *specific* behaviour (serving a Chinese couple accompanied by a white American). More appropriate would be to measure *specific* attitudes and then see how they relate to *specific* behaviours. The reason for the poor relationship between attitudes and behaviour may be the design of the experiment by the social psychologist; this is true of the La Piere study.

De Fleur and Westie (1958) attempted to relate specific attitudes to specific behaviours in order to overcome the problems of the La Piere study. They asked a large number of people specific questions about blacks and whites in order to gain a measure of prejudice. They then selected highly prejudiced people and asked them if they would be willing to pose for a photograph with a black. They found prejudiced people less willing to pose than unprejudiced people.

As well as trying to relate specific attitudes to specific behaviours, norms and habits need to be taken into account. Wicker (1969b) found that people's church-going behaviour was more related to what they thought the consequences of being seen going to church were (setting a good example to children, impressing others, etc.) than to their attitudes towards the church and religion. This is reminiscent of 'impression management' discussed earlier. Habits are also important, for example, Sugar (reported in Triandis, 1971) found the strongest predictor of smoking behaviour in a social situation to be amount usually smoked rather than a person's attitude to smoking.

The more recent approach of Fishbein and Ajzen (1975), described earlier in this chapter, suggests that behaviour may be accurately predicted if we know a person's attitude to that behaviour, the person's intention to perform that behaviour and what the person believes are the consequences of performing the behaviour. At the same time we need to know social norms with respect to that behaviour (i.e. is it desirable to act in that way or is that kind of behaviour socially unacceptable). Fishbein and Ajzen claim that only when knowledge of a person's attitude toward that behaviour and social norms are known is it possible to predict the *behavioural intention*. Knowing the intention should lead to a high degree of accuracy in predicting behaviour. This approach has proved more successful since the predictions for behaviour are based solely on beliefs, attitudes and norms about the behaviour, thus avoiding the general–specific trap that La Piere and other researchers fell into in the past. However, Fishbein and Ajzen's approach is very unlikely to produce very high predictive accuracy since the best of intentions often fail to result in behaviour; other things (distractions, crises, etc.) intervene to prevent intentions being carried out.

In summary, early research, such as that by La Piere, shows methodological problems for researchers attempting to predict behaviour from attitudes. Conceptual advances, such as those by Fishbein and Ajzen, have helped in understanding more precisely the questions being asked when relating attitudes to behaviour. The correlation will probably always be less than perfect but is much higher these days due to methodological improvements in research and detailed conceptual frameworks.

### 4.6.2 Personality variables

Behaviour may not be consistent with attitudes because some people may simply not behave in ways consistent with what they believe. If this is the case neither methodological or conceptual advances, as described above, will be of much use. Self-monitoring (Snyder, 1979) offers a way of accounting for poor attitude–behaviour relations by saying that some people *do* behave in consistent ways (low self-monitor) whilst others *do not* (high self-monitor). The behaviour of the high self-monitor is determined more by the demands of the social situation and behaviour appropriate to that social situation.

The low self-monitor exhibits a high degree of consistency between attitudes and behaviour since behaving according to one's own beliefs and attitudes is the prime consideration for this personality type. The high self-monitor, by contrast, may seem to others like a different person in different social situations with different people present.

The self-monitoring personality dimension has implications for research on cognitive dissonance. For example, in counter-attitudinal tasks *low* self-monitors would be expected to *change* their attitude to be consistent with their behaviour. High self-monitors would *not* change their attitudes as they would see it as appropriate to behave in that way in that kind of situation.

Predicting behaviour from attitudes is not as straightforward or simple a matter as would seem at first sight. Social psychologists have had to take account of the problem of specificity of attitude and behaviour, social norms and habits, and personality differences. Taking account of such factors allows for behaviour to be predicted more confidently and accurately, but by no means as accurately as social psychologists would deem desirable.

## 4.7 Summary

- Social psychologists regard attitudes as central and fundamental to understanding and explaining how people behave. Attitudes occupy an important place in our everyday social lives.

- The structural approach to explaining what attitudes are attempts to relate them to other concepts such as values, beliefs, intentions and behaviour.
  The functional approach suggests that attitudes serve four main functions for the individual: adaptive, knowledge, self-expressive, and ego functions.

- Attitudes have been measured by both indirect and direct means. Indirect means have proved less successful and more unreliable than direct means, which are self-report type rating scales.

- The principle of 'cognitive consistency' states that attitudes are related to other attitudes and behaviour in consistent ways. Balance, congruity and cognitive dissonance (the 'family of consistency theories') all reflect this principle. Attitudes are predicted to change when imbalance, incongruity or dissonance arises. Attitudes are often changed to be consistent with behaviour.

○ Self-perception theory, impression management and self-generated attitude change offer alternative approaches to understanding how attitudes change. They all, however, rely on the principle of cognitive consistency.

○ Predicting behaviour from attitudes is not simple, social psychologists have found a poor relationship to exist at times. To predict more accurately requires knowledge of norms, habits, as well as personality differences such as the self-monitoring scale.

## 4.8  Suggestions for further reading

Brown, R. *Social Psychology* (New York, Macmillan Co., 1965) Ch. 11.
Good, thorough coverage of the area, a little dated in some respects now but worthwhile for the full, critical discussion of consistency theories.

Eiser, J.R. *Cognitive Social Psychology* (London, McGraw-Hill, 1980), Chs. 2 and 5.
Up to date critical account of the traditional approaches to attitude measurement and theories of attitude change.

Festinger, L., Riecken, H. and Schachter, S. *When Prophecy Fails* (Minneapolis, Minn., University of Minnesota Press, 1956).
Classic participation-field study describing how a group of people predicting the end of the world reduced dissonance after world was supposed to end but did not. A compelling and illuminating insight into how dissonance theory applies to real situations.

Warren, N. and Jahoda, M. *Attitudes* 2nd Edition (Harmondsworth, Penguin, 1973).
Collection of journal articles representative of theory and research on attitudes and attitude change. Includes an interesting historical section.

# 5

# Prejudice and conflict

5.1    The scope of the problem
5.2    Three social psychological approaches
5.3    The individual approach
       *5.3.1 Personality differences   5.3.2 Frustration and aggression*
5.4    The interpersonal approach
       *5.4.1 Shared beliefs   5.4.2 Shared identities   5.4.3 Stereotypes   5.4.4 Conformity
       to values*
5.5    The intergroup approach
       *5.5.1 Intergroup competition   5.5.2 Social categorization*
5.6    Cultural, institutional and economic considerations
5.7    Reducing prejudice and conflict
5.8    Summary
5.9    Suggestions for further reading

## 5.1  The scope of the problem

Religion, race, ethnic minorities, sex, mental and physical handicap, to name
but a few, have all been, and still are, objects of prejudice and discrimination.
Reference to any daily newspaper or newscast on the television attest to widespread mistreatment of one person by another or one group by another group
of people. Human history is littered with appalling and horrific incidents of
mass slaughter arising from prejudice, and depressingly, it seems that prejudice and discrimination are unchanging features of civilized society and are
likely to remain so. Why are people prejudiced, and when does prejudice lead
to discrimination and conflict? This chapter will look at attempts by social
psychologists to explain: (a) how people become prejudiced; (b) what
function prejudice serves for the individual; and (c) how prejudice may be
reduced. It is assumed that prejudice is unjustified since there exist neither
logical nor scientific grounds for one person or group of people to categorize
themselves as either inferior or superior to another person or group of
people.

Prejudice may be defined as 'an attitude that predisposes a person to think,
feel, perceive and act in favourable or unfavourable ways towards a group or
its individual members' (Secord and Backman, 1974). Notice this definition
bears strong similarities to that given for attitudes in Chapter 4, hence prejudice may *predispose* a person to behave in either favourable or unfavourable
ways since it may manifest itself both as preferential treatment for oneself or
one's own group (referred to throughout this chapter as the '*ingroup*') and as
attempts to disadvantage the other group (the '*outgroup*').

Discrimination may be defined as 'the inequitable treatment of individuals considered to belong to a particular social group' (Secord and Backman, 1964). As this definition implies, discrimination is the actual *behavioural* consequences of a person's prejudiced attitudes.

Behaviour resulting from prejudicial attitudes can, and does, taken many forms resulting in varying degrees of inequitable treatment. This may be mild, as in the case of prejudiced talk and avoidance of people, to extreme, as in the case of massacres and pogroms. Conflict, then, is conceptualized as an extreme form of discrimination where either an intention to do harm is present or harm is actually inflicted.

This chapter concentrates on social psychological approaches to explaining prejudice and conflict. This is not meant to be, nor indeed should be, taken to imply that other types of explanations are not important or valid, they are: as we shall see, cultural, institutional and economic factors also need to be taken into consideration. A sociological perspective is of value since it sensitizes us to social, cultural and sub-cultural factors constituting the context of social psychological investigation.

## 5.2  Three social psychological approaches

Defining prejudice as an attitude that predisposes an individual to behave in certain predictable ways has led social psychologists to seek for explanations as to how such attitudes come to be held. Further, since not all prejudices lead to overt acts of discrimination or conflict social psychologists have also sought to delineate the circumstances and situations most likely to encourage such behaviour. Three broad approaches – the '*Individual*', '*Interpersonal*' and '*Intergroup*' – provide conceptual coherence to the many theories that have been suggested. Table 5.1, summarizes the essential characteristics of each of these social psychological approaches.

The '*individual approach*' places greatest emphasis (but not exclusive) on the personality of the individual and/or the emotional basis of prejudice. In looking at personality the central question asked is 'to what extent are people predisposed to being prejudiced?' i.e. is there such a thing as a prejudiced personality? We will look at two highly influential theories here – the 'authoritarian personality' and the 'open and closed mind'. The individual

**Table 5.1** Summary of the characteristics associated with the three social psychological approaches to prejudice and conflict.

| SOCIAL PSYCHOLOGICAL APPROACH | CHARACTERISTICS |
|---|---|
| *Individual* | Focus on processes *within* the individual: personality and emotions, also interest in differences between people. |
| *Interpersonal* | Focus on processes occurring *within* social groupings: shared beliefs and identities, prevailing stereotypes and conformity. |
| *Intergroup* | Focus on relationships *between* different groups of people: intergroup competition, social categorization and the consequences of these. |

approach also seeks to discover how stresses and strains of everyday life, resulting in frustration, may lead to prejudice: repeated experiences of frustration are thought to lead to aggression which is 'released' or displaced onto scapegoats.

The *'interpersonal' approach* focuses on what goes on *within* social groupings. This means it is relevant to discover the extent to which a person identifies with his or her own group (i.e. the ingroup). This approach also looks at how prevailing stereotypes within a society or sub-culture 'blind' one to the individual characteristics of a person. Finally, the approach seeks to discover the extent to which people conform to the dominant values of a particular social situation.

The *'intergroup' approach* is concerned with relationships *between* social groups, in consequence it deals with the effects of social categorization and group membership. Research examines the extent to which simply belonging to a social group causes its members to behave in favourably prejudicial ways to their own group (called 'positive ingroup bias') and unfavourably prejudicial ways to other groups ('negative outgroup bias').

This chapter deals with each of these approaches, detailing the theories and examining experimental evidence. Whilst it may be helpful to think of social psychological approaches to prejudice in this tripartite way it is important to remember that any complete account will need to consider all three in a complementary way since such a separation is artificial in the end.

## 5.3 The individual approach

The individual approach views the causes of prejudiced attitudes as resulting from the emotional dynamics of a person. Such and related behaviour fulfil certain needs for the person such as reducing tension or satisfying a need for order and control in his or her life. Within the individual approach two types of explanation are possible: where prejudice is seen to (a) result from a distinct type of personality; and (b) be rooted in the make-up of *all* human beings. With the former we search for *differences* in personality between people, with the latter people are regarded as essentially the same, since frustration is an inevitable feature of daily life for everybody. These two types of explanation share an important common feature though – they are both examples of what Pettigrew (1959) calls *externalization*. Externalization means that an individual deals with his or her inner problems, conflicts, tensions, etc. by discharging or projecting them onto other individuals or groups of people. That is, people do not recognize a problem or conflict as being within them but perceive the cause as external to them.

### 5.3.1 Personality differences

Is there a distinct personality style that is strongly associated with prejudiced attitudes? Adorno and his colleagues (Adorno, Fenkel-Brunswick, Levinson and Sanford, 1950) suggested that such attitudes are to be found in individuals with an *authoritarian personality*. The authoritarian personality, they claim, both submits to the authority of others higher in status or power and is, at the same time, authoritarian with those 'beneath' or lower in status than him or her. Authoritarian parents are authoritarian with their children who in turn tend to be authoritarian in bringing up their children. In short, such a personality is characterized by excessive and blind obedience to authority. To establish the validity of these claims two questions need to be answered: (a) does such a personality style exist? and (b) is such a personality style associated with prejudice?

Adorno *et al.* were initially concerned with constructing a questionnaire to measure antisemitism, this was in the early 1940s when antisemitism was most viciously expressed in Nazi Germany. From an attitude scale measuring a particular type of prejudice Adorno *et al.* turned their attention to constructing an attitude questionnaire measuring prejudice in general – known as *ethnocentrism*. Antisemitism, then, is simply one manifestation of ethnocentrism. Research with these two questionnaires led Adorno *et al.* to think a link existed between political ideology and personality. This was the authoritarian personality which was characterized as manifesting itself as anti-democratic and potentially fascist in beliefs and attitudes. Sanford (1956) called this the F-syndrome ('F' standing for fascist) and developed a personality questionnaire (known as the F-scale) to measure authoritarianism. Much of the theory used in constructing the questionnaire derived from Freudian theory. The F-scale is made up of nine components (such as conventionalism, authoritarian submission, superstition, preoccupation with power, puritanical sexual attitudes) with four or five questions to do with each component. (For example: conventionalism – 'Obedience and respect for authority are the most important virtues children should learn'; superstition – 'Some day it will probably be shown that astrology can explain a lot of things'; puritanical sexual attitudes – 'Homosexuality is a particularly rotten form of delinquency and ought to be severely punished'.) The F-scale was constructed, as these examples show, such that a positive answer scored a point and was taken as an indicator of an authoritarian personality. The higher the score the more a person was deemed to have an authoritarian personality.

Adorno *et al.* then looked at the extent to which a person with an authoritarian personality was likely to be antisemitic and ethnocentric. Both the original and subsequent research (Christie and Cook, 1958) have shown a consistent positive correlation between three factors measured by these questionnaires. A strong positive relationship was found to exist between authoritarianism and ethnocentrism, authoritarianism and political and economic conservatism, and authoritarianism and fascist potentials. However, two main criticisms have questioned the validity of such findings, these are (a) methodological problems; and (b) conceptual problems.

The major *methodological* problem is that the F-scale (and, for that matter, the ethnocentrism and antisemitism questionnaires) is worded in such a way that agreement with the item is taken as an indication of authoritarianism (or ethnocentrism or antisemitism with the other questionnaires). The danger with this is that it encourages what is known as an 'acquiescent response set' – the tendency people often display of agreeing with whatever is said. Hence we cannot be sure that a high score on the F-scale is a strong indication of authoritarianism, it could simply be a measure of the extent to which a person will acquiesce. To some extent authoritarianism and acquiescence are related, but the authoritarian personality, as conceptualized by

**Table 5.2** Percentage of subjects who agreed with various items on the F-scale questionnaire categorized according to education level. From Hyman and Sheatsley (1954).

| ITEM FROM F-SCALE QUESTIONNAIRE | COLLEGE | HIGH SCHOOL | GRAMMAR SCHOOL* |
|---|---|---|---|
| The most important thing to teach children is absolute obedience to their parents | 35% | 60% | 80% |
| Any good leader should be strict with people under him in order to gain respect | 36% | 51% | 45% |
| Prison is too good for sex criminals. They should be publicly whipped or worse | 18% | 31% | 45% |
| No decent man can respect a woman who has had sex relations before marriage | 14% | 26% | 39% |

*School intermediate between primary and high school.

Adorno *et al.*, is also politically conservative, intolerant of ambiguity, etc. Methodological problems can be overcome by reconstructing the questionnaire in a balanced way, but conceptual problems are less easy to deal with.

One conceptual problem, raised by Hyman and Sheatsley (1954), is that a personality type is *not* needed to explain ethnocentrism since education and socioeconomic status offer a more plausible explanation. Hyman and Sheatsley found that the authoritarian personality is more likely to exist amongst the less well educated and those of low socioeconomic status. Table 5.2 shows that the percentage agreement with sample questions from the F-scale decreases as educational levels increase.

A further problem is that the authoritarian personality was assumed to be associated solely with fascism or, more generally, extreme right-wing political conservatism. Rokeach (1960) has argued that authoritarianism can as easily be associated with the extreme left as extreme right political wings. Rokeach claims that the important feature of authoritarians of both the left and right is they have 'closed minds' i.e. rigid styles of thought with intolerance of views different from their own. This he calls *dogmatism*. Rokeach hypothesized that *both* Communists and extreme right-wing conservatives should score high on his dogmatism questionnaire. He administered this questionnaire to Conservative, Liberal, Labour and Communist English college students. Results supported the hypothesis that dogmatism is found at both political extremes since he found both Conservatives and Communists to score higher than the other political groups. However, this research is not without its problems since, for example, all 40 items on the dogmatism questionnaire are worded such that agreement indicates dogmatism. The problem of acquiescent response set, as with the F-scale, throws doubt on the validity of the questionnaire. Rokeach does, though, make an important step forward in the search for a prejudiced personality by separating authoritarianism from political ideology.

Eysenck (1954) proposed that *two* personality dimensions, not one as with Adorno *et al.* and Rokeach, were needed to characterize similarities and differences between extreme left-wing (radical) and right-wing (conservative) adherents. Eysenck called one dimension 'radicalism/conservatism' and the

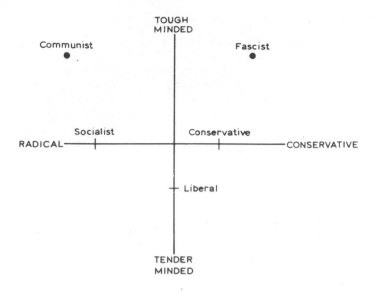

TOUGH
MINDED

Communist

Fascist

Socialist          Conservative

RADICAL ———————————————————————— CONSERVATIVE

Liberal

TENDER
MINDED

**Figure 5.1**  Eysenck's two personality dimensions of 'tough minded/tender minded' and radical/conservative showing the position of political parties.

other 'tough-minded/tender minded'. A tender-minded person believes in such things as the abolition of the death penalty, re-education of criminals and pacifism. A tough-minded person, by contrast, is seen as being in favour of, for example, the death penalty, prison and punishment, and compulsory sterilization of people with serious hereditary defects. With these two dimensions (radical/conservative and tough-minded/tender-minded) Eysenck located the positions of different political parties as shown in Figure 5.1. This shows that whilst Communists and Fascists are at different ends of the radical/conservative scale they are both very tough-minded. By contrast, Liberals are represented as rather tender-minded and neither radical nor conservative.

In terms of prejudice, and ethnocentrism generally, Eysenck's theory is such that prejudiced attitudes and discriminating behaviour are more likely to stem from tough-minded people. Little research, however, has addressed itself to such issues since the contention that Communists and Fascists are both tough-minded has not received great support. Rokeach's claim that the similarity between the two political extremes is that of dogmatism has enjoyed greater support and favour among psychologists.

In summary, research originally aimed at investigating antisemitism suggested a link between ethnocentrism and an authoritarian personality syndrome. Methodological and conceptual problems have cast doubt on this claim. Rokeach and Eysenck have both suggested authoritarianism to be characteristic of the extreme left and the extreme right political wings. The 'closed mind' style of thinking, suggested by Rokeach, and the tough-minded/tender-minded dimension of Eysenck have shown how these two ends of the political spectrum may be related.

### 5.3.2 Frustration and aggression

On countless occasions in our lives we experience frustration due to being unable to attain desired goals. Dollard *et al*. (1939) have claimed that the occurrence of aggressive behaviour *always* presupposes the existence of frustration and that frustration always leads to some form of aggression. Here our interest is with the extent to which frustration leading to aggression is enacted upon a 'scapegoat' (see Chapter 8 for a general treatment of aggression). Berkowitz (1969) has argued that frustration *may* result in aggression and that the less a person who frustrates you is able to retaliate the more likely you are to aggress against that person. This bears some similarity to scapegoating since a scapegoat is: (a) relatively powerless to retaliate to acts of aggression; (b) made to take the blame for actions which he/she or the group is not responsible for; and (c) is disliked or hated to begin with.

Experimental studies of scapegoating first attempt to frustrate subjects (by, for example, insulting them, stopping them from obtaining desired goals or ensuring they fail at some task) and then measure, on an attitude scale, the extent of prejudice after the frustrating experience. These results are then compared with a control group of subjects who did not go through the frustrating experience but just answered the attitude questionnaire. Miller and Bugelski (1948) first asked subjects their attitudes towards various minority groups. Half of these subjects were then frustrated by not being allowed to see a desired film they were told they were going to see. The 'frustrated' subjects were again asked about their attitudes to minority groups. Compared to the control group, the frustrated subjects showed an increase in prejudice.

Weatherley (1961) selected two groups of non-Jewish male college students, one group were those who scored high and the other low on an anti-semitic questionnaire. Half the subjects who scored high and half who scored low were insulted whilst filling out another questionnaire. The other half of the high and low scorers were the control groups since they were not insulted. Later all subjects were asked to write short stories about some pictures of men; two of these male pictures were given Jewish names. Two results were obtained: (a) highly antisemitic subjects who were insulted directed more aggression to the pictures with Jewish sounding names than did insulted subjects who scored low on antisemitism; and (b) subjects high and low in antisemitism and insulted did not differ in the amount of aggression directed at male pictures with non-Jewish sounding names. In short, this study supports the idea that highly antisemitic people direct their aggression towards Jews and not other groups of people.

Scapegoating as a consequence of frustration and aggression may derive from other sources such as a depressed economic climate, threat to a loss of status and other socioeconomic factors. Generally, it seems that when things go wrong and we get frustrated some suitable scapegoat is needed to avoid the painful experience of blaming ourselves.

## 5.4 The interpersonal approach

With the interpersonal approach psychologists have attempted to assess the importance of two issues: (a) whether *belief or race* similarity/dissimilarity provides us with criteria for accepting and rejecting other people, i.e. do people discriminate against others on the basis that they are of a different race or on the basis that they hold different beliefs? and (b) to what extent *conformity* to prevailing stereotypes and/or values may account for prejudice and discrimination. The issue of race or belief similarity/dissimilarity places emphasis upon peoples' perceptions of what is the same and different about others compared with themselves. Conformity, either to stereotypes or values, focuses more on the forces and pressures in social situations that cause people to fall in line with the dominant or accepted way of thinking or behaving. These issues will be explored in the following sub-sections.

### 5.4.1 Shared beliefs

Rokeach (1968) claims that 'differences in belief on important issues are more powerful determinants of prejudice or discrimination than differences in race or ethnic membership'. Put crudely, the contention is that social discrimination of blacks, for example, would not be because they are coloured but because they believe in different things.

To test this hypothesis Rokeach, Smith and Evans (1960) asked subjects to rate a number of stimulus persons according to whether or not they thought they would like to be friends with them. The stimulus persons were of either the same or different race and religion as the subjects and present in pairs as follows:

   1 (a) A white person who believes in God
     (b) A black person who believes in God
   2 (c) A white person who is a communist
     (d) A black person who is anti-communist

Results showed that subjects were more likely to say they would like to be friends with someone who believed in the same things as them *regardless* of race. For friendship, then, belief similarity would appear to be more important than racial similarity.

Rokeach (1968) conducted a field experiment, to test his theory further, in which 26 black and 26 white male job applicants acted as unwitting subjects whilst attending a job interview. Each job applicant was put in a waiting room with four confederates who the job applicant thought were also waiting for interview. The confederates were instructed to talk about treatment of mental patients with the real job applicants and took either a formal or informal approach to treatment. Things were arranged such that the confederates were either different or the same as the subject on race and belief. Two confederates were of the same race but one held different and one the same belief as the subject. The other two confederates were of different race with again one holding the same and one different belief to the subject. After the subject had been talking to the four confederates for about 10 minutes he was asked to indicate which two out of the four people he would most prefer to work with. Six possible combinations of two from four people to work with were available to the subject to choose from, these are given in Table 5.3. Subjects overwhelmingly chose potential workmates who shared the same

**Table 5.3** Possible combinations of partners subjects could choose to work with, where 'S' means the same race and 'O' means another race. ( + ) indicates same belief and ( − ) different belief to subject. Figures in the right-hand column show actual choices made by the subjects. Adapted from Rokeach (1968, pp. 69–71).

| COMBINATION OF PARTNERS | | DESCRIPTION | SUBJECT CHOICE |
|---|---|---|---|
| S + | O + | Two people who agree with the subject, one the same race and one the other race. | 30 |
| S − | O − | Two people who disagree with the subject, one the same race and one the other race. | 3 |
| S + | S − | Two people of the same race as the subject, one agreeing and one disagreeing with the subject. | 2 |
| O + | O − | Two people of the other race to the subject, one agreeing and one disagreeing with the subject. | 3 |
| S + | O − | One person of the subject's race agreeing and one of the other race disagreeing. | 4 |
| S − | O + | One person of the subject's race disagreeing and one of the other race agreeing. | 8 |
| | | TOTAL | 52 |

beliefs as them regardless of race (S + , O + in Table 5.3). Also there was some preference for workmates of the same and different race and same and different beliefs (S − , O + in Table 5.3) indicating a tendency for subjects to choose mixed groups of people to talk to. Generally, then, Rokeach's research supports his hypothesis that belief similarity or dissimilarity is a more important factor in social discrimination (positive discrimination for the same beliefs and negative discrimination for different beliefs) than is similarity or difference of race.

### 5.4.2 Shared identities

Two questions need to be addressed in order to ascertain the extent to which race itself may cause prejudice: (a) what evidence is there that race may be the *sole* cause of social discrimination? and (b) to what extent do people identify with their own race? We will deal with each of these questions in turn.

Triandis (1961) criticized the Rokeach, Smith and Evans (1960) study, and Rokeach's basic hypothesis, on the grounds that prejudice was measured solely in terms of friendship choice. To discover if race or belief was more likely, *generally*, to cause prejudice Triandis developed a 'social distance scale'. This measures the extent to which a person will associate with another in many different social settings. The social distance scale consists of items such as 'I would accept this person as a neighbour', 'I would not permit this person's attendance at our universities'. Subjects were asked whether they agreed or disagreed with each of the statements for a number of stimulus persons who varied according to race, religion, beliefs and occupation. Triandis found that as the stimulus person became *more different* from the subject there was a greater social distance. Detailed analysis showed that *race* was the most important factor in creating social distance with belief and occupation of equal importance but much less so than race. Further research by Triandis and Davis (1965) revealed a more complicated picture since race was found to be more important in intimate relationships between people and belief more important in more formal and less intimate relationships.

One reason why race does not assume overwhelming importance may be that people do not identify strongly with their own race. In a classic study by Clark and Clark (1947) white and black children were presented with a white and brown doll and asked to say which doll looked most like them. Virtually all white children identified themselves with the white doll but less than two thirds of the black children identified themselves with the brown doll. Habra and Grant (1970) replicated this study in an inter-racial setting and found an overwhelming majority of black children identified with the brown doll. Over the years then identification with one's own race has, so it would seem, become stronger. Perhaps this is a general phenomenon exemplified by the 'Black is Beautiful' movement of the late 1960s and early 1970s.

Perhaps, then, the research by Rokeach and Triandis needs to be interpreted in the context of the general social climate prevailing at that time. It may be that their research was done at a time when racial identity was just starting to become fashionable and that, particularly in more intimate relationships, race came to be a more important social discriminator since racial identity became stronger.

### 5.4.3 Stereotypes

Three features characterize stereotypes: (a) people are categorized on highly *visible* characteristics such as race, sex, nationality, bodily appearance, etc. (b) *all* members of that category or social grouping are attributed with possessing the *same* characteristics; and (c) any individual perceived to belong to that category is attributed with possessing those stereotypic characteristics. Stereotypes, then, are grossly oversimplified and overgeneralized abstractions about groupings of people and are usually highly inaccurate although they may contain a grain of truth, as Allport (1954) suggests.

Stereotypes are usually measured by giving people a list of adjectives (such as intelligent, industrious, lazy, etc.) together with a list of categories of people (categorized by, for example, race, nationality, sex) and asking subjects to indicate, on a five-point Likert-type scale, how those adjectives describe a particular group of people. Whilst people are less willing to engage in such an exercise than they once were Karlins, Coffman and Walters (1969) have shown how stereotypes have changed over the years. Table 5.4 shows that in 1933 Americans were seen as industrious, intelligent but not particularly materialistic, whilst in 1967 they were seen as materialistic but not particularly industrious or intelligent. What this study, and other similar ones, demonstrate is that whilst stereotypes may change the prevalence of stereotyping seems not to change. Two questions follow from this: (a) what consequences does stereotyping have for prejudice and discrimination?; and (b) since stereotyping occurs what function does it serve?

Campbell (1967) suggests four consequences of stereotyping for prejudice

**Table 5.4** Changing stereotypes of Americans, Jews and Negroes over a 40-year period. Adapted from Karlins, Coffman and Walters (1969).

| ETHNIC GROUP | TRAIT | PERCENTAGE CHECKING TRAIT | | |
|---|---|---|---|---|
| | | 1933 | 1951 | 1967 |
| *Americans* | Industrious | 48 | NA | 23 |
| | Intelligent | 47 | – | 20 |
| | Materialistic | 33 | – | 67 |
| *Jews* | Shrewd | 79 | 47 | 30 |
| | Mercenary | 49 | 28 | 15 |
| | Ambitious | 21 | 28 | 48 |
| *Negroes* | Superstitious | 84 | 41 | 13 |
| | Lazy | 75 | 31 | 26 |
| | Musical | 26 | 33 | 47 |

and discrimination. First, stereotypes operate to *overestimate* differences existing *between* groups. Second, stereotypes operate to cause *underestimation* of differences *within* groups. Third, stereotypes distort reality since the overestimation between groups and underestimation within groups bear little relation to the truth. Fourth, stereotypes are usually *negative attitudes* which people use to justify discrimination or conflict against others.

Why do stereotypes persist even when most people know them to be gross and erroneous distortions of reality? They serve the positive function of imposing some kind of order and structure on a potentially chaotic social environment. Without some way of 'pigeonholing' people it would be extremely difficult for social interaction to proceed as smoothly as it does. We simply cannot interact, get acquainted with, and develop friendships with everyone we meet, we have to have some rough and ready system to guide us. Stereotypes may also persist and be perpetuated through conformity to prevailing social norms or social values existing at that time or in a particular social context. It is to this we now turn.

### 5.4.4 Conformity to values

Minard (1952) noticed an apparent inconsistency in the behaviour of white miners toward black miners in a town in the south of the United States. He found that in the mines over 80 per cent of the white miners were friendly towards the black miners. Above ground, however, only 20 per cent of the white miners behaved in a friendly way. Pettigrew (1958) explains such findings by *conformity to values*, since a different set of values or norms operates underground compared to those that operate above ground. Generally, then, Pettigrew expects prejudice to depend upon the social context in which the behaviour takes place.

Pettigrew's (1959) own research supports such a conformity explanation of prejudice. He tested the hypothesis that people who are generally more conforming would also be more prejudiced. In a study investigating inter-racial tension in South Africa Pettigrew showed that white South African students who were higher than average in prejudice tended to conform more to social norms. Further research by Pettigrew in the north and south of the United States of America showed that high levels of prejudice were associated with churchgoing, upward mobility and low educational attainment in the southern but not northern United States. This confirms the conformity hypothesis since prejudice against blacks is less acceptable as a social norm in the north but more socially acceptable in the south.

Further support for the importance of conformity comes from Lieberman (1956) who found that a person's attitudes and values change to conform to changing norms. The attitudes of workers in a factory when they worked on the shop floor were compared with when they were promoted to either foremen or shop-stewards, 12 months later. Change in role (from shop floor worker to foreman or shop-steward) caused change in attitudes and values to those consistent with the job or role. For example, foremen became more favourable towards management, and shop-stewards more favourable to the union. Further, foremen who were subsequently demoted or shop-stewards who were not re-elected reverted back to attitudes held when they were shop floor workers.

The reasons why people conform are dealt with in detail in Chapter 10, the point to be made here is that people do not always behave in ways consistent with a distinct personality style, set of attitudes or stereotypes, racial or belief similarity because there are strong forces and pressures in the social situation causing people to conform to prevailing social norms. Norms change over time though, suggesting that conformity does not offer sufficient explanation for prejudice and discrimination.

## 5.5  The intergroup approach

Group membership may itself be an important contributing cause to prejudice and discrimination. So far we have largely ignored the effects and consequences group membership may have on how individuals treat members of their own group as opposed to members of other groups to which they do not belong or identify themselves with. Two questions are important: to what extent may prejudice and conflict arise from (a) two or more groups who are in *competition* for resources?; (b) social categorization *per se*, i.e. does group membership *by and of itself* cause people to treat their own group more favourably than other groups? Approaching prejudice by focusing on relationships between groups, rather than between individuals as with the interpersonal approach, means that such things as personality differences, conformity, etc. are viewed as playing only a minor role. To assess the two questions above we will look at research from two traditions: that which regards conflict as resulting from (a) intergroup competition (Sherif, 1966); and (b) social categorization (Tajfel, 1970). The terms 'ingroup' and 'outgroup' are used frequently: ingroup refers to a group of which an individual is a member, or perceives him or herself to be a member, outgroup to a group of which an individual is not a member, or perceives him or herself not to be a member.

### 5.5.1 Intergroup competition

In a series of pioneering experiments Sherif (1966) investigated intergroup conflict and cooperation in groups of 11–12 year old boys attending Summer School Camp in America. The field experiments lasted three weeks and were characterized by three stages each lasting a week:

*Stage 1*  In experiment (a) *all* boys spent a week together where they were involved in various informal activities. In experiment (b) the boys spent a week in one of the groups they were to be in in Stage 2 but the two groups were unaware of each other's existence.

*Stage 2*  The boys in experiment (a) were moved to the summer camp and divided into two groups. In experiment (b) the two groups were brought together at the summer camp. Sherif arranged a series of competitive events between the two groups with prizes or social advantages for the group which won.

*Stage 3*  Cooperation between the two groups was encouraged by the setting of 'superordinate' goals (goals which could only be achieved by *both* groups cooperating).

Stages 1 and 2 are concerned with the development of conflict; Stage 3 deals with the reduction of conflict and will be dealt with in more detail in a later section of this chapter.

In the experiment where all the boys were together in Stage 1 Sherif (1966) divided them into two groups such that about two thirds of any single boy's friends were in the other group. Sherif then compared changes in friendship patterns in Stage 1 and 2 of the experiment. Table 5.5 shows quite clearly that competition between groups in Stage 2 resulted in boys' friendship patterns changing, resulting in friendships being almost entirely restricted to the ingroup.

In experiments where the two groups were kept away from each other in Stage 1 Sherif observed dramatic changes in relationships *within* the groups as a result of intergroup competition. For example, the leadership of one group changed from a 'pacifistic' person to a 'bully'. Generally, behaviour and changes in friendship patterns were such as to increase solidarity in the ingroup.

Relationships between the two groups rapidly escalated into open conflict during Stage 2. This was evidenced by, for example, name-callings, raids on the other group's dormitory, taunting and jeering, refusing to eat with the

**Table 5.5**  Change in friendship choices before and after group competition. Adapted from Sherif (1966).

| FRIENDS CHOSEN FROM | BOYS MEMBERSHIP | | | |
| --- | --- | --- | --- | --- |
| | GROUP A | | GROUP B | |
| | *Before* | *After* | *Before* | *After* |
| Group A | 35% | 95% | 65% | 12% |
| Group B | 65% | 5% | 35% | 88% |

other group or sit and watch a film with them. At the end of Stage 2 Sherif summarized the situation thus:

> If an outside observer had entered the situation at this point with no information about preceding events, he could only have concluded on the basis of their behaviour that these boys (who were the 'cream of the crop' in their communities) were wicked, disturbed and vicious bunches of youngsters.
> (Sherif, 1966, p. 85)

We will return later to see how Sherif attempted to get these 'vicious and wicked youngsters' to be more friendly towards each other. The point to note from this research is that *group conflict arises because of competition between two groups for some prize, goal, resource, etc. that can only be achieve by one group at the expense of the other.* Sherif showed that whilst intergroup competition may start off in a friendly and sportsmanlike way it rapidly escalates into conflict and open hostility. The outgroup became stereotyped, the ingroup over-evaluated its positive achievements and became more 'tightly knit'. Competition for resources may result in conflict between groups; however, there are other reasons for the existence of prejudice between groups, as we shall see.

### 5.5.2 Social categorization

Tajfel (1970) showed that group membership itself, i.e. in the absence of competition, is a sufficient condition for intergroup discrimination to occur. Schoolchildren aged between 14 and 15 years were divided into two groups on the basis of some trivial criteria and asked to assign monetary rewards to *anonymous* members of their own (ingroup) and other (outgroup) group. Furthermore, subjects did *not* know who were members of their own and who were members of the other group; no face-to-face interaction took place between group members; no conflict of interest was said to exist between the two groups. These conditions are called the 'minimal group membership' paradigm, for obvious reasons. Disturbingly, Tajfel found quite strong evidence of ingroup–outgroup discrimination: subjects allocated greater monetary rewards to the ingroup and did it in such a way as to make the *difference* in monetary reward as great as possible between the two groups, even if this meant that the ingroup received less than it possibly could. So, for example, if a subject could choose between the following two options:

(a) allocating 18 points to a member of the ingroup and 12 points to a member of the outgroup (difference of 6 points) or,
(b) allocating 14 points to a member of the ingroup and 6 points to a member of the outgroup (difference of 8 points).

subjects would be more likely to choose option (b). Tajfel and Billig (1974) found that even when subjects are explicitly shown allocation to a particular group to be entirely random (they tossed a coin in front of the subjects and told them they would be allocated to a group according to whether the coin fell heads or tails) intergroup discrimination still resulted. Indeed, as will be seen later, it is exceedingly difficult to eliminate ingroup favouritism.

Turner, (1981) has offered two explanations as to why social categorization results in ingroup favouritism and negative outgroup bias: it causes individuals to (a) perceive *greater* similarities *within* their own group and *greater* differences *between* the ingroup and outgroup than actually exist; and (b) *evaluate* and *compare* themselves with reference to their own group in a search for *positive social identity*.

Tajfel and Wilkes (1963) demonstrated just how powerful an effect categorization has on perceptions of similarity and difference by asking subjects to make judgements about the length of a number of lines. They presented a series of eight lines of different length to three groups of subjects: Group 1 were presented with the four shorter lines labelled A and the four longer lines labelled B; Group 2 were shown the eight lines without the lines being categorized; and Group 3 were presented with the eight lines labelled A and B but randomly, i.e. not associated with length. Groups 2 and 3 were the control groups for comparing the effects of categorization (Group 1). Subjects in each group were asked to estimate the length of each of the eight lines. It was found that the longest line in the category of shorter lines (A) was perceived to be *much shorter* than it actually was and much shorter than that estimated by the control groups. By contrast, the shortest line in the category of longer lines (B) was perceived to be *much longer* by subjects in Group 1 than it actually was. The study leads us to infer that if objective stimuli, such as lines, can be seen to differ in length according to how they are categorized then social stimuli (personality traits, attitudes, etc.), since they are inherently more ambiguous, would be *even more* affected by categorization.

In the social world it has been found that people perceive a greater degree of similarity between themselves and others who they think believe in similar things or would act in similar ways to themselves. Equally, greater differences than actually exist are found when people think or believe in different things or would act in different ways to them (Ross, Green and House, 1977). In short, social categorization overemphasizes *both* differences between groups and similarities within groups.

Social identity theory (Turner, 1981) states that social categorization results in social discrimination as it causes people to make *social comparisons* between ingroups and outgroups. The theory further states that people make social comparisons because they need to provide themselves with a *positive social identity*. Positive social identity is important for a person since it provides both a sense of confidence (self-esteem, self-worth) and gives the person a sense of 'belonging' in the social world. Comparisons made by an individual between groups on such grounds as status and value, lead to *social competition*. Social competition embodies the idea that (a) people wish to be members of highly valued, high status, good, etc. groups; and (b) people strive to put their group in such a light as to believe it to be 'better' than the outgroup. False stereotypes, negative values, for example, are attributed to the outgroup in order to promote the ingroup. Such a sequence of events as this may be diagramatically represented as shown in Figure 5.2.

The final point to be made about social identity theory is that it is concerned with *social competition*, not *realistic competition*. Realistic competition is where groups compete for *real* resources and where one can only obtain the resource at the expense of the other group. With social competition no real or tangible resources are being competed for (or at least it

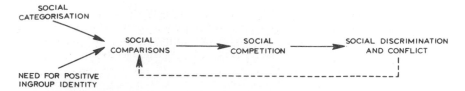

**Figure 5.2** Diagrammatic representation of the main features of Social Identity Theory. Notice how social discrimination and conflict can *feedback* to both maintain and increase social comparisons.

is not necessary that such resources are being competed for). Social competition is about, if you like, the need people have for a positive self-image which comes from obtaining a positive identity from the ingroup. This can only be achieved, it would seem, by overvaluing the ingroup and undervaluing the outgroup and social discrimination is a means of achieving this.

In summary, the 'minimal group' paradigm used by Tajfel demonstrates that social categorization *per se* is sufficient to produce social discrimination. Two explanations have been offered to account for this: social categorization causes people to (a) see greater differences between ingroups and outgroups, and greater similarities within groups, than actually exist; (b) compare themselves between and within groups because of a fundamental need for positive social identity.

## 5.6 Cultural, institutional and economic considerations

Social psychological explanations of prejudice and conflict sensitize us to aspects of the person, relationships between people and between groups but do, to a certain extent, ignore the *social context* in which such attitudes and behaviour take place. By social context is meant such sociological factors as culture/sub-culture, institutions (education, justice) and general economic factors. Without such factors supporting and perpetuating racism, sexism, etc. the extent and depth of such discrimination would be much less of a problem than it is. In considering the social context the historical background is of importance. Prejudice towards blacks in America, for example, needs to be considered in the historical context of slavery. It was only just over 150 years ago that William Wilberforce achieved the abolition of slavery in all British territories and possessions. Perhaps more relevant to an understanding of racial prejudice in Britain is its colonialism in the nineteenth century, when colonials were believed to be inferior both socially and intellectually (Gould, 1985). The historical backdrop sets the scene for how ethnic minorities, etc. are treated and how intergroup relationships may develop and change over time.

Cultural aspects include, for example, the tendency in technological societies for increased urbanization, upward mobility of certain groups of people, changes in the family structure and morality. The increasing tendency for people to live in large cities may result in prejudice towards ethnic minorities because cities are impersonal, experiencing rising unemployment and generally 'stressful' places to live in. Such factors provide ideal conditions for scapegoating, and emphasize the importance social identity comes to assume in such environments. Jones (1972, p. 106) says 'what emerges from strong ethnic affiliations is the sense of group position and development of strong group conflict'.

Institutional aspects of prejudice and discrimination concern two important systems in western society – education and justice. Jones (1972) shows two factors to contribute to the perpetuation of racism (particularly towards blacks) in America through the education system: (a) inferior education; and (b) miseducation about racial history and heritage. Perhaps the tremendous success of *Roots* by Alec Haley in the late 1970s was partially due to there being such a strong need to rectify the imbalance. Educational disadvantage to ethnic minorities may often be perpetuated for psychological reasons, for example, the continuing controversy over whether blacks score lower on IQ tests than whites (see Eysenck and Kamin, 1981 for a discussion of the controversy and problems with interpreting the evidence, such as it is) may filter through to the classroom. Suppose a teacher believes blacks to be less intelligent than whites, research has shown that teacher expectations have a strong influence on how pupils perform. A person (or ethnic minority) believed to be intellectually dull may be treated in such a way as to perform badly (Rosenthal and Jacobson, 1968), in a sense a form of self-fulfilling prophecy is operating. The Scarman Report on the Brixton riots in April 1981 reported on reasons why West Indians underachieved at school whilst Asians tended to do slightly better than white pupils. West Indians parents were dissatisfied with discipline in schools, lack of contact between parents and schools, failure of teachers to provide motivation and a failure to appreciate the value of different cultural traditions. Scarman (1982) recommended teachers to be given 'awareness' training in different cultural backgrounds, greater liaison between home and school, and greater provision of nurseries for the under-fives. Such measures, it is to be hoped, would go some way to reducing dissatisfaction through educating teachers as much as pupils and their parents.

The justice system, especially at the 'sharp end', also, unfortunately, reveals how prejudice and racism may be created and perpetuated. The Scarman Report again shows how insensitive enforcement of the law may cause resentment and hostility. For example, police harassment of West Indians happened at times because a police officer was young, inexperienced and frightened. At other times a general police policy of using Special Patrol Groups to stamp out street crime was seen as insensitive by local communities in Brixton. Occasionally, Scarman reports, police are simply racially prejudiced and use laws such as 'stop and search' in a discriminatory way on blacks. So, the police both as an institution and as individuals enforcing the law were seen to contribute to the Brixton riots. Scarman recommended, for example, more recruitment of ethnic minorities into the police force, 'sensitivity' training in law enforcement for new policemen, and liaison committees between police and the local community. These measures, Scarman hoped, would both reduce prejudice within the police force and reduce the feeling among West Indians that they were discriminated against by the police.

Economic factors also conspire to perpetuate prejudice, especially in the form of racism. Jones (1972) cynically remarks that in America in 1968 'a white skin is worth $2668 annually'. This was so because surveys revealed that a black man with a college education earned this much less than a white man with the same college education. Another way economics show prejudice is in the weekly rents that different groups of people pay for accomodation. Figures from the early 1960s in Britain showed West Indians, Indians and Pakistanis all to be paying well above average rents for accomodation compared to the total population (Rose, 1969). Furthermore, as Rose points out, these ethnic minorities paid higher rents for inferior accomodation.

Looking at the social context through cultural, institutional and economic factors suffers certain problems for explaining prejudice. First, do such factors create or perpetuate prejudice? It is not really possible to separate the two in the end, but unless there is some indication as to cause and effect it is difficult to know what would be effective in reducing prejudice and conflict. Second, not all individuals succumb to these sociological factors. To discover the reasons why psychology, more than sociology, will potentially be of greater use. We change emphasis now from the search for causes of prejudice and conflict to ways in which they may be reduced.

## 5.7  Reducing prejudice and conflict

It may seem that social psychologists have been obsessed with propounding and developing theories of prejudice and conflict whilst giving little attention to ways of reducing them. From our discussion of the three social psychological approaches, and bearing in mind some of the principles discussed in the preceding chapter on attitude change, indications of what might be successful can be suggested and evidence presented which will allow us to assess the validity of these suggestions. We will deal with the individual, interpersonal and intergroup approaches in turn using the theme of how *increased contact* between groups may reduce prejudice and conflict.

The authoritarian personality would appear to be self-perpetuating since research has shown (Byrne, 1966) that authoritarian parents tend to produce authoritarian children. However, Table 5.2 showed that the *higher* the level of educational attainment the *less* likely people were to be authoritarian. Clearly then it would seem to be in the interests of a more harmonious society for greater provision and access to be made to higher education. Campbell (1971) has shown that attempts to get different races, ethnic groupings, together are more likely to be viewed in a positive way the greater the level of education a person has had.

Increased contact, inter-racial mixing, desegregation, etc. has often been advocated not only be psychologists but also by politicians, civic leaders, etc. as a way of reducing prejudice and conflict. Why should such procedures work and what consequences do they have on people's attitudes and behaviour?

Interpersonally, increased contact should foster and encourage acquaintances and friendships between individuals of different groups. This should result in reductions in the perceptions of belief dissimilarity and increases in the perceptions of belief similarity between groups. Increased contact between prejudiced people should also arouse cognitive dissonance (see

Chapter 4), since it would be psychologically inconsistent to hold a negative stereotypical attitude about a certain race and have friends or acquaintances in that grouping. Two ways of reducing dissonance would be possible: either the person's attitudes can change or the person can terminate the friendship. The former would lead to a reduction in prejudice, the latter would maintain or even increase prejudice.

School desegregation policies in America offered psychologists a natural social experiment. Pettigrew, reviewing research on this spanning over 30 years, came up with the important point that desegregation was more likely to work only when it was perceived as *inevitable* by the people it was aimed at. Laboratory experiments provide support for this, Berscheid, Boye and Darley (1968), or example, demonstrated that even when we regard someone as socially undesirable we like them if we think we have to work with them. In this experiment female subjects were told that they had to work with another woman who was difficult and undesirable (moody, unclean and unpopular). Subjects accepted and liked the person since when they were later given the choice of another co-worker they often stuck with the 'difficult' person in preference to someone who was portrayed as intelligent, popular and generally desirable.

Stephan (1978) evaluated the short-term consequences of school desegregation and claimed there was *not* strong evidence to support the proposition that it was effective in reducing prejudice. Specifically, he concluded that white prejudice towards blacks showed little reduction whilst black prejudice towards whites was as likely to increase as decrease. Stephan did find one positive consequence of desegregation which was that blacks tended to achieve more academically at school. Such conclusions Stephan points out, should only be tentatively accepted since longer-term studies are required.

We saw with social identity theory that social competition was a cause of social discrimination. An important question, then, is what happens when groups are brought together in an atmosphere of *cooperation* rather than competition? Worchel *et al.* (1977) demonstrated that groups who initially interact in a cooperative way responded in a positive way to each other regardless of whether they experienced success or failure on a subsequent task. By contrast groups who initially interacted in a competitive way reacted very differently to success or failure. Competition between groups followed by failure at a task tended to result in each group keeping to themselves and attitudes towards the outgroup became more negative. Competition between groups followed by success at a task resulted in more positive attitudes and greater interaction with the outgroup. The point this research highlights is that the *history* of relations between groups needs to be taken into account before predictions can be made as to how attempts to reduce prejudice may fare. Table 5.6 summarizes the effects on prejudice of a competitive or cooperative history and success or failure at a task. Groups who have been cooperative in the past do not become prejudiced as a result of failure on a cooperative task. Groups that have been competitive in the past do become more prejudiced after experiencing failure on a cooperative task. Only success seems to reduce prejudice in groups with a competitive history. Such a theme was pursued in the earlier work of Sherif (1966).

**Table 5.6** Effects of cooperative or competitive history of relations between groups and success or failure at a cooperative task on prejudice.

| RESULT OF COOPERATION | HISTORY | |
| | *Cooperative* | *Competitive* |
| --- | --- | --- |
| *Success* | Little prejudice in evidence, groups not perceived as very different | Reduction in prejudice and reduction in differences perceived between groups |
| *Failure* | Little prejudice in evidence, groups not perceived as very different | Increase in prejudice and sharpening of differences perceived to exist between groups |

In the third stage, lasting a week, of Sherif's field experiments, described earlier in this chapter, intergroup conflict was reduced by setting the previously competing groups a series of cooperative tasks. Sherif set the groups *superordinate goals* – objectives which could *only* be achieved by *both* groups working together. Sherif stage-managed superordinate goals in the summer camps by causing, unknown to the boys in the groups, such events as the failure of the water supply and the breakdown of the camp lorry.

Generally, superordinate goals did reduce the intergroup hostility but only when the groups engaged in a *series* of such tasks. Just setting one superordinate goal did not have much effect, each group soon after completing one superordinate task returned to their hostile ways. At the end of the week when the groups had worked together on a number of superordinate tasks intergroup relations were quite friendly. There was a greater tendency for friends to be chosen from *both* groups, also groups were prepared to share things with each other, and aggressive hostile leadership was frowned upon by the group members. Sherif summarized the position as follows:

> In short, the findings suggest the various methods used with limited success in reducing intergroup hostility may become effective when employed within a framework of cooperation among groups working towards goals that are genuinely appealing and require equitable participation and contributions from all groups.
>
> (Sherif, 1966, p. 93).

Notice Sherif adds two important qualifications: (a) the superordinate goal must have genuine appeal to both groups, i.e. both groups must regard the task as worthwhile; and (b) there must be equitable participation and contribution from both groups – reduction of intergroup hostility will *not* occur when one group is of higher status or in command and one of lower status or subservient.

In summary, reducing prejudice and conflict is no easy or short-term matter. Changing attitudes, beliefs and behaviour by increasing contact between different groups of people is successful to a degree but not overwhelmingly so. Cooperation helps, but where groups have a history of being in competition many cooperative or superordinate tasks need to be undertaken with *success* for reductions in prejudice and conflict to be achieved. Two general points emerge from attempts to reduce prejudice and conflict: (a) no one way is successful, attacks have to be made at individual, interpersonal and intergroup levels; and (b) successful strategies produce change only slowly, no quick and easy way is possible.

## 5.8 Summary

O Prejudice is an attitude which predisposes a person to act in an unfavourable or favourable way to another person or group or people. Discrimination is the actual behaviour that occurs, conflict may result from unfair discrimination.

O Social psychology has investigated prejudice and conflict from individual, interpersonal and intergroup approaches. The individual approach focuses on processes *within* the individual; the interpersonal on processes *between* individuals; and the intergroup on relations *between* groups.

O The individual approach has looked at personalities of prejudiced people in terms of the authoritarian personality, dogmatism and the two dimensions of radical/conservative and tough/tender-minded suggested by Eysenck. Frustrations and aggression resulting in scapegoating has also been researched in this approach.

O The interpersonal approach has investigated the relative importance of differences in beliefs and differences in race; Rokeach showed belief differences to affect friendship choice, Triandis, however, found race more important in more intimate relationships. The interpersonal approach has also explained prejudice as a consequence of conformity to prevailing stereotypes and values shared by a group or sub-culture.

O The intergroup approach examines how group membership, rather than individual or interpersonal processes, affects how people in one group treat people in other groups. Sherif demonstrated prejudice and conflict arise when two or more groups compete for resources. Tajfel suggested group membership itself, i.e. in the absence of intergroup competition, was sufficient to explain discrimination.

O Turner explains discrimination resulting from social categorization (group membership) as due to: (a) greater similarities being perceived by ingroup members and greater differences between in and outgroup members than actually exist, (b) a search for positive social identity.

O Cultural, institutional and economic factors constitute the social context in which prejudice and discrimination take place, such factors both maintain and perpetuate racism, sexism, etc.

O Sherif reduced intergroup conflict by setting groups superordinate goals, these are goals in which *both* groups have to cooperate to achieve a certain objective. Sherif found numerous superordinate tasks were required for a reduction in conflict to remain effective. Increasing contact between different groups of people was considered from the individual, interpersonal and intergroup perspectives and it was argued that attacking prejudice and discrimination at these three levels would be more successful than if an approach aimed at only one level was attempted.

## 5.9 Suggestions for further reading

Allport, G.W. *The Nature of Prejudice* (Reading, Mass: Addison Wesley 1954.)
*The* classic social psychological text on prejudice and discrimination, although written over 30 years ago the book is still highly relevant. Covers the vast range of psychological approaches and includes a final section on reduction of conflict.

Baron, R.A. and Byrne, D. *Social Psychology: Understanding Human Interaction* (Boston: Allyn and Bacon Publishers, 1977).
This is an introductory text, however, Chapter 4 deals with prejudice and discrimination specifically in relation to women; worth reading because it provides a sustained look at sexist attitudes and behaviour drawing on many of the perspectives outlined in this chapter.

Davey, A. *Learning to be Prejudiced: Growing Up in Multi-Ethnic Britain* (London: Edward Arnold Publishers, 1983).
This book shows how prejudice is taught and socialized into children from very early ages, citing original research the author demonstrates how children as young as six or seven display prejudiced attitudes and know when to apply them in a particular social context.

Jones, J.M. *Prejudice and Racism* (Reading, Mass: Addison-Wesley Publishing Company, 1972).
Powerfully written book outlining the extent and meaning of racism in the United States of America; the book gives quite a detailed historical insight into how racism developed. Different theoretical perspectives within psychology are described and much space is devoted to institutional and cultural racism. This book is probably the best one to go to after this chapter.

# 6

# Social cognition I: Perception of ourselves and others

6.1    Introduction
6.2    Fundamentals of perception
       *6.2.1 Object perception   6.2.2 Social perception*
       *6.2.3 Individual differences in perception*
6.3    Forming impressions of others
       *6.3.1 Central and peripheral traits   6.3.2 First impressions*
       *6.3.3 Implicit personality theory   6.3.4 Stereotyping*
6.4    Self-perception
       *6.4.1 Self-perception of emotion   6.4.2 Self-concept*
6.5    Perceptual processes
       *6.5.1 Attention   6.5.2 Person memory   6.5.3 Social inference*
6.6    Accuracy in person perception
6.7    Summary
6.8    Suggestions for further reading

## 6.1 Introduction

This and the following chapter introduce a particular approach in social psychology known as *Social Cognition*. Cognition, or more precisely cognitive psychology, is to do with how people acquire, organize and use knowledge or information; thus the central concerns are with perception, attention, memory, thought and language. Social cognition is concerned with the same topics but in a social context – how people perceive, attend to and remember things about themselves and other people, and how different social situations and contexts influence such cognitive processes in people. The following two chapters introduce this new and growing field: this chapter deals with how we perceive ourselves and others by looking at what perception is; how we form impressions of others; self-perception; and the issue of whether some people are more accurate than others in their perceptions. Chapter 7 deals with one important approach in social cognition: attribution theory, the central concern of which is to understand how people attribute causes or reasons to their own and/or others behaviour. What factors, social situations, etc. tend to lead people to say that their behaviour was caused by something in the environment (i.e. *external* to them), and to say that their behaviour was a result of their own personality dispositions (i.e. *internal* to them)? This internal/external distinction is central to attribution theory and something we shall have much more to say about in the next chapter.

The cognitive approach generally, and that of social cognition in particular, attempts to understand thought, attention and memory, but not

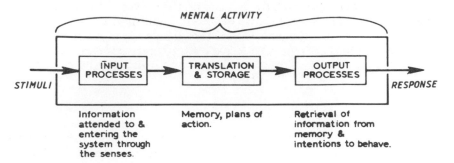

**Figure 6.1** Diagram showing how behaviour (response) results from processing of information (stimuli) reaching the senses and retrieval of information from memory.

through the use of introspection (self-reflection on our own cognitive processes) but through careful and controlled scientific experimentation. For experiments to be meaningful there has to be a general framework in which they can be interpreted – this is achieved by using a fundamental model in cognitive psychology: that which views people as *processors of information*. Applying the computer analogy to human cognitive activity means that the flow of information through the mind is charted from input (what enters the system), through translation and storage to output (what leaves the system) and finally to some response – behaviour. Figure 6.1 gives a diagramatic representation of this and shows that stimuli entering the mind do so first through the various senses. The senses, such as vision and hearing, do not faithfully represent the world but distort it to some extent, focusing on *changing* rather than unchanging aspects of the environment. Thus we are likely to notice the clothing of people we know well if they have just bought something new, but not if they are in the same old pair of jeans. What is different and changing receives the most attention and is more likely to proceed to the next stage of the process, that of translation and storage. This is where information is stored in memory and plans of action are conceived. So, for example, you store in memory the information that your friend has bought a bright pink pair of trousers which may lead you to attempt to find out more about why this may be so on some future occasion. Finally, information is retrieved from memory at some later date and intentions to behave are formed. Suppose then, that you have met your friend again some days later, you remember he bought a pair of pink trousers and also recall that this is highly uncharacteristic as this has never happened before, as far as you can remember. As a consequence you form the intention to find out more about such novel behaviour, this may result in a response – you actually ask your friend why he bought such outrageous clothes!

Whilst this example, explaining the diagram, does oversimplify matters it does serve to highlight two important points about viewing people as processors of information. First, we interpret things in the light of what we already know: our friend usually wears the same old denim jeans but now is wearing something very different. Second, how we act depends on what is retrieved from memory and how it is evaluated: pink trousers are out of character and outrageous relative to our own style of dress. In short, in order to account for how people behave we need to know how they perceive their social world and what determines their perceptions. The former issue occupies much of our time in the first half of this chapter, the latter is dealt with when we come to consider the *processes* involved in social perception later in the chapter.

## 6.2 Fundamentals of perception

The important point was made above that we interpret the world in which we live in the light of what we already know. This, in essence, captures the fundamental nature of both object and social perception. Furthermore, not only does our pre-existing knowledge allow interpretation, it also acts as a guide to selection, attention and organization of information. Perception then is both an *active and constructive process* which we may define as 'a complex response to a sensation (where a sensation is an immediate experience of stimuli) in the light of past experience, expectations, etc.' In general terms perception results from an *interaction* of how we expect the world to be and how it is actually presented to us through our senses: this is why perception is thought to be a complex response. The world in which we live is not passively responded to but actively interpreted before a response is made; this will become clearer when we come to look at object and social perception in more detail.

### 6.2.1 Object perception

Characterizing perception as an active process implies that it is selective both in terms of what is attended to and how what is attended to is interpreted. Take a look at Figure 6.2, what do you see? The picture on the left of the figure can either be seen as the moon or a man's face; the picture on the right as a vase or two faces looking at each other. The point these well known examples make is that we control which of the two interpretations we see through deciding what is there (moon or face; vase or faces) and selecting the appropriate parts to attend to. Gestalt psychologists (who regard the whole as greater than the sum of the parts) call this selection *figure and ground* (figure is what is prominent, ground is what is background). Figure and ground can be interchanged, as with the pictures in Figure 6.2, to arrive at different perceptions of one drawing. Notice, however, that you cannot see both interpretations at once.

Leeper (1935) provided an experimental demonstration showing that past experience strongly influences how one perceives things on subsequent occasions. Leeper used an ambiguous drawing which could either be seen as a young woman or an old hag (Figure 6.3a). To demonstrate the effect of past experience one group of subjects were first presented with a redrawn version of the ambiguous picture which emphasized the young woman (Figure 6.3b); another group or subjects were presented with a redrawn version which emphasized the old hag (Figure 6.3c). Later, both groups of subjects were shown the ambiguous drawing and asked to report what they saw. All subjects who had first seen the old hag reported seeing the old hag in the

**Figure 6.2** Demonstration of the figure–ground relationship in perception. Depending on what you choose to be the background, in (a) you can see either a moon or a funny face, in (b) either a vase or two faces looking at each other.

ambiguous drawing, whilst 95 per cent of subjects saw the young woman in the ambiguous version after having first seen an unambiguous drawing of the young woman. The experiment provides a simple demonstration of how past experience not only directs selection of information but may blind us to other possible interpretations.

Our perceptions of objects may also be influenced by the *value* that we associate with an object, as shown in a classic study by Bruner and Goodman (1947). They asked children to adjust the size of a circle to what they thought various denominations of coins, held in the researcher's hand, actually were in size. High-value coins were greatly overestimated in size and low-value coins slightly underestimated. Sub-cultural differences were also found: children of working-class parents overestimated the size of high-value coins more than children of middle-class parents. The phenomenon of size distortion resulting from value has been called *perceptual accentuation*.

Perception of objects may also be influenced by the emotional significance attached to that object. McGinnies (1949) presented female subjects with

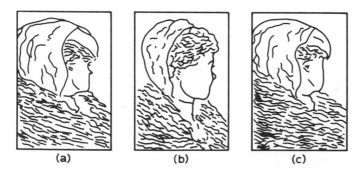

(a)                              (b)                              (c)

**Figure 6.3** Two perceptions from a single, ambiguous drawing; (a) can be seen as either an old hag or a young woman. Diagrams (b) and (c) depict the unambiguous young woman or old hag respectively.

socially taboo words (such as swear words) and asked them to recognize the words. The emotional response was monitored by measuring their galvanic skin response (a measure of electric activity of the skin associated with arousal). Taboo words produced a strong galvanic skin response but were recognized less often than neutral words. McGinnies argued that *perceptual defence* was causing the women to try to deny the existence of something emotionally disturbing. We may extend this idea to explain why people who deny certain emotions in themselves (because it would be too disturbing to acknowledge their existence) are insensitive to those same emotions in other people.

Object perception, as the above experiments indicate, is affected by past experience, value and emotional attachment. Ambiguity in our environment is selectively interpreted according to expectations, perceptual accentuation and defence. That this happens in our perception of objects suggests that perception of behaviour is going to be even more influenced by such things since behaviour is often highly ambiguous and needs both past experience and social context to render it meaningful.

### 6.2.2 Social perception

Social perception, how we perceive our own and other people's behaviour, takes place according to the same fundamental principles as object perception. Hastorf and Cantril (1954) experimentally demonstrated: (a) that people select different behaviours to attend to; and (b) interpretation of the same behaviour is often very different. Two groups of American football supporters looked at a video recording of a match they had just seen live. The supporters, Dartmouth and Princetown students, were asked to keep a note of the number of fouls perpetrated by each side. Table 6.1 summarizes the findings and shows that Princetown supporters perceived the Dartmouth team to perpetuate more than twice as many fouls as their own team. Dartmouth students thought their own team committed slightly fewer fouls than the other team. The same match, then, was perceived very differently depending on supporters' affiliations.

**Table 6.1** Average number of fouls perceived to have been perpetrated by each team by supporters of each team. From Hastorf and Cantril (1954).

| | NUMBER OF FOULS | |
| --- | --- | --- |
| FOULS PERCEIVED BY: | *Dartmouth Team* | *Princetown Team* |
| *Dartmouth students* | 4.3 | 4.4 |
| *Princetown students* | 9.8 | 4.2 |

Motivation can also influence perception of another's behaviour as was shown in the experiment by Pepitone (1949). Subjects were given the opportunity to win tickets for a basketball game which they were either greatly interested in or not particularly interested in. To win a ticket subjects had to

**Table 6.2** Amount of influence perceived to have been exerted by each coach in the decision to grant a free ticket by high and low motivation subjects. The higher the number the greater the perceived influence. Adapted from Pepitone (1949).

| | BEHAVIOUR OF COACH | | |
| --- | --- | --- | --- |
| MOTIVATION OF SUBJECTS | *Friendly* | *Neutral* | *Unfriendly* |
| *High* | 6.7 | 4.2 | 3.9 |
| *Low* | 5.4 | 4.1 | 3.7 |

answer questions put to them by a group of three basketball coaches. The coaches were confederates of the experiment (but subjects did not know this) and they treated subjects in one of three ways: one was friendly, one neutral and one unfriendly to each subject. The coaches, after putting the questions, determined the quality of answers given and decided whether or not to award a free ticket.

Each subject was asked to indicate how approving each coach had been towards them and how influential each had been in the decision to award or not award a free ticket. Results showed, summarized in Table 6.2, that whilst the 'friendly' coach was perceived as more influential by both high and low-motivation subjects, the high-motivation subjects perceived this influence to be much greater than the low-motivation subjects.

These experiments demonstrate how social perception is similar to object perception in that commitment, affiliation, motivation, etc. all affect what is perceived. However, a number of important differences exist between object and social perception; these stem from the fact that how we perceive and interact with another person is, in part, dependent upon how the other person perceives and interacts with us. Some of the more important differences are as follows:

(a) People are causal agents, they have *intentions* and attempt to control their world. Objects do not have intentions and are not causal agents.

(b) How others perceive us influences how we behave; knowing somebody has categorized us in a certain way may cause us to *change*.

(c) Many of the things we perceive about others (and ourselves) are not directly observable: personality traits, emotions, etc. have to be *inferred* or *attributed*. Generally, characteristics of objects are observable and can be reliably measured.

(d) Accuracy in social perception is difficult if not impossible to establish: we often find it difficult enough to know ourselves, and psychologists do not find it easy to measure personality even when highly developed statistical techniques are to hand. By contrast it is easier to establish and agree upon attributes and characteristics of objects.

### 6.2.3 Individual differences in perception

So far we have been concerned to highlight the important aspects of object and social perception that are common to all people. However, people do differ, in predictable ways, in how they perceive the world they live in.

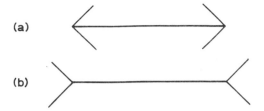

**Figure 6.4** The Mueller-Lyer illusion: line (a) looks shorter than line (b), but in reality they are the same length.

The particular environment in which a person is raised and lives has a strong influence upon perceptions. This was demonstrated by Segall *et al.* (1966) who showed that the famous Mueller-Lyer illusion, where the enclosed line (Figure 6.4a) is perceived as being shorter than the open line (Figure 6.4b), did not occur in cultures where straight lines and right-angles were not a prominent environmental feature. Certain African tribes were shown the two lines (a) and (b) but did *not* see them as different in length, in contrast, virtually everybody in western society succumbs to the illusion.

Witkin *et al.* (1962) showed how the ability of people to perceive embedded figures in a picture may have consequences for how people behave in, and perceive, the social world. Figure 6.5. has 12 items embedded in it (for example, a pumpkin, cat, witch's hat) some people are very quick to spot all the embedded figures and others very slow. This has formed the basis of a proposed personality dimension of field-dependent/field-independent. Field-independent people are fast at spotting the embedded figures since they are not 'locked' into the content of the whole picture. Field-dependent people are slow as they are 'locked' into the whole picture and are less able to look at each part of the picture independent of the other parts.

Witkin *et al.* found, from administering a number of personality question-naires, that field-independent people generally perceived themselves as separate from other people and see many differences between themselves and others. By contrast, field-dependent people perceived themselves to be similar to others as they saw their identity in relation to others and not to individual aspects of themselves. These differences in social perception lead people to behave in different ways with other people. Field-independent people look for, select, and attend to *differences* between themselves and others; field-dependent people, by contrast, select and attend to similarities between themselves and others. We might expect, then, that if the same individual interacted with a field-independent and field-dependent person he or she would be perceived quite differently in terms of, e.g., impressions formed and personality characteristics attributed. This will occur because each type of person will have searched for different types of information when in social interaction; the different types of information gathered by each will result in different impressions being formed. The point is that individual differences in perception arise not only from differing environmental and cultural or sub-cultural experiences but also from differences in personality.

**Figure 6.5** Example of an 'embedded figures' test used to measure field independence/field dependence. There are twelve embedded figures in the drawing, see if you can spot them all and see how long it takes you! Some people are quick and some slow at this kind of task.

## 6.3 Impression formation

Forming impressions of other people (and ourselves) is a common, everyday activity we all engage in. First impressions are often important, for example at interviews. However, first impressions are often inaccurate and reflect prejudice, as in the case of stereotyping (see Chapter 5). Moreover, impressions, as the word implies, only give a very rough and highly selective view of what a person is really like. Not surprisingly then, social psychologists have spent much time trying to establish the influences upon the impressions we form of other people.

In this section we will deal with four themes that have been of main concern: first, the idea that knowledge of certain personality traits is more important than knowledge of other traits – some are *central* to forming impressions, others *peripheral*. Second, the question of how enduring first impressions are and how they may change over time. Third, a brief outline of 'implicit personality theory' – the idea that we all have some preconception of which personality traits go together. Fourth, when impressions lead to stereotyping: this involves both why stereotypes may form and why they are perpetuated.

### 6.3.1 Central peripheral traits

The idea that the impression a person forms of another is not simply the sum total of all the information the person has about the other was first investigated by Asch (1946). Asch, using principles from Gestalt psychology, argued that the impression formed of another is a *dynamic* product of all the information and where some information is perceived to be of greater significance than other information. In terms of Gestalt psychology, the overall impression formed is greater than the sum of the parts. This dynamic approach to perception led Asch to put forward the idea of 'central traits' – personality traits which are highly influential in the final impression formed because they allow many other inferences about the person to be made.

Asch (1946) pioneered an experimental method which has been used on countless occasions to investigate impression formation. Basically, a list of adjectives describing a person (stimulus traits) are given, then subjects are asked to indicate, on the basis of this description, how another set of adjectives (response traits) best describe this target person. Asch, investigating central and peripheral traits, gave subjects slightly different lists of adjectives describing an imaginary person. There were four experimental conditions and a control condition. In the control condition subjects were given just six stimulus traits, in the experimental conditions seven were given. The additional stimulus traits were ones Asch thought to be central: all these conditions are shown below:

Control Group: intelligent, skilful, industrious, determined, practical, cautious

Experimental: intelligent, skilful, industrious, *warm*, determined, practical,
Group A cautious.

Experimental: intelligent, skilful, industrious, *cold*, determined, practical,
Group B cautious.

Experimental: intelligent, skilful, industrious, *polite*, determined, practical,
Group C cautious.

Experimental: intelligent, skilful, industrious, *blunt*, determined, practical,
Group D cautious.

As you can see Groups A and B were given additional traits opposite to each other (warm or cold), as were Groups C and D (polite or blunt). Subjects were then asked whether they thought the target person would also be generous, wise, happy, good-natured, reliable and important. Table 6.3 summarizes the results and shows that subjects given the adjective trait of 'warm' thought the person would be generous (91 per cent), happy (90 per cent) and good-natured (94 per cent). By contrast, those given the trait 'cold' did not think the person would possess such traits. Subjects given either the 'polite' or 'blunt' trait make less extreme judgements. This is shown, for example, by

**Table 6.3** Percentage of subjects who thought the target person possessed the characteristics of generous, wise, happy and good-natured. Adapted from Asch (1946).

| RESPONSE ADJECTIVE | % SUBJECTS INDICATING TRAIT IS CHARACTERISTIC OF THE PERSON | | | | |
|---|---|---|---|---|---|
|  | CONTROL GROUP | GROUP A | GROUP B | GROUP C | GROUP D |
| *Generous* | 55 | 91 | 8 | 56 | 58 |
| *Wise* | 49 | 65 | 25 | 30 | 50 |
| *Happy* | 71 | 90 | 34 | 75 | 65 |
| *Good-natured* | 69 | 94 | 17 | 87 | 56 |

the fact that only 58 per cent and 56 per cent thought the stimulus person would be generous and good-natured, respectively (compare this with the percentages for these traits in Groups A and B). Asch argued, on the basis of these results, that warm/cold are central traits whilst polite/blunt are peripheral.

Many subsequent studies have supported these findings. For example, Kelley (1950) introduced a guest lecturer by giving students either the trait description of Group A or Group B in Asch's experiment. After the lecture Kelley found more students stayed behind to talk and interact with the guest lecturer who was provided with the 'warm' rather than 'cold' central trait embedded in the trait list. Students also made ratings of the lecturer on traits similar to those used by Asch; similar differences between 'warm' and 'cold' in Asch's study were found by Kelley. Maier (1955) extended the central/peripheral idea to encompass descriptions of a person's employment: different impressions of a person were formed depending upon whether that person was depicted as a treasurer of a trade union or a manager of a small company.

In summary, these, and many other studies, demonstrate that certain adjectival descriptions have strong influences upon the impressions of people that are formed. This theme will be developed in the section dealing with implicit personality theory. Before this we need to look at factors influencing first impressions.

### o.3.2 First impressions

Common wisdom has it that first impressions are of paramount importance and endure: this implies that not only is information (central/peripheral traits) we receive about another person important but that we have to take into account the *order* in which such information is presented. Where information presented first has more influence over impressions formed a *primacy* effect is said to occur: where information presented last has more influence a *recency* effect is said to occur. A primacy affect, then, is where first impressions endure. Asch initiated research into this and, again, used lists of adjectives to present to subjects.

Asch (1946) presented two groups of subjects with the same list of six adjectives, however, one group received the adjectives in one order, and the other in a different order, as shown below:

Subject Group A: intelligent, industrious, impulsive, critical, stubborn, envious.
Subject Group B: envious, stubborn, critical, impulsive, industrious, intelligent.

The order of adjectives given to group A presents the imaginary person in good light to start with and a negative one later on. This is the other way around for group B. Asch found a primacy effect when subjects were asked to check a list of response adjectives, i.e. a more positive evaluation was given to the imaginary person by subject group A than subject group B. For example, only 10 per cent of subjects in group B rated the person as generous or humorous compared to 90 per cent in group A.

Luchins (1957) showed a primacy effect when subjects were presented with two one-paragraph descriptions of a person – one paragraph portrayed the person, Jim, as extrovert in character, the other as introvert, as shown below:

### Extrovert paragraph

Jim left the house to get some stationery. He walked out into the sun-filled street with two of his friends, basking in the sun as he walked. Jim entered the stationery store which was full of people. Jim talked with an acquaintance while he waited for the clerk to catch his eye. On his way out, he stopped to chat with a school friend who was just coming into the store. Leaving the store, he walked toward school. On his way out he met the girl to whom he had been introduced the night before. They talked for a short while, and then Jim left for school.

### Introvert paragraph

After school Jim left the classroom alone. Leaving the school, he started on his long walk home. The street was brilliantly filled with sunshine. Jim walked down the street on the shady side. Coming down the street toward him, he saw the pretty girl whom he had met on the previous evening. Jim crossed the street and entered a candy store. The store was crowded with students, and he noticed a few familiar faces. Jim waited quietly until the counterman caught his eye and then gave his order. Taking his drink, he sat down at a side table. When he had finished his drink he went home. (Luchins, 1957, p. 35).

Subjects, instead of checking response adjectives, as with Asch's studies, were asked a number of questions, for example, whether or not they liked Jim, how they thought Jim would look and talk. Subjects were also asked to imagine the following situation:

Jim was waiting his turn in a barber's shop. The barber overlooked him to call on another customer who had just come in. What did Jim do?

Luchins found that subjects who read the extrovert paragraph *followed* by the introvert paragraph thought Jim would tell the barber it was his turn next. Subjects in this condition also thought they would like Jim a lot and that he would be good-looking. By contrast, subjects who read the paragraphs in the opposite order thought Jim would not insist on his turn at the barber's, did not think they would like him and did not think he would be particularly good-looking. These results demonstrate a *primacy* effect.

Luchins found that when there was a time delay between reading the two paragraphs (subjects spent 15 minutes reading a comic between reading the two paragraphs) a *recency* effect occured.

Primacy or recency effects may be important with jurors in criminal trials: Pennington (1982) showed that the order of appearance of witnesses and the order in which the witnesses presented their testimony can affect whether a guilty or not-guilty verdict is returned. In this experiment subjects were given a fairly substantial summary of a rape trial to read. More guilty verdicts resulted from putting the more important witnesses for the prosecution (i.e. those most strongly suggesting the defendant to be guilty) first rather than last: a primacy effect.

Three explanations have been put forward to account for primacy effects: first, a change of meaning hypothesis – later information is interpreted to be consistent with information first received. Second, attention decrement – later information is paid less attention to due to such things as fatigue and boredom. Third, discounting – later, inconsistent information is discounted because it contradicts with what came earlier.

### 6.3.3 Implicit personality theory

Why should a person described as warm also be perceived as generous, happy and good-natured (Table 6.3), and why should, when primacy effects occur, later information be perceived to change meaning so as to be consistent with information which came earlier? Bruner and Tagiuri (1954) suggested that everybody has their own, naive 'implicit' theory of personality. This means, essentially, that we all have an idea of which personality characteristics go with, or are consistent with, other personality characteristics.

Wishner (1960), in a correlational study, showed the relationships people perceive to exist between different traits. Two hundred subjects rated their teachers on 53 pairs of adjectives (ones used by Asch, 1946). Wishner correlated each adjective trait with every other trait and discovered three things: first, the correlation between warm/cold and the other six traits (included in the 53 pairs of adjectives) on Asch's list was low, indicating that warm/cold provides a lot more information than the other traits. Second, the correlation of the other six traits in the stimulus list with the traits in the response list was low. This means that knowledge of these stimulus traits does not lead to judgements of how a person may be on the response traits. Third, correlation between warm/cold and the other remaining 53 traits was high, indicating much can be inferred about a person from knowing he or she is warm or cold. Wishner further demonstrated that the centrality of a trait is *relative*, i.e. whether a given trait is central or peripheral depends on what else is known about the person. For example, warm/cold is central in relation to generous, wise and good-natured, but peripheral in relation to, for example, a person's vanity and reliability.

Rosenberg *et al.* (1968) added greater detail to the idea of implicit personality theory by estimating the degree of relationships people perceived traits to have. Their findings are depicted in Figure 6.6, here traits are shown to fall into two dimensions – good intellectual/bad intellectual and good social/bad social. Figure 6.6 also shows those traits which are closely associated with each other and which would be central or peripheral in relation to other traits. We can now understand why, for example, 'warm' leads people to perceive a person as being good-natured and happy; we would also expect that person to be perceived a helpful and sincere. Another point to emerge from this is that warm is towards the 'bad' end of the intellectual dimension and the 'good' end of the social dimension. 'Cold' on the other hand is 'good intellectual' and 'bad social'. This would lead to the expectation that 'warm'

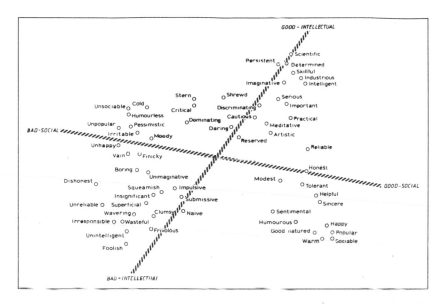

**Figure 6.6** Two major trait dimensions (bad-social/good-social and bad-intellectual/good-intellectual) proposed by Rosenberg *et al.* (1968). Notice how knowledge of one trait, such as warm, leads to numerous other trait attributions being made, for example, happy, sincere and popular.

people are perceived as less intellectually capable than 'cold' people.

Generally, knowing where a trait lies on these two dimensions allows predictions to be made. For example, knowing a person to be superficial (bad intellectual and bad social) also means we should predict the person to be perceived as foolish, irresponsible and frivolous (intellectually undesirable traits), as well as vain, boring and dishonest (socially undesirable traits).

### 6.3.4 Stereotyping

Whilst impressions of other people are simplified perceptions which attempt an accurate assessment of a person, albeit in a rather oversimplified way, stereotypes are attempts to force people into certain categories or 'pigeon-holes' without paying attention to how they actually are. Stereotypes represent distortions of reality and are in error because they fail to accommodate the actual personality traits that a person possesses. In Chapter 5 we looked at how stereotypes relate to and may be the cause of prejudice and discrimination – the reader is referred back to the relevant section to refresh his or her memory.

Stereotypes may result in bias and prejudice but persist because they offer ways to simplify and predict how people behave. One of the fundamental principles of perception, as we saw at the beginning of this chapter, is that people process information in a way which selectively reduces a potentially overwhelming number of stimuli coming from what people say and do. As such, stereotypes serve as useful *guides*, but only sometimes, since in using them people should constantly be aware of the limitations such devices of 'cognitive economy' may offer.

The dimensions of traits in Figure 6.6 can be seen as a form of stereotyping. However, the important difference with implicit personality theory is that trait inferences are made on the basis of what is known about a person; with stereotypes, perceptions of a person are distorted in an attempt to force someone into a preconceived mould. Taylor *et al.* (1978), for example, showed that when subjects were asked to remember how certain people were who had previously been described to them, mistakes were made in the direction which tended to confirm the stereotype. Snyder (1978) has further shown that stereotypes may perpetuate because people tend to seek out information which tends to confirm rather then refute the stereotype. Such a confirmatory approach to testing the validity of a stereotype when applied to an individual may turn into a self-fulfilling prophecy. Stereotypes, then, represent the less acceptable face of impression formation.

## 6.4 Self-perception

How far is it possible to know oneself? Generally great value is placed upon increasing self-knowledge; indeed behaviour is thought to be more rational if people have explored their own motives, intentions, etc. Careful, considered actions are praised whilst spontaneous, wild outbursts are often condemned. How we perceive ourselves, then, will have important consequences for how we act and interact with other people. In Chapter 4 Bem's self-perception theory of attitude change was described: Bem makes the point that often our behaviour determines the attitudes we hold. This idea applies more widely in that emotional experience is often only given meaning by the social context in which it occurs. Our perception of ourselves in terms of how we evaluate our abilities, characteristics, etc. – known as our self-concept – has important consequences for the quality and nature of our interaction with others. This section looks at how we perceive our own emotional experiences and how our self-concept may affect our social behaviour.

### 6.4.1 Self-perception of emotion

Psychologists have had little success in relating physiological response (such as heart rate, sweating, galvanic skin response) to *particular* emotional experiences. It has been possible to measure the intensity of an emotion but not what the emotion is. To account for this Schachter (1964) proposed a *two-factor* theory of emotion stating that specific bodily sensations and feelings are interpreted as a particular emotion because of the social situation in which they occur. The two factors involved are:

(a) General physiological arousal: intensity of bodily sensations, such as increased heart rate, tremor, flushing.
(b) Cognitive label: perception of the appropriateness of a particular emotion in a given social context. Social rules and norms are often used as guides here.

Schachter and Singer (1962), in a widely cited social psychology experiment, recruited subjects for an experiment which the subjects were told was concerned with the effects of a vitamin supplement (called Suproxin) on visual acuity. Subjects were told they would receive an injection of Suproxin and then have their vision tested. In fact, subjects had been misled since some were actually injected with epinephrine and some with a placebo. Epinephrine mimics the feelings found to occur in intense emotion – increased heart rate, tremor, flushing, etc. Subjects were divided into four groups and told different things: the *informed* group, as Schachter and Singer called them, were told that the vitamin supplement caused increased heart rate, tremor, etc. The *ignorant* group were given no information about possible side-effects: the *misinformed* group were told the drug would cause numbness of the feet. The fourth group, injected with a *placebo* – a neutral liquid with no effect – were told nothing about possible side effects.

After being given an injection subjects were asked to wait in a room while the vitamin supplement took effect; in the room was a confederate of the experiments, however subjects were led to believe this person was another subject in the same experiment. Whilst the subject waited in the room the confederate acted in one of two ways: (a) euphorically – throwing paper planes, dancing around, playing hula-hoop; or (b) angrily – speaking critically of the experimenters and showing extreme displeasure whilst filling out a questionnaire. After being exposed to the confederate acting in one of these ways subects were asked to identify and rate their own emotional state.

The prediction from the two-factor theory is that subjects injected with epinephrine and *informed* about side-effects would be little affected by the 'euphoric' or 'angry' confederate, since they could sufficiently justify their bodily sensations to themselves. 'Ignorant' and 'misinformed' subjects, however, would be influenced by the social situation, and subjects injected with a placebo should be unaffected by the confederate's behaviour. Generally, these predictions were supported. Figure 6.7 shows that subjects'

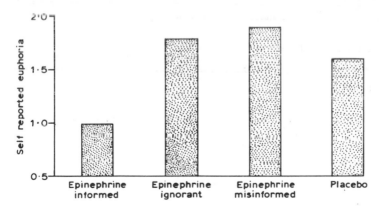

**Figure 6.7** Self-reports of euphoria by subjects in different experimental conditions. Those subjects misinformed reported the most euphoria when placed in a situation with another acting euphorically, subjects in the control condition (placebo) were more affected by the other person's behaviour than those informed of the effects of epinephrine. Adapted from Schachter and Singer (1962).

own rating of euphoria were highest in the ignorant and misinformed conditions and lowest in the informed condition. Subjects injected with a placebo reported some feelings of euphoria as the injection itself is physiologically arousing.

Valins (1966) extended the two-factor theory to show that it is only necessary for a person to *believe* he or she is physiologically aroused for a socially appropriate emotion to be felt. Male college students were shown slides of semi-nude women, with certain slides subjects were given *false feedback* about their heart rate – that it increased. After viewing the slides subjects rated the attractiveness of each woman; results showed greater attraction to those women subjects associated (falsely) with increases in heartbeat. This is known as the *Valins effect* – the effect of false feedback on emotional experience; it is thought to work because belief in increased arousal causes subjects to attend to what they are doing more closely (Parkinson and Manstead, 1981).

Nisbett and Schachter (1966) showed how important the cognitive label attached to the feeling is by looking at how relabelling of emotional states increases tolerance to pain. Subjects were either told electric shocks would be painful (high fear) or not painful (low fear). Half the subjects in each condition were given a pill which they were told would produce side-effects similar to electric shocks, the remaining subjects were given a similar pill and told of side-effects irrelevant to electric shocks. Subjects were then given electric shocks and asked to indicate when the shocks became too strong to bear. Results showed, as predicted, that subjects expecting shock-like side-effects from the pill would tolerate more pain than those not expecting such side-effects. Table 6.4 shows this to be the case in the 'low fear' condition but not the 'high fear' one. This is to be expected since subjects in the high-fear condition were expecting painful shocks, those in the low-fear condition were not.

In summary, these experiments demonstrate that how we *label* an emotion depends on what we believe our body to be doing and how we think such sensations are most appropriately perceived or interpreted.

**Table 6.4**  Tolerance of shocks by subjects in 'low' and 'high' fear conditions and led to believe the pill either did or did not produce shock-like side effects. Higher numbers indicate subjects tolerated higher levels of shock. Adapted from Nisbett and Schachter (1966).

| | SIDE-EFFECTS OF DRUG | |
| FEAR CONDITION | *Shock-like* | *Non-shock like* |
| --- | --- | --- |
| *Low* | 25.8 | 15.8 |
| *High* | 26.3 | 28.2 |

### 6.4.2 Self-concept

Self-concept is a general term describing how we think about or evaluate ourselves, it consists of how we think of ourselves physically, morally, personally, in relation to family, and the social self (Fitts, 1964). The many facets of self-concept are strongly influenced by our sense of identity – in Chapter 3 we saw how important successful identity-formation is for the way we approach the world generally and engage in social relationships in particular. Two things have powerful effects on our self-concept: (a) the opinions and judgements other people make of us; (b) social comparisions – perceptions of the ways in which you are similar to and different from other people. A particular aspect of self-concept that has been widely investigated is that of *self-esteem*. If people perceive themselves to be intelligent, competent and well-adjusted their self-esteem is said to be high; however if their self-perception is that of being unintelligent, incompetent and poorly adjusted their self-esteem is low.

Gergen (1965) showed how self-esteem is affected by other people's reactions by asking subjects to talk about themselves as openly and honestly as possible. Half the subjects were treated in a positive way and half in a negative way by a clinical psychologist; other subjects in a control condition were treated neutrally.

Subjects' self-esteem increased dramatically as the talk progressed when responded to positively; decreased when responded to negatively and remained roughly the same in the control condition. Subjects were interviewed some time later and the changes in self-esteem were found to persist. Generally, others make us feel good when they agree with what we think is good about us and disagree with what we think bad about us. Bergin (1962), however, showed that we do not believe people who disagree wildly with our self-evaluations.

In uncertain and/or anxiety-arousing situations our self-esteem may be subject to quite rapid changes. Morse and Gergen (1970) investigated subjects' change in self-esteem whilst waiting for a job interview in the presence of another candidate who dressed in one of two ways:

(a) 'Mr Clean' – dressed in a smart suit, carried a new brief case which he opened to reveal books and a slide rule.
(b) 'Mr Dirty' – dressed in an old T-shirt and jeans, slouched in a chair and read a cheap sex novel.

The self-esteem of subjects was found to increase when in the presence of Mr Dirty, and decrease when Mr Clean was waiting with the subjects. Unfortunately, Morse and Gergen did not go on to see how subjects performed in the interview. Since level of self-esteem has been found to affect performance at numerous tasks (Coopersmith, 1967) we might predict that subjects who sat with Mr Dirty and experienced an increased in self-esteem would be more likely to give a good account of themselves at the interview and so stand a better change of getting the job than subjects who sat with Mr Clean.

Whilst self-esteem may fluctuate in certain social situations there are times, it seems, when we continue to believe in good things told about us even when evidence to the contrary exists. This is known as the *perseverance effect*; Ross, Lepper and Hubbard (1975) showed that people who believed they possessed socially desirable characteristics persisted in holding such beliefs when given contrary evidence by the experimenters. Such a perseverance effect would probably not hold if we were told negative things about ourselves, but this might depend on our level of self-esteem. For example, people low in self-esteem are more likely to believe negative things about themselves than people high in self-esteem. A perseverance effect should occur for low, but not high, self-esteem people in such circumstances.

## 6.5 Perceptual processes

At the beginning of this chapter the idea was introduced that people process information in self- and other-perception. Figure 6.1 diagramatically represents the way in which information from the outside world enters the mind, then retrieved at some later time when planning how to behave. In this section we shall look a little more closely at how these processes affect social perception. In particular the perceptual processes of attention, memory and social inference will be deal with.

### 6.5.1 Attention

Attention is whatever we are presently conscious of or aware of; we attend only to highly *selective* aspects of all the potential information available. Furthermore, whether our attention is directed outwards or inwards (memories, thoughts, etc.) the *intensity* or degree of mental effort we make is also important. Within this framework social psychologists have investigated three major determinants of what influences attention in social settings – salience, self-awareness and self-consciousness (a personality difference).

Anything that stands out and attracts our attention, such as novel, extreme or loud stimuli, is salient to us. For example, if you walk into a bar and find a crowded room in which there is just one woman, that woman will be salient. People who 'stick out' in a crowd are salient. A person perceived as salient has social consequences: such people are perceived as more influential in group interaction – resulting in salient people attracting more extreme and exaggerated judgements. The latter is shown in a study by Strack, Erber and Wicklund (1982) where subjects were given a biography to read. Some subjects were told the person depicted in the biography was socially influential and others that the person was susceptible to social influence. Some of these subjects also saw a videotape of the person whilst reading. Subjects who saw the video tape, the high-salience manipulation, perceived the person to be much more socially influential (or susceptible to influence depending on the biography they had been given) than subjects who did not see the video tape. Taylor and Fiske (1975) found that observers of a conversation perceived the person they sat opposite to as more active and influential in the group than people sitting either to their left or right, and more influential than they actually were.

The extent to which we attend to our social surroundings or to ourselves as social objects has consequences for how we perceive ourselves. Factors which enhance *self-awareness* (which is the amount of attention focused on yourself as a social object) increase the extent to which we perceive ourselves as responsible for our behaviour. Self-attention in the form of self-awareness was increased in a study by Duval and Wicklund (1972) by getting subjects to work at a task whilst looking at themselves in a large mirror. Subjects who worked at the same task but did not look at themselves in a mirror were much

**Table 6.5** Items from the self-consciousness scale of Fenigstein, Scheier and Buss (1975). Indicate in the right-hand column whether you generally agree or disagree with each question.

| SELF-CONSCIOUSNESS SCALE | AGREE / DISAGREE |
|---|---|
| 1  I'm always trying to figure myself out | . . . . .    . . . . . . |
| 2  I'm concerned about my style of doing things | . . . . .    . . . . . |
| 3  Generally, I am now very aware of myself | . . . . .    . . . . . |
| 4  I reflect about myself a lot | . . . . .    . . . . |
| 5  I'm concerned about the way I present myself | . . . . .    . . . . . . |
| 6  I'm self-conscious about the way I look | . . . . .    . . . . . |
| 7  I never scrutinize myself | . . . . .    . . . . . |
| 8  I'm generally attentive to my inner feelings | . . . . .    . . . . . |
| 9  I usually worry about making a good impression | . . . . .    . . . . . |

less concerned with or 'tuned into' their personality characteristics than those working in front of the mirror. Generally, anything which increases self-awareness will increase a person's concern with managing the impression he or she gives to others (Schlenker, 1980).

Personality differences exist in the way people direct their attention; sayings such as 'he is always absorbed with his own thoughts' and 'I don't think he ever stops to think before acting' reflect this. Fenigstein, Scheier and Buss (1975) produced a questionnaire to measure how people differ with respect to both private and public self-consciousness. The former is where a person is aware of his or her own thoughts, the latter where there is awareness of how he or she is behaving and the opinions others might be forming from that behaviour. Table 6.5 reproduces some items from the questionnaire – you might like to find out your own degree of public and private self-consciousness by indicating whether you agree or disagree with each statement. To do this score a point for each time you agree with questions 1, 4 and 8 and a point each time you disagree with questions 3 and 7 – the higher you score the more *privately* self-conscious you are. For *public* self-consciousness score a point each time you agree to questions 2, 5, 6 and 9; again a high score indicates greater public self-consciousness.

Scheier (1980) showed that people who score high on public, but low on private, self-consciousness are more likely to behave in ways to please other people with whom they disagree than subjects who score low on public and high on private self-consciousness. The latter type of people are more likely to behave in ways consistent with their attitudes, this is so because inconsistencies between attitudes and behaviour will receive greater attention by such people.

### 6.5.2 Person memory

Suppose you are in a bank when two armed men walk in, demand cash from the cashier, and run out when the alarm bell sounds. Later police question you about such things as what the men looked like, how they were dressed, how they behaved and talked, etc. In short, you are asked to draw upon your memory when giving eye-witness testimony.

Memory, for people and social events, is thought to be of two types: episodic and semantic. Episodic memory consists of specific, concrete events such as the bank robbery you were asked to imagine witnessing. Semantic memory is abstract and concerned with general properties and meanings, for example, what you know about bank robberies in general. In attempting to give an account of some social event you have witnessed you would need to draw solely on episodic memory. Since no one's memory is perfect, and you have not attended to everything that happened (due to attention being selective), people tend to 'fill-in' the gaps in their actual memories with information from semantic memory. In the case of the bank robbery you may not be able to remember if the two men carried shot guns or rifles, but since most armed bank robbers you have heard of use shotguns, it is highly likely you will think you remember the men carrying shotguns.

Memory for people (person memory) tends to fall into three categories – memory for appearance, behaviour and traits (Fiske and Cox, 1979): when asked to remember what they can about another person, people usually start with an account of appearance, followed by what took place (the behaviour) and finally what kind of person (personality traits) he or she might be. Appearance is directly observable and retrieved from episodic memory; traits, by contrast, have to be inferred and so come from semantic memory. If one of the bank robbers wore bright pink trousers, a frilly shirt and white shoes you might infer him to be extroverted (among other things!), this might be so because semantic memory tells you what extroverts are usually like. Memory for personality traits are of two types – social desirability and competence characteristics (Rosenberg and Sedlak, 1972); these reflect the two trait dimensions, in Figure 6.6, found in implicit personality theory.

The context in which one tries to remember is also important, attempts by police to reconstruct crimes are often effective in 'jogging' memory. Empathizing is also a useful technique for enhancing person memory. Harvey *et al.* (1980) found people to remember more about another when they were asked to imagine themselves in the 'other person's shoes' and share the other's feelings. Person memory is also improved when we try to form a general impression of another rather than attempt to memorize only how another behaves (Hamilton, 1981).

### 6.5.3 Social inference

Information about a person which has been attended to and remembered forms the basis of social inference. By social inference is meant the way in which judgements are made about: (a) personality characteristics a person possesses; and (b) predictions about the way a person is likely to behave. Tversky and Kahneman (1974), in a highly influential paper, suggest that people use *heuristics* when making judgements. These are short-cuts or aids to rapid reasoning, since it is not possible for us to consider all potentially relevant information when making a judgement. Two heuristics are important for social inference – *availability* and *representativeness*. Most time will be devoted to the former heuristic of availability.

The availability heuristic reflects memory: it is used to judge the frequency or likelihood of some social event by the ease with which relevant instances can be brought to mind. For example, imagine trying to decide how common heated arguments are between married couples. One could conduct a survey of a large number of married couples; however, if the question comes up in conversation with a friend what you will probably do is think of all married couples *you know* who argue a lot and make an inference of commonness of heated arguments on that basis. If many such instances come to mind or are *available from memory* then you will think heated arguments are relatively common between married couples. If only few instances come to mind then you will infer heated arguments to be relatively rare. The availability heuristic reflects your own experience of the social world and as such may lead to quite serious errors of social inference. This was highlighted by Coombs and Slovic (1978) who showed that newspaper reporting of more dramatic and 'exciting' causes of death (violent accidents, deaths from catastrophic disasters) result in these causes being perceived as much more frequent than they actually are. Conversely, rarely reported but common causes of death (such as diabetes, emphysema) are perceived as much less frequent than they actually are.

Kahneman and Tversky (1982) have extended the availability heuristic to encompass inferences made about the likely behaviour of a person based on what we might *imagine* a person to do. This is called the *stimulation* heuristic; its use can be seen from the following example used by Kahneman and Tversky:

> Mr Crane and Mr Tees were scheduled to leave the airport on different flights, at the same time. They travelled from town in the same limousine, were caught in a traffic jam, and arrived at the airport 30 minutes after the scheduled departure time of their flights. Mr Crane is told his flight left on time. Mr Tees is told that his flight was delayed and left five minutes ago. Who is more upset? Mr Crane or Mr Tees?

Most people think Mr Tees will be the most upset since, Kahneman and Tversky argue, people are able to imagine many ways in which five minutes could have been saved in the car journey but not 30 minutes. Whilst a 'near miss is as good as a mile' it certainly is not perceived by people in that way.

The representativeness heuristic is used to make judgements of similarity. Suppose you are given the following information:

> Steve is very shy and withdrawn, invariably helpful but with little interest in people or in the world of reality. A meek and tidy soul, he has a need for order and a passion for detail. (Tversky and Kahneman, 1974).

You are now asked to indicate whether you think Steve is a former trapeze artist, librarian, driver or surgeon. How would you go about doing this? Most likely you would make a judgement as to how *representative* the description is of the stereotype or image you have of the occupations given above. Tversky and Kahneman found most subjects thought Steve to be a librarian, even when they had additional information which should have led to a different inference being made.

Heuristics of thinking, such as availability and representativeness, are aids to making *rapid* social inferences but do not always result in accurate judgement being made. The question of whether or not people can be accurate in their judgements of others is the topic we now turn to.

## 6.6  Accuracy in person perception

The question of accuracy in person perception, i.e. whether some people are more accurate in their perceptions than others, has a long tradition in social psychology. In the light of what you have already read in this chapter you will, perhaps, not be surprised to learn that evidence is mixed and inconclusive on this issue. The finding that different aspects of the social environment cause different people to attend to different things, for example, would suggest that to talk about accuracy in person perception may be mistaken. Furthermore, to know that one person is more accurate than another in his or her perceptions means that some objective (or at least acceptable) criterion against which to compare different people's perceptions is needed. Such a yardstick has not been, and is probably not likely to be, forthcoming in social psychology. Nevertheless, the question of accuracy has been researched, particularly from the point of view of emotions and personality traits.

In *The Expression of Emotion in Man and Animals* Charles Darwin made the claim that facial expressions were innate and had evolved from facial movements that once served specific functions for the species. The expression of disgust, for example, evolved from the expression made when vomiting. This claim leads to the hypothesis that people should be accurate in recognizing emotional expression in other people – since everybody should exhibit identical expressions for the same emotion. Early studies did not find this (see Ekman, Friesen and Ellsworth, 1972 for a summary) because too many emotional expressions were used. More recent research (Ekman, Sorenson and Friesen, 1969; Izard, 1972), however, has found strong and consistent evidence that people perceive emotional expression accurately but only for a very *limited number* of emotions and if those emotions are *unambiguously* displayed (Chapter 9 deals with this issue in more detail). Ekman restricted his studies to six emotions – happiness, sorrow, anger, fear, disgust and surprise. Actors unambiguously displayed these emotions as well as they could (see the pictures for four of these in Table 6.6), photographs of these emotional expressions were then shown to subjects who were asked to identify which emotion they thought was being expressed. Ekman and Friesen (1975) showed these photographs to people from different cultures and found high levels of agreement. This occurred even when people had little or no contact with westerners, as was the case, for example, with certain tribes in New Guinea. As Table 6.6 shows, all four emotional expressions were accurately perceived by Americans, and happiness was accurately perceived by all cultures tested by Ekman and Friesen. However, people in New Guinea were less able to identify fear, disgust and anger. Generally, though, the results show quite high agreement and accuracy in identifying emotional expression.

Accuracy in the perception of personality traits has fared much less well. One of the most common ways social psychologists use to assess this is to compare a test of personality filled in by person X with how another person thinks person X would fill in that questionnaire. Another method has been to compare ratings made by a subject with those of an 'expert', usually a clinical psychologist. Vernon (1933), for example, attempted to discover if some people had a general ability accurately to judge personality traits in others.

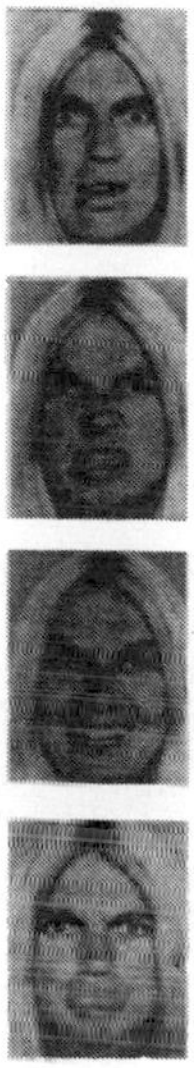

| | | UNITED STATES | BRAZIL | CHILE | ARGENTINA | JAPAN | NEW GUINEA |
|---|---|---|---|---|---|---|---|
| | Fear | 85% | 67% | 68% | 54% | 66% | 54% |
| | Disgust | 92% | 97% | 92% | 92% | 90% | 44% |
| | Happiness | 97% | 95% | 95% | .98% | 100% | 82% |
| | Anger | 67% | 90% | 94% | 90% | 90% | 50% |

**Figure 6.8** Percentage agreement in the identification of emotional expressions by people from different countries. Adapted from Ekman and Friesen (1975).

Forty eight male students filled in a number of personality and intelligence questionnaires, these students were then asked to rate themselves, friends and strangers on the same characteristics. Vernon did not find a general ability, but that some people rated themselves, others their friends, and yet others strangers more accurately. Subjects found to be accurate self-raters, for example, were found to be humorous, intelligent and moderately artistic; those who more accurately rated friends were found to be less intelligent and more artistic. Cronbach (1955) criticized this and other similar studies by correctly arguing that such an approach throws greater light on how subjects perceive people to be than on how people actually are. The point really reflects many of the issues already covered in this chapter: for example, the idea that everyone has his or her own implicit theory of personality.

Little recent research has addressed the accuracy question for three main reasons: (a) problems of methodology outlined above; (b) the question of accuracy is mistaken in the first place – Mischel (1968) argues that behaviour results from both personality and the social situation; (c) research in social cognition has produced a major shift in emphasis to look at error and bias in social inference – this is brought out more fully in the next chapter.

In summary, research on accuracy in person perception has found good evidence that people can recognize expressions of common and unambiguous emotions. However, accuracy in the perception of personality traits has produced little, if any, evidence for the idea that some people are more accurate than others.

## 6.7 Summary

○ Perception of objects and people (including ourselves) involves information processing. This means that we selectively attend to only a limited amount of our social environment.

○ Object and social perception share certain similarities but are different since person perception is a two-way, interactive process.

○ People readily form impressions of other people: central traits allow people to make more judgements than do peripheral traits. Primacy effects in impression formation are quite common and relatively enduring, recency effects occur when there is a delay between presentation of two types of information.

○ People have an 'implicit personality theory' which guides the personality traits associated with one another. Personality traits are perceived by people on two dimensions – good/bad intellectual and good/bad social.

○ The Two-Factor theory of emotion – how we believe our body to be responding and the cognitive label applied – has been put forward to account for our self-perception of emotional experience.

○ Self-concept is how we evaluate ourselves. High and low self-esteem affects our performance at certain tasks and is influenced by various social situations, e.g. ones arousing anxiety.

○ The perceptual processes of attention and memory are important components of social cognition. Salience, self-awareness and self-consciousness affect what we attend to about other people. Person memory consists of episodic and semantic memory.

○ Judgemental heuristics, such as availability and representativeness, are used to make rapid inferences about other people, but may result in error and bias.

○ Accuracy in person perception has been looked at from the perspectives of emotions and personality traits. People are quite accurate in recognizing a limited number of emotional expressions. However, accuracy in perception of personality traits is less accurate for both methodological and theoretical reasons.

## 6.8 Suggestions for futher reading

Cohen G. *The Psychology of Cognition* (London, Academic Press, 1983).
Highly readable introduction to the area of cognitive psychology. This field is becoming increasingly important, and, with the development of Artificial Intelligence through advances in computer technology, an understanding is now essential for a grasp of contemporary psychology.

Schneider, D.J., Hastorf, A.M. and Ellsworth, P.C. *Person Perception* Second Edition (Reading, Mass, Addison Wesley, 1979).
Thorough introduction to the area, not easy reading but necessary if you wish to develop a further appreciation of this aspect of social psychology, an aspect I think will become increasingly important in the future.

Wegner, D.M. and Vallacher, R.R. *Implicit Psychology: An Introduction to Social Cognition* (New York: Oxford University Press, 1977).
Excellent introduction to the issues covered in this and the next chapter. The first source to go to if you wish to explore the issues raised in this chapter more fully and more broadly.

Wegner, D.M. and Vallacher, R.R. *The Self in Social Psychology* (New York, Oxford University Press, 1980).
Again an excellent introduction to this more specialized area of social psychology, these authors have an enviable ability to present difficult ideas in an interesting and non-technical way.

# 7
# Social cognition II: The attribution approach

7.1    Introduction
7.2    Fundamental concepts
7.3    Theories of attribution
       7.3 1 Covariation model   7.3.2 Causal schemata   7.3.3 Correspondent inference
7.4    Attributional biases
       7.4.1 Fundamental attribution error   7.4.2 Actor/observer differences
       7.4.3 Self-serving bias
7.5    Personality differences
7.6    Attributions in a social context
7.7    Application – depression
7.8    Summary
7.9    Suggestions for further reading

## 7.1 Introduction

The central concern of the attribution approach in social psychology is to understand and explain how people attribute *causes* to their own and other people's behaviour. A few examples may help clarify the objectives of such an approach. Suppose you have just been for a job interview, performed very poorly in that interview and did not get offered the job. How might you explain to yourself, and to your friends, why you made such a mess of the interview and so did not get the job? That is, what *causes* might you attribute to your poor performance? A host of possibilities present themselves, for example, you may have been very anxious, or had a late night, or found the interviewer aggressive and patronizing. Doubtless you can think of other possible causes which all offer some explanation and justification for the poor performance. Take another example: suppose, this time, you are walking along a busy shopping precinct and a stranger collapses on the pavement just in front of you. You may automatically go to the person's assistance but at the same time you will probably be speculating about what caused the person to collapse. How you *perceive* the behaviour to be caused may affect the amount and quality of help you are willing to offer. For example, if the person was dressed in a rather shabby way and smelt of alcohol you may attribute the cause to the person being drunk. By contrast, if the person was smartly dressed, did not smell of alcohol, and appeared to you rather 'old for his age', you may think the cause to be a heart attack. None of this can be known for certain at the time, the point is, though, that you would probably be less willing to help if you attributed the cause to drunkenness than if you attributed the cause to a heart-attack.

127

The perception of the cause of another's behaviour also has consequences for the degree of responsibility attributed to the person for his or her actions. The distinction between murder and manslaughter is a good example of this. Somebody who, in cold blood and with aforethought, plans to kill somebody and then goes out and commits the deed is held to be highly responsible for that act (excepting, of course, when that person is judged to be insane). On the other hand, a woman who has a violent drunkard for a husband and in a fit of temper and exasperation kills him will most likely be convicted of manslaughter. This may be so since the killing of her husband is not perceived to be entirely caused by her: his violent drunkenness reduces her responsibility.

These examples serve to demonstrate three points about the attribution approach: first, people *seek* to explain their own and other people's behaviour. This is because attributing causes to behaviour serves the important function of *reducing uncertainty* about how that person is likely to behave in the future. People, it would seem, generally need to feel that they can predict and have some control over the world in which they live. Second, both examples demonstrate how people *search for and use information* when attributing causes. Information about the person in question and the social context in which the behaviour takes place is used to produce an attribution. Third, in characterizing people as seeking to explain and understand social behaviour we may regard them as '*naive scientists*'. We may think of scientists searching for the cause of physical events such as the weather, electricity, etc. Psychologists, as scientists, attempt to explain why people behave as they do by constructing theories and testing them experimentally. In a similar but much less rigorous and objective way, the lay person acts as a scientist, albeit a 'naive' one, since the objectives are the same: prediction and control.

This chapter develops the themes and ideas introduced here by, first, looking at fundamental concepts in the attribution approach then moving on to describe three major attribution theories. It then examines biases and errors people often make when attributing causes. Then we look at the effect of personality differences, social context and end by considering an application of the attribution approach to the understanding and treatment of depression.

## 7.2　Fundamental concepts

The conceptual foundation on which theories of attribution have been built was provided by Heider (1944). He advanced three points concerning the way people understand their social environments: (a) people perceive behaviour as being caused; (b) it is important to understand people's perceptions; and (c) the locus of the causes of behaviour is perceived to be with the person, the situation, or some combination of both. We will deal with each of these points in turn.

Claiming that people perceive behaviour as being caused may seem rather obvious and trite on first acquaintance, however, the important point is that we attribute causes to virtually *all* human behaviour. People appear to be ill at ease or loath to admit or believe that behaviour happens because of chance events. All and everything that others, and ourselves, do is believed to result from one or a number of particular causes.

How people *perceive* behaviour to be caused, rather than how it is actually caused (if this can ever be known), is of interest to attribution theorists. Consider again the example, given earlier, where you were asked to imagine having a poor job interview. We considered possible causes you might give such as being anxious, having a headache from being up late, etc. However, the reasons for your bad performance might be perceived in an entirely different way by the person who interviewed you; for example, the interviewer may regard you as incompetent and of low intelligence. Discrepancies in perceptions of the causes of behaviour, such as this, happen frequently in our social life. Attribution researchers are concerned to discover if there are distinct patterns in the different ways in which people, from different perspectives, attribute causes to behaviour. If you think back to what was said in the previous chapter, on social perception, it is not hard to see why different people with different perspectives may offer different causal attributions for the *same* behaviour. In Chapter 6 we saw that perception is an active process in which we selectively attend to only limited features of our social environment. Heider (1958) claimed that perceptions of the causes of behaviour, as with our perception of physical objects, depends on three things: (a) the characteristics of the perceiver; (b) the features of the behaviour perceived; and (c) the social context in which the behaviour takes place. Referring back to the old hag/young woman depicted in Figure 6.2 you should be able to see what Heider meant. The figure provides a simple demonstration of how what you *expect* to see has a strong influence on what you *do* see. Similar ideas apply to the ways in which people see behaviour to be caused since ambiguity exists just as strongly in this domain.

The third point by Heider, and one of central importance, which will be encountered again and again in this chapter, is that people attribute causes, primarily, to either *the person or the situation*. Consider the example, given earlier, of the distinction between murder and manslaughter: for a person to be convicted of murder the cause of the behaviour has to be attributed entirely to the person by referring to such things as personality traits, motives, intentions, etc. Such attributions are known as *internal causes* since they refer to causes of behaviour located within the individual whose behaviour we are concerned to explain. By contrast, our example of the circumstances under which a person may be found guilty of manslaughter tend to emphasize *external* causes. Generally, these are forces located outside the person and in the social situation which, as it were, compel or incline a person to act in those ways. External causes are those which most people think would compel them to act in a similar way in such a situation. In our example of manslaughter, the external cause was a violent drunkard for a husband.

The distinction of internal and external causes is of fundamental importance to the attribution approach, because theories have been developed to predict when people make internal attributions and when they make external attributions. The internal/external distinction is a relative one, and it is important to bear this in mind. An example, discussed by Ross (1977), highlights this: suppose we are interested in knowing why Jack has just bought the house that he has. One person might say that Jack bought the house 'because it was so secluded', implying that it is something about the house (external attribution) that caused Jack to buy it. Another person, however, might say that Jack bought the house 'because he wanted privacy' emphasizing something about Jack's need for seclusion (internal attribution) that caused him to buy the house. Notice, however, the latter implies that the house is secluded and the former implies that Jack likes privacy (he would be hardly likely to buy such a house if he did not!) An internal attribution may, then, have external implications and *vice versa*; but of interest is the emphasis a particular person gives when attributing the cause of behaviour.

## 7.3  Theories of attribution

Three attribution theories will be looked at in this section, it is important to realize that each theory does *not* offer a different explanation of behaviour but offers an explanation depending upon the information available and the kind of explanation we are interested in. The three theories are: (a) *the causal schemata model* (Kelley, 1972) which is most appropriate to use when we have information about a person behaving on only a single occasion; (b) *the covariation model* (Kelley, 1967), which requires much information about the person and how others behave in similar situations; and (c) *the correspondent inference model* (Jones and Davies, 1965) which is concerned solely with understanding when and under what circumstances people make internal attributions.

### 7.3.1  Causal schemata model

In many everyday social situations we make attributions about the cause of a person's behaviour based on no more than a single observation of that person behaving. Take the example, given earlier, of the stranger collapsing on the pavement in front of you; uppermost in your mind, perhaps, will be attempting to explain why the stranger collapsed. What information can be used to assist you in making an attribution? Since you do not know the person you cannot think back to how he behaved in the past; to make an attribution you have to rely on your knowledge (called 'schemata') of how people behave in general. To continue with the example, you might infer the person collapsed through being drunk because he was shabbily dressed, smelt of alcohol, etc. In a sense, making attributions based on single acts means that people often draw on stereotypes, implicit personality theory, etc. These are the kind of things meant by Kelley's term 'causal schemata'.

A causal schema is defined by Kelley (1972) as 'a general conception the person has about how certain kinds of causes interact to produce a specific kind of effect' (p. 151). However, as the above example also demonstrates, we need some guidelines to tell us how we arrive at one type of causal explanation (drunkenness) rather than another (heart-attack).

One of the main strategies used, Kelley (1972) suggests, is what he calls the *discounting* principle. Simply put, this is where other causes are discounted if one is known to be present. For example, suppose I have an accident in my car on a bend in the road and this happens late at night. You might be tempted to say I had been drinking since it was about the time the pubs shut. However, you might well discount this causal explanation as you also know that it had been snowing and the road was very slippery. Given that you know one cause to be present (road conditions) you are likely to discount other causes (drinking). The discounting principle demonstrates, as was seen in the previous chapter, the tendency people have towards *simplicity* in social perception. Whilst it may be the case that the accident was a result of both these factors people often give just one causal explanation when possible.

### 7.3.2 The covariation model

Kelley (1967) proposed a theory of attribution to apply when the attributor has information about: (a) how the person in question has behaved in the past; and (b) how other people behave. Kelley says that people use *three* types of information when making an internal or external attribution – consistency, distinctiveness and consensus information.

Suppose we were interested to explain why someone we know, called Jane, behaved in a friendly way to another person, Anne. Table 7.1 describes each of the three types of information and gives examples. As you can see from the table, *consistency* information is concerned with whether or not the person behaves in a similar or consistent way at *different times* to the same person. High consistency is where similar behaviour has been shown at different times; low consistency is where behaviour in the past is different to that shown now. *Distinctiveness* information is concerned with how the person has behaved with other people. Highly distinctive behaviour is when, with our example, Jane has *not* behaved in a similar way to other people. Behaviour low in distinctiveness is where Jane *does* behave in a similar way with others. The final piece of information, *consensus*, concerns how people other than Jane behave towards Anne. In our example, are most other people friendly (high consensus) or not (low consensus) towards Anne? Kelley calls

**Table 7.1** Three types of information – consistency, distinctiveness, and consensus – Kelley suggests people use when making internal or external attributions about the causes of behaviour.

| TYPE OF INFORMATION | QUESTIONS ASKED ABOUT BEHAVIOUR | EXAMPLES |
|---|---|---|
| Consistency | Does the person behave in the same way to the other person at different times? | *High:* Jane nearly always acts in a friendly way towards Anne. *Low:* Jane has rarely acted in a friendly way towards Anne. |
| Distinctiveness | Does the person behave in a similar way to other people? | *High:* Jane does not behave in a friendly way to other people. *Low:* Jane does behave in a friendly way to other people. |
| Consensus | Do other people behave in a similar way to that person? | *High:* Most other people behave in a friendly way towards Anne. *Low:* Not many other people behave in a friendly way towards Anne. |

this a *covariation model* since whether an internal or external attribution is made depends upon how these three pieces of information covary to give an overall picture.

An internal attribution (in our example, 'Jane is a friendly person') would, according to Kelley, result from the following combination of information:

High consistency:      Jane is almost always friendly towards Anne.
Low distinctiveness:   Jane is friendly to most other people
Low consensus:         Not many other people are friendly towards Anne

By contrast, an external or situational attribution (Anne makes others behave in a friendly way towards her) would result from:

High consistency:      Jane is almost always friendly towards Anne.
Low distinctiveness:   Jane is rarely friendly towards other people.
High consensus:        Most other people are friendly towards Anne.

Kelley allows for attributions other than internal or external ones, most notably he suggests that sometimes it is neither just the person or the situation, but a combination of *circumstances* operating solely at that time. A circumstances attribution results from the following combination of information:

Low consistency:       Jane has rarely acted in a friendly way towards Anne in the past.
High distictiveness:   Jane is rarely friendly towards other people.
High consensus:        Most other people are friendly towards Anne.

Given this combination of information it would be inferred that there was some unusual set of circumstances operating, for example, that Jane was drunk or was in a particularly good mood because she had just won a large sum of money, etc.

McArthur (1972) experimentally investigated Kelley's covariation model by giving different subjects different combinations of the types of information given in Table 7.1. Overall, McArthur found support for the combinations of information specified by Kelley under which people make internal, external and circumstances attributions. However, there were findings not quite in accord with the model and which have been important for later research on attributional biases (dealt with later). McArthur found subjects made more internal than external attributions overall. Also, distinctiveness information was perceived to be the most important type of information by subjects, consistency the second most important and consensus the least important. With external attributions distinctiveness was seen as most and consensus as least important. The covariation model says that people use all three types of information equally, McArthur's work suggests this not to be the case.

The covariation model misleadingly suggests that people use only these three types of information, Garland *et al.* (1975) showed that when people are allowed to ask for *any* information they wish, only 23 per cent of requests were for consistency, distinctiveness and consensus information. Twenty-nine per cent of requests were for other types of dispositional (personality traits) information. If you think back to the last chapter we might expect this because people would want more information in line with the 'implicit personality' idea. Garland (1975) also found that 25 per cent of requests were concerned with the other person (in our example, Anne). Whilst the covariation model may accurately characterize how we use consistency, distinctiveness and consensus information it fails to include other information that people find just as important to know when making attributions.

In summary, the covariation model is an elaborate theory for how people perceive the causes of behaviour, but does require a lot of information about the person's past behaviour and about the behaviour of other people. The model also attempts to predict when we will make internal, external and circumstances attributions. However, if we are solely concerned with the more detailed factors regarding when an *internal* attribution is made the correspondent inference model of Jones and Davis is appropriate.

### 7.3.2 Correspondent inference model

Jones and Davis (1965) were concerned to discover precisely the conditions that result in a person making an attribution about another's personality characteristics. The correspondent inference model attempts to account for how the behaviours and intentions behind the behaviours *correspond* to stable and enduring aspects of personality. Two factors are taken into account: the *non-common effects* of a person's behaviour, these are concerned with the distinctive features of behaviour: suppose, for example, you are trying to choose which of three colleges to go to and the important aspects of each college are those shown in Table 7.2. If you chose College A your reason for this choice is unlikely to be that it is far from home or of good academic status, since all three colleges have this in common. The main reason is likely to be the isolated campus as this is the *non-common* aspect of your choice of college. If, however, you chose to go to College C the non-common effect would be the location in a large city, from this it might be inferred that you were a gregarious sort of person. However, before an internal attribution can be made (gregariousness) a second factor needs to be taken into account – the *social desirability* of the behaviour.

Knowledge of the social desirability of the behaviour (in our example, choice of college) is important for two reasons: (a) it is assumed that we intend desirable effects to follow from what we do; (b) people who perform socially desirable acts provide little information about their own personality characteristics since such behaviour does not distinguish one person from the next. To take our college choice example again, if it was the 'in thing' that

**Table 7.2** Common and non-common consequences from choosing which of three (A, B or C) colleges to go to.

| COLLEGE A | COLLEGE B | COLLEGE C |
|---|---|---|
| Isolated campus | In a small town | In a large city |
| Good academic status | Good academic status | Good academic status |
| Far from home | Far from home | Far from home |
| Poor sports facilities | Good sports facilities | Good sports facilities |

year to go to College C, then we can say little about the person who makes the choice, except that he or she wants to be 'in'. If, on the other hand, College C was definitely out of favour, and you chose to go there, we could be reasonably certain, since the choice is low in social desirability, that you like large cities and are a gregarious person.

A correspondent inference (internal attribution) is made, then, when a behaviour is *both* low in social desirability and when there are *few* non-common effects. In terms of the covariation model of Kelley this amounts to behaviour high in distinctiveness with the added knowledge about its social desirability. In a sense Jones and Davis put attribution in a more social context because they consider the variable of social desirability.

## 7.4 Attributional biases

The three attribution models we have just been looking at – causal schemata, covariation and correspondent inference – all assume that people make attributions in a logical and rational way. For example, Kelley's covariation model tells us which combinations of information (consistency, distinctiveness and consensus) *should* result in an internal or an external attribution being made. The correspondent inference model states the conditions under which internal attributions *should* be made. The question arises, however, as to whether people do *actually* make attributions according to these prescriptions or whether they are subject to bias and error in their perception of the causes of behaviour. In this section we shall look at three attribution biases: the fundamental attribution error, actor/observer differences and a self-serving bias.

### 7.4.1 Fundamental attribution error

Findings from MrArthur's (1972) research, described earlier, which tested Kelley's covariation model suggested that people make more dispositional (personality characteristics) than situational attributions. This has been called the *fundamental attribution error* and is defined by Ross (1977) as follows: 'the tendency to underestimate the importance of situational determinants and overestimate the degree to which actions and outcomes reflect the actor's dispositions' (pp. 193-4). People's attributions are in error because forces in the situation are often ignored; the error is a fundamental one since the internal/external division of causes of behaviour is fundamental to the attribution approach.

Ross, Amabile and Steinmetz (1977) investigated this in an experiment where subjects were either assigned the role of 'questioner' or 'answerer' in a general knowledge quiz game. The questioner was asked to make up a number of questions from his or her own general knowledge, and then put them to the other subject to answer. The answerer is at a strong disadvantage here since the questioner can draw on his own idiosyncratic general knowledge. Another group of subjects observed this quiz game and were instructed to pay attention to both the questioner and answerer. After the quiz questioners, answerers and observers rated the general knowledge of the questioner and answerer. It was found that both answerers and observers rated the questioner as having *superior* general knowledge to the contestants. This is a fundamental error since, as Ross *et al.* argue, the perceivers (answerers and observers) ignored the situational determinants (structure of the game) which gave such power to the questioner, and put too much emphasis on the personality characteristics of the questioner when assessing evidence for general knowledge.

Further evidence for the fundamental attribution error is from Bierbrauer (1979) who had subjects watch a re-enactment of Milgram's (1963) famous experiment on obedience to authority (described in Chapter 10). Briefly, Milgram had 'teachers' deliver progressively stronger electric shocks to 'learners'. The teachers, who were subjects, were not actually delivering a shock but led to believe they were. Milgram found all subjects delivered shocks up to 300 volts, as shown in Figure 7.1, with only 12.5 per cent refusing to deliver a 315 volt shock, and 35 per cent refusing to deliver the maximum shock. Milgram put strong social pressures on the teachers to continue delivering shocks, resulting in the teachers' behaviour being strongly influenced by situational (external) factors.

Bierbrauer (1979) asked subjects who watched a re-enactment of one 'teacher' delivering the maximum shock to indicate the percentage of disobedience they thought would occur at various levels of electric shock. As Figure 7.1 shows, subjects consistently *underestimated* the extent to which 'teachers' would yield to situational forces demanding obedience. For example, they thought 60 per cent of the teachers would refuse to give a shock of 300 volts and over 80 per cent would refuse to deliver the maximum shock.

The idea that such results constitute an attributional error has not gone unchallenged. Harvey, Town and Yarkin (1981) argue that in order to say an

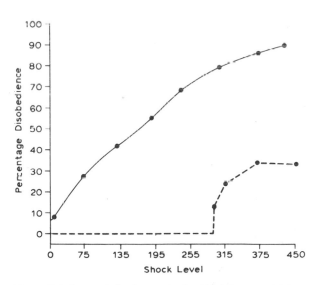

**Figure 7.1** Rates of obedience obtained by Milgram (1964) compared with predicted disobedience rates (continuous line) made by subjects who watched a re-enactment of the Milgram experiment. Adapted from Bierbrauer (1979).

attribution is in error we need first to know what a correct attribution would be. Furthermore, as Locke and Pennington (1982) point out, people from different perspectives may emphasize different reasons for the behaviour which may be justified given the perspective and interests of the attributor.

### 7.4.2 Actor/observer differences

The fundamental attribution error occurs when people attribute causes to *another's* behaviour; however, when we attribute causes to our *own* behaviour we tend to emphasize stiuational factors. This is known as the actor/observer difference: the actor is the person attributing causes (mainly external) to his or her *own* behaviour; the observer is the person attributing causes (mainly internal) to another's behaviour. Actors give largely external and observers internal causes.

Nisbett *et al.* (1973) showed this in an experiment where subjects were asked to explain, both for themselves and a friend, reasons for their chosen course of study at college. Their attributions of reasons for their *own* course of study gave as much emphasis to their own interests and personality traits as to the quality of the courses. However, when explaining why a fried had taken a certain course of study they emphasized dispositional factors.

Why should actor/observer differences occur and is there evidence of bias in such a pattern difference? The differences may arise simply because we have more 'privileged' information when explaining our own rather than another person's behaviour. By this is meant that we know a lot more about how we have acted in the past than how any other person has (even a very close, long-standing friend). It might follow, then, that we would be inclined to say the actor is correct and the observer wrong since the former has more information on which to base the attribution.

Against this, though, we need to remember that the *salience* of causal factors is different for actors and observers. The actor is more sensitive to forces in the environment than his or her own personality characteristics: when in a social situation one is typically more aware of others than oneself. The observer finds the individual more salient since more attention is focused on that person and less on the surrounding social situation (Taylor and Fiske, 1975).

If this line of argument is valid we would predict that *any* technique which changes what is salient for actor and observer would result in a corresponding change in attributions made. Storms (1973) showed actor/observer attributions could be *reversed* by showing the actor a videotape of him or herself. In this experiment two subjects took part in a conversation and two observers watched – one observer watched one subject and one the other subject. Storms videotaped the conversation and played it back to subjects in one of two ways. Half the subjects (actors who were the subjects in conversation and observers) saw the same videotape to that which they saw live. That is, the actor saw a videotape of the person he was in conversation with, the observer saw the person he was originally assigned to watch. This is the *same orientation* condition of the experiment. The other half of the subjects saw a videotape from the *opposite* orientation. That is, actors watched *themselves* in conversation and observers watched the person they had been instructed *not* to watch initially in the 'live' conversation. There was also a control group of subjects who watched only the live conversation but not the video playback. All subjects were then asked to rate the extent to which friendliness, nervousness and dominance of the person they watched initially or themselves was due to either dispositional or situational factors.

Figure 7.2 summarizes the results: it shows, first, that the traditional actor/observer difference is present in the control condition, as expected. Second, subjects who saw the videotape in the *same* orientation produced even greater actor/observer differences (actors gave more external and observers more internal attributions). Third, and most importantly, subjects who were in the *opposite* orientation for the video playback *reversed* the traditional attributional difference. Actors tended to see their behaviour strongly in dispositional terms and observers in situational terms. Similar results have been found by Regan and Totten (1975) simply by asking subjects to empathize with the person they were assigned to observe.

It would appear, then, that in the normal course of events actors emphasize situational and observers dispositional factors when making attributions. *Anything* which forces a change of perspective on the attributor is likely to

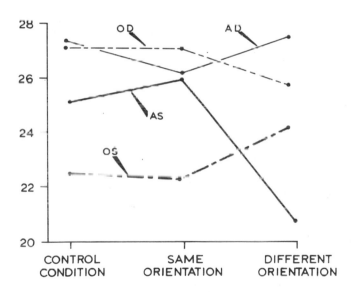

AD  *Dispositional Attributions by Actors*
AS  *Situational Attributions by Actors*
OD  *Dispositional Attributions by Observers*
OS  *Situational Attributions by Observers*

**Figure 7.2** Situational and dispositional attributions made by actors and observers in the same or different orientation. Higher numbers indicate greater attributions. Notice the *greater* situational attributions for observers in different orientation and *lesser* situational attributions for actors in different orientation. Adapted from Storms (1973).

result in the perceptions of the causes of behaviour being changed to accord with the new perspective.

### 7.4.3 Self-serving bias

A self-serving bias is where people attribute causes to their own or others' behaviour in such a way as to enhance their abilities and/or preserve their self-esteem. For example, people who experience success at some task might attribute that success to personal (internal) characteristics such as ability and effort. By contrast, people who experience failure may attribute the failure to external factors such as task difficulty and bad luck. With the former a person is saying he or she is responsible for that success but with the latter the person is saying that it is not his or her fault. If you had just failed an exam your self-esteem would be 'dented', to bolster your opinion of yourself it would be self-serving to think and claim that the examination paper was a particularly hard one that year (external attribution).

Initial support for a self-serving bias in attribution came from Johnson *et al.* (1964) who used educational psychology students as subjects and asked them to teach arithmetic to two pupils. The students were then told one pupil had performed well and one poorly on test. Students were then asked to teach more arithmetic to the same two pupils. Subsequently the subjects were told that the pupil who had done well the first time had continued to do so, the pupil who had done badly the first time had either (a) continued to perform badly or (b) improved. Students were then asked to account for the performance of the two pupils. It was found that the student-teachers attributed improved performance in the initially poor pupil to themselves and continued poor performance to the pupil.

However, later research using experienced rather than student teachers failed to produce consistent findings. Ross *et al.* (1974) had professional teachers coach 11-year olds to spell words correctly which are often misspelt. Teachers were then informed that the pupil had done very well or very badly on a subsequent spelling test. The teachers were then asked to indicate how important they thought teaching ability and scholastic ability of the pupil were in determining the pupil's test performance. As Table 7.3 shows, teachers who were told their pupil performed badly thought teaching ability *more* important than scholastic ability of the pupil. By contrast, teachers who were told pupils had done well thought the pupils' ability to be more

**Table 7.3** Ratings by teachers of the importance of teaching and pupil's scholastic ability after their pupil had either succeeded or failed at a spelling test. The higher the number the more that factor was deemed important by teachers. Adapted from Ross *et al.* (1974)

|  | PUPIL PERFORMANCE | |
|---|---|---|
|  | *Success at the spelling test* | *Failure at the spelling test* |
| *Teaching ability* | 7.1 | 8.2 |
| *Pupil's scholastic ability* | 9.1 | 7.5 |

important than the teaching they received.

Other research has pointed out the importance of *expectations* in attributing success or failure. Feather (1969), for example, showed that subjects who expected to be either successful or unsuccessful at an anagram-solving task tended to make *internal* attributions. When people were led to believe they had performed in ways opposite to their expectations attributions tended to be external in nature.

Much more could be said about when people do and do not exhibit self-serving biases, the main point to result from this brief survey of research is that evidence is less than consistent and requires other factors such as expectations, and previous experience to be taken into account. Of the three attribution biases discussed in this section it should be apparent that evidence is weakest and more controversial for self-serving biases than for the fundamental attribution error or actor/observer differences.

## 7.5 Personality differences

The concern so far in this chapter has been to discover the conditions under which *all* people make internal and external attributions. At the beginning of the chapter we saw that people attribute internal and external causes in order to make the social world a more predictable place in which to live: being in a position to predict how other people will behave has the implication that a certain amount of *control* is possible. The two themes of control and internal/external attributions are claimed to constitute a single personality dimension, suggested by Rotter (1966), and called *Locus of Control*.

Rotter suggested that some people perceive behaviour (both theirs and others') to be largely under external control – called 'external locus of control'. This means that people who fall towards the 'internal' end of the locus of control personality dimension see their own behaviour as controllable by themselves. Hence, the consequences of certain behaviours, such as success or failure at an examination, pleasure or pain, are perceived to result from what they do. By contrast, people who are 'external' perceive themselves to have little control over how they are, what they do and the consequences which follow their actions. So, for example, success or failure at an examination would not be attributed to effort and ability (internal) but more to other people's behaviour (good teachers) and/or chance or luck (the right questions came up), both external attributions.

A personality questionnaire was developed by Rotter (1966) which consisted of 29 items, five of which are given in Table 7.4. You may wish to see if you are an 'internal' or 'external', to do this, circle the option in each question, either (a) or (b), which most accurately represents your views. The notes given in the caption to Table 7.4 tell you how to score each item and how to find out where you might be on this personality dimension (remember this is only an indication).

The theory Rotter used in developing the idea of locus of control was not derived from the attribution tradition of Heider but from the *behaviourist* tradition in which all behaviour is seen as a product of either *reinforcement* and *punishment*. Rotter originally called the scale the 'internal versus external control of reinforcement', emphasizing the point that it is the

**Table 7.4** Examples of items from Rotter's (1966) Locus of Control Scale questionnaire. To score yourself simply add up the number of times you agreed with a statement (a or b) which is underlined. A score of 5 (maximum here) indicates *external* locus of control, a score of 0 (minimum) indicates *internal* locus of control.

---

ITEMS ON THE LOCUS OF CONTROL SCALE

---

1   a   Many of the unhappy things in people's lives are partly due to bad luck.
   b   People's misfortunes result from the mistakes they make.

2   a   In the long run people get the respect they deserve in this world.
   b   Unfortunately, an individual's worth often passes unrecognized no matter how hard
     he tries.

3   a   In the case of the well-prepared student there is rarely if ever such a thing as an unfair
     test.
   b   Many times exam questions tend to be so unrelated to coursework that studying is
     really useless.

4   a   In my case getting what I want has little or nothing to do with luck.
   b   Many times we might just as well decide what to do by flipping a coin.

5   a   Sometimes I can't understand how teachers arrive at the grades they give.
   b   There is a direct connection between how hard I study and the grades I get.

---

internal or external control of reinforcement that was of central concern. Fortunately, the idea of internal versus external locus of control has readily lent itself to an attribution approach. We shall see, later in this chapter, how it may apply to both the understanding and treatment of depression. Locus of control has been widely related to understanding how people attribute responsibility; Phares and Wilson (1972) found that people who were 'internals' perceived a driver of a car to be more responsible for an accident than people who scored as 'externals'. Phares *et al.* (1971) showed that when there was no obvious explanation available for subjects to attribute exam failure to, internals blamed themselves whilst externals blamed situational factors.

One area of importance for perception of locus of control is that of health. Wallston and Wallston (1978) have shown that people who believe themselves to be in control of their health generally (as opposed to the control being with professionals such as doctors, consultants, etc.) tend to cope better with chronic illnesses such as diabetes. This is a fairly new area for attribution theory to enter into but one which, in all probability, will grow as it reflects a general consciousness among people that they need to take 'charge' of themselves and be more involved with their own well-being. Further support for this comes from the growing number of self-help groups ranging from self-help groups for cancer sufferers to victims of incest. The message seems to be that no matter what misfortune might befall you in life, if you feel in control of yourself you are going to be in a better position to cope than if you feel out of control, perceiving the control to reside with other people or factors in the environment external to yourself.

## 7.6 Attributions in a social context

The attribution approach has, up to now, been characterized as an attempt to understand how *one* person attributes causes to *another* person or himself. Such an approach ignores many social aspects of everyday life, hence it is of relevance and interest to ask whether social groupings or social categories affect the attributional process: for example, do people who belong to a particular social group (such as class, race, etc.) differ in the attributions they make about people they know belong to their own group and people who belong to other groups? We might expect consistent differences in the light of the research discussed in Chapter 5 on intergroup relations and social identity. There it emerged, you may remember, that members of *ingroups* favour themselves at the expense of the *outgroups*. From this it might be predicted that people will make 'self-enhancing' or 'ingroup-enhancing' attributions to the ingroup.

A number of studies have investigated this idea (see Hewstone and Jaspers, 1984, for a summary), the variables to have received most attention are skin colour, schooling and religious groupings. Taylor and Jaggi (1974) conducted an experiment in southern India using Hindus as subjects. Hindus were asked to make attributions to a person either of their own religion or a different religion (Moslem). The target of the attribution was described as being treated in a socially desirable way (praised by a teacher) to half the subjects and a socially undesirable way (scolded by a teacher) to the other half of the subjects. The design of the experiment and results are summarized in Table 7.5. It was found that Hindus tended to make internal attributions (ingroup enhancing) to other Hindus who were treated in a socially desirable way and external attributions for Hindus who were treated in a socially undesirable way. By contrast, attributions to Moslems were the reverse of this, for example, socially desirable treatment of Moslems was attributed to external factors. Overall, the pattern of results supports the idea that attributions are made so as to enhance the ingroup and degrade the outgroup. Unfortunately, the study is flawed since Taylor and Jaggi did *not* get Moslem subjects to make attributions about members of their own and other (Hindu) religions.

Duncan (1976) asked white subjects to make attributions about violent behaviour perpetrated by either a black or white person on either a black or white victim. Subjects were shown a videotape of two males talking (one black, one white), the conversation became heated and resulted in one person violently pushing the other. Half the subjects saw a videotape where the 'pusher' was black, and half where the 'pusher' was white. Subjects were

**Table 7.5** Design of the experiment by Taylor and Jaggi (1974) and types of attributions made according to religion of target person and how that person was treated.

| RELIGION OF TARGET PERSON | | TYPE OF ATTRIBUTION MADE |
|---|---|---|
| *Hindu* | Socially desirable | Internal |
| | Socially undesirable | External |
| *Moslem* | Socially desirable | External |
| | Socially undesirable | Internal |

asked to make attributions about the perpetrator of the violent act. Results indicated that white subjects made external attributions (pusher was provoked, etc.) when the pusher was white, and internal (violent personality, etc.) when the pusher was black.

Finally, a study by Hewstone and Jaspers (1982) investigated how working-class West Indian and white youths made attributions for racial discrimination towards blacks. Subjects could make either internal negative attributions about blacks or 'system' (external) attributions reflecting the exercise of social authority. Black subjects, as predicted, tended to attribute discrimination more to the 'white system' and less to dispositions of blacks. By contrast, white subjects did *not* perceive blacks to be more responsible for discrimination than whites. Overall, both types of subjects tended to attribute the cause to the 'system' and not internal dispositions, a finding which, perhaps, reflects more the working-class nature of the subjects than anything else.

We have looked at a number of experiments dealing with the effect of social groupings or social categorization on attributions. Generally, results support the idea, as expected from work on intergroup relations (Chapter 5), that people tend to make attributions which enhance the value of the ingroup. The attempt to make the attribution approach more social has, then, distinct implications for increasing our understanding of prejudice and conflict.

## 7.7 Application – depression

Depression is something we all suffer from at times – it varies in intensity from just having the 'blues' or feeling a little down to chronic states where a person sees the whole world as a useless evil place in which to live and has little or no self-esteem or feeling of self-worth. Attribution theorists and clinical psychologists have developed a model and therapy for understanding and treating depression (Abraham and Martin, 1981). Before going into this it is important to bear in mind that the approach applies only to what is called '*unipolar*' depression, not '*bipolar*' depression. Bipolar depression is where an individual *alternates* between periods of depression and mania; unipolar depression is where somebody only has depressive episodes with *no* history or indication of mania.

The approach has been developed from the 'learned helplessness' model of depression (Seligman, 1975) which states that depressed people believe themselves to have little or no control over what happens to them in their lives. This makes people feel helpless, becomes a normal way of viewing oneself, and results in people being unable to help themselves. However, lowered self-esteem is also an important aspect of depression which the learned helplessness model fails to account for on its own. This was reformulated in attribution terms, and Abramson *et al.* (1978) suggested that *how* people make attributions for this *lack of control* over what happens to them in their lives has important consequences for their depressive state in general and their self-esteem in particular.

Weiner's (1979) model for success and failure at school performance was considered appropriate to apply to depression. This model has three attributional dimensions as follows:

| | | | |
|---|---|---|---|
| (i) internal/external | : | whether the behaviour is attributed to the person or the environment. | |
| (ii) stable/unstable | : | whether the perceived cause of the behaviour is a constant or changing feature of the person or environment. | |
| (iii) global/specific | : | whether the perceive cause is specific to that behaviour or occurs in many different aspects of a person's life. | |

An example may clarify these dimensions: imagine you have just broken up with your girlfriend/boyfriend and you are very depressed by this, how might you attribute the cause of the break-up of the relationship? Abraham and Martin (1981) suggest that a person who was chronically depressed would give an internal, stable and global attribution which might be as follows:

| Chronic depression at break up of the relationship | (i) internal attribution | it's my fault | results in lowering of self-esteem |
|---|---|---|---|
| | (ii) stable attribution | that's the way I will always be | results in lack of motivation to change |
| | (iii) global attribution | that's how I am with everybody | results in lack of motivation to change |

Such an *attributional style* for a *negative* event means that (a) self-esteem would be very low (I am not worth knowing, I always cause arguments); (b) you would think you were unable to control this in the future (I'm never going to be worth knowing because I will always cause arguments); and (c) that this will happen no matter who you are with (I'm like this with everybody).

For a *positive* event (success at forming an enduring relationship, for example) a depressed person's attributional style would be to make an external, unstable and non-global attribution. The external attribution might be – 'the relationship works because she always gives in to me'; the unstable attribution – 'the good things only result from her being in a good mood'; the non-global attribution – 'this relationship would not work with anybody else.' The depressive person makes attributions such that negative things are seen as his or her own fault and good things to result only from other people's efforts. Together they result in the individual believing him or herself to be helpless in bringing about positive things in life and viewing himself as of very little worth.

Seligman *et al.* (1979) developed a questionnaire for assessing a person's *attributional style*. This questionnaire presents a person with 12 different hypothetical situations. For each situation the person has to say what the major causes would be, then, on 7-point scales, a question relating to each of the three dimensions – internal/external, stable/unstable and global/specific – has to be answered. The person has also to indicate, again on a 7-point scale, how important each of the 12 situations would be for him or her. This latter is included as attributional style is only significant for what people

**Table 7.6**  Attribution Style questionnaire from Seligman *et al.* (1979).

HYPOTHETICAL SITUATIONS

(a) *Positive Achievement Items*
   (i)   You become very rich
   (ii)  You apply for a job (college place) that you badly want and get it
   (iii) You get a raise

(b) *Negative Achievement Items*
   (iv)  You have been looking for a job unsuccessfully for some time
   (v)   You give an important talk in front of a group and the audience reacts negatively
   (vi)  You can't get all the work done that others expect of you.

(c) *Positive Interpersonal Items*
   (vii)  You meet a friend who compliments you on your appearance
   (viii) Your spouse (boyfriend/girlfriend) has been treating you more lovingly
   (ix)   You do a project which is highly praised

(d) *Negative Interpersonal Items*
   (x)   A friend comes to you with a problem and you don't try to help him
   (xi)  You meet a friend who acts hostilely toward you
   (xii) You go out on a date and it goes badly

QUESTIONS ASKED ABOUT EACH ITEM

(i)   Write down *one* major cause . . . . . . . . . . . . . . . . . . . . . . . . . . .
(ii)  Is the cause of your friend's compliment due to something about you or something about the other person or circumstances? (Circle one number)

| Totally due to the other person or circumstance | 1 | 2 | 3 | 4 | 5 | 6 | 7 | Totally due to me |
|---|---|---|---|---|---|---|---|---|

(iii) In the future when you are with your friends, will this cause again be present? (Circle one number)

| Will never again be present | 1 | 2 | 3 | 4 | 5 | 6 | 7 | Will always be present |
|---|---|---|---|---|---|---|---|---|

(iv)  Is the cause something that just affects interacting with friends or does it also influence other areas of your life? (Circle one number)

| Influences just this particular situation | 1 | 2 | 3 | 4 | 5 | 6 | 7 | Influences all situations in my life |
|---|---|---|---|---|---|---|---|---|

(v)   How important would this situation be if it happened to you? (Circle one number)

| Not at all important | 1 | 2 | 3 | 4 | 5 | 6 | 7 | Extremely important |
|---|---|---|---|---|---|---|---|---|

consider to be important in their lives. Table 7.6 gives each of the 12 items and the set of questions a person would have to answer about each.

Knowing the attributional style of a depressed person (along the lines described earlier) offers suggestions for a therapy aimed at changing how a person thinks about the world generally and makes attributions about behaviour in particular. Abramson and Martin (1981) suggest *four* ways in which depressives need to change their approach and thinking about the world. First, the most important task for the therapist is to *reverse* how the person perceives control over the outcomes of his or her behaviour – the person has to be encouraged to think and believe that he or she *can control* what happens. This should result in a change in attributional style from, for example, internal, stable and global for negative events (such as the ones on the questionnaire in Table 7.6) to external, non-global and unstable. The change from helplessness to believing one can help oneself is crucial. Second, depressives must set themselves *realistic* goals in life rather than unattainable goals – the latter often occurs as it serves to perpetuate the feeling of helplessness. Third, the importance of unattainable, but often desirable, goals must be *decreased*; the therapist must try to make the person find attainable goals rather than unattainable goals desirable and attractive. Fourth, in feeling helplessness the depressive perceives other people to have control; this has to be changed to a more healthy balanced position whereby the amount of control another is perceived to have is at most only equal to the amount of control one perceives oneself to have.

Whilst this particular attribution approach, developed from Weiner's (1979) model, makes sensible and relatively clearcut suggestions for therapy, as with most things results of treating depressives in this way have not been convincingly effective. For example, although depressives do seem to improve as a result of such a therapy it is not clear whether each of the three dimensions (internal/external, global/non-global, stable/unstable) needs to be taken into account or whether just one is most important. It has been suggested that the controllability of behaviour (i.e. the internal/external dimension) is the really crucial one to be worked on with depressives. Evidence shows that reversal from external to internal for positive events, and internal to external for negative events, is most effective in increasing self-esteem and alleviating depression. This is still a matter of controversy, though, and future research will be needed to clarify the position.

## 7.8 Summary

O The attribution approach is concerned with how the ordinary person attributes causes to his or her own behaviour and the behaviour of other people.

O Heider laid the conceptual foundations by claiming that people perceived behaviour as being caused and that the cause was either something to do with the person (internal) or something to do with the social situation (external).

O The causal schemata model of attribution applies when we have information about a person behaving on only one occasion. The covariation model requires knowledge about how a person has behaved in the past (consistency), in different situations (distinctiveness) and how other people behave (consensus). The correspondent inference model looks at non-common effects of behaviour and social desirability of that behaviour to determine conditions for making internal attributions.

O Three attributional biases were described: (i) actor/observer differences: actors give more external and observers more internal attributions. (ii) the fundamental attribution error: the tendency for people generally to give internal attributions when external ones might be more appropriate. (iii) self-serving bias: people give attributions for success and failure, for example, which serve to enhance or maintain their self-esteem.

O Rotter developed the 'locus of control' personality dimension in which some people perceive behaviour to be caused by internal factors and others perceive behaviour to result from external causes.

O The social context affects the types of attributions made. Attributions to ingroups tend to enhance and attributions to outgroups tend to devalue that group.

O The idea of 'learned helplessness' has been reformulated in terms of Weiner's attribution model, this consists of three dimensions (internal/external, stable/unstable, and global/specific). Depressives have a particular attributional style – for positive events: external, unstable, non-global; for negative events: internal, stable, global. Therapy is based on trying to change and reverse these perceptions.

## 7.9 Suggestions for further reading

Schneider, D.J. Hastorf, A.M. and Ellsworth, P.C. *Person Perception*, (Reading, Mass, Addison-Wesley, 1979).
Fairly advanced text, up to date and the best book to go to if you want to take a much more detailed look at the full breadth and depth of the attribution approach.

Shaver, K.G. *An Introduction to Attribution Processes*, (Cambridge, Mass, Wintrop, 1975).
Good, brief introduction to the attribution approach, traces some of the historical developments and relates attribution to the general field of perception well.

Tedeschi, J.T. and Lindskold, S. *Social Psychology: Interdependence, Interaction and Influence*, (New York, Wiley & Sons, 1976).
Advanced introductory text to social psychology generally. Chapter 4 provides a thorough treatment of the attributional approach. Best place to start if you want to read more about the area.

Wegner, D.M. and Vallacher, R.R. *Implicit Psychology: An Introduction to Social Cognition*, (New York, OUP, 1977).
Excellent introduction to the issues covered in this and the next chapter. The first source to go to if you wish to explore the issues raised in this chapter more fully and more broadly.

# 8

# Interpersonal attraction

8.1    Introduction
8.2    Need for other people
       *8.2.1 Total isolation    8.2.2 Social isolation    8.2.3 Fear and affiliation*
8.3    Formation of relationships
       *8.3.1 Physical attractiveness    8.3.2 Proximity    8.3.3 Reciprocity    8.3.4 Similarity*
8.4    Development of relationships
       *8.4.1 Byrne-Clore reinforcement model    8.4.2 Balance theory*
       *8.4.3 Social exchange    8.4.4 Self-disclosure*
8.5    Intimate relationships
       *8.5.1 Companionate love    8.5.2 Romantic love*
8.6    Summary
8.7    Suggestions for further reading

## 8.1  Introduction

Why are we attracted to some people, repelled by others and indifferent to many? Is love ineffable and incapable of being understood or explained? What causes friendships to turn to hatred or love to hate? These, perhaps, are some of the questions often asked of social psychologists interested in interpersonal attraction and constitute some of the issues explored in this chapter.

Interpersonal attraction may be defined as 'an individual's tendency or predisposition to evaluate another person in a positive way' (Walster and Walster, 1976). In the broadest sense, then, interpersonal attraction is a specific type of attitude. Attitudes, as we saw in Chapter 4, are predispositions to behave and are made up of beliefs and values. This definition of interpersonal attraction means there are implications for how a person thinks, feels and behaves towards someone he or she is attracted to. How a person thinks and feels (positive evaluation of the other person) and behaves (seeking the other's company, avoiding conflict, etc.) should, as discussed in Chapter 4, conform to the principle of consistency.

However, such a definition does not offer any characterization of the range of relationships that people engage in, nor does it capture the range of intensities of feelings that people have for others. Levinger (1974) offers a useful way of conceptualizing both the range of relationships that exist and the way relationships develop from acquaintance to friendship or love. As shown in Figure 8.1, Levinger views relationships between two people as progressing through four levels. At the first level there is no contact between two people: the two people do not even know of each other's existence. This is the state of affairs for most of humanity since we only form relationships with

147

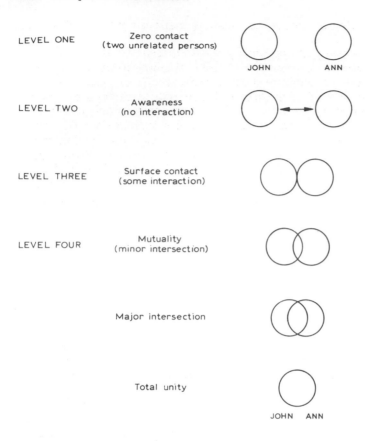

LEVEL ONE    Zero contact
(two unrelated persons)

JOHN        ANN

LEVEL TWO    Awareness
(no interaction)

LEVEL THREE    Surface contact
(some interaction)

LEVEL FOUR    Mutuality
(minor intersection)

Major intersection

Total unity

JOHN  ANN

**Figure 8.1**  Levels of relatedness between two people. Adapted from Levinger (1974).

very, very few of the total population. At the second level two people become aware of one another, this is before any interaction takes place. It is a crucial point since factors such as physical attractiveness, perceived similarity of attitudes, etc. determine whether interaction will take place and a relationship form. If each person feels circumstances to be right they proceed to level three – that of surface contact. Here each person begins to find out about the other in terms of such things as likes and dislikes, beliefs, values, etc. These first two levels are to do with the *formation of relationships* which will be discussed in more detail later in the chapter. Level four, mutuality, is concerned with the *development of relationships*. Levinger characterizes this on a continuum ranging from acquaintance (minor intersection) to strong friendship (major intersection) to deep and enduring love (total unity). A section in this chapter discusses social psychological variables affecting whether a relationship will develop further or remain at a given level. A later section deals with more intimate relationships – companionate and romantic love – where major theories together with experimental evidence will be discussed. Levinger (1974) proposes a useful framework for thinking about how two people relate to one another and how relationships may mature and develop.

Attempts to measure interpersonal attraction, apart from arousing suspicion and distaste in some people, present similar difficulties to those encountered in trying to measure attitudes generally. Techniques of attitude measurement were described in Chapter 4, here only an example of a direct and indirect approach will be given. The direct approach, simply asking how one person feels about another, is best exemplified by Byrne's (1971) *Interpersonal Judgement Scale*. This scale measures how one person views another in terms of intelligence, general knowledge, current affairs and three measures of attraction. These three are (a) personal feelings of like or dislike; (b) feelings about working with the other person; and (c) romantic attraction. Each are measured on seven-point scales, that for romantic attraction is as follows:

1  very sexually unattractive,
2  sexually unattractive,
3  slightly sexually unattractive,
4  neither particularly sexually attractive or unattractive,
5  slightly sexually attractive,
6  sexually attractive,
7  very sexually attractive.

To find out how much a person is attracted to another a subject would simply circle the number which most closely expressed how he or she felt. The higher the score on each of the three scales measuring interpersonal attraction the greater the attraction felt for the other person.

*Unobtrusive* or indirect measures offer a useful complement to the direct approach or a replacement where it is impractical to administer such a questionnaire. The amount of eye-contact, for example, that two people engage in, amount of touching and interpersonal distance (see Chapter 9) are often good guides as to whether two people like each other or not. Rubin (1970) found lovers to engage in much more eye-contact than strangers; Bryne, Ervin and Lamberth (1970) found couples stood closer together the more they liked each other.

With Levinger's (1974) conceptualization of relationships and knowledge of how psychologists go about measuring interpersonal attraction we are in a position to look at how relationships form and develop. Before doing this, however, it will prove useful and of interest to consider why people may need others and how they fare when alone.

## 8.2  Need for other people

Other people provide us with rewards and when they do so we subsequently seek their presence. The rewards others provide us with take many forms – for example, increase in self-esteem, reassurance when frightened or anxious, comfort when sad or depressed, increase in our enjoyment of life. Most of these functions we take for granted and later in this section we will consider experimental confirmation of the rewards others provide. This does not necessarily imply we need other people's company: psychologically a need is a fundamental requirement that an individual must satisfy in order to continue existing. Food and water are obvious needs, but do people need stimulation generally and other people specifically? To answer these questions we will look at research on being alone: this falls into two categories (a) isolation from *all* stimuli, and (b) isolation from other people only.

### 8.2.1  Total isolation

The most extreme and the most distressing form of isolation is where an individual is not only isolated from other people but from *all* sensory stimuli. Total isolation has been used as an effective means of torture for many thousands of years. However, simply locking somebody in a dark room does not isolate them totally from their environment – the person can still smell, feel and hear noises. To know more precisely the effects of total isolation scientifically controlled conditions are required. Bexton, Heron and Scott (1954) recruited subjects from an American university and paid them to do nothing for as long as they possibly could. Each subject was put in a separate room which was comfortable, of even temperature, contained no television, radio, stereo, or books, but did have some chairs and a bed. There were no windows in the room, the floor was thickly carpeted and the air was conditioned. Subjects wore frosted glasses so that they could not see anything distinctly, they wore ear muffs to deaden sounds and their hands were gloved with thick mittens In short they could not see, hear or touch anything. Subjects were then left until they asked to be removed from these conditions back to the normal world.

   Bexton *et al.* found three days to be the maximum subjects could last, the majority, however, lasted less than 24 hours. Effects of total isolation were dramatic – inducing a transient psychosis and temporary mental disturbances such as hallucinations, disorientation and confusion of thought. Those who lasted longest seemed to set themselves mental tasks such as playing chess in their head. Generally, people seem ill-equipped to deal with such isolation. This is perhaps not surprising since the human nervous system has evolved to respond to *change* in the environment. Deprive people of change (increases and decreases in light, colour changes, sound changes, etc.) and the nervous system *makes up* or invents its own stimulation in the form of hallucinations. Our nervous system needs stimulation, without it we quite literally go mad!

### 8.2.2  Social isolation

Personal accounts from people, who for one reason or another, have experienced extended periods of social isolation attest to how unpleasant the experience is. Religious hermits, prisoners of war and castaways all seem to report an early 'unbearable period' followed by apathy which is often accompanied by dreams and hallucinations about other people. Daniel Defoe's *Robinson Crusoe* provides a compelling, though fictional account, of what it must be like to be alone. How well do people fare, though, if asked to remain alone for as long as possible?

   Schachter (1959) put subjects into rooms where they were removed from the presence of other people but *not* deprived of physical stimulation: they were allowed books, etc. and their visual, auditory and tactile senses were not impaired. Of five subjects one lasted for only two hours, three for two days, and one for eight days, before asking to return to the normal world. Compared to results from research on total isolation people seem, generally, to be able to tolerate social isolation for longer.

Schachter found similar symptoms to be displayed by those in social isolation as those in total isolation: three trends characterizing social isolation seem to occur:

(a) Most people's first reaction is that being away from others is unbearable. This pain decreases and is often followed by withdrawal, a general feeling of apathy and, in more extreme cases, schizophrenic reactions may be observed.
(b) People's thoughts, both whilst awake and asleep, seem to be dominated by other people: they think, dream and hallucinate about others.
(c) Differences in the ability to cope relate less to personality differences and more to the extent to which they are able to set themselves goals, instituting regimes, etc. People successful at this suffer less and are less likely to become apathetic.

Research on social isolation, whilst demonstrating how disturbing being alone is, does not indicate why the absence of other people is painful. Have we been socialized to find the company of others comforting or have we evolved as social animals and hence have an instinct to be in the company of others? Experiments on primates other than humans, for example Harlow and Harlow (1959) described in Chapter 2, suggest a firm biological basis to the need we experience for the presence of others. Humans are more affected by their social environment so the extent of biological influences is more difficult to ascertain.

In summary, research on isolation (both total and social) supports the view that people require stimulation generally and the presence of others in particular. Given that people need other people what is that others provide? Is the mere presence of others rewarding and desirable in certain circumstances? It is to such questions that we now turn.

### 8.2.3 Fear and affiliation

Schachter (1959) demonstrated that people in whom fear had been induced preferred, when given the choice, the presence of other people rather than being alone. Schachter obtained volunteers for an experiment who were told it was concerned with investigating the effects of electric shocks. Half the subjects were allocated to a *high-fear* condition in which vivid and anxiety raising descriptions of the pain and consequences of the electric shocks were given. The other half of the subjects were in a *low-fear* condition where they were told that the electric shocks were mild, not painful and that they would only experience a tickling sensation. Schachter then assessed the desire subjects had to affiliate with other people. This was done by telling subjects there would be a 10-minute delay to receiving electric shocks as the equipment had to be wired up. During this delay they were asked whether they preferred waiting in a room alone, waiting with others or had no preference. Results are

**Table 8.1** Percentages of subjects choosing to wait with others, alone or having no preference in the high and low fear conditions of Schachter's (1959) study on fear and affiliation.

| EXPERIMENTAL CONDITION | CHOICE OF WAITING CONDITIONS | | |
| --- | --- | --- | --- |
| | *With other* | *Alone* | *No preference* |
| *High fear* | 63% | 10% | 27% |
| *Low fear* | 33% | 7% | 60% |

shown in Table 8.1. As you can see, the majority of subjects in the 'high-fear' condition preferred to wait with others whilst less than a third in the 'low-fear' condition preferred this option.

A refinement of this experiment showed that people do not simply desire the presence of others but prefer to be with others who are in the same predicament. Schachter offered the following choices to a group of subjects in the high-fear condition:

either (a) waiting alone or with others taking part in the same experiment
or (b) waiting alone or with other people who had nothing to do with the experiment.

Sixty per cent of the subjects preferred to wait with others in the same experiment, no subject wished to wait with other people who had nothing to do with the experiment.

Sarnoff and Zimbardo (1961) showed the presence of others is desirable when people are fearful but not when people feel anxious. (Fear is a response to an event which has happened and anxiety is the emotional response to the expectation of a future event.) They found highly anxious people preferred to wait alone in a modified version of Schachter's (1959) experiment.

Schachter proposed that fear induces people to affiliate for two reasons: first, others act directly to reduce the fear felt by providing comfort and reassurance; and second, to provide a means by which to evaluate oneself and what it is appropriate to feel and do in the situation.

In summary, having established that people find it extremely unpleasant and psychologically disturbing to live in isolation, we also find that people have a particular desire to be in the company of similar others when fearful. Given that we need and desire other people for those and many other reasons, what determines whom we form relationships with?

## 8.3  Formation of relationships

We do not form relationships with everybody we find attractive: often people we find attractive or desirable do not reciprocate our feeling, if they do this may form the basis of a lasting friendship. In attempting to understand and explain who we actually form relationships with, social psychologists have focused attention on four main variables – physical attractiveness, proximity, reciprocity and similarity.

### 8.3.1 Physical attractiveness

It is hardly surprising to learn that a person's physical appearance has a strong influence on interpersonal attraction. Although beauty is, to some extent, in the eye of the beholder there does seem to be broad agreement as to what constitutes a beautiful woman or handsome man in a particular culture at a particular time. Physical attractiveness is important, but since only very few people are viewed as being very attractive it is obvious that not everybody can or indeed does form relationships with such people. It has been suggested (Berscheid and Walster, 1978) that people form relationships, particularly intimate ones, with people who are similar in physical attractiveness to themselves. This is called the *matching hypothesis*; it means that very attractive people tend to form relationships with each other, as do moderately attractive, unattractive and ugly people. This is an example of *equity theory* (looked at in more detail later in this chapter), which, baldly stated, says that people get 'what they think they deserve out of life' (Berscheid and Walster, 1978, p. 126). According to equity theory, for a relationship to form (and endure) each person must offer the other enough benefits to make it worthwhile to stay together.

Walster *et al.* (1966) experimentally investigated the matching hypothesis by recruiting over 700 students to attend a dance at which they would be assigned a partner by computer matching. Subjects were led to believe they were being computer matched as they filled out a number of personality and intelligence questionnaires, in fact Walster *et al.* assigned partners at random. Each student was rated in terms of physical attractiveness by four of Walster's colleagues. It was predicted that the more physically attractive a student was the more he or she would expect the partner to be physically attractive. Results confirmed this but did not show that the greater the match in attractiveness between the two partners the more likely the relationship was to endure. It was found that physically attractive partners were liked more regardless of the other person's own physical attractiveness.

A study by Berscheid *et al.* provided stronger support for the matching hypothesis. When people were allowed to choose their partners and knew that that partners might reject them, the more attractive men chose more attractive women for a date. The study also showed that because of the possibility of rejection subjects lowered their aspirations and chose a partner whom they thought would agree to a date with them.

Silverman (1971) provided further support for the matching hypothesis in a study where observers rated the physical attractiveness of couples who were actually going out with each other. The greater the degree of physical attractiveness existing between the two people the more physical intimacy (touching, kissing, holding hands) was displayed.

In summary, physical appearance is an important factor in interpersonal attraction, however, when it actually comes to forming relationships an equity or matching principle seems to operate.

### 8.3.2 Proximity

Do we actively choose our friends and/or partners or do circumstances where people are 'thrown together' exert a strong influence on the formation of relationships? Research tends to show that we form relationships with people we are in close proximity with, and that stronger relationships are formed with those we live nearer to or work with at school, college, etc.

Proximity (or propinquity as it is often called) can be of two types: (a) the *actual* physical distance that exists between two people; and (b) the *functional* distance between two people. The latter is the more important for the formation of relationships since we may actually be physically close to somebody but functionally distant. For example, sitting in a classroom the person to your side (left or right) may often be the same distance away from the person behind you but you are more likely to interact, and hence form a relationship with a person to your side. Interpersonal communication is easier with the person to your left or right; it is functionally easier to interact and functionally hard to interact with the person behind you, even though *physical* distance may be the same.

Festinger, Schachter and Back (1950) showed how the architecture of a housing project for married students exerted a strong influence over formation of friendships. The houses were arranged in U-shaped courts such that all but the end ones faced inwards, these faced outwards. It was found that those who lived in the end houses had, on average, half as many friends as those who lived in the inward facing houses. Also, friendships rarely formed between couples more than four houses apart.

Allocation to seats in a classroom at the beginning of a course affects who forms friends with whom. Segal (1974) investigated the friendship patterns that formed between police recruits who were assigned seats according to alphabetical surname order. After a few weeks of the training course had elapsed Segal asked trainees who were their closest friends. Friendships predominantly formed between those whose surname was alphabetically close rather than far apart. Segal found that knowledge of a person's surname was a better predictor of friendship choice than religion, age, education, hobbies, etc. Clarke (1952) found that more than 50 per cent of people who marry in Columbus, Ohio lived within walking distance of each other. Deutsch and Collins (1951) found that assigning people to public housing without regard to race produced many interracial friendships.

Festinger *et al.* (1950) suggested that the smaller the functional distance between people the more surface contact (in Levinger's scheme) will take place and repeated contact will lead to relationships developing. Saegert, Swap and Zajonc (1973) tested the prediction that the more a person comes into contact with another the more the person will like the other. Subjects, who thought they were in an experiment to rate the tastes of various drinks, came into contact with another person on either one, two, five or ten different occasions. Afterwards subjects were asked, on a seven-point scale, how much they liked the other person. As Figures 8.2 shows, the more frequently a subject came into contact with another the greater they seemed to like them.

Generally, proximity or propinquity increases the likelihood that people form relationships with one another. The closer the functional distance between people the more likely a relationship is to form since contact between people will take place more often, which tends to lead to liking.

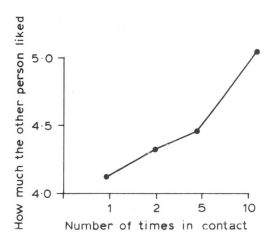

**Figure 8.2** Results of a study by Saegert, Swap and Zajonc (1973) showing greater liking to result from an increase in the number of occasions one person came into contact with another person.

### 8.3.3 Reciprocity

If I like you and you like me there is a sound basis for the formation of a relationship. But how does this mutual liking or *reciprocity* of liking come about? There are two possibilities: (a) we first discover that somebody likes us and *then* reciprocate that liking; or (b) we like another person and then assume, rightly or wrongly, that the other person also likes us.

Backman and Secord (1959) investigated the validity of the first form of reciprocity by getting subjects who were strangers to talk to one another. However, before putting the subjects together in groups they told them that certain members of the group would like them very much. Each group met and talked on six different occasions; at the end of each session subjects were asked which individuals in their own group they most preferred. After the first two sessions subjects were found to prefer most those they were told would like them. However, by the end of the sixth session subjects were found to prefer those group members who they discovered *really* liked them, who were not necessarily those they were *told* would like them.

Further research has presented a slightly more complicated picture since reciprocity of liking has been shown to depend on whether or not the other person makes an *accurate* evaluation of us – we like those who see us as we see ourselves. Deutsch and Solomon (1959) demonstrated this by using female telephone operators as subjects and informing them of their performance at their jobs. Half the women were told they performed poorly (regardless of how they actually performed), and half that they performed well. The women were then shown an anonymous evaluation by one of their colleagues which was either consistent or inconsistent with how they were told they performed. Women who performed well and were evaluated as such by the colleague liked that colleague; women who were told they performed badly gave an unfavourable evaluation to the colleague who gave a favourable evaluation of their performance.

This study does not, it should be noted, take account of how a person feels about his or her abilities. Dutton (1972) found that subjects who were certain they performed well or badly at a task were most attracted to another person's evaluation which was consistent with their own. However, subjects who were uncertain of how they performed were most attracted to the person giving a positive evaluation.

The claim that we like those who like us needs some qualification: as research described above shows, we only reciprocate liking if another person's evaluation of us is consistent with our evaluation of ourselves. Reciprocity of liking is also affected by physical attractiveness. Sigall and Aronson (1969) showed that male subjects evaluated in a positive way by a physically attractive woman were more likely to reciprocate liking than if evaluated by a physically unattractive woman.

So far we have been concerned to detail how we react to other people's personal evaluations of us. Looking at the other side of the coin, where we assume other people like us because we like them, would appear tenable also. However, research has tended to show (Taguiri, 1958) that we tend to overestimate the extent to which other people like us if we like them (and presumably overestimate the extent to which others dislike us if we dislike them). Perhaps this is a special case of a generally observed phenomenon – known as the 'false consensus' effect – where people who we know are similar to us are seen as being more similar than they actually are (this is discussed in more detail in Chapter 7)

### 8.3.4 Similarity

The old proverb 'birds of a feather flock together' is really too general to be of much use since it does not tell us what types of birds of a feather flock together. Attention has focused on two types of similarity – attitude and personality. Attitude similarity as an influence in interpersonal attraction may take two different forms: (a) we may see ourselves as more similar to those we like than is actually the case; or (b) we tend to like those we perceive to be similar to us. Research, as we shall see, supports both propositions, although the latter has been more extensively researched.

Byrne and Wong (1962) asked people who were strongly prejudiced towards blacks and people who were not prejudiced to assess the extent to which their own attitudes were similar to those of both a black and white person unknown to them. Unprejudiced subjects thought they would be as likely to share the same attitudes with either of the strangers. By contrast, prejudiced subjects believed they would be more in agreement with the white rather than the black stranger.

Byrne and his colleagues have conducted many studies, all showing that as attitude similarity increases between two people then so does the degree of attraction. Byrne and Nelson (1965), for example, measured subjects' attitudes to such things as religion, music and politics. Two weeks later they presented the same subjects with a similar attitude questionnaire filled in by another student. The questionnaire presented to subjects was manipulated

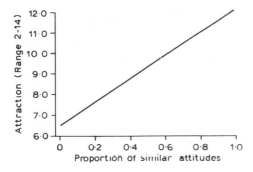

**Figure 8.3** Graph showing that as similarity of attitudes increases then so too does attraction between two people. Adapted from Byrne and Nelson (1965).

such that one group of subjects received a filled-in questionnaire in which the attitudes expressed were the same as their own, another group of subjects were presented with attitudes opposite to their own, and other groups were presented with varying degrees of attitude similarity. Subsequently all subjects filled in Byrne's Interpersonal Judgement Scale. Byrne and Nelson then correlated the attitude similarity with interpersonal attraction. As Figure 8.3 shows, attraction towards a stranger increases in a straightforward linear way as the proportion of similar attitudes between subject and stranger increases.

Exceptions to the rule that attitude similarity induces liking have been reported. For example, Byrne has shown (1961) we are more likely to be attracted to those who share our attitudes on important rather than trivial matters. Novak and Lerner (1968) demonstrated that although subjects preferred initially to interact with people portrayed as being similar to themselves, they changed their minds upon hearing that the person had a long history of emotional disturbance. So marked was this that subjects preferred to interact with people portrayed as holding very different attitudes to themselves.

The claim that people with similar personalities are attracted to each other has also received a good deal of support. Reader and English (1947) administered personality questionnaires to friends and strangers and found a stronger degree of resemblance in personality between the former than the latter. Cattell and Nesselrode (1967) found that stable marriages were more likely to exhibit personality similarity between partners than unstable marriages.

Perhaps, as is often claimed, people *become* more similar the longer they have been together, however there is little support for this idea. Hoffeditz (1934) measured dominance, self-sufficiency and neuroticism and found no evidence that husband and wife became more alike on these dimensions with length of marriage. Perhaps a further study should be conducted where stable and unstable marriages are distinguished. We might predict that there will be increasing similarity in personality over time in stable marriages but not in unstable ones.

In summary, a great deal of support has been found for the idea that similarity (whether of attitudes or personality) leads to attraction between people.

Generally, the more similar we perceive people to be to ourselves the more we will like them; there are exceptions and qualifications to this rule though.

## 8.4 Development of relationships

Physical attractiveness, proximity, reciprocity of liking and similarity of attitudes and/or personality have all been shown to be important factors influencing the formation of relationships. We move now from factors assisting in initiating the acquaintance process to consider how relationships develop, change and terminate. Four topics will be dealt with: first, the *Byrne–Clore reinforcement-affect model* will be used to explain relationship development. Second, *balance theory* (described in Chapter 4 in the section dealing with attitude change) will be used to understand how relationships grow and change when disagreements occur. Third, *social exchange* theory will be used to consider the circumstances under which a relationship is likely to continue and when it is likely to end. Fourth, and finally, we will look at how people get to know one another as a relationship becomes more intimate, this will be achieved by looking at research on *self-disclosure*.

### 8.4.1 Byrne–Clore Reinforcement-Affect Model

Byrne and Clore (1970) claim that we need to know the rewards and punishments that other people provide in order to know when a relationship, once formed, will grow and develop. The basic idea of the reinforcement-affect model is very simple: *we like those who reward us and dislike those who punish us.* This is the 'reinforcement' part of the model, the 'affect' part is the feelings we associate with another person and this comes about through a process of *conditioning*.

The reinforcement-affect model contains the following four basic principles:

---

(a) Most stimuli from other people (what they say or do to us) are either rewarding or punishing. We approach stimuli that are rewarding and avoid punishing stimuli.
(b) Stimuli we find rewarding arouse positive feeling in us, punishing stimuli arouse negative feelings. This is on a continuum for extremely positive to extremely negative.
(c) Stimuli that arouse positive or negative feelings are evaluated – on a continuum from like very much to dislike very much.
(d) Through conditioning, any neutral stimuli associated with a reward or punishment becomes similarly evaluated. A neutral person near us when something good happens will be liked, and disliked if around when something bad happens.

---

One important point about this model, mentioned in (d), is that if we happen to be in a certain situation by chance, and that situation is rewarding to us (for example, a party at which we are having a good time), then we will like that person since good feelings will be associated with him or her. Hence, in many situations it is not the attributes of the person (looks, attitudes, personality, etc.) that are important for interpersonal attraction but simply the association of positive and pleasant feelings with that person.

So far the model has characterized a person's relationship with another in terms of simple like or dislike. This is not very realistic as most people we know we have mixed feelings about, i.e. another person provides both rewards and punishments. Byrne and Clore accept this and suggest that attraction increases and relationships develop as the proportion of different positive feelings increases. If there is a greater number of positive than negative feelings a relationship will develop, but if the other way round a relationship is unlikely to continue unless something changes.

Veitch and Griffith (1976) tested the hypothesis that something making a person feel good would cause that person to be attracted to another more than if the person felt depressed. Subjects were asked to wait in a room for a few minutes; half listened to a radio news broadcast (pre-recorded by the experimenter) consisting of entirely good news (for example, a new breakthrough in the treatment of cancer, food prices going down), whilst the other half of the subjects listened to entirely bad news (cancer breakthrough had fatal side-effects, food prices would increase substantially). Subjects were then taken to another room for the experiment 'proper' and asked to rate their feelings about a stranger after interaction with him. In line with predictions, subjects who heard bad news disliked the stranger, those who heard good news liked the stranger.

The reinforcement-affect model explains why relationships, once formed, are likely to develop: the more a person provides us with rewards in proportion to punishments the more likely a relationship is to endure. The model does not, however, tell us how two people deal with a disagreement that may arise between them – for this we look to balance theory.

### 8.4.2 Balance theory

Balance theory, as proposed by Heider (1958), was described in some detail in Chapter 4 – the reader is referred back to the appropriate section in that chapter to refresh his or her memory of the basic principles. Here we will only be concerned with Newcombe's (1971) reformulation of the theory as it applies to interpersonal attraction. Newcombe said that three states, not two as with Heider, exist between the three entities (P, O and X) – these are balance, imbalance and non-balance. Balance and imbalance are the same as in Heider's formulation except only two triads are in each category (both where *P likes O*). Four triads are in the non-balanced state, as shown in Figure 8.4, and are where *P dislikes O*. Newcombe introduced a state of non-balance because in cases where P dislikes O it is usually of little concern to P what O thinks about X. Since, as Newcombe claims, P feels indifference in triads (c) to (f), P should feel little or no motivation to change the state of affairs. Non-balanced states are, then, stable states of affairs. Imbalanced states, by contrast, are experienced as unpleasant by P and provide motivation to change *one* of the three relationships in order to achieve either balance or even non-balance.

An example might make matters clearer. Suppose Philip to be good friends with Oliver (P ___+___ O), Philip to like cricket (P ___+___ X), and Oliver (so Philip believes) to dislike cricket (O ___−___ X). This is triad (g) in Figure 8.4. Four possible ways are open to Philip to remove the unpleasant feelings coming from this state of imbalance. These are:

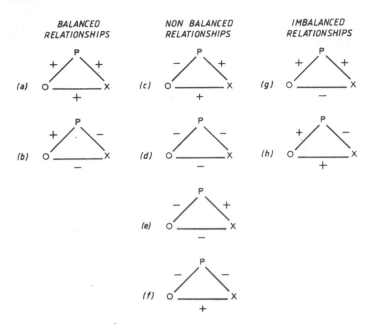

**Figure 8.4** Newcombe's reformulation of Heider's theory of balance, showing balanced relationships (experienced as pleasant and harmonious), non-balanced relationships (experienced with indifference) and imbalanced relationships (experienced as unpleasant). Imbalanced states will motivate P to achieve balance if possible (if not possible a state of non-balance may be the best solution for P).

(a)  Philip may try to change how Oliver thinks about cricket – resulting in triad (a), a balanced state of affairs.

(b)  Philip may change his own mind about cricket and decide he does not really like it – resulting in triad (b), again a balanced state of affairs.

(c)  Philip may simply have misperceived how Oliver feels about cricket (Philip may, for example, think Oliver does really like cricket but is saying he does not just to be awkward) – resulting in triad (a), a balanced state.

(d)  Philip may see there to be no way of reconciling his views with Oliver's over cricket and decide to end his friendship with him – resulting in triad (e), a non-balanced state of affairs but a stable one.

Rosenberg and Abelson's (1960) principle of 'minimum effort', described in Chapter 4, would help in predicting which of these four possibilities Philip would take to remove the state of imbalance.

Newcomb (1961), in a classic field study, tested his reformulation of balance theory by recruiting male college students to live, rent free, in a cooperative housing unit for a term. Development of friendships, Newcomb found, was strongly determined by how two people felt about other individuals in the housing unit. Friendships were most likely to develop when two people agreed about whom they liked and disliked amongst the others. As term progressed and the students became better acquainted the number of balanced friendships increased and the number of imbalanced friendships decreased.

Balance theory, as developed by Newcomb, offers further support for the contention that attitude similarity between two people is likely to provide a stable foundation for the development of a relationship. Disagreement over an issue may only become apparent as a relationship develops – how the disagreement or imbalance is resolved will depend on how important the issue is for both people. An important difference incapable of resolution between two intimate friends might well result in a 'cooling off' or lessening of intimacy. The more precise conditions under which a relationship is likely to continue or not, especially if an alternative relationship is available, is more the concern of *social exchange theory*.

### 8.4.3 Social exchange theory

Simply knowing the rewards another person provides us with is not enough to predict whether a relationship will develop and become more intimate or whether it will terminate or slowly become more distant. The social exchange approach (Thibaut and Kelley, 1959) characterizes relationships as an exchange of rewards and costs: the *satisfaction* a person feels in a relationship (and this is the predictor of whether it will endure or not) can be predicted if we know two things:

(a) how much reward the person gains from being with the other.
and
(b) how the *actual* rewards another person provides compare with the rewards *expected* from the other person, called the Comparison Level.

The comparison level predicts the amount of satisfaction the person has with the relationship. If the actual rewards *surpass* the expected rewards the person will be highly satisfied with the relationship. However, if the actual rewards *fall below* the expected rewards the person will be dissatisfied with the relationship. Dissatisfaction with a relationship is not enough to predict the future course of the relationship; to do this Thibaut and Kelley claim we need to know what alternative relationships are available.

This leads to the *comparison level for alternatives*: a relationship will end or the level of intimacy greatly decrease if a better or more satisfactory relationship is available. This applies even if a person is in a satisfactory relationship but an even more satisfactory one presents itself. However, if an alternative relationship is more unsatisfactory (or less satisfactory) than the existing one the latter will endure. The comparison level for alternatives suggests that we compare the alternatives available, if there is no alternative an unsatisfactory relationship is likely to endure; only where a more satisfactory (or less unsatisfactory) relationship is available will the already existing one be likely to end or change in nature.

Kiesler and Baral (1966) showed that as a relationship develops and the two people come to know each other better they become better able to predict the other's behaviour. This, Kiesler suggests, is rewarding and serves to make the comparison level between the actual and expected rewards more favourable. People often stay in a relationship because an alternative offers too high a degree of uncertainty about the likely behaviour of the other person (intimate knowledge, as the next section on self-disclosure will show, of another person takes time and trust to acquire). 'Better the devil you know' characterizes what is going on here perhaps.

One problem with the social exchange approach is that it does not specify when somebody will opt out of a relationship in the *absence* of alternatives. Some relationships are so unsatisfactory, where there is a vast discrepancy between expectations of and actual rewards, that a person is better off on his or her own. Perhaps the social exchange approach needs to incorporate some notion of *general expectation* where people have a general expectation of what constitutes a satisfactory and unsatisfactory relationship regardless of whom the relationship is with. This would lead to a general/actual comparison of relationships – if the actual relationship fell below what was acceptable at a general level it would be terminated regardless of whether or not an alternative was available.

In summary, the social exchange approach characterizes relationships in terms of rewards and whether the relationship is satisfactory (exceeds expected rewards) or unsatisfactory (falls below expected rewards). In some ways the approach is more applicable to intimate relationships rather than friendships since people usually only engage in one of the former at a time but often have a number of friendships at any one time.

### 8.4.4 Self-disclosure

The process of getting to know another person, as conceptualized by Levinger and described at the beginning of this chapter, means people must reveal more and more about themselves as the relationship develops – this has been investigated in a research tradition known as *self-disclosure*.

It is important to distinguish between self-disclosure and self-description. Self-disclosure refers to 'an individual explicitly communicating to one or more persons information that he believes others would be unlikely to acquire unless he himself discloses it' (Culbert, 1967). Self-description, on the other hand, designates self-data that an individual is likely to feel comfortable in revealing to most others (Culbert, 1967). Self-disclosure, then, concerns the sharing of private and personal information about oneself with another person. As such, self-disclosure carries a risk since another person may criticize or use that which is being revealed.

Much is known about the variables which influence whether people will disclose information about themselves. For example, Jourard (1971) found that women are not only higher disclosers but that they are more likely to disclose on the basis of liking whilst men are more likely to disclose on the basis of trust. Children are most likely to disclose to their mothers (Rivenbark, 1971) and parents perceived as supportive and nurturant are more likely to receive disclosures from the children (Doster and Strickland, 1969). The most consistent and intimate disclosures occur within the marital relationship, as one might expect.

In the development of relationships two general trends have been observed: (a) as the relationship becomes closer disclosures become less superficial and more intimate (Rubin and Schenker, 1978) (b) as a relationship becomes more intimate the disclosures by one person are 'matched' by the other in terms of breadth and depth (Altman and Taylor, 1973). By

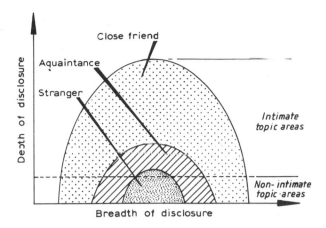

**Figure 8.5** Diagram showing how a person reveals more and more and at greater depth about him or herself and the relationship changes from stranger to casual acquaintance to best friend or lover. Adapted from Altman and Taylor (1973).

'matching' is meant that each partner *reciprocates* the other's disclosure in terms of level of intimacy. Matching of disclosures has been found, by Altman and Taylor, to be more important in the early stages of the development of a relationship. A well-established relationship is more tolerant in expecting immediate reciprocation of disclosures (Morton, 1978). As a relationship grows and develops so too does the depth and breadth of disclosures. Altman and Taylor (1973) have called this *social penetration theory*: Figure 8.5 depicts this by showing that as relationships become more intimate they are characterized by disclosures greater in both depth and breadth. The theory is called social penetration because closer relationships penetrate deeper and deeper into the private, social and mental life of the self.

Self-disclosure is the very stuff of which relationships are made. If we are not prepared to tell another about our 'real' self (our fears, likes, embarrassments in life, etc.) and have that other reveal highly personal things about him or herself to us then the relationship will remain at a superficial level (Level Four, a minor intersection in Levinger's scheme given early on in this chapter). Perhaps a willingness to disclose everything about oneself to another is one essential aspect of what total unity would be in Levinger's scheme.

## 8.5 Intimate relationships

Berscheid and Walster (1978) distinguish between liking, companionate love and romantic or passionate love. Liking and companionate love represent two extremes of a continuum as can be seen from the following definitions:

Liking: The affection we feel for casual acquaintances

Companionate Love: The affection we feel for those with whom our lives are deeply entwined

Companionate love refers to very close friends and marriage partners of course, the latter are often close friends. Passionate or romantic love is a powerful emotional state, not often experienced and defined by Berscheid and Walster as follows:

> A state of intense absorption in another. Sometimes lovers are those who long for their partners and for complete fulfilment. Sometimes lovers are those who are ecstatic at finally having attained their partner's love and, momentarily, complete fulfilment. A state of intense physiological arousal.

This kind of love is qualitatively different from companionate love since it involves both a powerful physiological (bodily) effect and domination of one person's thoughts by another. Such relationships do not, generally, remain in such an intense state for extended periods of time. In what follows we will look at some of the major theories, together with evidence, put forward to account for companionate and romantic or passionate love.

### 8.5.1 Companionate love

Two theories of companionate love, where this is taken to mean choice of a person to live with for a large part of one's life, will be presented – Winch's (1958) theory of 'complementary needs' and equity theory (Walster, Berscheid and Walster, 1976). Whilst these theories were developed to explain conventional heterosexual relationships, there is no reason why they should not apply to homosexual or lesbian relationships.

The basic idea in Winch's (1958) theory is that people select a partner to live their life with whose personality *complements* their own. There are two principles involved:

(a)  people are attracted to, and love those, who provide them with most gratification of their needs.
(b)  people prefer those who needs complement rather than mirror their own.

There are two ways in which another could complement one's needs: first, the difference in needs between two people may only be one of *degree*, for example, a person who needs to dominate may get along well with someone who feels little need to dominate. Second, the difference in needs between two people is one of *kind*, for example, a protective person may seek out a partner who needs to be protected, or a dominant person may seek out a person who needs to be dominated, or *vice versa*.

It is the second of these that has received attention. In Winch's initial research 25 married couples were interviewed and had a number of personality questionnaires to complete. The findings were largely supportive of the theory; however, little subsequent research has been so kind to the theory. Winch (1967) has since modified his theory to take both psychological (needs) and sociological (cultural roles of husbands and wives) factors into account. Both factors are used to predict the *stability* of a marriage: a stable relationship is most likely where both partners complement each other's needs in accordance with the cultural roles of husband and wife. An unstable relationship is where the roles of each partner are opposite to cultural norms.

Equity theory (Walster, Berscheid and Walster, 1976) offers a very

**Table 8.2** Endurance of a relationship as a function of the extent to which the relationship is equitable or inequitable. Adapted from Walster *et al.* (1977).

| | ENDURANCE OF THE RELATIONSHIP | | | | |
|---|---|---|---|---|---|
| | *Still together* (a) | | *How long been going together* (b) | *How certain together in future* (c) | |
| DEGREE OF EQUITY IN THE RELATIONSHIP | Time 1 | Time 2 | | 1 year | 5 year |
| Person is getting far *less* than he or she deserves | 1.4 | 1.3 | 3.9 | 1.3 | 1.0 |
| Person is getting slightly *less* than he or she deserves | 1.6 | 1.4 | 5.4 | 1.9 | 1.4 |
| Person is getting just what he or she deserves | 1.7 | 1.7 | 5.6 | 2.5 | 2.1 |
| Person is getting slightly *more* than he or she deserves | 1.7 | 1.6 | 5.2 | 2.2 | 1.6 |
| Person is getting far *more* than he or she deserves | 1.4 | 1.4 | 4.2 | 1.4 | 1.2 |

(a) A score of 1 = No; 2 = Yes
(b) Higher the number, longer been together
(c) Higher the number, more certain relationship to endure into the future

different, and to my mind, rather cynical approach to explaining choice of marriage partners. The basic idea is that people are selfish and act to achieve maximum reward from another at the smallest cost to themselves. An equitable relationship, and hence stable one, is where each person feels he or she is getting what he or she deserves from the other. An inequitable relationship is where one partner feels he or she is getting less than he or she deserves from the other.

Walster *et al.* (1977) tested the hypothesis that equitable relationships would be more stable and enduring than inequitable ones by interviewing over 500 men and women who were 'going out' with each other. They asked each of the partners to estimate how much they thought (a) they contributed to the relationship; and (b) their partner contributed to the relationship. They then asked each partner how much they thought (a) they got out of the relationship; and (b) their partner got out of the relationship. The measures of contribution to and benefit from a relationship allowed an assessment to be made of the extent to which a relationship was equitable or not – this was done on a five-point scale shown in the extreme left-hand column of Table 8.2.

Fourteen weeks later the same men and women were asked: (a) if they were still going out with the same person or not; (b) how long they had been going out with the person (if they were still going out with the same person) or how long did they go out with that person if they were no longer with them: and (c) how certain they felt they would be with that person in one and five years time. Results are shown in Table 8.2 and demonstrate that the more equitable a relationship the more a person was likely still to be with the same partner, the longer they had been together and the more sure they felt about being together in the future.

Equity considerations seem, generally, to be an important factor in choice of partner, as Berscheid and Walster (1978) put it 'choices appear to be a delicate compromise between our desire to capture an ideal partner and one's realization that we must eventually settle for what we can get' (p. 191).

### 8.5.2 Romantic love

In many ways romantic love is a non-rational state for a person to be in, sayings such as 'love is blind' and 'it was love at first sight' attest to this. Such love often brings about suffering, for example, a man married for many years may abandon a companionate relationship for a romantic one – often at high personal cost. A parent's opposition to their teenage son's or daughter's romance usually serves to fuel the passion rather than dampen it. Driscoll, Davis and Lipitz (1972) showed this by interviewing 91 married couples and 49 dating couples all of whom were seriously committed to one another. They found the more adverse parental influence there was the more the couple said they were in love; this was more pronounced with the unmarried couples. Six to 10 months later the same couples were interviewed and it was found that where parental interference had increased so had romantic love. Caution is needed in accepting these results since it may have been that parental interference had been a reaction to the couple falling more deeply in love rather than a cause of it.

This, and similar experiments, together with anecdotal evidence from common sayings in our culture show that romantic love is difficult to explain in terms of a reinforcement or reward model, such as outlined earlier in this chapter. This is because we need to focus more on the *thoughts and feelings* of a person rather than rewards others provide. Theories of romantic love reflect this since most derive from clinical psychology where the fantasy-idealization of the loved one is of central concern. We will look briefly at Freud's and Maslow's theories.

Freud (1914) described two types of love based on his view that every person originally possesses *two* love objects: (a) the person him or herself; and (b) the person who cared (usually the mother) for him or her when young. The latter, Freud claims, results in the person searching for a substitute mother to fall in love with as an adult – this Freud called *dependency love*, an' is more often found in men than women. The former love object resul' erson looking for him or herself in others: he or she loves another ther is similar to how the person would like to be. This Freud *tic love*, and is to be found more in women than men.

proposed two kinds of love as well – one called 'D' love d the other 'B' love (being love). 'D' love is where a person loves another because the other gratifies needs deficient in the person. This bears similarities to Winch's theory of complementary needs, and Freud's dependency love. However, for Maslow 'D' love is negative and not to be regarded as true love which is 'B' love. 'B' or being love is where a person loves another simply for what that other is. Maslow further claims that people who are dissatisfied with themselves and/or have not fulfilled their own needs are not likely to experience 'B' love, but are more likely to love another for what the other gives them ('D' love).

Both Freud and Maslow's theories have attracted little experimental research aimed at either refutation or confirmation. Perhaps because they have developed from a clinical background accounts for this and is why they are still popular since they offer useful frameworks for treating psychologically disturbed people.

Experimental social psychology has produced a theory of romantic love which combines how a person both *feels* and *thinks* – this is known as the *'two-component'* theory, for obvious reasons. This is really a special case of Schachter's (1964) two-component theory of self-perception of emotions (described in Chapter 6). The basic point is that physiological arousal (which occurs with any strong emotional experience) does not mean anything to the person by and of itself. The physiological arousal (the affective component) is given meaning by the social context in which it occurs. How we understand or perceive (the cognitive component) the social context determines the emotion attributed to our bodily sensations. The emotional experience, then, depends on the situation – if in one situation it is appropriate to feel fearful then that is what will be felt, if in another situation euphoria is appropriate then that is what will be experienced. Schachter and Singer's (1962) classic study, described in Chapter 6, demonstrated how the social situation determines the way a person interprets physiological arousal caused by the injection of epinephrine. Subjects put in a situation where others acted in an angry way felt anger themselves, different subjects put in a situation where others acted euphorically felt euphoria themselves.

Berscheid and Walster (1974) predicted that people would be most vulnerable to love when both physiologically aroused and in a social context appropriate for falling in love. Most experimental work testing the two-component model of love has measured interpersonal attraction and liking rather than love itself. For example, Berscheid, Stephan and Walster (1971) told male subjects they were going on a blind date with a female student who had been allocated to them on a random basis. Subjects then had to read a passage of prose and rate it for its potential to cause sexual arousal. Half the subjects read a highly sexually arousing passage and half a dull passage. Later, subjects were given information and shown a photograph of either the woman they were going on a blind date with or a woman another person was going on a blind date with. Subjects had to make various ratings of the photograph. It was found that: (a) those who had read the more arousing passage rated the female depicted in the photograph as more attractive than those who read the dull passage; (b) the more 'aroused' subjects thought *their* blind date would be more sexually receptive than when the woman in the photograph was someone else's blind date.

Dutton and Aron (1974) tested the two-component model in a highly original field study in which the reactions to a female experimenter by men crossing one of two bridges was measured. Bridge 1 was five feet wide and 450 feet long, it was a wooden suspension bridge which tilted and swayed, had low handrails and was perched 230 feet above the canyon floor. Bridge 2 was shorter, firmer and only 10 foot above a small stream. As unsuspecting male subjects reached about half-way across a bridge they were approached by either a male or attractive female experimenter. The experimenter introduced him or herself by saying they were doing research on the 'effects of exposure to scenic attractions on creative expression' and asked them to fill out a questionnaire whilst still standing in the middle of the bridge. When this had been completed the experimenter gave the subject his or her telephone number and encouraged the person to contact them if they wanted to know more about the project. The questionnaire was designed to measure sexual arousal.

It was found that sexual arousal was lowest in the conditions with a male experimenter, higher with the female experimenter on a safe bridge and highest with the female experimenter on the dangerous bridge. Furthermore, hardly any male subjects phoned a male experimenter back, but 2 out of 33 of the subjects on the safe bridge phoned the female experimenter back, whilst 9 out of 33 who had been on the dangerous bridge phoned the female experimenter to ask for more information about the project!

These, and numerous other experiments, demonstrate that people tend to be more attracted to another when experiencing high physiological arousal. Research has yet to extend to romantic love itself; the two-component model has been tested using male college students and/or male subjects generally and taking measures of interpersonal attraction *not* romantic love. To this extent the model looks like a plausible candidate for explaining romantic love but needs to look directly rather than indirectly at romantic love.

## 8.6 Summary

○ People need each other – research on total isolation and social isolation show people experience great difficulties when alone and/or without stimulation for long periods. One reason for people needing others is that others reduce fear when in uncertain or threatening situations.

○ Physical attractiveness, proximity, reciprocity of liking and similarity of attitudes and/or personality have all been found to be important factors determining who we form relationships with. Whilst most people are attracted to physically attractive people, relationships are much more likely to form on the basis of a 'matching' rule.

○ The Byrne–Clore reinforcement-affect model accounts for why relationships may develop; balance theory, as reformulated by Newcombe, shows how developing relationships may cope with disagreements. Social exchange outlines the conditions under which relationships are likely to continue or terminate. Self-disclosure demonstrates how people disclose, both in terms of breadth and depth, private information about themselves as a relationship becomes more intimate.

○ Companionate love is affection felt for somebody we spend much of our life with and has been investigated from the perspectives of Winch's complementary needs theory and equity theory. Romantic or passionate love, which is defined as a state of intense absorption in another, is qualitatively different from companionate love. Freud saw love as either 'dependency' or 'narcissistic' in nature; Maslow conceptualized love as 'D' or deficiency love and 'B' or being love. The two-component model of romantic love says that both thoughts (concerning the perception of a social situation) and sensations (physiological arousal) are needed to explain love.

## 8.7 Suggestions for further reading

Berscheid, E. and Walster, E.M. *Interpersonal Attraction*, (Reading, Mass,. Addison-Wesley, 1978), 2nd edition.
Very readable introductory book covering in more detail the topics covered in this chapter. Much of the book devotes itself to different aspects of reward associated with the Byrne–Clore reinforcement-affect model.

Murstein, B.I. *Theories of Attraction and Love*, (New York, Springer Publishing Company, 1971).
Collection of different theories dealt with in each chapter of the book, worth consulting for the more 'clinical' theories of love briefly described at the end of this chapter.

Proust, M. *Remembrance of Things Past*, (Harmondsworth, Penguin, 1983), Vol. 1.
In this long self-analysis of Proust's past there is a long and detailed account of obsessive love given in *Swann in Love*. This has also been made into a film.

# 9

# Non-verbal communication and interpersonal behaviour

9.1      Introduction
9.2      Significance in animals
9.3      Cross-cultural consistencies
9.4      Channels of non-verbal communication
         *9.4.1 Looking and eye-contact    9.4.2 Facial expression    9.4.3 Body language*
         *9.4.4 Personal space    9.4.5 Self-presentation    9.4.6 Paralanguage*
9.5      Methodological issues
9.6      Visual interaction
         *9.6.1 Structural aspects    9.6.2 Functional aspects    9.6.3 Looking, seeing and*
         *cuelessness*
9.7      Non-verbal behaviour and conversation
         *9.7.1 Spontaneous speech and hesitations    9.7.2 Interruptions*
9.8      Social skills
9.9      Summary
9.10    Suggestions for further reading

## 9.1 Introduction

We spend much of our social lives interacting, face-to-face, with another person or small group of people. On first reflection it may be thought that communication between two people occurs via the medium of spoken language, however *non-verbal communication* is also of great importance. Verbal communication may be defined as the actual words spoken; non-verbal communication is everything else that takes place and includes both *vocal* and *non-vocal* behaviour. Vocal behaviour refers to aspects of speech such as intonation, pitch, speed and hesitations. Non-vocal behaviour includes all other communicative behaviour that is not to do with speech, such as looking and eye-contact, facial expressions, interpersonal distance, dress, etc. Figure 9.1 depicts these conceptual distinctions.

The distinction between verbal and non-verbal communication is made because each has been thought to fulfil different functions (Patterson, 1977). Verbal communication, in the form of language, is better for conveying logical or abstract ideas; non-verbal communication is regarded as better for conveying emotions, the type of relationship existing between two people and regulating/manipulating interpersonal interaction. Such a functional distinction is useful but it should be remembered that it does not rigidly apply, since people often say what they feel and talk about the kind of relationship they have with another person. It is also clear that effective communication takes place in the absence of, or with little, non-verbal support, such

170

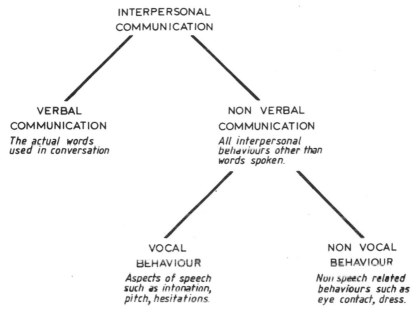

INTERPERSONAL
COMMUNICATION

VERBAL
COMMUNICATION
*The actual words
used in conversation*

NON VERBAL
COMMUNICATION
*All interpersonal
behaviours other than
words spoken.*

VOCAL
BEHAVIOUR
*Aspects of speech
such as intonation,
pitch, hesitations.*

NON VOCAL
BEHAVIOUR
*Non speech related
behaviours such as
eye contact, dress.*

**Figure 9.1** Components of interpersonal communication showing how non-verbal communication is made up of vocal behaviour and non-vocal behaviour.

as in telephone conversations and the written word. In some ways it is easier to do without non-verbal rather than verbal communication – conveying abstract ideas non-verbally can prove extremely difficult, as you may know if you have played charades.

Verbal and non-verbal behaviour differ, but what does it mean to say a behaviour is communicative? Wiener *et al.* (1972) proposed that three features need to be present: an encoder, a code and a decoder. This means, in interaction between two people, that one person (the encoder) conveys a message through a system (the code), mutually understood by both participants, and interpreted by the second person (the decoder). Intention and awareness on the part of the encoder are not necessary prerequisites since we often convey non-verbally that which we do not wish or intend to reveal about ourselves. Philosophically this presents difficulties since non-verbal codes are not written or well-defined but are socially shared norms which are implicitly adhered to. Perhaps one of the best ways of becoming aware of such 'unwritten rules' (Goffman, 1963) is to break them or act in ways unexpected by others in a specific social situation.

This chapter outlines non-verbal behaviours by first considering the different 'channels' or types of non-verbal communication. Since visual interaction is often regarded as the most important we will look at this in some detail, focusing on how such behaviour synchronizes with speech to allow smooth speaker changes when two people are conversing. Finally, non-verbal behaviour as a social skill will be considered because research has led to the development of therapeutic procedures in clinical psychology.

However, we need first to consider the biological significance of and the extent to which humans may have evolved a common set of non-verbal behaviours.

## 9.2 Significance in animals

One, if not the, most striking difference between humans and other animals is that we possess a language which allows us to think, talk and write about what we see and feel, imagine and represent the world in which we live. Other animals possess communication systems but none as elaborate, well-developed or formally learned as with humans (Hockett, 1960). In the light of Wiener's prerequisites for behaviour to be classified as communicative, we should refer to animal behaviour as *signalling* rather than communication. Research on many different species of animals suggests a strong biological basis to their signalling systems; however, in the absence of exposure to adult signalling behaviour (of the same species) they do not become so elaborate or complex.

Among invertebrates the 'dance' of the honey-bee, first described by von Frisch (1954), stands out as the most elaborate system for communicating the

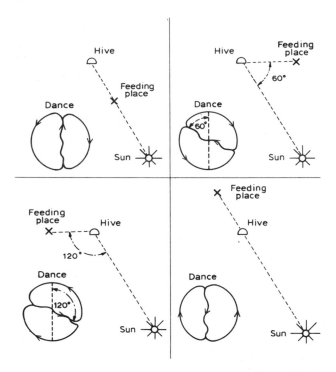

**Figure 9.2** Diagram showing the dance of the honey bee used to communicate the direction of a food source to other bees in the hive. Notice how the overall orientation of the dance changes to indicate direction of the food source in relation to the hive and the sun. Distance of the food source from the hive is indicated by the vigour with which the bee performs the dance. From von Frisch (1954).

direction and distance of a rich source of nectar to other bees. The 'figure of eight' dance, portrayed in Figure 9.2, communicates the direction of the nectar by bees dancing at an angle to the vertical which then has to be transposed by other bees relative to the sun outside the hive. Distance is communicated by the vigour of the dance – the more vigorous the further away the nectar.

Birds use 'song' to communicate between parents and offspring, when searching for a mate, to protect territory and to warn both their own and other species of nearby predators. Learning seems to play an important role – Marler (1970) has suggested there are many similarities between the development of human speech and the development of bird songs. The initial 'cheepings' of a chick are transformed into species-specific songs as it becomes an adult. Hinde (1970) has shown that not only does a chaffinch know another male chaffinch is in it's territory but the *particular* male that has invaded is recognized. Without hearing other birds of the same species chicks do not develop such an elaborate system: a good example of biological predispositions requiring experience and learning to become fully realized.

Sub-human primates exhibit elaborate and complex non-verbal behaviour associated with territorality, mating, and dominance hierarchies. Van Hooff (1967), tracing the evolutionary significance of smiling and laughter in humans, claims the majority of primates have a 'bared teeth' and 'relaxed open-mouth' display. These are shown in Figure 9.3. The bared teeth display occurs when the monkey is threatened: when submissive the monkey is silent, when defensive and not fleeing from a threat the display is accompanied by hissing and spitting. The relaxed open-mouth display is shown in play and mock fighting. In humans Von Hoof has suggested that the silent bared teeth display is similar to smiling and the relaxed open-mouth display to laughter. Shared evolutionary roots between human and non-human primates is further evidenced by the observation that chimpanzees often reciprocate a relaxed open-mouth display (laughter) given by a human.

Perhaps the most dramatic example of non-verbal communication *across*

**Figure 9.3** The 'bared-teeth' display, and 'relaxed open-mouth' display of the chimpanzee. The former occurs when the chimp is threatened, the latter in play and mock-fighting. After van Hooff (1967).

species comes from a study by Exline (1972). It has been found that prolonged eye-contact (looking at each other in the region of the eyes) between
monkeys is often interpreted as threatening, and aggressive behaviour may
follow. Exline was interested to discover whether this would be the case when
humans engaged rhesus macaques in eye-contact. Male rhesus macaques
were put in individual observation cages and an experimenter initiated eye-
contact by staring in the region of the eyes of a monkey. Once eye-contact had
been established the experimenter either continued to stare at the monkey (a
'challenging look') or looked away (a 'deferrent look'). Three stages of threat
were found to be displayed by monkeys subjected to a challenging look:
staring with open mouth and bared teeth, head bobbing back and forward,
and finally either an attempt to attack the experimenter or running away. No
threat display was observed with the deferrent look. Exline concluded that
prolonged eye-contact, even between human and monkey rather than two
monkeys, acts as a dominance challenge resulting in either fight or flight.
Later in this chapter we will look at evidence suggesting prolonged staring
and/or eye-contact between humans is often interpreted as a threatening or
aggressive act.

This brief look at the significance of non-verbal behaviour in animals has
demonstrated both how such behaviour is 'communicative' and may be
inherited as a product of evolution but requiring experience to become
developed fully.

## 9.3　Cross-cultural consistencies

To what extent is human non-verbal behaviour innate and hence a product of
evolution? One important research strategy used to answer this question is
to look for similarities or consistencies, particularly in the facial expression
of emotions, between different cultures. If it can be shown that different
cultures both display (encode) and interpret (decode) facial expressions in a
similar way then the innateness hypothesis, first suggested by Charles
Darwin, may be accepted. The validity of such evidence relies upon one being
confident that one culture could not have learned such expressions by contact
or exposure to the other culture (usually Western) that is being used as a comparison. Isolated cultures with minimal or no contact with westerners would
be ideal comparison groups – unfortunately such scientifically exact requirements are difficult to achieve. Nevertheless, evidence from a number of
sources lends credibility to an innateness hypothesis in the human expression
of emotions.

Ekman and Friesen (1971) conducted an experiment in which subjects were
told a story concerning a single emotion, subjects were then required to indicate which of three photographs, depicting different facial expressions, best
fitted the emotion represented in the story. One story concerned the death of
a child and after hearing this subjects were asked how they would be if it was
their child that had died. Three photographs from a range depicting happiness, sadness, disgust, surprise and fear were shown to subjects from two
very different cultures, American and an isolated tribe from New Guinea.
For the latter minimal contact was where they had 'seen no movies or magazines, they neither spoke nor understood English or Pidgin, they had not

**Table 9.1** Percentage agreement between Americans and New Guineans over the appropriate picture to ∷ t a story concerning a single emotion. Adapted from Ekman and Friesen (1971).

| | PERCENTAGE AGREEMENT | |
|---|---|---|
| EMOTION DESCRIBED IN THE STORY | *Adults* | *Children* |
| Happiness | 92 | 92 |
| Sadness | 79 | 81 |
| Anger | 84 | 90 |
| Disgust | 81 | 85 |
| Surprise | 68 | 98 |
| Fear | 80 | 93 |

lived in any Western settlements, and they had never worked for a caucasian' (Ekman, 1982, p. 135).

Percentage agreement with American subjects was calculated, the results are given in Table 9.1, which shows overall agreement to be high and children to agree more than adults between cultures.

The above study investigates the *decoding* of emotions, another study by Ekman *et al.* (1972) investigated cross-cultural consistency in the *encoding* of emotions. In this study other members of the New Guinea tribe were asked to give an appropriate facial expression to an emotion depicted in a story. Photographs were taken and given to American college students to judge the emotion expressed. Agreement between cultures was less good, as shown in Table 9.2, in particular the emotions of surprise and fear were poorly identified by Americans.

**Table 9.2** Percentage agreement by American college students of emotions expressed by New Guineans. Adapted from Ekman *et al.* (1972).

| EMOTION RATED BY AMERICAN STUDENTS | PERCENTAGE AGREEMENT |
|---|---|
| Happiness | 73 |
| Anger | 51 |
| Disgust | 46 |
| Sadness | 68 |
| Surprise | 27 |
| Fear | 18 |

Eibl Eibesfeldt (1972) has looked for gestural cross-cultural similarities. In greetings, for example, photographic evidence shows the 'eyebrow flash' to be commonly used. This has been observed in many cultures – French, Balinese, Samoan, Waika Indian and Papuan – as shown in Figure 9.4.

Eibl-Eibesfeldt (1970) also made detailed observations of the facial expressions of deaf and blind-born children – such children all display the basic facial expressions of laughter, smiling, crying, surprise and anger. These children are unable to learn such expressions from seeing other people, consequently they would appear to be of innate origin. One might argue that the expressions could be learned by touch; however, this may help in more

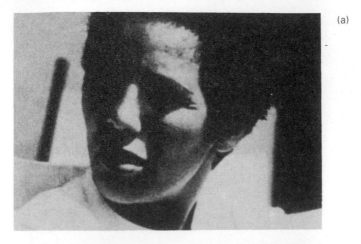

(a)

(b)

**Figure 9.4** Example of the eyebrow flash, a universal sign of greeting (a) shows the lowered eyebrow which occurs just before the greeting, (b) the greeting where the eyebrows are maximally raised. From Eibl-Eibesfeldt (1972).

fully expressing the emotion but it is unlikely to explain the *origins* of the facial expression. Further evidence supports this since these expressions are found in thalidomide children born without arms, and in deaf- and blind-born children with severe brain damage affecting motor coordination (Eibl-Eibesfeldt, 1970).

Cross-cultural and deprivation studies indicate a strong innate basis to emotional expression. Such research suggests an interaction between biology and environment such that biology provides the basic expressions and cultural experiences serve to give them their full and subtle characteristics.

## 9.4  Signals of non-verbal communication

Social interaction is characterized by many types or 'channels' of signals of non-verbal communication – looking, facial expression, gestures, personal space, etc. – occurring simultaneously. It is convenient to identify the main non-verbal channels but important to remember that one rarely occurs in isolation. The notion of signals of non-verbal communication pursues the encoder–code–decoder analogy described at the beginning of this chapter. By signal is meant the means by which the message or information is conveyed. People pay more attention to some signals than others, for example, we spend much time looking at another in the region of the face, especially the eyes, and upper shoulders, in contrast we spend little time looking at their feet and legs. The nature of the interaction often determines the signals we pay attention to – telephone conversations, for example, only allow para-language (aspects of prosody such as pitch, stress, timing and pauses, and tone of voice, accent and speech errors) to be attended to. A short description, together with the significance, of the main channels of non-verbal communication follows.

### 9.4.1 Looking and eye-contact

Looking and eye-contact have often been regarded as the most important signals of non-verbal communication. Looking is where one person looks at another in the region of the eyes whether the other person is looking back or not. Eye-contact occurs when both people are looking at each other in the region of the eyes. Typically periods of eye-contact are brief. When prolonged, or an attempt is made to prolong eye-contact by one of the inter-actants staring, anxiety is caused and may be interpreted as a threat (Ellsworth and Carlsmith, 1973). Looking and eye-contact have also been shown to be synchronized with speech, especially speaker changes between two people (Kendon, 1967). This will be described in detail later in the section on Visual interaction.

The great significance attributed to eye-contact (by, for example, Michael Argyle) has recently been questioned (Rutter, 1984) and it is now suggested that eye-contact may simply be a chance product of individual looking and that what is important is *seeing* (visual access to various non-verbal behaviours) another person. All this is taken up later in this chapter.

### 9.4.2 Facial expression

Facial expression is largely concerned with the communication of emotional states (Argyle, 1983). Whilst the English language has hundreds of words to describe emotions and their nuances only a small number of such emotional words are recognized in the absence of any social context. Ekman (1972) claims people recognize only seven basic emotions – happiness, fear, anger, disgust, contempt, sadness and interest. Thayer and Schiff (1969) demonstrated this by asking subjects to identify schematic faces in which only the configuration of the mouth and eyebrows varied. The mouth and eyebrows are regarded as conveying the greatest information in the face about emotional states. As can be seen from Table 9.3, Thayer and Schiff found the schematic representations of happiness and anger to receive the highest degree of agreement from subjects, whilst the 'sad' face received only a low

**Table 9.3** Categorization of schematic faces of emotions where eyebrow and mouth configurations only were varied. Adapted from Thayer and Schiff (1969).

| EMOTIONS RATED BY SUBJECTS | SCHEMATIC EMOTION | | | |
| --- | --- | --- | --- | --- |
| | *Neutral* | *Happy* | *Sad* | *Angry* |
| Neutral | 39 | 0 | 0 | 0 |
| Happy | 33 | 81 | 0 | 0 |
| Sad | 8 | 0 | 42 | 0 |
| Angry | 0 | 0 | 13 | 65 |
| Afraid | 3 | 0 | 0 | 0 |
| Other | 17 | 19 | 45 | 35 |

level of agreement. Research by Ekman and Friesen (1972), described earlier, would lead us to predict greater agreement if a specific social context is given (as by telling a story).

From this and other research the impression might be gained that peoples' facial expressions are simply 'books to be read'. This is mistaken since, as you must know, people often hide their true emotions and attempt to appear calm and relaxed or express a different emotion to be one actually being experienced. Also, social constraints and norms operate to suppress emotional expression, for example, men rarely cry in public. If you find yourself in conversation with someone who 'bores you to tears', you are unlikely to tell the person, or express what you are feeling. Most likely you will wait for an appropriate cue to end the encounter in a reasonably polite way.

### 9.4.3 Body language

Body language is a generic term covering the non-verbal signals of touch, body orientation, posture, hand gestures and head nods. Touch, or bodily contact generally, varies with the degree of intimacy existing between two people: good friends and lovers touch each other a lot whilst more distant acquaintances touch each other far less frequently. The most common form of touch is when we meet or say goodbye: the handshake or embrace are often used on these occasions. Cultural variations in touch exist, in British and Japanese societies touching is relatively uncommon whilst in African and Arab cultures people touch each other frequently.

Body orientation and posture is important in social interaction, normally we orient our body towards the person we are talking to so that turning away from the person requires body movement. Sommer (1965) found body orientation to vary with social context: people in a cooperative situation tend to sit side-by-side whilst face-to-face is preferred in a competitive situation. We tend to orient our body towards somebody we like by facing the person, moving towards them and nodding agreement with what they are saying (Clore *et al.*, 1975). Disliked people tend to be treated by orienting the body away, looking at one's hand and playing with one's hair. Body posture can also be a good indicator of whether a person is tensed or relaxed, for example, hunched shoulders and 'leg swinging' indicate tension.

Hand gestures are important complements to facial emotional expression, a clenched fist may signify anger and an open-hand gesture signal a call for help or submission. Generally, hand gestures are coordinated with speech and are used to emphasize or give more precise detail to what is being said (Bull, 1983).

Head nods occur frequently when two people are in conversation, and function to provide feedback to the speaker (indicating that what is being said is understood) and reinforce the speaker so that the speaker continues (Argyle, 1983). Head nods may also be used to indicate to the listener that he or she is being offered the 'floor' (i.e. being offered the chance to speak).

### 9.4.4 Personal space

Personal space is the 'area with invisible boundaries surrounding a person's body into which intruders may not come' (Sommer, 1969). The crucial variable is what counts as an intruder since this determines whether we feel our personal space has been invaded: here much depends on the social context and the type of relationship between the person being invaded and those doing the invading. Hall (1968) outlines four interpersonal distances:

| | |
|---|---|
| Intimate | up to about 18 inches |
| Personal | up to about 4 feet |
| Social | up to about 12 feet |
| Public | up to about 18 feet |

Intimate or good friends do not make us feel uncomfortable if they come within 18 inches of us, such a distance is encouraged so we are able to touch each other easily. Acquaintances or strangers are usually kept at the personal distance in more social surroundings where there are more than two people, and people within 12 feet are often conversed with. The public distance is usually too great for conversation but is one at which recognition and initial greetings take place. The social context may change these distances, for example, in a crowded shopping street people stand closer together when talking than if the street is relatively devoid of people.

A popular method employed to demonstrate the 'unwritten rules' of personal space is to violate what are thought to be the norms. Garfinkel (1964), Felipe and Sommer (1966) demonstrated that avoidance, embarrassment and/or bewilderment often follows personal space violations. Felipe and Sommer invaded peoples' personal space in libraries, on benches in public parks, etc. and found, for example, sitting right next to a person on an otherwise empty park bench caused the person to either move further along the bench or get up and walk away.

Invasions of personal space initiate threat with the likely response of flight, but what happens in a situation where a person cannot immediately move away? This question was investigated in a field study, which raised ethical questions, by Middlemast, Knowles and Matter (1976). Using a male public lavatory with three urinals side-by-side on the same wall, they hypothesized that delay in onset of micturation would be greater, and length of micturation shorter when a male was forced to use a urinal next to one already occupied (close distance) than when there was an empty urinal separating the two men

**Table 9.4** Effects of personal space invasions on the delay in onset and persistence of micturation in a male lavatory. Adapted from Middlemast *et al.* (1976).

| PERSONAL SPACE | DELAY IN MICTURATION (SECS) | PERSISTENCE OF MICTURATION (SECS) |
|---|---|---|
| *Close* | 8.4 | 17.4 |
| *Moderate* | 6.2 | 23.4 |
| *Control* | 4.9 | 24.8 |

(moderate distance) or only the male subject at the three urinals (control). Taking observations from a toilet stall using a periscope to observe micturation, their results, as shown in Table 9.4, upheld predictions.

In the close distance – invasion of personal space – both delay in onset and persistence of micturation were significantly affected when compared with the moderate and control conditions. Middlemast *et al.* explained this effect in terms of physiological arousal: when threatened by an invasion of personal space the body is aroused. In a different context, imagine how you would feel if you were sitting alone on the top deck of a double-decker bus, the bus stops, picks up a passenger, a stranger who comes upstairs and sits down beside you! What would you do? Look fixedly out of the window and feel distinctly anxious, I suspect. In humans then, as with animals, invasions of personal space represent invasions of what one considers to be one's own territory. Territorial invasions are threatening and responded to by flight or fight or arousal and anxiety if either of these options are not possible.

### 9.4.5 Self-presentation

The clothes we wear, the way we style and colour our hair, use make-up and adorn our body with other artifacts all represent self-expression. The way we choose to present ourselves to other people provides information about, for example, social class, ethnic identification, sub-cultural affiliation and whether we are married or single. Personality characteristics may also be inferred – a person who dresses in bright, showy clothes may give the impression of being an extrovert; a person dressed in dull, conventional clothing may be thought to be an introvert.

People may choose to dress and present themselves in certain ways to manage the impressions others form of them with the function of maintaining or enhancing self-esteem.

### 9.4.6 Paralanguage

'It's not what you say, but the way that you say it'. How often have you heard this said or said it yourself? Paralinguistic aspects of speech include prosody (pitch, stress, timing and pauses) and emotional tone of voice, accent, and speech errors such as stuttering 'ums' and 'ers', etc. Tone of voice can have important consequences. For example, Milmoe *et al.* (1967) found, in doctor–patient relationships, doctors to be more successful at getting alcoholics to take further treatment if they spoke in an anxious rather than angry voice. In mother–child relationships Milmoe found children to behave more irritably when the mother spoke in both an anxious and angry voice.

The speed at which a person talks may be an indicator of emotional stress, for example, highly anxious people often speak very quickly (Davitz, 1964). More serious, perhaps, are our expectations of speech rate, people suffering from a speech defect (stuttering) or who can only talk very slowly (as happens after a stroke sometimes) often get extremely frustrated by impatience shown by a 'normal' talker. The latter often interrupt, attempt to complete what the afflicted speaker is saying, or simply cease to continue with the conversation. Often people who speak in an abnormal way are also attributed as being of low intelligence, when there is no information to this effect.

## 9.5 Methodological issues

Research on non-verbal communication offers a good opportunity to examine methods used by social psychologists and provides a useful context for becoming aware of the problems and shortcomings associated with these methods. Three aspects of methodology will be dealt with: (a) encoding and decoding studies; (b) field studies and laboratory experiments; and (c) fine-grained measurement.

At a number of points in this chapter *encoding* and *decoding* research strategies have been referred to. The *encoding* approach focuses on the person who sends or encodes the non-verbal behaviour. Experiments here vary the relationship between the sender and receiver then measure the effect of the manipulation on the former. For example, Exline (1971) found that a person in an inferior position (low power) looks more at a high-power person than if power is evenly distributed in the dyad. With the *decoding* approach the focus of attention is on the receiver (decoder) and non-verbal behaviour becomes the independent, rather than dependent variable (see Chapter 1), so the perceptions of the receiver to variations in non-verbal behaviour are measured. Turning Exline's (1971) study around, a *decoding* experiment would test the hypothesis that a person who looks a lot will be perceived to be low in power. It is important to demonstrate consistent results using both encoding and decoding approaches because non-verbal behaviour can only be considered communicative when *both* the encoder and decoder make the same interpretations of the specific non-verbal behaviour.

Research on non-verbal communication employs both field studies and laboratory experiments. Field studies (as described in Chapter 1) may be of two sorts – field experiments and naturalistic observation. These give ecological validity and provide evidence, if results are consistent, that findings from laboratory experiments are generalizable and occur in the 'real world'. Laboratory experiments provide high levels of control over independent and intervening variables, whereas field research offers only low levels of control and so may result in findings that are due to a variable not controlled for. For example, if you were to conduct a study on personal space invasions, over a number of days, in the High Street and it was cold and rainy one day and hot and sunny the next, it would be difficult to tell whether the sex of the 'invader' (if that was your independent variable) or variations in the weather would best account for your findings. Counterbalancing would get rid of

| | NL SPEECH | EYES | BROWS | MOUTH | HEAD | GAZE | GAZE | HEAD | MOUTH | BROWS | EYES | JH SPEECH |
|---|---|---|---|---|---|---|---|---|---|---|---|---|
| 352 | and um | | | | | | | | | | | |
| 3 | sometimes | | | | | | | | | | | |
| 4 | of course it's | | | | | | | | | | | |
| 355 | only one of | | | | | | | | | | | |
| 6 | parents in which | | | | | | | | | | | |
| 7 | case you can | | | | | | | | | | | |
| 8 | take it | | | | | | | | | | | |
| 9 | away and | | | | | | | | | | | |
| 360 | | | | | | | | | | | | |
| 1 | let the | | | | | | | | | | | |
| 2 | other one feed them | | | | | | | | | | | |
| 3 | | | | | | | | | | | | |
| 4 | itself | | | | | | | | | | | |
| 5 | | | | | | | | | | | | |
| 6 | | | | | | | | | | | | some breed |
| 7 | | | | | | | | | | | | ers |
| 8 | | | | | | | | | | | | um |
| 9 | | | | | | | | | | | | pair |
| 370 | | | | | | | | | | | | with |
| 1 | | | | | | | | | | | | infer- |
| 2 | | | | | | | | | | | | -ior |
| 3 | | | | | | | | | | | | birds for |
| 4 | | | | | | | | | | | | this purp |
| 5 | | | | | | | | | | | | -ose |
| 6 | | | | | | | | | | | | |
| 7 | | | | | | | | | | | | em I mean |
| 8 | | | | | | | | | | | | |
| 9 | | | | | | | | | | | | |
| 380 | | | | | | | | | | | | those that don't |

Key:

HEAD □ erect, pointing forward; turned left; turned right; tilted left; tilted right; tilted back; tilted forward

BROWS normal; raised; W puckered or "frowning"

EYES o fully open; narrowed; closed

MOUTH — closed, lips relaxed; O lips relaxed, mouth open; lips pouting; = lips drawn tight at corners; lips forward, open mouth

GAZE P looking at Q

**Figure 9.5** Extract from a series of frames (numbers on the extreme left) where one long utterance ends (person NL) and another starts (person JH). The key shows the different non-verbal behaviours measured and the different ways in which each behaviour was coded. The main diagram depicts the non-verbal behaviours of each interactant frame-by-frame. From Kendon (1967).

confounding variables – but not all potential confounds can be taken into account.

Analysis and measurement of non-verbal behaviour are often very detailed: the *pictographic* system used by Kendon (1967) in his frame-by-frame analysis of two people in conversation will be described. Kendon (1967), as we shall see later in this chapter, was interested to discover if looking and eye-contact were synchronized with speech (particularly endings and beginnings of long utterances). He developed a system relating non-verbal behaviour to speech and measured head position, mouth, eyebrows, eyes, and looking of each person when they were in conversation. Seven measures of head position, three of eyes, five of mouth and three of eyebrows were taken, these are shown in the key to Figure 9.5. To see how this pictographic system works consider frame 367, JH has just started speaking and NL has just finished, i.e. a 'floor change' has occurred. NL has eyes fully open, normal eyebrows and closed, relaxed lips, NL's head is erect, face pointing forward and is looking (in the region of the eyes) at JH. JH is not looking at NL, has an erect head which tilts to left and right quickly, lips are pouting, eyebrows puckered and eyes narrowed. Kendon analysed seven two-person conversations lasting five minutes, frame-by-frame using this pictographic system.

Such analysis is very time consuming and because of this limits the number of non-verbal behaviours that can be sampled. For example, paralanguage, hand gestures and body orientation were not analysed by Kendon. To discover rules and patterns of non-verbal behaviour such detailed measurement is necessary.

## 9.6 Visual interaction

Many social psychologists regard visual communication as one, if not the, most important channel of non-verbal communication. Visual communication refers not only to looking and eye-contact but to the available and usable social cues gained from our being able to *see* another person when we interact with them. We will first consider structural aspects of visual interaction, followed by suggestions concerning function. Finally, the importance of eye-contact will be questioned by considering Rutter's (1984) view that visual access to the person with the availability of numerous non-verbal cues is of greater functional importance.

### 9.6.1 Structural aspects

For any face-to-face interaction between two people three measures of looking can be taken – duration of looking, number of looks and mean length of looks; the same three measures can be taken for eye-contact. It may also be of interest to take these measures for looking whilst listening and looking whilst speaking.

Argyle and Dean (1965) and Kendon (1967) pioneered research in this area. From their and many subsequent studies it has been found that, on average, during conversation people spend about 50–60 per cent of their time looking at the other person. Of this about twice as much time is spent looking whilst listening than looking whilst speaking, also the mean length of the former is greater than the latter. Individual variation is large, ranging from 30 to 70 per cent of the time looking – some people look a lot and others little. On average about 35 per cent of the time is spent in eye-contact, again individual variation is large – ranging from 10 to 40 per cent of the time. Eye-contact is usually brief, averaging about one second (with a range 0.7 to 1.5 seconds) whilst the mean length of looks is around three seconds.

Looking and eye-contact have been found to vary with topic of conversation (less when the topic is more intimate), proximity (less when close to another person), sex of the interactants and personality characteristics (Argyle and Cook, 1976 for a review). Argyle and Ingham (1972) found women in female–female dyads to look more than men in male–male dyads. The same research showed men to look more and women less in mixed-sex dyads than they do in single-sex dyads. Levine and Sutton-Smith (1973) found similar sex differences in children ranging from 4 to 11 years in age. The relationship between two people results in different amounts of looking and eye-contact. Rutter and Stephenson (1979) found that friends look less and engage in less eye-contact than strangers. However, if two people are in love looking, and eye-contact particularly, is much higher than in any other social relationship (Rubin, 1970).

Numerous personality variables have been found to affect visual inter-action. Exline (1971), for example, compared dominant and dependent people's looking behaviour when interviewed by a continuously staring con-federate of the experimenter. Dominant subjects looked more than dependent subjects at the interviewer. Also, dependent subjects looked less whilst listening than dominant subjects. Rutter, Morley and Graham (1972) found that extroverts look more and show a higher incidence of eye-contact than introverts.

People suffering mental illness, such as schizophrenics and depressives, have often been thought to look less and engage in less eye-contact than 'normal' people. Early research tended to support this view, but it was often based on impressions gained from clinical interviews. More recent research (summarized in Rutter, 1984) has questioned the validity of such a generaliza-tion: looking behaviour has been found to depend on the social context. When the topic of conversation is of a personal or intimate nature gaze aversion occurs, however, normal patterns of looking and eye-contact are found when the topic is impersonal. Who the schizophrenic interacts with also affects looking behaviour – looking and eye-contact is less in patient–nurse dyads than in patient–patient dyads, the latter producing normal levels of looking. Personal topics of conversation and low status (as in patient–nurse dyads) may produce anxiety and embarrassment resulting in gaze aversion with mentally ill patients.

### 9.6.2 Functional aspects

Visual communication serves two main functions: (a) expressive – the conveying of attitudes and emotions; and (b) informational – the regulation and monitoring of social encounters. Argyle pioneered theoretical thinking about the former function with the intimacy model, which was highly influential for a decade. Argyle and Dean (1965) proposed the intimacy model suggesting eye-contact plays an important role in establishing the nature of the relationship between two people. The intimacy model makes two assumptions: first, eye-contact is characterized by *both* approach and avoidance forces. The approach forces are needed for feedback and affilia-tion; the avoidance forces are fear of rejection and fear of revealing personal and private mental states. Second, since both forces are operating at once a balance or equilibrium should exist reflecting the degree of intimacy between two people, hence an equilibrium for intimacy develops and is a function of numerous non-verbal behaviours, as shown in Figure 9.6.

If the equilibrium appropriate to a certain level of intimacy is disturbed along one or more of these non-verbal dimensions, compensation should take place along the other dimensions. For example, if two strangers are made to sit too close to one another (at the intimate distance of 18 inches, for example) a reduction in eye-contact may occur to compensate for this. Con-versely, sitting two people farther apart than appropriate (say 10 feet) should result in greater levels of eye-contact to compensate for the relative lack of intimacy induced by distance. Argyle and Dean (1965) tested these predic-tions by using naive subjects and continuously staring confederates engaging in conversations at two, six and 10 feet. Results confirmed predictions but

$$
INTIMACY \ IS \ A \ FUNCTION \ OF \ \begin{cases} PHYSICAL \ PROXIMITY \\ EYE \ CONTACT \\ FACIAL \ EXPRESSION \ (SMILING) \\ TOPIC \ OF \ CONVERSATION \\ TONE \ OF \ VOICE \\ ETC. \end{cases}
$$

**Figure 9.6** The intimacy model of Argyle and Dean (1965).

because of methodological problems (conversation were not video-recorded) and because all looking on the part of the subject resulted in eye-contact (because of a continuously staring confederate) research using two naive subjects and video recording using split-screen and zoom lens was needed. This was introduced by Stephenson and Rutter (1970), and Pennington and Rutter (1981) tested the intimacy model using such a procedure. In this experiment 11-year-old pairs of boys and girls engaged in conversation at either two, six or 10 feet. Measures of both looking and eye-contact were taken. Figure 9.7 shows that both duration and mean length of looks increased with distance whilst the number of looks decreased. Duration of eye-contact also increased with distance.

One shortcoming of the intimacy model is its lack of predictive precision – it does not predict how equilibrium is restored in a specific way. Disequilibrium, caused, for example, by getting strangers to engage in a highly intimate conversation, may be restored by increasing interpersonal distance, smiling less, etc, instead of or as well as reducing eye-contact. The intimacy model also characterizes non-verbal behaviour as serving mainly emotional functions: Kendon (1967) proposed that looking and eye-contact function to regulate and monitor social interactions – informational functions. In a classic paper, Kendon showed looking and eye-contact to be synchronized with speech and function to assist in smooth floor changes or speaker switches.

Using frame-by-frame analysis (described earlier) of two people in conversation Kendon found that during long utterances (lasting five seconds or more) the listener looks at the speaker, but the speaker tends to look away (particularly during hesitant speech). Kendon observed that as the speaker came to the end of an utterance he would tend to look up at the listener. Since the listener would probably be looking at the speaker, eye-contact would occur. Kendon suggested this look from the speaker, resulting in eye-contact, is equivalent to non-verbally 'offering the floor' to the listener. If the listener took the floor, the new speaker tended to look away until well into the utterance and the old speaker, now the listener, continued to look. Kendon found 70 per cent of long utterances conformed to such a pattern.

Rutter *et al.* (1978) pointed out that Kendon's analysis did not specifically investigate floor changes, it investigated all long utterances which may or may not have ended in a floor change taking place. Rutter *et al.* (1978) argued that for Kendon to be correct three conditions needed to be fulfilled: (a) speakers should look more at the end of floor-change utterances than at the

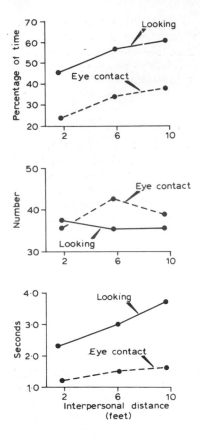

**Figure 9.7** Graphs showing how looking and eye-contact change with interpersonal distance. Graph (i) shows how percentage of time spent looking and eye-contact increase with increased interpersonal distance. Graph (ii) shows how the number of looks decreases with increased interpersonal distance. Graph (iii) shows how the average length of looks and eye-contact increases with increased interpersonal distance. From Pennington and Rutter (1981).

beginning of such utterances; (b) eye-contact should be high at the end of these utterances; and (c) low levels of eye-contact should be found at the beginning of new utterances.

To test these predictions an experiment was run in which six male, six female and six mixed-sex pairs of subjects discussed themselves and their interests for 20 minutes. The interactions were videotaped, 195 floor changes were recorded, and it was found that eye-contact occurred only about 50 per cent of the time at the beginning of new and the ending of old utterances. Looking by speakers occurred 66 per cent of the time at the end of an old utterance and 68 per cent of the time at the beginning of a new utterance. Looking by listeners occurred 76 per cent of the time at the end of an old utterance and 66 per cent of the time at the beginning of a new utterance.

For Kendon to be correct eye-contact should occur more often at the end of

an old utterance. If only about 50 per cent of floor changes are so characterized the listener is often missing the look of the speaker offering the floor.
Rutter (1984) argues that visual communication allows two people to *see* each
other and that it is the number of social cues available that is important, *not*
the specific non-verbal cues of looking and eye-contact.

### 9.6.3 Looking, seeing and cuelessness

Further evidence that eye-contact may be less functionally significant than
generally thought came from Strongman and Champness (1968). They ask us
to imagine, instead of two people interacting two robots have been pro-
grammed to look at and away from each other randomly and independently.
In such a situation eye-contact would simply be a *chance product* of each
robot's individual looking. The amount of eye-contact would be predicted
by:

$$\text{Amount of eye-contact} = \frac{A \times B}{T}$$

> where A is the duration
> of one robot's looks
> > B is the duration
> of the other robot's looks
> > > T is the duration
> of the interaction

If this chance formula is correct then knowledge of two people's individual
looking can be used to predict the *expected* amount of eye-contact, this can
then be compared with the *actual* amount observed. Rutter *et al.* (1977)
analysed all his previous research in this way and found extremely high correlations (around 0.98) between the actual eye-contact and the amount predicted by the chance formula.

This finding does not mean that eye-contact is not a significant event but
suggests that the degree of visual access to another person, called seeing,
rather than the specific individual components, is the most important thing
(the more we can see of another's non-verbal behaviour the more social cues
will be available). This led Rutter (1984) to predict that as the number of
social (non-verbal) cues available decreases (the degree of *cuelessness*) the
conversation should become more depersonalized and task oriented; this is
suggested by the cuelessness model of Rutter (1984), shown in Figure 9.8. The
model states that the fewer social cues available to a person the greater will he
or she experience a feeling of psychological distance. This will affect the
content of what is said (more depersonalized and task oriented) which in turn
will affect the style of speech (a less spontaneous conversation) and the
outcome of the interaction.

Experiments on negotiation by Morley and Stephenson (1969, 1970)
demonstrated how a reduction in social cues affected the outcome. Subjects
were assigned to be either management or union representatives and
instructed to attempt a settlement to a dispute. In one experiment the
management were given the stronger case, in the other the union had the
stronger case. In both experiments half the pairs of subjects negotiated face-

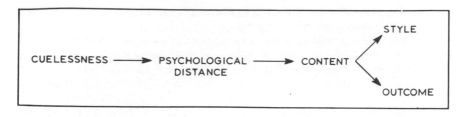

**Figure 9.8**  The cuelessness model of Rutter (1984).

to-face and the other half over an audio link only, the latter being similar to a telephone conversation. Morley and Stephenson found settlements in the face-to-face condition, regardless of who had the stronger case, resulted in compromise. However, in the audio condition the side with a stronger case usually obtained a settlement in their favour. In terms of Rutter's model the audio condition is greater in cuelessness, causing content to be both depersonalized and task oriented. Focusing so much on the tasks results in a favourable outcome in the manner outlined above. By contrast, a face-to-face situation is likely to evoke more sympathy from the person with the stronger case, resulting in a less favourable outcome for that person.

Other research (summarized in Rutter, 1984) testing the cuelessness model has confirmed style of conversation to be less spontaneous (interruptions occurred less frequently) the greater the degree of cuelessness. Content is affected by being more task oriented and depersonalized, evidenced by greater exchange of task-related information, discussion of outcomes and avoidance of irrelevant (personal) information. Rutter and Robinson (1981) compared the content and style of Open University tutorials conducted either face-to-face or over the telephone. Tutorials in both conditions were task oriented and impersonal, however, telephone tutorials were characterized by tutors seeking more contributions from students and students responding more. The style of conversation was less spontaneous and more structured in the telephone tutorials.

In summary, early theorizing with the intimacy model of Argyle and Dean wrongly assumed eye-contact to be of central importance in dyadic face-to-face interaction. Rutter (1984) argued that seeing and being seen is the crucial variable, seeing another allows many social cues to become available. This change in emphasis led to the cuelessness model, which states that as the number of non-verbal cues decreases (increasing cuelessness) greater psychological distance is felt. This results in a change in the content of what is said, which in turn affects the style of the conversation and its outcome.

## 9.7  Non-verbal behaviour and conversation

It is quite clear that conversations do not break down between two people when they are unable to see one another. We have all held telephone conversations and most of the time speaker changes take place quite smoothly. Consequently, other aspects of non-verbal behaviour must assist in smooth speaker changes since we rarely say to another 'now it is your turn to speak' or some such thing.

Duncan (1972) proposed three cues to be important for smooth speaker switches: (a) verbal cues – completion of a clause and sociocentric sequences such as 'you know'; (b) intonational cues – rising or falling intonation, drawl on the final syllables and a drop in loudness; and (c) gestures – particularly hand gestures signifying the end of an utterance. Note that both verbal and non-verbal cues are involved and all but one (gestures) do not require we see another person.

Beattie (1983) analysed speaker switches from conversations with six pairs of subjects. Smooth speaker switches were defined as the absence of simultaneous claims to speak by both people. In over 200 smooth turn takings, 13 per cent took place in the absence of any of the cues suggested by Duncan (1972). In no instances were five or six cues cojointly present, however half the speaker switches occurred when three cues were present. This was a much higher percentage than for one, two or four cues which were each present about 15 per cent of the time. The most common cue was syntactic clause completion, which was present about 60 per cent of the time. Finally, well over 90 per cent of speaker switches occurred when both clause completion *and* change in pitch of the voice were present. Generally, the results of this study support Duncan's proposals and refine them since three cues are present for most smooth speaker switches and two of these are almost always present. Hence, both vocal and non-vocal aspects of spontaneous speech contribute to smooth floor changes.

### 9.7.1 Spontaneous speech and hesitations

The spontaneous speech that takes place in social interaction differs markedly from written language or when written text is read aloud: spontaneous speech is peppered with hesitations.

Hesitations are of two types – filled or unfilled. Unfilled hesitations or pauses are silences between words or clauses of more than 200 milliseconds. These silences are significantly longer than normal spaces between words. Filled hesitations can be of four types:

| | |
|---|---|
| (a) Repetitions | – repeating the same word of phrase without adding to the meaning. |
| (b) Parenthetic remarks | – words or phrases that do not add to the meaning such as 'I mean', 'Well', 'you know'. |
| (c) Filled pauses | – 'Ah', 'er', 'um', etc. |
| (d) False starts | – errors of speech quickly corrected by the speaker. |

Goldman-Eisler (1968) showed unfilled pauses to account for between 4 and 50 per cent of spontaneous speech time. Hesitations serve two functions: filled hesitations help the speaker to keep the floor since it is difficult to interrupt on these occasions. Unfilled hesitations assist the speaker in planning what he or she is going to say (Beattie, 1983). Goldman-Eisler (1968) found unfilled pauses occurred more frequently and lasted longer when subjects had to interpret rather than give a description of a cartoon. Generally, tasks requiring more thought and attention result in more and longer unfilled pauses than simple tasks or when talking about things we know a lot about.

If this is the case it should follow that distractions result in an increase in the frequency of hesitations. To test this prediction Beattie (1983) had a continuously staring confederate interview 10 subjects separately. Having someone continuously stare at you whilst you are talking should be distracting since more eye-contact will take place than the speaker would like when he or she is concentrating on and planning what to say next. Distraction should result in less fluent speech, i.e. more hesitations. Beattie found an increase in filled hesitations, especially false starts compared to subjects who were looked at normally. However, the number and mean length of unfilled pauses was not greater.

The necessity of unfilled hesitations for planning spontaneous speech was demonstrated in a study by Beattie and Bradbury (1979). Subjects were asked to tell a story and in one condition they were 'punished' whenever they paused (unfilled) for more than 600 milliseconds. Subjects were found to reduce the number of such unfilled pauses as storytelling proceeded; however, as this happened the frequency of repetitive speech increased. A compensatory mechanism seems to be working – deprived of the normal way of planning spontaneous speech people employ other types of hesitations in compensation.

Given that planning time is needed continuously in spontaneous speech it is pertinent to ask whether this time is more crucial at some points rather than others. Beattie (1983) analysed hesitations in speech with this question in mind and found three things: (a) alternations between hesitant and fluent speech; (b) long clauses contained more hesitations than short ones; and (c) hesitations were more likely to occur at the beginning of a clause rather than towards the middle or end. Planning, then, takes place at the beginning of an utterance, and the longer the utterance the more planning time the speaker requires.

### 9.7.2 Interruptions

Smooth speaker-switches often work because the speaker is willing to yield the floor. However, if the listener wishes to speak and the speaker is unwilling to let him do so, the listener may interrupt. Interruptions often indicate a breakdown in social interaction since they violate turn-taking rules and, whilst often effective, incur penalties such as being perceived as rude or domineering.

Personality characteristics have been related to the tendency to interrupt; for example, people high in neuroticism (Rim, 1977) and extroversion (Natale, 1979) tend to interrupt a lot. People who fear negative social evaluation interrupt less than those without such an anxiety. Zimmerman and West (1975) found men interrupted more in conversations between mixed-sex pairs. This may be explained by the tendency for men to dominate and attempt to exercise power in conversations with women.

But what precisely are interruptions? Most researchers have simply regarded instances of spontaneous speech as interruptions, Beattie (1983) though, has identified the following four categories of interruptions:

(a) Overlap – successful speaker switch, presence of simultaneous speech and the first speaker's utterance is complete.
(b) Simple interruption – successful speaker switch, presence of simultaneous speech and the first speaker's utterance is incomplete.
(c) Silent interruption – successful speaker switch, absence of simultaneous speech and the first speaker's utterance is incomplete.
(d) Butting-in interruption – unsuccessful speaker switch, presence of simultaneous speech.

Three types of interruptions (a, b and c) result in successful speaker switches, the silent interruption takes place during a speaker's unfilled pause.

In dyadic conversations Beattie (1983) found 10 per cent of speaker switches to involve interruptions, in groups of three or more people the frequency increased to over 30 per cent. In the latter, overlap interruptions were the most common (42 per cent), followed by simple interruptions (33 per cent), butting-in (15 per cent) and silent interruptions (10 per cent). Status of speaker affected the frequency of interruptions: students interrupted tutors 37 per cent of the time, tutors interrupted students 26 per cent and students interrupted other students in 51 per cent of speaker switches. Greater incidence of interruptions in groups larger than two may be expected since more listeners would be wanting to take the floor from the speaker. Overlap interruptions, the most polite form, were the most frequent because the listener is 'jumping in' almost as the speaker has finished.

Beattie (1983) made a novel extension to his study of interruptions by analysing videotapes of live political interviews shown on television prior to the 1979 general election. The politicians were James Callaghan (the then Prime Minister) and Margaret Thatcher (then leader of the Conservative Party). Beattie was interested to discover if different turn-taking styles were exhibited by the politicians.

The videotapes were analysed to compare the frequency of smooth speaker switches with interruptions, Table 9.5 summarizes the findings. As can be seen, D. Tuohy interrupted Margaret Thatcher (19 times) more than L. Gardner interrupted James Callaghan (14 times). Margaret Thatcher interrupted D. Tuohy less (10 times) than James Callaghan interrupted L. Gardner (23 times). Overlap interruptions were more common by politicians

**Table 9.5** Relative frequency of smooth speaker switches and interruptions by politicians and interviewers. Adapted from Beattie (1983).

| SPEAKER 1 – SPEAKER 2 | SMOOTH SPEAKER SWITCHES | INTERRUPTIONS | | | | |
|---|---|---|---|---|---|---|
| | | Total | Simple | Overlap | Butting in | Silent |
| M. Thatcher – D. Tuohy | 17 | 19 | 4 | 4 | 11 | 0 |
| D. Tuohy M. Thatcher | 16 | 10 | 1 | 8 | 0 | 1 |
| J. Callaghan – L. Gardner | 28 | 14 | 4 | 6 | 4 | 0 |
| L. Gardner J. Callaghan | 19 | 23 | 8 | 11 | 4 | 0 |

(19) than by interviewers (10) – this type of interruption is made more by dominant people (Ferguson, 1977).

An intriguing difference was that Margaret Thatcher did not butt in on D. Tuohy, but D. Tuohy butted in on Margaret Thatcher 11 times. Further analysis revealed that Margaret Thatcher's speech style to be such that people thought she had come to the end of an utterance (indicated by clause completion and change in pitch of voice) when in fact she had not. Margaret Thatcher has developed a particularly skilled interviewing style which leads the interviewer to predict the end of an utterance and expect a floor change when this is not the case. It was also found that Margaret Thatcher would engage in simultaneous speech much longer than is usual when interrupted in order to retain the floor. Most people engage in simultaneous speech for, on average, 500 milliseconds, by contrast Margaret Thatcher would spend as long as five seconds in simultaneous speech.

Margaret Thatcher has developed a turn-taking style which allows her to hold the floor for long periods, force the interviewer to interrupt her and not allow interruptions to result in floor changes. It is hardly surprising that she is regarded as dominant in interviews!

## 9.8  Social skills

Much of this chapter has examined the structure and function of interpersonal communication between two people in normal, social interaction. We have found that listeners look more than speakers, eye-contact may assist smooth turn-taking, visual access (seeing) to another's non-verbal behaviour is important for spontaneous conversation and making the conversation more personal. The ability to notice verbal and paralinguistic cues is important for smooth speaker-switches (Duncan, 1972). Hesitations, both filled and unfilled, help a speaker plan what he or she wants to say, and interruptions (overlap) demonstrate the skill of the listener to predict the end of a speaker's utterance. Such findings can be viewed from the perspective of telling us what normally takes place in effective, rewarding and satisfying social interactions. This would not be the case if we were unable to make appropriate interpretations and responses to another's non-verbal cues as well as make those responses ourselves. Failure at these aspects of interpersonal communication may result in loss of friends and acquaintances leading, in extreme cases, to social isolation and rejection.

Thinking of interpersonal communication in this way has led social psychologists to regard social interaction as a *skilled* performance and the behaviours that take place as *social skills*. This has led to an understanding of and therapeutic treatment (Social Skills Training or SST) for people considered socially inadequate. SST is used not only with psychiatric patients and criminal offenders but also with managers, supervisers, interviewers, etc. to make them more competent in their social performance.

Michael Argyle (1983) suggests that social skills are similar to motor skills, which implies five things: (a) they are directed towards some end, such as changing another's attitudes, conveying emotional states, or impressing, etc.; (b) they are selective – only a small number of the available non-verbal cues are attended to; (c) control – people have control over what they say and how they say it; (d) feedback is of vital importance – monitoring how what you say and do is being received by the other person; and (e) timing of responses – anticipating the correct or appropriate responses from the other person and timing your responses to fit these.

There are three additional aspects of social skills not present with motor skills: (a) each person acts independently and exerts influences upon each other; (b) you are able to put yourself in another person's shoes, i.e. empathize with what the other person is thinking and feeling; and (c) other people are attracted to us if they find us rewarding to be with.

To summarize, being socially skilled involves *perceptual sensitivity*, 'meshing' with the other's non-verbal behaviour, control over your own behaviour and the ability to take the role of another.

To appreciate how social skills training is used, a study assessing the effects of such training on adolescent male offenders living in a short stay Regional Assessment Centre will be described. Spence and Marzillier (1979) had five boys, ranging in age from 10 to 15 years, referred to them for SST because of difficulties with staff and peer interaction. Typically, the boys had few close friends, tended to be aggressive and were often rude to staff. The social skills performance of these boys was assessed in three ways: (a) administering questionnaires to staff; (b) interviewing the boys; and (c) analysis of videotapes of the boys talking with an adult. These assessments revealed avoidance of eye-contact, inappropriate head movements, excessive hand fiddling movements, lack of verbal acknowledgements ('yes', 'mm', 'I see', etc.) and a lack of verbal feedback ('did you?', 'really?', 'Oh?', etc.). Generally, the boys were unresponsive, disinterested and did little to maintain social interactions.

Each boy received 7 to 10 training sessions using modelling, role-playing, videotaped feedback and social reinforcement. Modelling consists of showing the person appropriate and normal non-verbal behaviour, which then has to be imitated by the trainee. Video feedback involves videorecording the person in social interaction, playing this back and pointing out inappropriate behaviour. Social reinforcement consists largely of verbally rewarding ('good', 'well done') the person for desired behaviours. The training sessions were split up such that just one of the deficiencies, outlined above, was concentrated on in each session.

Results showed mixed success with SST: eye-contact increased and hand fiddling decreased, however little change was found with inappropriate head movements and increasing the incidence of verbal acknowledgements. Verbal feedback questions were the most difficult to train with the boys. In a follow-up study two weeks later, Spence and Marzillier found improvements to be maintained and staff reported positive changes. It would have been useful to have conducted a follow-up study after a long period of time, say six months, to see if the changes were still present.

Clinicians who practice SST assume improvements in social skills result in successful social interaction across a wide range of social situations. Spence (1981) attempted to relate 13 measures of social skill to friendliness, social anxiety, perceived employability and social skills performance. Seventy adolescent male offenders were each interviewed by an adult stranger for five minutes, the interviews were videotaped. Independent judges rated the boys, on 10-point scales, on the above four variables. These ratings were then correlated with the 13 behaviours (for example, gestures, fiddling, eye-contact, smiling, interruptions, questions asked) thought to be important in social skills performance.

The measures of eye-contact and verbal initiations correlated highly with all four variables. Friendliness and employability correlated best with fluency of speech and smiling; frequent head movements were indicative of social anxiety. A high frequency of questions asked and interruptions correlated positively with social skills performance and employability. The general point this study makes is that clinicians should know what they are training a person for so that the most appropriate behavioural deficits can be attended to and remedied.

Ineffective social interaction by psychiatric patients (depressives, schizophrenics, neurotics) centres around two problems: (a) an inability to sustain a friendly, cooperative and rewarding interaction; and (b) they themselves find social encounters stressful and unrewarding. SST attempts to break this vicious circle by teaching appropriate social skills in the hope that the latter problem will be ameliorated. People who have been incarcerated in a psychiatric hospital for years, even decades, are given extensive SST to help ease their transition back into the outside world. Such training focuses on helping people cope with the everyday demands of life such as shopping, going to the post office, asking directions, etc. Techniques used differ very little from those outlined above.

Social skills training has not been without its critics: three will be mentioned here. The first concerns the general idea of conceptualizing social interaction in terms of a social skill, where the term 'skill' connotes achieving an objective or end result, whilst this is true of motor skills (riding a bicycle, driving a car) it may not be true of social interactions. People often engage in social encounters because they are valuable and pleasurable in their own right. Second, the social skills approach implicitly assumes there is a desirable norm or ideal 'social person'. The approach suggests it is desirable to be socially active, warm, friendly, assertive and empathic, and that being cold, self-interested and introverted is undesirable. Such a moral judgement over how we should be is a dangerous one for social psychologists to make and culture-bound. Furnham (1979) cites research to show how other cultures (particularly eastern ones) value humility, subservience and tolerance in preference to assertiveness. Within our own culture prescribing how we should be denies individual choice – if a person wishes to lead a secluded life and behave antisocially why shouldn't he or she provided this does not cause harm to others? Third, it has often been found (Rutter, 1984) that psychiatric patients are *competent* at social skills but that when mentally ill it is their *performance* that suffers. It is as if such people know the appropriate social behaviour but are unable to engage in it because of their degree of mental distress. If this is the case social skills training is redundant or even counterproductive, since such training may serve to promote even greater confusion.

## 9.9 Summary

O Non-verbal communication includes both vocal (but not verbal) and non-vocal aspects of behaviour that occur in social interaction. Verbal communication is better for communicating logical or abstract ideas, non-verbal communication conveys emotional states and regulates interpersonal interaction.

○ Non-human animals communicate both within and between species using non-verbal behaviour, such behaviour is a product of evolution but requires experience for the innate potential to be fully realized.

○ Cross-cultural consistencies provide evidence for the inheritance of expression of emotion in man, decoding studies produce stronger evidence for this than encoding studies. Studies on deaf and blind born children suggest basic emotional expression to be innate.

○ The main channels of non-verbal communication are looking and eye-contact, facial expression, body language (touch, posture, hand gestures, etc.), personal space, self-presentation and paralanguage.

○ Visual interaction has been regarded as the most important aspect of non-verbal behaviour in social interaction. Looking and eye-contact were thought, in the intimacy model of Argyle and Dean, to convey emotional states.

○ Eye-contact was shown by Kendon to be important for smooth speaker switches to take place, the speaker looks up at the end of an utterance, and so engages in eye-contact with the listener, to offer the floor to the listener.

○ Subsequent research by Rutter suggested seeing to be more important since this gives access to numerous non-verbal cues. The cuelessness model states that greater psychological distance is felt as the number of social cues decreases, this results in changes in the content and subsequently the style and outcome of the interaction.

○ Duncan proposed that both verbal and non-verbal cues contributed to smooth turn-taking, the most common being clause completion and change in pitch of the voice. Hesitations in spontaneous speech assist the speaker in planning what he is going to say and help him retain the floor.

○ Non-verbal behaviour in social interaction has been conceptualized as a social skill, this involves perceptual sensitivity, meshing, control over behaviour and the ability to empathize with the other person. Social Skills Training (SST) is used by clinical psychologists to assist people in becoming more effective socially; psychiatric patients and criminals offenders are often trained in this way.

## 9.10 Suggestions for further reading

Argyle, M. *The Psychology of Interpersonal Behaviour* (Harmondsworth, Penguin, 1983) 4th edition.
This is probably the best book to go to if you wish to pursue matters discussed in this chapter in greater depth. Michael Argyle is one of the leading researchers in this field and his book is readable and up to date.

Argyle, M. *Social Encounters: Readings in Social Interaction* (Harmondsworth, Penguin, 1973).
Edited by Argyle, this book contains some of the more influential papers contributing to the development of this area. Many of the readings are journal articles so they may be difficult to understand in places, especially for those without statistical knowledge.

Beattie, G. *Talk: An Analysis of Speech and Non-Verbal Behaviour in Conversation* (Milton Keynes, Open University Press, 1983).
Highly readable, and at times entertaining, account of Beattie's research on the relationship between speech and non-verbal behaviour. Has a chapter devoted to the analysis of political interviews.

Rutter, D.R. *Looking and Seeing: The Role of Visual Communication in Social Interaction*. (Chichester, John Wiley & Sons, 1984).
A more technical book and, in places, presents rather a lot of data to assimilate. However, the book does represent the 'state of the art' of theory and research in this area. Reads rather like a detective story, since it traces development of theories on looking and their demise.

# 10

# Social influence

10.1    Introduction
10.2    Compliance
10.3    Conformity
        *10.3.1 The autokinetic effect   10.3.2 The Asch paradigm   10.3.3 Factors
        affecting conformity   10.3.4 Resisting group pressures*
        *10.3.5 Explanations   10.3.6 A child of the times?*
10.4    Group polarization
        *10.4.1 The polarization phenomenon   10.4.2 Explanations*
10.5    Obedience to authority
        *10.5.1 Milgram's experiments   10.5.2 Further findings   10.5.3 Defying authority*
10.6    The influence of roles
10.7    Is there a conforming personality?
10.8    Minority influence
        *10.8.1 Status and power   10.8.2 Behavioural style*
10.9    Summary
10.10   Suggestions for further reading

## 10.1 Introduction

Throughout our lives attempts are made, either directly or indirectly to influence the way we think, feel and behave. Similarly, we spend much time in social interaction attempting to influence others to think, feel or act as we do. Indeed the continuance of any society demands a degree of *conformity* to social norms; society also demands people *comply* with requests and *obey* authority at times. However, people are not sheep, they do not blindly conform, comply or obey whenever the opportunity arises. As we saw when considering Erikson's theory of identity (in Chapter 3) it is of fundamental importance for an individual to feel a unique sense of identity. Yielding to social influence of whatever type or form, is counter to this. Hence, the individual is often placed in the conflicting situation of needing to maintain his or her own sense of identity and independence whilst at the same time being required or expected to conform, obey or comply with other people's wishes, prevailing norms, or standards. Failure to fall in with the 'crowd' may incur painful penalties – ranging from ostracism to imprisonment if a law has been broken; whilst failure to achieve and maintain a sense of identity may result in low self-esteem, low self-confidence and, in more extreme cases, depression and apathy. Social influence may be either readily accepted by a person, both consciously and unconsciously, or yielded to reluctantly or resisted. This chapter explores different types of social influences and factors likely to increase or decrease influence, and explanations of why people comply, conform and obey.

This chapter also addresses the question of whether a certain personality type is associated with high levels of conformity, compliance and obedience. In looking at this issue we again, as in other chapters, consider how the social situation in which a person finds him or herself and the psychological make-up of the person *interact* to determine behaviour (Endler and Magnusson, 1976). Finally, the chapter changes emphasis from majority influence, which is the main concern up to this point, to minority influence. The issue addressed here is how an individual or small group of people holding views opposed to the majority or the prevailing norms come to influence the majority and change the status quo.

## 10.2 Compliance

Compliance may be defined as 'a response to a direct attempt to influence someone by means of a request' (Baron and Byrne, 1977). The important point here is that one person explicitly asks (not commands or exercises authority) another to act in a certain way.

Four main variables have been found to affect compliance – reciproca-tion, foot-in-the-door technique, transgressions and self-esteem. Apsler (1975) found lowering of self-esteem, by getting people to say and do foolish things, resulted in high levels of compliance; this occurs, he suggested, in an attempt to recover loss of face. Wallace and Sadalla (1966) found people caught in the act of doing something wrong complied more when subse-quently asked than people who had done something wrong but had not been caught. Regan (1971) demonstrated reciprocation by finding greater compli-ance from people who had previously been done a favour than a control group not done a favour.

The foot-in-the-door technique, where a person first makes a small request followed by a large request, is often effective in getting people to comply with the large request. Freedman and Fraser (1966) asked homeowners if they would display a very *large* sign in their front garden which read 'DRIVE CARE-FULLY'. There were two experimental conditions and a control group. The control group were simply asked to display the large sign without a prior smaller request. Experimental Group A were first asked to display a *small* sign reading 'DRIVE CAREFULLY' (same type of request); experimental Group B were first asked to sign a petition about a conservation matter (different type of request). Greatest compliance for the large request (displaying the very large sign) was found when the small request had been of the same type – here 75 per cent complied. When the smaller request was different compliance dropped to around 50 per cent, in the control group compliance was only 17 per cent. The most likely explanation for the success of the foot-in-the-door technique is that people are basically helpful and do not mind complying with small requests. Having complied with the small request and attempting to be consistent with this self-image of being helpful, people feel impelled to go along with subsequent requests (Freedman and Fraser, 1966).

Cialdini (1975) has demonstrated the contrary approach also to be effective in getting a person to do what you want. First, a request is made which is large enough to be unreasonable, this is followed by a more reasonable request and one that you really wish the person to comply with. This technique appears only to work when the same individual makes both requests, the foot-in-the-door technique works equally well when the same or different individuals make the small and large request (Cann, Sherman and Elkes, 1978).

## 10.3 Conformity

Conformity differs from compliance in two ways: it involves (a) a change in behaviour *towards* a group or social norm; and (b) pressure from a *group of people* rather than a request from an individual. Conformity is defined as 'a change in behaviour or belief toward a group as a result of real or imagined group pressure' (Keisler and Keisler, 1972, p. 1). This implies two things; first, the change toward the group is that accepted and approved by the group. Conforming to the expectations and norms of one group may be deviant in reference to another social group: for example, dressing like a 'punk' with a coloured, mohican hair style, torn clothing, etc. conforms to the punk sub-culture but is deviant to a Hell's Angels group. Second, the person has a choice in how to respond to group pressure. Crutchfield (1955) suggests three responses are possible: conformity, independence and anti-conformity. The latter is where an individual deliberately does the opposite to group expectations; independence is where the individual does what he or she would do in the absence of group pressure.

In what follows we will first look at experimental techniques used to measure and demonstrate conformity, then at factors affecting conformity and resistance to group pressures, finally some explanations offered by social psychologists of why people conform will be considered.

### 10.3.1 The autokinetic effect

Sherif (1936) demonstrated people conform to group norms when they find themselves in highly ambiguous, novel situations. To show this he made use of what is known as the *autokinetic effect*: placed in an otherwise dark room with a spotlight projected onto a screen, the stationary spot of light appears to move. Subjects asked to make judgements about the extent of 'movement' when alone in the room show great variability. A single subject repeating the task many times develops a standard range into which most judgements fall, however, *different* subjects develop different ranges. For example, one subject may develop a range of 20–30 cm whilst another a range of 60–80 cm. The influence of group norms was investigated by putting three subjects together, two whose standard range was very similar and one whose range was very different, and asking them to announce aloud their individual estimates of movement of the light. Sherif found that over numerous trials at this task in these conditions, the group converged on a common range and the range was very similar to that of the two subjects initially sharing a similar range. In effect, the 'deviant' person conformed to the group norm. In a further study Sherif found conformity to the majority group judgement to occur much more quickly when subjects had no prior experience of the task and hence had not already developed a 'frame of reference'. In such a situation, where an inexperienced subject sat in the darkened room with two subjects experienced and sharing the same standard range for movement of the spot of light, the group norm becomes the frame of reference for the person new to the situation.

Generally, the more ambiguous the situation and the less experience a person has had in such a situation the more powerful will be the influence of a group with pre-existing, established norms.

### 10.3.2 The Asch paradigm

Solomon Asch (1955) devised an experimental set-up to investigate conformity which has been used and modified by numerous subsequent researchers. The basic experiment involves presenting a subject with a standard line and three comparison lines, the subject then has the seemingly simple task of judging which comparison line is closest to the standard line in length. Figure 10.1 gives an example of the stimuli typically used by Asch: as you can see the task is an *unambiguous one*. To study conformity Asch put a subject in a room with seven other people who were confederates of the experimenter but thought to be other subjects by the naive subject in the room. Things were arranged so the naive subject sat at the end of the row. Each person in the room had to state publicly which comparison line was most similar to the standard line. Since the naive subject sat at the end of the row he or she had to listen to the judgements of the confederates before giving his or her judgement.

A typical experiment would proceed as follows: each person in the group would be presented with 18 pairs of cards similar to those shown in Figure 10.1. On the first two of these 18 trials all the confederates would give the *correct* response. Thereafter on 12 of the remaining 16 trials *all* the confederates would give the same *incorrect* response. A control group of subjects performed the 18 judgement trials on their own and hence in the absence of group pressure. Asch was interested in whether subjects would conform to the unanimous but incorrect majority.

Subjects in the control group conditions made correct judgements 95 per cent of the time, in contrast, in the presence of unanimous, incorrect judge-

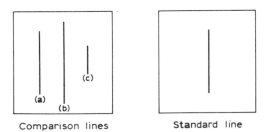

Comparison lines     Standard line

**Figure 10.1** Example of the line judgement task used by Asch (1955). Notice how easy, i.e. unambiguous, the task is.

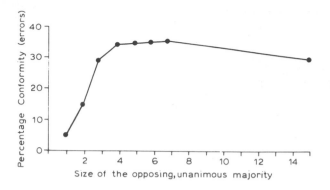

**Figure 10.2** Effect of the size of a unanimous, incorrect majority on conformity in naive subjects. Adapted from Asch (1955).

ments 80 per cent of subjects agreed at least once with the incorrect majority. Eight per cent of subjects agreed with the incorrect majority all the time, and on average subjects conformed between four and five times on the critical 12 trials. Asch interviewed each subject after the experiment: those who agreed with the majority most of the time gave various reasons for their behaviour. For example, that the group was actually correct, that they did not want to spoil the experimenter's results, and that they went along with the majority to avoid creating disharmony and conflict. Subjects who never conformed gave the following reasons for maintaining independence: confident their judgement was correct, and thinking the majority was correct but could not agree with them since that was not what they saw.

Asch conducted numerous experiments using this paradigm to investigate conformity, for example, the size of the unanimous majority giving a wrong judgement was varied from between one and 15 people. As can be seen from Figure 10.2 the effect of one person is very small (only about five per cent conform), this increases to 15 per cent conformity with two people, to 30 per cent with three and 35 per cent with four. Above four group size makes very little difference to conformity levels. In another series of experiments Asch varied the length of the *difference* between the comparison lines. In one experiment he made the difference between the longest and shortest line 7 inches, in another the difference was less than two inches. Conformity decreased as the difference in length between the lines increased. Generally, the more difficult and ambiguous the task the more people conform (Moscovici and Faucheux, 1972).

Crutchfield (1955) and Deutsch and Gerard (1955) devised an experimental procedure which allowed for a number of subjects to be tested at once and where the subject does not have to give his or her response verbally and in the presence of others. The Asch paradigm is costly in terms of time and the number of confederates needed and requires good acting from the confederates. Crutchfield (1955) had five subjects sit in separate booths, side by side. In front of each subject was a box with lights and switches on it, as shown in Figure 10.3. The stimulus material – which varied from line judgement, dot

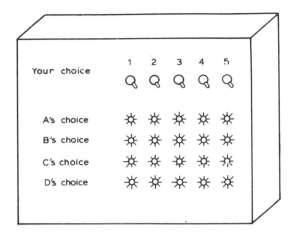

**Figure 10.3** The Crutchfield apparatus placed in front of a subject in a booth. Other subjects, in separate booths, would have a similar device in front of them.

counting, and statements of opinion – was presented on a screen in front of the subjects. The experimenter then turned on the lights, via a remote control device, of 'subjects' A to D according to a prearranged schedule. The subjects sitting in the booths would then be required to indicate their choice by flicking one of the five switches.

Conformity using this procedure was found to be lower than in the Asch paradigm, for example, only about 50 per cent conformed to a wrong judgement where the task involved estimating whether a particular circle had a larger area than a star. With statements of opinion conformity was found to be even lower, for example, only 37 per cent of subjects (military men in this case) agreed with the statement 'I doubt whether I would make a good military leader' when given cause to believe four other people had agreed with this statement.

Comparison of the Asch and Crutchfield procedures suggest different processes might be operating since subjects in the former procedure are required to state publicly their judgements – in the latter this is done in private. This is explained by Kelman (1958) who distinguishes between public compliance and private acceptance (internalization). Public compliance is where somebody publically conforms to group norms but privately maintains a different opinion; here the individual is said to be under *normative* pressure to conform. Internalization or private acceptance is where the person believes the group to be correct and believes those opinions him or herself. Conformity here is due to *informational* pressure – the group provides information about how reality is to be interpreted. Generally, the more ambiguous a situation the greater the informational pressure to conform; the less ambiguous the situation or task the greater will normative pressure exert a conforming influence.

### 10.3.3 Factors affecting conformity

Normative social influence might be expected to be greater in face-to-face situations rather than in situations where individuals give responses in private. Deutsch and Gerard (1955) confirmed this in an experiment using the judging task of Asch but where subjects had either to give their responses in the presence of others or privately.

Other variables found to affect conformity are: (a) the attractiveness of the group for the individual – the more attractive the greater will be conformity to group norms (Festinger, Schachter and Back, 1950); (b) reference groups – groups whom we both like and compare ourselves to – are particularly powerful sources of social influence (Newcombe, 1943) (c) self-esteem was shown to be important in an experiment by Stang (1973). Here subjects were divided into those with high and those with low self-esteem, each was then put in the Crutchfield set-up. Subjects high in self-esteem conformed less than those with low self-esteem. Weisenthal *et al.* (1976) found people who perceived themselves as competent or skilled at certain tasks were less likely to conform than those less skilled or experienced at that task. Presumably, informational influence is stronger for those less skilled or less competent than the other people in the group.

Asch (1955) investigated the effect of an incorrect *non-unanimous* majority in two ways: (a) where one of the confederates always gave the correct judgement and others the same incorrect judgement; and (b) when a confederate first gave a correct judgement but subsequently defected to the incorrect, majority view. Conformity in (a) occurred only 5 per cent of the time compared with over 30 per cent when the majority was unanimous. Conformity was found to increase when the 'supporter' defected to the majority view – condition (b) above.

Reinforcement has been shown to increase conformity: Endler (1966) gave positive reinforcement (reward) to subjects who agreed with the majority; a control group were given no rewards at all when making judgements. Conformity was greatest when subjects were rewarded for agreeing with an incorrect majority; it was also found that conformity was highest when subjects were rewarded *every* time they agreed with the majority rather than every *other* time.

### 10.3.4 Resisting group pressure

Asch (1955) showed, as we have just seen, how the support of one person has a considerable effect on another to resist social pressure. Further research has shown both the timing (Morris and Miller, 1975) and quality (Allen and Levine, 1971) of that support to be of importance.

Morris and Miller (1975), using the Crutchfield technique, had one condition in which the supporter (confederate giving the correct judgement) made the correct response before a majority gave the same incorrect response. In another condition support was given after the majority opinion had been expressed. A control group of subjects was exposed to an incorrect unanimous majority. It was predicted that conformity would be least when the supporter responded *after* the incorrect majority. Results, shown in

**Table 10.1** Effect of social support (given either before or after the majority) upon conformity. Note that any kind of support is better than none at all. Adapted from Morris and Miller (1975).

| | NO SOCIAL SUPPORT: (UNANIMOUS INCORRECT - MAJORITY) | TIMING OF SOCIAL SUPPORT | |
| --- | --- | --- | --- |
| | | *Before majority* | *After majority* |
| Percentage conformity | 46.3 | 23.0 | 28.3 |

Table 10.1, were in the opposite direction: conformity was least when the supporter responded *before* the majority. Morris and Miller explained this by suggesting support before the majority provides the subject with immediate confirmation of his or her own judgement upon first viewing the stimulus material.

Allen and Levine (1971) looked at the effect of either credible or noncredible social support. The task was one involving visual perception and the supporter was presented in one of two ways to the subject: where (a) he wore glasses with thick lenses and said he had a sight problem: or (b) the person did not wear glasses and made no reference to his sight. Results confirmed predictions: conformity was lowest when the supporter's credibility was doubtful – condition (a). The above two experiments demonstrate: (a) timing and credibility of support help people resist group pressure; and (b) any support, ill-timed or of doubtful credibility, is better than none at all since it results in less conformity than where there is a unanimous incorrect majority.

Most experiments on conformity have controlled for sex of subjects, usually by ensuring half to be male and half female. Comparisons between males and females have found the latter to conform more than the former. Sistrunk and David (1971) claimed this occurs not because females are more conforming but because the tasks given subjects tend to have masculine connotations. They conducted an experiment in which sex of subject and gender normally associated with the task was varied (masculine items, feminine items and neutral items were used). They found, as shown in Table 10.2, three things: (a) males and females showed no difference in levels of conformity for neutral items; (b) males conformed *more* than females on feminine items; and (c) females conformed more than males on masculine items. These differences are explained in terms of familiarity and confidence subjects had with the test materials prior to taking part in the experiment.

**Table 10.2** Percentage conformity by male and female subjects on neutral, masculine and feminine test items. Adapted from Sistrunk and McDavid (1971).

| SEX OF SUBJECT | ASSOCIATED GENDER OF MATERIAL | | |
| --- | --- | --- | --- |
| | *Neutral* | *Masculine* | *Feminine* |
| *Male* | 39.5 | 34.0 | 44.0 |
| *Female* | 39.0 | 42.0 | 34.5 |

## 10.3.5 Explanations

Why do people yield to group pressure and conform? In a highly ambiguous or novel social situation conformity may be readily explained by *informational* influence – other people provide information about appropriate or expected behaviours. For example, suppose you are attending an important, formal dinner, you take your seat and find laid neatly in front of you numerous knives, forks and spoons of different sizes. You panic – which go with which course? You could guess, but the best bet would be to observe what others do. Looking to others for appropriate behaviour is known as *social comparison* (Festinger, 1954). The above example characterizes social comparison in terms of informational influence, it encompasses *normative* social influence as well. Festinger claims people need to evaluate their opinions, beliefs, abilities, etc. by reference to other people – when we doubt ourselves (our convictions or actions) we use others as a reference point to provide a guide to appropriate behaviour. Social comparison theory, then, offers an explanation of conformity based on the idea that others provide us with a means of self-evaluation. Positive self-evaluation increases our self-confidence and self-esteem (Gruder, 1971).

Asch (1955), when interviewing subjects after they had taken part in his experiments, found numerous reasons given for conforming – such as to please other people, avoid creating dissent, wishing to avoid conflict. Conforming to *avoid conflict* entails two things: (a) group harmony is desirable and dissent undesirable: and (b) pleasing others is more important than giving correct, or what are thought to be correct, judgements. The latter is a form of ingratiation: conforming to social norms or group expectations is one way of making people like you. But is it? Jones (1965) found people to be disliked if they totally disregarded truth and honesty when conforming to group norms. Maintaining group harmony may also have negative consequences as we shall see, in Chapter 11, when we deal with *groupthink* (Janis, 1972). Effective decision-making necessitates a degree of dissent and conflict within a group.

Another explanation for conformity is that people feel uncomfortable and highly self-conscious if they stick out in a crowd (Duval and Wicklund, 1972). Being overly self-conscious, or self-aware, may have negative consequences since it may cause people to focus on their failings and shortcomings. Duval (1972) demonstrated this in an experiment where subjects observed themselves on video whilst giving their opinions on various topical matters. A control group gave opinions without observing themselves on video. Those made self-aware (by watching themselves) conformed more to group opinions than those not made self-aware.

In summary, three explanations of conformity have been briefly described – social comparison, conflict avoidance and self-awareness. Neither explanation is sufficient on its own, but one may be more appropriate than another depending on the social context. For example, social comparison processes are likely to be operating when we find ourselves in a novel or strange social situation, and self-awareness where our self-esteem or self-confidence is perceived to be threatened.

### 10.3.6 A child of the times?

Numerous criticisms have been directed at the Asch and Crutchfield para-digms. For example, they do not distinguish between compliance and personal acceptance; neither provides a situation of relevance to subjects; there are problems of knowing how the findings generalize to the 'real world'. Perrin and Spencer (1980) have criticized Asch's research findings as reflecting the particular social and cultural climate in the USA in the 1950s during and shortly after the McCarthy era. Conformity in that decade, they claim, was both expected and encouraged: subjects in Asch's experiments called Asch 'sir', an extremely unlikely form of address in contemporary social psychology experiments. Perrin and Spencer (1980) claim students these days are encouraged continuously to call the status quo into question. If Perrin and Spencer are correct we would predict conformity to group pressure to be less pronounced these days. Perrin and Spencer replicated some of Asch's experiments using engineering, chemistry and mathematics students. They found conformity to a unanimous incorrect majority in only *one* of 396 trials. Interviews with subjects afterwards showed them to feel doubt, puzzlement and conflict, as was the case with Asch's subjects, but they did not yield to the unanimous incorrect majority view.

Doms and Avermaet (1981) point out that failure to replicate the Asch effect does not necessarily mean conformity does not exist. It may well be the Asch paradigm is too well known amongst the student population for it to be a valid technique for measuring conformity any longer. Using the Crutch-field technique, Doms and Avermaet (1981) obtained conformity around 35 per cent of the time, similar to Asch's results back in the 1950s.

Recent research questions the extent to which people yield to group pressure in the cultural milieu of the 1980s. However, as other recent research shows, people do still yield to group pressure. It is the task of future research to map out more precisely the different *social* conditions under which people do and do not conform to group pressure.

## 10.4 Group polarization

Both the Asch and Crutchfield techniques involve individuals making judge-ments, expressing opinions, and becoming aware of what others think but in the *absence* of social interaction. Neither discussion of, nor talk about how such a judgement was arrived at takes place or, indeed, is even permitted. In many respects this is unrealistic, especially for reference groups, as discus-sions, exchange of views, etc. are often an important means of social influ-ence. It is of importance, then, to enquire into the effects of group discussion upon individual and group opinion and to discover whether other social influence processes occur in such contexts.

### 10.4.1 The polarization phenomenon

Research on group decision making (looked at in more detail in Chapter 11) had, up until the early 1960s, found groups to be conservative and cautious in comparison with individuals. Stoner (1961) investigated risk-taking by individuals and groups, he found, much to his and many other social psychologists' surprise, that groups took *riskier* decisions than the average individual group member. This became known as the 'risky shift' effect. Stoner's procedure will be described since much subsequent research has been based on it.

Groups of six people acting as subjects were given a number of dilemmas (called choice dilemma questionnaires or CDQs) in which a person is portrayed as having to choose between a risky or cautious alternative. The risky alternative would lead to a desirable outcome if successful but a highly undesirable outcome if unsuccessful. Subjects were first asked, as individuals, to indicate the advice they would give the person in the dilemma by stating the *lowest probability of success* acceptable before advising the person to take the risky option. The following is an example of a CDQ given to subjects:

> Mr A, an electrical engineer, who is married and has one child, has been working for a large electronics corporation since graduating from college five years ago. He is assured of a lifetime job with a modest, though adequate, salary and liberal pension benefits upon retirement. On the other hand, it is very unlikely that his salary will increase much before he retires. While attending a convention, Mr A is offered a job with a small, newly founded company which has a highly uncertain future. The new job would pay more to start and would offer the possibility of a share in the ownership if the company survived the competition of the larger firms.
>
> Imagine you are advising Mr A. Listed below are several probabilities or odds of the new company's proving financially sound. PLEASE CHECK THE LOWEST PROBABILITY THAT YOU CONSIDER ACCEPTABLE TO MAKE IT WORTHWHILE FOR MR A TO TAKE THE NEW JOB.
> -   The chances are 1 in 10 that the company will prove financially sound.
> -   The chances are 3 in 10 that the company will prove financially sound.
> -   The chances are 5 in 10 that the company will prove financially sound.
> -   The chances are 7 in 10 that the company will prove financially sound.
> -   The chances are 9 in 10 that the company will prove financially sound.
> -   Place a check here if you think Mr A should *NOT* take the new job no matter what the probabilities.

After indicating their response individually subjects would be brought together in a group and instructed to discuss each dilemma in turn until they had reached a *unanimous* decision on each. Finally, subjects were required again to indicate their own individual decision in light of the group discussion and the decision reached by the group. Stoner compared the *average* individual pre-discussion choice with the group decision and found the latter to be *riskier* than the former. Comparison of the average individual pre-discussion and post-discussion decision showed the latter also to be riskier, but less so than the group decision. Numerous studies replicated these findings and the idea that groups take *riskier* decisions than individuals quickly became accepted. This became known as the *risky-shift* (Kogan and Wallach, 1967).

However, right from the start Stoner had noticed some CDQs consistently produced shifts in the opposite direction (i.e. shifts towards caution) as a product of group discussion. The following is an example of one such CDQ:

> Roger, a married man with two children of school age, has a secure job that pays him about £10,000 a year. He can easily afford the necessities of life, but few of the

luxuries. Except for a life insurance policy he has no savings. Roger has heard from reliable sources that the stock of a relatively unknown Company X might triple its present value if a new product currently in production is favourably received by the buying public. On the other hand, if the product is unfavourably received, the stock might decline considerably in value. Roger is considering investing his life insurance money in this company.

Subsequent research reported consistent shifts to caution (Frazer, Gouge and Billig, 1971). Moscovici and his colleagues (Moscovici and Zavalloni, 1969) found the phenomenon to apply more generally using attitudes towards, for example, General de Gaulle and Americans as stimulus material. With these and other types of attitude statements Moscovici found group discussion to result in *shifts* towards the *extreme* of the attitude scale (usually a 5- or 7-point Likert scale) used to measure individual and group attitudes. It was soon realized that psychologists had been wrong to focus on the 'risky' aspect of the risky-shift; instead the focus should have been on the 'shift' aspect. In view of this Moscovici proposed a *group polarization* hypothesis: 'the average post-group response will tend to be more extreme in the same direction as the average of the pre-group responses' (Myers and Lamm, 1976, p. 603). To understand what is being suggested it is important to distinguish between *group polarization* and *extremization*: the latter is simply where there is a shift to an extreme position regardless of the initial views of the individuals. Polarization is where there is a shift towards the already preferred pole. Figure 10.4 makes this distinction more clearly.

Myers and Lamm, (1976), in a major review of research in this area, showed widespread support for the polarizing effect of group discussion. It was reported to occur in jury decision making, person perception and ethical decision making. Much, if not most, of this research was carried out in the laboratory with groups of five to six strangers who met only once. Field

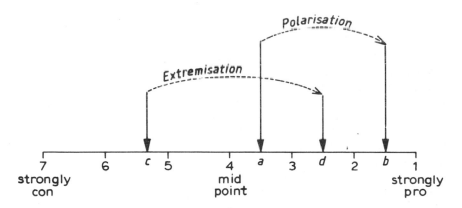

**Figure 10.4** Likert scale, used for measuring attitudes, showing *extremization* and *polarization*. With group polarization the average individual attitude (a) is on the 'pro' side of the midpoint, group discussion serves to polarize this tendency to produce a stronger 'pro' group position (b). With extremization, the average individual position is on one side of the midpoint (c) and the group position on the other side of the midpoint (d). *Polarization only occurs where a pre-existing tendency is strengthened.*

research using 'real' groups (committees and exam boards, for example) has produced little evidence for group polarization (Frazer, 1984), instead averaging effects have been found. Frazer (1978) suggests polarization might be expected to occur when people come together as a group for the first time but not in established functioning groups. The latter will have group norms and expectations over numerous matters, whilst the former will not have achieved this. If the development of group norms goes hand in hand with the tendency for group polarization to decrease we may view group polarization as a form of social influence.

### 10.4.2 Explanations

The 'risky shift' attracted two main explanations: (a) diffusion of responsibility; and (b) value of risk theory. The former proposes that since no one individual is responsible for the group decision, responsibility is diffused over each member. But why should risk rather than caution be diffused? Risk is something society, or at least Western society, values since it is desirable to be seen taking risks and succeeding. Shift to risk occurs, according to this explanation, because group discussion acts as a social comparison process whereby one individual compares his or her riskiness with that of the other group members. This shows some individuals to be more cautious than they initially thought they were being. These individuals increase their willingness to take a risk which results in both the group decision and post-discussion individual decision being more risky than the pre-discussion individual decision.

The existence of consistent cautious shifts undermines these explanations, hence the diffusion of responsibility theory becomes untenable. The value of risk theory has to be modified to a general 'value theory' in a rather *ad hoc* way since it is difficult to predict in advance which CDQs produce shifts to risk and which shifts to caution.

Viewing group polarization as a product of social influence suggests normative and informational majority influence may be operating. Informational social influence in this context involves being influenced by persuasive arguments supporting the already preferred direction (Vinokur, 1971). Groups favouring a particular direction (or pole on the Likert scale) produce more arguments in favour of that direction during group discussion than arguments in the opposite, opposing direction. Normative social influence operates on the minority in the group adopting neutral or opposite positions to the majority. Social pressures to conform to the expectations of others may be of two sorts here: (a) conforming to other group members' expectations; and (b) conforming to external social norms. A consistent finding supporting the normative influence explanation is that individuals show a degree of *recidivism* compared to the group view when making post-discussion choices. That is, after group discussion the individual shows less polarization than evidenced by the group. Conformity to the prevailing majority view here is, then, a mixture of both public compliance and private acceptance. The degree of public compliance is determined by the amount of recidivism taking place when a person gives his decision or opinion after group discussion.

## 10.5 Obedience to authority

Social influence as obedience to authority is where a person or group of people obey the direct commands, missives or orders of an authority. The authority may be another person, as with parental authority, or may be institutionally based as with the police or army. Generally, for people to obey authority they must perceive, to a greater or lesser extent, it legitimate for the authority to make such a request of them. Much of the time obedience is benign and constructive – complex societies require a certain level of obedience to function and continue. However, 'blind obedience' is often destructive – the mass slaughter of millions of Jews by the Nazis during the Second World War, the My Lai massacre during the Vietnam War, the Khmer Rouge's mass execution of Cambodians in the 1970s all attest to this. Depressingly, such a list is almost endless. Common to all these, and many other, events is that numerous people low in a hierarchy obeyed the orders of their superiors. Why? Does fear of punishment cause people to do such things, is there a personality characteristic associated with the tendency to obey, or are there external, situational factors to account for such obedience? Stanley Milgram, in the early 1960s, conducted an extended and detailed research programme in an attempt to discover the circumstances resulting in obedience to authority.

### 10.5.1 Milgram's experiments

In a series of perhaps the most controversial experiments ever in social psychology, Milgram sought to discover why and how often people would continue to obey authority when those people thought they might be endangering the life of another person.

Milgram recruited subjects by placing an advertisement in local papers requesting volunteers for an experiment in learning. Respondents were taken to the psychology department of Yale University and told the experiment required one person to act as a 'teacher' and another as a 'learner'. A coin was tossed in the presence of two subjects (actually one was a confederate of Milgram's) and each assigned accordingly to one of the two roles. This was always rigged so the real subject, the person who had responded to the newspaper advertisement, was always assigned to the role of teacher. Milgram then explained to the teacher that he had to read a series of word pairs (such as blue–girl, fat–neck, etc.) to the learner. After this the teacher read the first word of each word pair to the learner, the learner had to indicate from a set of four words which one was originally paired with the word read by the teacher. If the learner gave the wrong answer the teacher had to give the learner an electric shock. This continued over many trials and each time the learner gave an incorrect response the teacher had to give a shock of *increasing intensity*. A sophisticated looking piece of equipment was placed in front of the subject (the 'teacher') which he was instructed to use to administer the shocks. On the front panel of this equipment was a voltage scale ranging from 15 to 450 volts with an indication of the severity of the different voltages as follows:

| | |
|---|---|
| slight shock | 15–60 volts |
| moderate shock | 75–120 volts |

| strong shock | 135–180 volts |
|---|---|
| very strong shock | 195–240 volts |
| intense shock | 255–300 volts |
| extremely intense shock | 315–360 volts |
| danger, severe shock | 375–420 volts |
| XXX | 425–450 volts |

There were 30 switches on the front panel, the teacher flicked the next one up each time the learner gave the wrong answer.

Prior to beginning the experiment subjects were given a sample shock of 45 volts (which is quite painful) to give them some idea of what they thought they were inflicting on the learner. In Milgram's original experiments the learner and teacher were put in separate rooms, however, the teacher watched whilst the learner had electrodes placed on his arms. At the same time the learner informed the experimenter, in the presence of the teacher he had a weak heart and was worried in case the shocks were strong. Of course, no shocks were actually given but the teacher did not know this!

Imagine yourself to be the teacher, you have seen the man wired up, he has complained of a weak heart, and you are to give him progressively strong electric shocks as he gets answers wrong. The experiment starts, the learner gets the first few words right then he makes a mistake, you give the lowest level of shock (15 volts). The learner keeps getting words wrong, and you give increasingly strong shocks. At 75 volts you hear the learner 'grunt', at 125 volts he says 'that really hurts', at 180 volts he complains of his weak heart, at 285 volts he gives an agonized scream and at 315 volts and beyond there is silence. All the time the experimenter is urging you to continue even though you protest. How far up the 30-switch 450 volt scale do you think you would go before refusing to continue?

Milgram put this question to psychiatrists, college students and middle-class adults then compared their estimates with what he actually found from running the experiment. The results are shown in Table 10.3. As you can see,

**Table 10.3** Expected and actual behaviour of 'teachers' in Milgram's experiment. Results are shown as cumulative percentages. The column of actual shocks at which subjects refused to continue indicates 65 per cent administered shocks to the maximum level. Adapted from Milgram (1974).

| SHOCK LEVEL | PREDICTIONS OF LEVEL AT WHICH WOULD REFUSE TO ADMINISTER SHOCK | | | ACTUAL SHOCK LEVELS AT WHICH SUBJECTS REFUSED TO CONTINUE |
|---|---|---|---|---|
| | *Psychiatrists* | *Students* | *Middle class adults* | |
| *Slight shock* | 10.3 | 0.0 | 12.5 | 0.0 |
| *Moderate shock* | 48.7 | 25.8 | 42.5 | 0.0 |
| *Strong shock* | 92.3 | 96.8 | 82.5 | 0.0 |
| *Very strong shock* | 97.4 | 100.0 | 90.0 | 0.0 |
| *Intense shock* | 100.0 | 100.0 | 100.0 | 12.5 |
| *Extremely intense shock* | 100.0 | 100.0 | 100.0 | 23.5 |
| *Danger, severe shock* | 100.0 | 100.0 | 100.0 | 35.0 |
| *XXX* | 100.0 | 100.0 | 100.0 | 35.0 |

predictions fell grossly short of what actually took place. All groups predicted subjects would not go beyond the 'intense shock' level; in reality just over 12 per cent refused at this level. Sixty-five per cent (26 subjects) continued to give shocks up to the maximum intensity.

Milgram investigated many variations on the basic experiment, we will look at these in the next section. First, some of the criticisms levelled at the basic experimental paradigm will be considered. Critics have suggested that the 'teachers' did not really believe the learner was receiving electric shocks, and if this were true Milgram's findings would be invalid. Detailed extracts of conversations Milgram had with subjects both during and after the experiment lead one to think the 'teacher' believed he was hurting the learner. Debriefing of subjects gave some indication of their involvement with and belief in the reality of the experiment, as the following passage from Milgram (1974) shows:

> *Experimenter*: 'At what point were you most nervous or tense?'
> *Subject*: 'Well, when he first began to cry out in pain, and I realized this was hurting him. This got worse when he just blocked and refused to answer. There was I, I'm a nice person, I think, hurting somebody and caught up in what seemed a mad situation . . . and in the interests of science one goes through with it. At one point I had an impulse to just refuse to continue with this kind of teaching situation.'

Another criticism of these experiments is that they are unethical: they involve deception and inflicting severe stress and anxiety on subjects. It is doubtful if such experiments could be conducted now, they would probably fall outside the ethical guidelines for research published by the British Psychological Society and American Psychological Association (extracts of which were given in Chapter 1). A third and final criticism is the extent to which these results generalize beyond the laboratory to the real world. Mixon (1972) argues the results only generalize if we take the roles and the rules that operate in a particular social context. The role of 'teacher' is adopted by the subject, a process which relegates personal identity and personal responsibility to second place. The role of a teacher often necessitates punishment when learners do something wrong: giving shocks in the above experimental set-up would be consistent with this. This does ignore, however, the principle of making the punishment appropriate to the transgression.

## 10.5.2 Further findings

Milgram (1974) investigated various situational and social factors affecting people's willingness to obey authority. Using the same learner/teacher paradigm he looked at legitimacy of authority, proximity of the learner to the teacher, proximity of the authority figure, and sex of subjects.

Legitimacy of authority was manipulated by using a run-down office in a less respectable part of the city and telling subjects the research was sponsored by a private commercial concern. This 'low legitimacy' resulted, as can be seen from Table 10.4, in a lower level of obedience (48 per cent of subjects delivered the maximum shock) than when the research was conducted at Yale University, giving 'high legitimacy'. When the authority figure was of

**Table 10.4** Percentage of subjects giving maximum shock under different conditions. In the original experiment with the learner in a different room to the teacher, 65 per cent of subjects gave the maximum shock. Adapted from Milgram (1974).

| SITUATIONAL OR SOCIAL FACTOR | PERCENTAGE OF SUBJECTS GIVING THE MAXIMUM SHOCK |
|---|---|
| LEGITIMACY OF AUTHORITY: | |
| (a) Seedy building | 47.5 |
| (b) Ordinary man giving orders | 20.0 |
| PROXIMITY OF THE 'LEARNER': | |
| (a) In same room | 40.0 |
| (b) Hand on the metal plate | 30.0 |
| PROXIMITY OF THE EXPERIMENTER: | |
| Experimenter leaves the room | 20.5 |
| CONFLICTING COMMANDS BY TWO EXPERIMENTERS | 0.0 |
| FEMALE SUBJECTS | 65.0 |

questionable legitimacy, here Milgram had another subject giving the orders rather than a psychologist in a white laboratory coat, obedience dropped dramatically. Only 20 per cent administered shock to the maximum level.

In Milgram's original experiment the learner was in a different room to the teacher. When both were in close proximity, i.e. in the same room, fewer subjects administered maximum shock. This decreased even more when the teacher had to take the hand of the learner and put it on a metal plate for the shock to be delivered.

When the authority figure – the experimenter dressed in a white coat – left the room after instructing the subject on how to proceed, only 20 per cent obeyed the experimenter's initial request to continue giving increasingly strong levels of shock. Two authority figures giving conflicting commands (one telling the subject to continue the other urging him to stop) resulted in obedience dropping dramatically. No subject gave maximum shock, and 19 out of 20 stopped at the 150 volts level – the point at which conflicting commands were given to the subjects.

Finally, when females were used as teachers 65 per cent, the same as with male subjects, gave shocks to the maximum level. However, Milgram did find greater conflict to be experienced by female than male subjects. Kilman and Mann (1974) reported similar findings when they found women tended to resist harming the victim more then men.

### 10.5.3 Defying authority

Milgram's studies reveal high levels of obedience to authority even when people are experiencing severe misgivings about obeying a command they believe results in harm being inflicted on another person. Obedience reduces, but still remains relatively high, when the authority seems less than legitimate, the victim is in close proximity, etc. Only when authority figures are in conflict (giving different orders) does obedience to injure another cease.

What other factors result in our defying authority?

One of the strongest sources is if our peers show rebellion and resistance. Social support from others we perceive to be similar to ourselves may allow us to do what we think is right rather than obey instructions when we think we should not.

Milgram (1974) investigated this in an experiment where subjects were told that the concern was with 'the effects of collective teaching and punishment on memory' (p. 116). Three of the participants, unbeknown to the fourth naive subject, were confederates: two confederates and the naive subject were assigned to teacher roles, the other confederate to the 'learner' role. The three teachers were seated together before the shock generator and proceeded with the experiment giving progressively stronger shocks to the learner as the learner gave the wrong answers. At 150 volts one of the confederate teachers rebelled and refused to participate any further. The experimenter urged him to continue but he refused. At 210 volts the second confederate teacher refused to continue, leaving the naive subject alone.

Most naive subjects continued to give shocks up to the 150 volt level. However, when the first confederate rebelled 80 per cent continued, but when the second confederate rebelled over 60 per cent of the subjects rebelled themselves and refused to continue. Ten per cent of subjects still continued to give shocks up to the maximum level. This experiment demonstrates that social support decreases a person's tendency to obey authority but does not lead to everybody being defiant.

This overall programme of research by Stanley Milgram has cast important light on factors affecting people's tendency to obey authority. Two findings stand out: (a) authority exerts a powerful influence over everybody, more perhaps than we realize; and (b) destructive obedience may be reduced by the presence of certain variables, but rarely is it eliminated. The experiments have been and continue to be controversial among psychologists and those studying psychology: I leave it to you to make up your own mind about whether you think they were worthwhile.

## 10.6 The influence of roles

So far social influence has been viewed from the perspective of one person or a group of people either directly (compliance and obedience to authority) or indirectly (conformity) changing the behaviour of another in a desired direction. Often social influence operates when a person takes on a role: the roles of parent, teacher, policeman, etc. all have norms and expectations of behaviour associated with them. An important psychological effect of taking on a role is that individual identity is replaced by a group or role identity: this offers a person anonymity. This may lead to *deindividuation* (Zimbardo, 1969): the loosening of social, moral and societal constraints upon behaviour.

Zimbardo (Haney, Banks and Zimbardo, 1973) investigated the deindividuating influence of roles in a controversial study commonly known as the Stanford prison experiment. The basement of a university building was converted into a 'prison': there were three cells, a solitary confinement cell and an observation room for guards. Twenty-one subjects were selected from a pool of volunteers, these were judged to be 'stable' (physically and mentally), most mature and least involved in antisocial behaviour (p. 73). Nine were randomly assigned to be prisoners, and 12 randomly assigned to be guards. Prisoners were told 'they would be under constant surveillance, some civil rights would be suspended, but there would be no physical abuse'. Guards were instructed to 'maintain the reasonable degree of order within the prison for its effective functioning'.

Subjects assigned the role of prisoner were arrested in their homes by the police, brought to the 'prison', stripped and made to take a shower, then all dressed in the same loose fitting smocks and nylon caps. Guards were dressed in khaki uniforms, mirror sun-glasses and each given a wooden baton and whistle.

To the surprise and horror of the researchers things quickly got out of hand and the experiment had to be terminated after only six days. Observations revealed behaviour patterns to quickly emerge: prisoners evaluated themselves negatively, became very passive and talked about harming the guards. Guards became increasingly aggressive and sadistic, exercising total control over the prisoners by, for example, making going to the toilet a privilege rather than a right. Such was the dehumanizing effect on prisoners that five had to be 'released' because of depression, crying and acute anxiety. When the experiment was terminated prisoners expressed great relief, but the guards were unhappy because they found the sense of power exhilarating.

Providing an overall evaluation the researchers commented: 'in less than a week middle class, caucasian, of above average intelligence and emotionally stable Americans became pathological and anti-social' (p. 89). Prisoners and guards quickly took on the stereotypic behaviour associated with these roles, displaying personality characteristics and behaviours that are normally alien to them. This study vividly demonstrates how a role can take over a person and relegate personal and ethical standards to second place.

## 10.7　Is there a conforming personality

Zimbardo's research reminds us of the error of attributing behaviour (see Chapter 7) to personality characteristics when powerful *external* forces may be sufficient to account for the person's behaviour. In everyday life, however, we often hear people say 'he will agree to anything' or 'he follows like a lamb to the slaughter'. These and other similar phrases suggest certain people possess particular personality traits which result in them being more susceptible to social influence than people who do not possess these traits.

Perhaps the prime candidate is the authoritarian personality described in Chapter 5, whose central features are rigid adherence to conventional values and a submissive, uncritical attitude towards authority (Adorno *et al.*, 1950). Elms and Milgram (1966) found weak evidence supporting the proposition that those scoring high on the F-scale (indicating authoritarianism) were more likely to continue obeying the experimenter and continue 'administering' electric shocks than those who scored low on the F-scale. One of the components of this scale measures acquiescence (the readiness of a person to agree with what another says or asks regardless of the content of the request); an acquiescent person may have a need for social approval and to be seen in a good light by others. From this it would be predicted that people who have a high need for social approval will be more yielding to social influence than those whose need is low. Moeller and Applezweig (1957) tested this and found greater conformity in the Asch situation with those high in need for social approval; low self-esteem is often correlated with such people. Rosenberg (1963) found greater conformity in people with low self-esteem; and highly anxious people are also found to exhibit high levels of conformity. Need for social approval, low self-esteem and high anxiety may form a cluster of traits resulting in a person being highly susceptible to social influence.

Zimbardo, in the Stanford prison experiment, administered numerous personality tests to the subjects; he found no differences between prisoners and guards on such traits as authoritarianism and machiavellianism. However, he did find that those prisoners who remained for the full six days scored twice as high as on measures of conventionalism and authoritarianism than those released early. Zimbardo claimed the more conforming prisoners were able to adapt better to the prison environment than those of a less conforming personality. Caution is needed with these results since Zimbardo's sample was small; 10 were assigned the role of prisoner so his findings are based on comparing two groups of five.

This brief survey of research would tend to indicate certain personality traits associated with conformity, however more substantial research is needed for us to feel more confident about some of these claims. Perhaps the most that can be said is that personality is a contributing factor, but is often swamped by powerful situational forces.

## 10.8 Minority influence

We tend to think of social influence in terms of attitudes, beliefs, behaviours, etc. changing in the direction of the majority. Majority influence (as manifested in compliance, conformity, group polarization and obedience) *reduces conflict* between individuals or groups. Occasionally, though, a small group of people or a single person effects a strong influence over the majority: Galileo, Darwin, Einstein and Freud each put forward views against the then existing prevailing majority view. Each changed the pre-existing dominant view and replaced it with their own views. We will look at two social psychological processes suggested to account for effective minority influence: (a) the status and power of the minority; and (b) the behavioural style of the minority.

### 10.8.1 Status and power

Individuals occupying positions of high status or who are able to exert power over others may use such resources to make their, initially, minority view a majority one. Hollander (1964) proposes the following: the problem for the person with a minority view is first to achieve a position of status and power. This is attained by conforming with the status quo and demonstrating competence in the general area. Conformity to social norms and group expectations allows the individual to accumulate 'idiosyncrasy credits'. Idiosyncrasy credits permit the individual to express his own deviant, minority view; the more credits accumulated the more a group will tolerate deviant, original and/or innovative ideas from the person.

Unfortunately, matters are not this simple since numerous other variables affect the extent to which a majority are prepared to accept a minority view. Homans (1961) has shown that both high and low-status persons in a group conform least to group norms. High-status people have little to lose by acting independently: if wrong idiosyncracy credits are used up, if right even more credits are accumulated and greater legitimacy is added to the high-status position resulting in the person being heeded when putting forward a minority view in the future. However, high-status people are not tolerated for long by a group if a deviant or minority position impedes the group from achieving its goal (Wiggins, Dill and Schwartz, 1965).

The use of idiosyncracy credits by those with high status and power is a resource not available to minorities lacking such attributes. Nevertheless, such minorities do change social norms and majority views by, it is suggested, their *behavioural style* (Moscovici, 1976).

### 10.8.2 Behavioural style

Sigmund Freud was the object of derision, verbal abuse and rejection by much of the Victorian scientific community when he first propounded his theory of childhood sexuality. Freud did not yield to the opposing majority view, but persisted in propounding and developing his theory. His success at influencing people has been so great that much of his terminology is now integrated into everyday language, with common use of terms such as 'Freudian slips' (Gellner, 1985). According to Moscovici and Nemeth (1974) persuasion is successful in the absence of status and power because of the 'behavioural style' of the minority group or person.

The behavioural style of influential minorities has four main components: (a) consistency; (b) certainty in the correctness of the ideas or views they are propounding; (c) appearing to be objective and unbiased; and (d) resisting social pressure and abuse. In contrast to majority influence, minority influence *creates* conflict rather than avoiding or reducing it. Consistency (defined as 'a firm, systematic, coherent and autonomous repetition of one and the same response – Mugny, 1984) creates conflict by unsettling people's accepted views and making them question and doubt their assumptions. A pioneering experiment by Moscovici, Lage and Naffrechoux (1969) provided empirical support for these contentions.

This experiment was in two stages: in the first stage female subjects were formed into groups of six, in which two were confederates of the experimenter, and shown coloured slides which were all blue in colour, but the brightness was varied. In one condition the confederates said the slides were green on every trial; in the control group there were no confederates in the groups of six. A pronounced influence was found by a minority consistently saying the slides were green: 32 per cent of the naive subjects said they saw green at least once. In the control group only a quarter of one per cent of responses were green. In the second stage of the experiment subjects were put into a cubicle by themselves and shown a further sequence of coloured slides. In this sequence three were obviously blue, three obviously green and

10 were blue/green. Subjects exposed to a minority consistently saying green in Stage 1 of the experiment tended to see the blue/green slides as green. This tendency was absent in subjects who had been in the control group in the first stage of the experiment. Furthermore, 68 per cent of subjects who reported only seeing blue but exposed to a different minority view in Stage 1 saw the blue/green slides as green in Stage 2. The experiment shows consistent minorities effect influence in two ways: (a) at the time at which the minority is espousing its view; and (b) after the minority view has been made and when the minority is absent.

Moscovici, Lage and Naffrechoux (1969) showed an inconsistent minority to have little effect. In a similar experiment to the one described above confederates in Stage 1 said they saw green on 24 trials and blue on 12 trials. Overall, subjects gave a response of green on only 1.25 per cent of occasions (compared to over 8 per cent with a consistent minority).

Moscovici and Nemeth (1974) point out that consistency of responses itself is not the cause of minority influence but it is necessary that there is *recognition* by others that a position is consistent. This suggests others attribute confidence, autonomy and distinctiveness to the minority. Nemeth and Wachtler (1973) demonstrated the effect of autonomy and distinctiveness (focus of attention) in an experiment where groups of five people, four subjects and a confederate, had to make 'jury' deliberations. Of interest was the effect of a confederate who put forward a minority view, either assigned (no autonomy) or choosing (autonomy) to sit at the head or side of the table. Figure 10.5 shows the seating arrangements, the seat assigned or chosen was either position Q, R or S. Results showed a confederate's minority position exerted no influence when assigned to a seat regardless of whether the seat was at the head of the table (S) or not (Q and R). However, when the confederate had chosen his seat he was highly influential when seated at the head of the table, but not when seated in one of the side positions.

If a minority consistently espouses a position without making any concessions to the majority this may be perceived as dogmatic and inflexible and so reduce minority influence. Mugny (1984) has shown, in a series of experiments, that flexibility exerts more influence than dogmatism and inflexibility

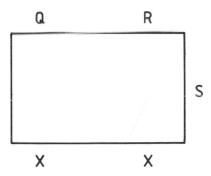

**Figure 10.5** Seating positions (Q, R and S) of a confederate adopting a minority view in the group. From Nemeth and Wachtler (1973).

on the part of the minority. Mugny defines flexibility as 'when some concessions were made to the population so as not to accentuate the conflict, while the break with authority remained consistent' (p. 508). Such a strategy prevents the minority from being socially categorized as an outgroup (see Chapter 5). Flexibility stops dissimilarities between the minority and majority being accentuated whilst at the same time similarities are attended to.

In summary, the behavioural style of a minority, rather than exercise of power and status, may successfully influence a majority when the style is consistent but tempered with a degree of flexibility to prevent being categorized as an outgroup, resulting in ostracism by the rest of the group.

## 10.9  Summary

○ Compliance is agreeing to a direct request, where the request is not a command or made by authority. People are more likely to comply if they are acting in reciprocation, have made a transgression, or have low self-esteem. The foot-in-the-door technique increases compliance.

○ Conformity is a change in behaviours towards a group norm as a result of group pressure. Sherif used the autokinetic effect to demonstrate how group norms strongly influence a person in ambiguous or novel situations. Asch investigated the effect of group pressure in a relatively unambiguous situation involving line judgements. A unanimously incorrect majority exerts considerable influence over an individual. This influence decreases when the majority is not unanimous and/or if credible social support is provided.

○ Crutchfield devised an experimental procedure allowing numerous subjects to be tested at once. The Asch procedure requires public expression of opinion, the Crutchfield procedure allows subjects to express their opinions privately. Conformity in the former may be due more to normative pressure, in the latter due to informational pressure.

○ Group polarization is where group discussion serves to strengthen or polarize already existing tendencies of the individuals in the group. Group polarization occurs because of both normative and informational social influence.

○ Milgram investigated obedience to authority by getting subjects to administer, so they believed, increasingly strong electric shocks to a learner when he answered wrongly. Sixty-five per cent of subjects gave the maximum shock when urged to do so by the experimenter. If the authority was of dubious legitimacy, or the learner in close proximity to the teacher or rebellion shown by peers, obedience was much reduced. Only conflicting commands resulted in all subjects refusing to continue to give electric shocks.

○ Zimbardo investigated the deindividuating properties of roles in the Stanford prison experiment. Guards and prisoners took on their roles so realistically the experiment had to be stopped. Guards became aggressive and inhuman, prisoners submissive and distraught.

○ Some evidence exists to support the idea of a conforming personality. People scoring high on the F-scale and those in need of social approval, low in self-esteem and anxious have a tendency to be more conforming.

○ Minority influence may be achieved by people high in status and power using 'idiosyncracy credits' to get minority opinions accepted. In the absence of status and power, the behavioural style of a minority may successfully influence a majority. Behavioural style includes consistency, certainty, objectivity and resisting majority social pressure.

## 10.10  Suggestions for further reading

Brown, J.A.C. *Techniques of Persuasion* (Harmondsworth, Penguin, 1963).
Good, broad survey of different approaches to changing people's attitudes, beliefs and

behaviour as well as their personality. The book deals with more sinister aspects of enforcing change such as propaganda and brainwashing.

Kiesler, C.A. and Kiesler, S.B. *Conformity* (Reading, Mass., Addison-Wesley, 1969).
Highly readable and accessible introduction to psychological explanations of conformity and research conducted to test the validity of these explanations. This would be the best book to read if you wanted to find out more about the issues and topics raised in this chapter.

Milgram, S. *Obedience to Authority: An Experimental View* (New York, Harper & Row, 1974).
Detailed exposition of Milgram's views and experiments conducted to investigate why people obey authority and the degree of obedience found in different situations.

# 11

# Groups and group performance

11.1    Introduction
11.2    Individuals and groups
11.3    Group composition
11.4    Group structure and influence
        *11.4.1 Group cohesiveness    11.4.2 Status and roles    11.4.3 Communication structure*
11.5    Analysing group processes
11.6    Leadership
        *11.6.1 'Great man' theory    11.6.2 Leadership style    11.6.3 Fiedler's contingency theory    11.6.4 Leadership skills*
11.7    Decision making
        *11.7.1 Individuals versus groups    11.7.2 Group decision making    11.7.3 When decisions go wrong – groupthink    11.7.4 Countering groupthink*
11.8    Summary
11.9    Suggestions for further reading

## 11.1  Introduction

We all belong to a diverse variety of groups – family groups, work groups, clubs and friendship groups – such groups are either formal or informal in character, usually small in size and come together to achieve a common goal. Small groups may be defined as 'involving at least three persons who communicate with one another to coordinate their activities in the pursuit of common goals. The structure of a group typically consists of role differentiation, leadership, a set of norms and rules of membership' (Tedeschi and Lindskold, 1976). This definition makes three important points: (a) group members communicate and interact – known as group processes; (b) groups come together to perform certain tasks or achieve goals – the task performance; and (c) groups are structured – which means individuals occupy roles, have status and power, and conform, to a greater or lesser extent, to group norms. Such an approach forcuses more on the systems of relationships existing within a group and less on the individual group members.

Small groups may be understood in terms of group composition, group structure, group process and the effects this has on individual change and group development, as well as task performance. Figure 11.1 shows the relationships between these components. There are two feedback loops: loop (a) acknowledges group performance on a task may affect future group composition – poor performance may result in membership changes; loop (b) shows how group structure may change, for example, a leader may emerge or

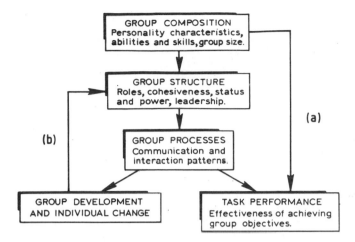

**Figure 11.1** Relationships between the different aspects of small groups. After McGrath (1964).

the leadership may change to accommodate changing demands on the group.

Conceptualizing, as the definition above does, small groups composed of at least three members imposes no upper limit on size. As your experience and knowledge may tell you, groups in industry or institutions rarely exceed about 20 members, if they do there is a strong tendency for sub-groups or sub-committees to form. Generally, as groups get larger there are increases in centralization of authority and formality, greater variation in the degree of individual member satisfaction and individual participation, and an increased need for effective leadership (McGrath, 1964). As a result we commonly find working parties, decision-making groups, etc. to be composed of between five and 12 members. Groups of five or six members allow active participation from each member, as well as clear role differentiation and effective use of each individual's abilities and skills.

This chapter looks at small groups in terms of performance and effectiveness at achieving objectives by viewing a group as an interrelated system. We will look at the three central components given in Figure 11.1; before this it is of importance to consider how individual performance is affected by the presence of others and how individual and group performance may differ. It is to this we now turn.

## 11.2 Individuals and groups

The prevalence of groups at all levels and in all contexts in society reflects two assumptions: first, individuals perform better when other people are around; and, second, groups are better or more effective at performing a task than an individual working alone. Research investigating the validity of the first assumption is known as *social facilitation* and was one of the earliest areas of study in social psychology.

Social facilitation was first demonstrated by Travis (1925) who trained subjects for several days on a hand-eye coordination task (a pursuit rota device) until a set standard of performance was reached. Subjects performed 10 more trials of the task in front of a passive audience, this was compared with subjects' performance on the best 10 trials done alone. Eighteen of the 20 subjects performed better in front of a passive audience, and 16 achieved their best score under such conditions. Many subsequent studies have shown social facilitation effects to occur on well learned, simple *motor tasks*, however, audiences detract or *inhibit* the learning of new and complex *conceptual tasks*. Pessin (1933) had subjects learn a series of seven nonsense syllables either alone or in front of a passive audience. Subjects took longer to learn and made more errors in the presence of an audience. Alper (1952) measured the time subjects took to match a word, from two possible words, with a passage of prose. Subjects did this in one of three conditions: alone, before an audience they could see, and before an unseen audience. Decision times were shortest for subjects alone and longest when in front of an audience they could not see.

Zajonc (1965) suggests audiences increase arousal, and, when a task is familiar and/or well learned (dominant behaviour), the arousing effects of an audience facilitate performance. With new or poorly learned tasks (non-dominant) audience arousal inhibits performance.

Social facilitation looks at the effects of passive audiences upon performance, but how do individuals perform on a task in the presence of others doing the same task? *Coaction effects* were investigated by Allport (1924) who compared the performance of subjects working along with subjects working at the same table, but not interacting, on tasks such as multiplication problems, word associations and production of arguments. On each of these tasks *quantity* of work was greater when subjects were coacting, but *quality* was higher when working alone. Kelley and Thibaut (1969) suggest coaction increases a person's motivation and arousal, resulting in a competitive urgency speedily to complete the task set: hence quantity increases but quality decreases.

So far individual and group performance have been compared without allowing interaction to take place between individuals. The latter has been studied in many ways, three will be mentioned here: problem solving, learning and brainstorming.

A classic experiment by Shaw (1932) gave individuals and four-person groups 'eureka'-type problems to solve, the Tartaglia is the best known of this type:

> Three missionaries and three cannibals are on one side of the river, and they want to get to the other side of the river. They have a boat which will only carry two persons. All the missionaries and one of the cannibals can row. However, under no circumstances must the number of cannibals outnumber the number of missionaries.

The problem for subjects, as individuals and in groups, is to devise a method of getting everyone safely across the river in the *fewest* number of trips. Shaw found groups solved more problems in a given time than individuals; this was because errors were identified more quickly and incorrect solutions rejected faster by groups than individuals. Does this mean groups are better? The answer depends on how 'better' is conceptualized: if it is in terms of number of problems solved in a given time then groups are better. However, if it is in terms of number of man-hours taken to solve a task groups are less efficient, and become even more so as group membership increases (Taylor and Faust, 1952).

Perlmutter and de Montmollin (1952) showed groups learned nonsense syllables faster than individuals. In one experiment half the subjects worked first in three-person groups, had a 15 minute break, then worked alone but in the presence of others. The other half of the subjects first worked alone but in the presence of others, had a break, then worked in groups of three. Two findings emerged: (a) groups learned more and faster regardless of whether individuals worked in groups before or after working alone; (b) individuals who first worked in groups learned faster than individuals who first worked alone. Subsequent research has consistently confirmed these findings.

Brainstorming is where a group attempts to solve problems in new and creative ways and has found to be most effective when: (a) no comment or evaluation of an idea is given; (b) evaluations are only given when no new ideas are forthcoming; and (c) elaboration of all ideas is encouraged by all group members and in the absence of criticism. Osborn (1957), who introduced the approach, claimed groups would be better at producing more creative ideas. Support has been mixed: Taylor, Berry and Block (1958) compared production of ideas by four-person groups and the combined product of four individuals working alone (called nominal groups). Nominal groups produce a greater number of and more novel ideas than interacting groups. If groups have been previously trained in brainstorming or are allowed to choose who they want in their group, performance is superior to individuals.

In summary, research does not consistently support the view that working in the presence of others (passive audience or coacting) results in better performance than when working alone. The nature of the task, previous experience and how one conceptualizes 'better' have all to be taken into account.

## 11.3 Group composition

Imagine you have been asked to serve on a committee, your first question might be to enquire into the purpose of the group. The next set of questions, I suspect, will be to do with finding out who the other members of the group are and how many people are in the group. These two aspects of group composition, size and membership, have important influences on group performance.

Individual satisfaction with the group is likely to decrease as size increases. Slater (1958) had groups, ranging in size from two to seven, meet for discussion on four separate occasions. Greatest individual satisfaction was found in the group of five, larger groups became more competitive and impulsive. A low level of satisfaction may cause decrease in motivation. Bales *et al.* (1951) found larger groups to be characterized by greater disparity in individual contributions; in large groups some people spoke a lot and some spoke hardly ever, in small groups contributions by each individual were more uniform.

Hemphill (1950) found leadership style to change with size of group: leaders of large groups (over 31 members) had greater demands placed on them and were more influential than in smaller groups. In larger groups, leaders were more authoritarian, less tolerant of deviations from group norms, less likely to explain changes and more likely to make decisions for the group in the absence of prior consultation. Group size may both facilitate and inhibit individual performance: Gibb (1951) found that whilst larger groups produced more ideas on problem solving tasks, productivity – time taken to generate each idea – decreased. Interviews with individual members revealed greater experiences of being inhibited about contributing and participating in discussion as group size increased.

Are groups which are composed of homogeneous or heterogeneous individuals more effective? As might be expected, there is no simple answer. Schutz (1958) found compatible rather than similar pairs to be better at complex problem solving and no difference between such groups on relatively easy tasks. Compatible groups were where each had different but complementary personality characteristics along the dimensions of need to be included, need to control and need to give affection. A compatible group would be where, for example, person A has high needs to be included, control events and give affection, and person B has high needs to receive inclusion, be controlled and receive affection.

Groups composed of individuals having similar attitudes towards authority show less internal conflict, less disruption and are more productive. A general mix of personalities results in better task performance overall (McGrath, 1964), however homogeneity for some traits may be more effective for performance than heterogeneity. A group composed entirely of dominant people is liable to result in conflict amongst members: a group of entirely submissive people is likely to result in poor performance since no one would take initiatives or leadership roles when required.

Overall, the search for consistent correlations between effective group performance and individual abilities, personality and intelligence has been disappointing. Groups requiring specialist skills perform less well if those skills are absent; low levels of motivation for achieving group goals result in poor performance. All this suggests factors over and above individual abilities, personality, etc. operate to make groups perform well or poorly: this leads us to look at groups as wholes not as collections of individual members.

## 11.4 Group structure and influence

In the previous chapter (Chapter 10) we saw how people's attitudes and behaviours could be influenced by others, even when those other people were obviously wrong in their judgements. In the experiments of Sherif, Asch and Crutchfield interaction was not allowed: simply listening to or being informed of other people's views exerts powerful social influences. When individuals in groups are free to interact with each other a further set of variables operate to influence individual members' behaviour. These variable are properties of the *group structure*, which is defined as 'the relatively stable patterns of relationships that exist among members of the group' (McGrath, 1964, p. 72). Three aspects of group structure, variables influencing member behaviour, will be looked at: *group cohesiveness, roles and status,* and *communication structure.*

Knowledge of a group's structure will give a good idea of the *dynamics* of that group: the dynamics of a group are processes by which change takes place. Change can be of two sorts: (a) at an individual level it refers to changes in attitudes, opinions and willingness or not to conform to group expectations or role demands;and (b) at a group level referring to altering patterns of relationships – changes in leadership, membership and morale of the group.

Groups that endure over time, even though membership may change, are continually changing at both individual and group levels to accommodate changes in the environment, the task and within the group.

### 11.4.1 Group cohesiveness

Group cohesiveness refers to the extent individual members of a group are attracted to each other and attracted to the group as a whole. One way of assessing group cohesiveness is the frequency with which the word 'we' is used by individuals to refer to the group: highly cohesive groups use 'we' very often. Cohesiveness is important for group performance since, to take an extreme example, if each member disliked every other member the group would perform ineffectively and not remain together very long. However, highly cohesive groups may also perform badly – as we shall see towards the end of this chapter in the section on 'groupthink'.

What makes membership of a group attractive to an individual? Cartwright and Zander (1968) claim the prime reason is that the group satisfies the interests of the members. This may become self-perpetuating since working harder to achieve group objectives will produce success and result in increased cohesiveness. Research conducted in an industrial setting demonstrated how cohesiveness affects worker behaviour. Kerr *et al.* (1951) found absenteeism to be less, productivity and morale to be higher in more rather than less cohesive groups. Cohesiveness was also affected by communication: workers allowed to converse freely with each other showed increased productivity, job satisfaction and, as a consequence, were more cohesive than workers restricted in the conversation they could have with each other.

Highly cohesive groups extert strong influences upon individual members to behave in accordance with group expectations and norms. In one experiment Schachter (1951) formed groups in which members were told they would get on well with each other (high cohesiveness) or would not (low cohesiveness). Subjects had to cut out cardboard shapes in order to make checkerboards, they did this working alone in separate rooms. Attempts to influence productivity were made by giving notes to subjects who were led to believe these notes had come from other group members. Productivity increased when the notes urged an increase in productivity for both high and low cohesive groups; however, members of high cohesive groups were much more likely to *reduce* productivity when urged to do so than were members of low cohesive groups. The experiment demonstrates that highly cohesive groups may follow negative injunctions from group members even when this may result in disapproval from people outside the group. Group cohesiveness, then, is important for influencing people, their productivity, and providing job satisfaction.

### 11.4.2 Roles and status

The behaviour of a person in a group is influenced by the role he or she is expected to adopt and the status of that person in relation to others in the group. A role is usually defined as 'the behaviours expected of a person occupying a certain position in a group', for example, the roles of father and mother differ in a family group, the roles of leader and expert differ in a work group. Roles are normative in that people occupying them are expected to conform to group or cultural expectations.

A tripartite distinction may be made between *expected role, perceived role* and *enacted role* (Shaw, 1971). The perceived role is the behaviour the occupant of the position thinks he or she *should* enact; the enacted role is the *actual* behaviour engaged in by the person occupying the position; and, the *expected* role is the behaviours thought appropriate by others in the group. When these three are in accord there will be little, if any, conflict between the occupant of the role and other members of the group. However, disparity between any two or all three may often result in group conflict: if perceived and/or enacted roles differ greatly from member expectations the person occupying the role may either be put under pressure to conform, asked to vacate the position or, unusually, attempt to change the expectations of other members of the group.

In the previous chapter we saw how the roles of 'guard' and 'prisoner' in Zimbardo's (1969) prison simulation study exerted powerful influences over behaviour, so much so that the experiment had to be stopped after only six days. Notice in this study that no external pressure was put on subjects to conform to role expectations, their perceived and enacted roles were consistent with stereotypic expectations existing in society.

A study by Schachter (1951) demonstrates how the role a person adopts in a group affects patterns of communication within the group. Schachter had groups consisting of five to seven members where three were confederates of the experimenter and the others naive subjects. Each member was given a case history of a delinquent to read, after which they had to give their opinions about what ought to be done with the delinquent. The group then had to discuss this for 45 minutes. The confederates adopted one of three roles: (a) *the deviate*, where an extreme and different position from the rest of the group was taken; (b) *the mode*, where the position of the most common view of the group was taken; and (c) *the slider* who first took an extreme and different position to the rest of the group but changed during the course of the discussion to that of the common view of the group. Schachter found that at the start of group discussion communications in the group were mainly directed at people occupying extreme positions (the deviate and slider). As discussions proceeded less and less communications were directed at the slider as his position gradually came to conform to the common group view.

However, communications to the deviate, who did not change his position, were high to start with then decreased dramatically: as soon as the group discovered they were not going to change his opinion they ceased attempting to do so and tended to exclude him from further discussion. In reality though, as the Asch studies demonstrate, a lone deviate in the face of an otherwise unanimous group view is unlikely to maintain his or her position for very long, particularly if the person values membership of that group.

Usually a person occupies different roles in different groups: when behaviours demanded of each role differ but occur at the same time there will be *role conflict*. This is resolved by the person enacting the role in the group which has greatest attraction and importance for him or her. Killian (1952) investigated this in policemen when oil refineries in their home city caught fire. Role conflict was between acting as a policeman by serving the community and acting as a father by ensuring the safety of their family. Every policeman whose family lived in the city threatened by the fire resolved role conflict in favour of the role of father.

The role or position a person occupies in a group has an evaluation attached to it, this is the *status* of that position. A distinction is made between *ascribed* and *achieved* status: the former does not reflect individual merit or achievement but comes through, for example, age, sex or social standing of the family into which the person is born. The latter does reflect abilities and achievements (or failures) of the person. The status of a person influences the extent to which he or she conforms to role expectations and group norms. High-status people both conform to, and deviate more from, group norms than low-status people. Greatest conformity to group norms and expectations comes from people occupying the second highest status position (Harvey and Consalvi, 1960). In the previous chapter we saw how minority influence may be achieved by a high-status person accumulating 'idiosyncracy credits' (Hollander, 1964).

Status affects the pattern and content of group communications: Back *et al.* (1950) provided a novel demonstration of this by planting a rumour in a factory with five statuses of workers. The researchers were interested to find who reported the rumour to whom. They found the vast majority of reports were upwards in the status hierarchy, with very few communications of the rumour between people of the same status or downwards to people of low status. Kelly (1951) found two status effects upon the content of communications: (a) low-status people make more comments irrelevant to the group task; and (b) less criticism of a role is made if it is occupied by a high rather than low-status person.

The status of a person can influence both group product and opinions of group members. Strodtbeck (1957) investigated the effects of socioeconomic status of jurors with respect to leadership, participation and influence. Subjects acted as jurors and heard a tape-recording of a court case, afterwards they were asked to reach a verdict as a jury. Three findings emerged: (a) high socioeconomic-status jurors were more likely to be elected as chairperson; (b) high-status jurors participated more and had greater influence in pressing their views on others; and (c) high-status jurors were better liked than low-status jurors.

### 11.4.3 Communication structure

In the preceding sections we have seen how group structure may influence both the pattern and content of communications. In these groups members were allowed to communicate freely and face-to-face: it is of interest to discover how group performance and satisfaction with the group are affected when a communicative structure is imposed and restrictions are placed upon who can communicate with whom. Time, distance, etc. restraints may not permit a group to come together face-to-face, and communication may take place via the telephone, or computer linkages or by letter/memorandum. In such circumstances allowing each group member to communicate with every other group member would lead to gross inefficiency in terms of time and duplication. It may, then, be necessary to impose a certain communication structure upon the group.

Bavelas (1950) introduced the notion of *communication networks* in which five-person groups were restricted in with whom they could communicate. The most commonly researched networks are given in Figure 11.2, the crucial difference between each is the degree of *centralization*. The most centralized network is the wheel since person C can communicate with everyone else, but

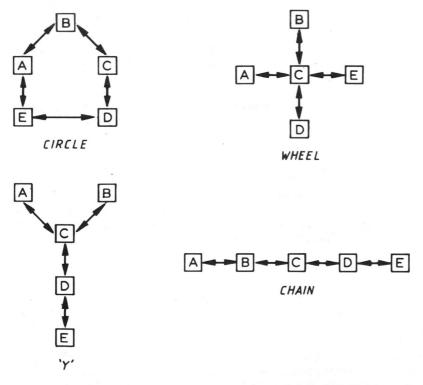

**Figure 11.2** Examples of five-person communication networks, boxes represent positions and arrows permissible communication channels between people in the group. The wheel is the most centralized, and circle the most decentralized network. After Bavelas (1950).

the four peripheral members (A, B, D and E) can only communicate to person C. The most decentralized network is the circle as each person communicates with two other people, here all members are equally central. The chain and 'Y' networks are moderately centralized positions where person C in both is central, and A, B, E in the 'Y' and A, E in the chain peripheral, B and D in the chain and D in the 'Y' are moderately central positions.

Leavitt (1951) experimentally investigated the effects of these communication networks on performance at problem solving tasks, member satisfaction and morale. Problems given to groups were to discover which symbol (for example, asterisk, addition or subtraction sign) from a possible six was common to each group member. Each member of a five-person group was given a card with six symbols on it, with a different symbol of the six omitted from each of the five cards given to them. Group members could only communicate to others as dictated by the communication network they worked within, and communication was by written message only. Measures were taken of time to solve problems, number of problems solved, number of incorrect solutions, how much subjects enjoyed the task and whether subjects perceived the group to have a leader.

Two main sets of findings emerged: (a) for task performance the more centralized networks solved the problems faster and made fewer errors. The wheel produced the fastest and greatest number of accurate solutions, the circle the slowest and fewest number of accurate solutions. (b) Satisfaction of individual members was highest in the most decentralized network, overall subjects in the circle expressed greatest enjoyment of the task, whilst peripheral members of the wheel, chain and 'Y' enjoyed the task the least. Subjects perceived person C in the latter three networks to be the group leader, no leader was perceived to exist in the circle network.

Subsequent research has confirmed these findings for relatively simple tasks such as those used by Leavitt, however, for more complex problems the more decentralized networks produced superior performance, the circle being the best. Shaw (1964) explains this as due to more complex tasks placing excessive demands or information overload on the central person in centralized networks. Decentralized networks allow a more even distribution of the workload among group members. Member satisfaction for those in peripheral positions in centralized networks can be increased by giving these people more relevant and important information than those occupying more central positions (Gilchrist *et al.*, 1954).

Much research on communication networks has simply brought a group together to solve problems on one occasion only and for a short period of time. Guetzkow and Simon (1955) found the better performance of centralized networks on simple problems disappeared after about 20 or so problems had been solved by a group. In the more decentralized networks it was found that group members developed their own substructures to compensate for the relative inefficiency of such networks.

In summary, communication structure in the form of networks affects both group performance and member satisfaction. More centralized networks produce better group performance but lower member satisfaction, varying the complexity of the task or nature of information possessed by peripheral members changes this, and groups working together for a considerable time develop their own substructures in decentralized networks.

## 11.5  Analysing group processes

We have seen how various aspects of group structure, such as cohesiveness, roles and status, affect the content and pattern of communications; Figure 11.2 diagrammatically shows this as well. However, no systematic method has been used, as yet, to measure and analyse interaction between individuals in groups. Bales (1950) has developed a comprehensive and important coding system for this called 'Interaction Process Analysis' or IPA.

Interaction Process Analysis assumes that all behaviours, both verbal and non-verbal, occurring in small groups can be allocated to one of *four* main areas: positive and negative socio-emotional behaviour and attempted answers and questions concerning the task area. Each of these four areas is broken down into three specific categories of behaviour, this yields a total of 12 categories as shown in Figure 11.3. IPA provides a very powerful tool for

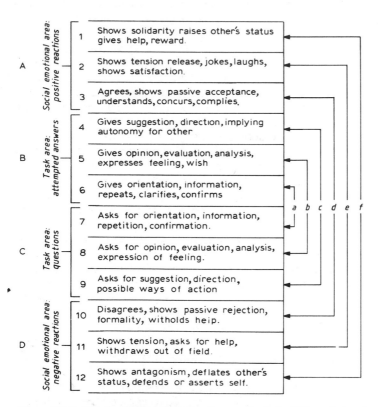

**Figure 11.3** Bales's (1950) Interaction Process Analysis (IPA); verbal and non-verbal behaviours are categorized into one of the four main areas, each area has three components. Notice pairs of components *nest* together, these are shown by the lower-case letters on the right of the figure.

social psychologists since it not only allows the measurement of patterns and content of communications but also gives information about the relative contribution of each member, a profile of the group, leadership styles and the nature of conflict (if it exists within the group). Additionally, IPA has been used to depict the ways in which a group develops over time and how role differentiation takes place.

To use IPA requires experience and training, this is to ensure coders are reliable in consistently recording similar behaviour into the same categories. Reliability must be achieved in two ways: (a) *inter-rater* reliability – different coders code similar behaviour in the same way: and (b) *intra-rater* reliability – the same coder codes similar behaviour at different times in the same way. With some assurance that both these forms of reliability can be achieved IPA can be a powerful tool for analysing group processes.

Bales and Strodtbeck (1951) found a fixed sequence of identifiable stages to occur in problem solving groups. First, the group would orient itself to the problem (categories 6 and 7), next would be an evaluation phase where the group decides what its goals are (categories 5 and 8), in the third phase the group discusses ways of achieving these goals (categories 4 and 9). Whilst the group is organizing itself over the task, role differentiation (discussed in more detail below) and divisions of labour take place. As a consequence, tensions and conflicts may arise. When this happens socio-emotional communications (both positive and negative) come to dominate group behaviour as attempts are made at resolutions and settlements. Increased conflict will be evidenced by an increase in the frequency of behaviours in categories 10, 11 and 12. Prolonged interaction of this sort may, eventually, lead to the group disbanding. Typically, though, negative socio-emotional behaviour is responded to with positive socio-emotional behaviour. Bales proposes a *nesting* hypothesis in group interaction over time: groups move from central categories (6 and 7) to extremities (1 and 12). The nesting hypothesis states that *pairs* of categories tend to occur together in group interaction – the pairs that nest together are shown by the lower-case letters in Figure 11.3. In summary, problem solving groups first get on with matters related to the task, this causes a build-up in tension and conflict which is dealt with next, satisfactory resolution allows the group to return to the task it has been set. The picture Bales and Strodtbeck (1951) paint of group processes is a cyclic one in which task and socio-emotional behaviours interact and alternate.

Bales and Slater (1955) used IPA to show how role differentiation takes place in problem solving groups: over time three roles were found to emerge and become differentiated in initially *unstructured* groups. First, the role of *task leader* emerges, communications by this person are mostly confined to categories 4 to 9, i.e. the two task areas. Second, the role of group harmonizer or *socio-emotional leader* emerges, this person attempts to reduce group tension and conflict; communications are mainly in categories 10 to 12 and, to a lesser extent, categories 1 to 3. The third and final role to differentiate is that of the *high participator*: this person contributes most to the group and acts to maintain momentum. Sometimes this role is taken by the task leader but it is rarely performed by the socio-emotional leader, most often the high participator is a different person to those occupying the two different leadership roles.

Bales and Borgatta (1956) showed how communications changed with the size of the group: as size increases so too does the frequency of communications showing tension release and giving suggestions. There was also a decrease in the showing of tension, showing agreement and asking for opinions. Slater (1958) found small groups to express less disagreement and dissatisfaction than large groups.

Interaction Process Analysis can be used to provide a group profile; for example, does a group concentrate mostly on task-related matters (categories 4 to 9) or concern itself with socio-emotional issues (categories 1 to 3 and 10 to 12)? By the same token, IPA can also be used to produce profiles of individual group members. This will allow the researcher to discover, for example, whether one person or many people are responsible for producing group conflict. IPA, then, provides a systematic and reliable method for analysing the many and varied aspects of group processes.

## 11.6 Leadership

Because of the practical utility attached to selection and training of leaders social psychology has devoted much effort in attempting to answer such questions as: 'What makes a good leader?', 'Can effective and ineffective leaders be distinguished?' 'Do different situations demand different leadership styles?' From simple beginnings theory and research have evolved to demonstrate how complex a topic leadership is. Contemporary perspectives suggest the following variables all need to be taken into account: the leader's personality and behaviour, composition and function of the group, the situation and group structure, the nature of the task and whether the leader is effective or ineffective. Early research looked for personality characteristics separating leaders from non-leaders, failure here led psychologists to focus on the situation rather than the person. This too failed and theorizing became increasingly complex to encompass all the variables mentioned above. Given the number of variables now acknowledged to be important you will not be surprised to discover that no one single definition of leadership has been forthcoming. However, three components have achieved a degree of consensus (Tedeschi and Lindskold, 1976). Leadership as *social influence* refers to the extent to which a person or persons can direct and control the behaviours of others by changing attitudes and opinions and getting members to conform to roles and group norms. Leadership *behaviour* refers to what the leader does in terms of clarifying group objectives, making decisions and suggesting ways of achieving objectives. Leadership as *authority* concerns the power the leader is invested with or is perceived to have by other group members in order to achieve the group's goals and institute change when necessary. The weakness of attempting a definition along these lines is that it does not tell us what makes leaders effective in some situations and not others. For example, we need to know why Winston Churchill made a good leader during World War II, but not before or afterwards.

**Table 11.1** Percentage of positive and negative relationships between personality traits and leadership. Adapted from Mann (1959).

| TRAITS | NUMBER OF FINDINGS | % GIVING A POSITIVE RELATIONSHIP | % GIVING A NEGATIVE RELATIONSHIP | % YIELDING NO RELATIONSHIP |
|---|---|---|---|---|
| Intelligence | 196 | 46 | 1 | 53 |
| Adjustment | 164 | 30 | 2 | 68 |
| Extroversion | 119 | 31 | 5 | 64 |
| Dominance | 39 | 38 | 15 | 46 |
| Masculinity | 70 | 16 | 1 | 83 |
| Conservatism | 62 | 5 | 27 | 68 |
| Sensitivity | 101 | 15 | 1 | 84 |

### 11.6.1 'Great man' theory

Historically and traditionally a leader has been viewed as a person possessing a distinct set of personality characteristics – this view is encapsulated in the saying 'leaders are born not made'. Early research looked for traits distinguishing leaders from non-leaders and found, at best, leaders to be slightly more intelligent than non-leaders! Mann (1959) reviewed over a 100 studies seeking to correlate personality characteristics with leadership; some of the findings are summarized in Table 11.1. From this table it can be seen that weak evidence exists supporting the claim that leaders are more intelligent, more extrovert, more dominant and more sensitive than non-leaders.

McGrath (1964) offers five reasons as to why the trait approach has been and always will be unsuccessful: (a) there are no agreed upon personality traits by which to compare leaders and non-leaders; (b) there is no agreed upon definition of leadership – researchers using different definitions may select different people from the same group as leaders; (c) the trait approach ignores relationships between leaders and followers – are relationships good or bad and are different people more effective in these different situations? (d) the situation generally is ignored; and (e) the approach assumes a single leader exists in a group when quite often, as we saw with Bales's IPA, two types of leaders often emerge.

Lack of success with the trait approach led researchers to focus on the situation and how this affects the person who becomes the leader. Being *appointed* to the position of leader, as opposed to a leader *emerging*, may shape the person's behaviour because of role requirements stemming from that position and different behaviour by group members to the leader than to other group members. In a study by Bell and French (1950), acting petty officers were *randomly* assigned from a pool of new recruits: they were subsequently found to be retained in that position and perceived to be leaders by their fellow recruits. The study demonstrates that mere occupancy of a role, even if arrived at randomly, results in that person being treated as and perceived to be the leader.

The communication structure, as we saw earlier in this chapter, may determine the leader: Leavitt (1951) found occupants of the central positions in the wheel, chain and 'Y' were perceived to be and became group leaders.

Similarly, Sommer (1969) found people who occupied central positions at a table were often treated as and became the group leader.

Crisis situations often result in the emergence or replacement of a leader. Hamblin (1958) demonstrated this in an experiment in which college students working in groups of three were asked to play a game in which they had to work out some of the rules of the game for themselves. Upon correctly discovering a rule the experimenter turned on a green light, when wrong a red light was switched on. All groups had to play the game six times; for half the groups the rules to be discovered remained the same throughout, for the other half the experimenter changed the rules after the third game. The latter condition resulted in a crisis for the groups on the fourth game since rules they thought were correct were now wrong. Hamblin took two measures: (a) the frequency of suggestions made by each person in the group; and (b) the frequency with which suggestions made by one person were accepted by the other two group members. Individuals who had been influential in 'pre-crisis' games became much more so in the 'crisis' games – they made more suggestions and had their suggestions accepted more often. The person who emerged as leader in the crisis period was also challenged and criticized less often. In short, a crisis situation resulted in members of a group being more willing to be led and influenced than in a non-crisis situation.

In summary, there is some evidence to suggest situations make leaders: this occurs not because of any inherent personality characteristics of the leader but because the situation demands greater directiveness and members are more willing to be guided by one person. The emergence of a leader may be because the person talks and contributes the most or may simply be due to the person occupying a central position in the group.

### 11.6.2 Leadership style

Regardless of whether a leader is appointed or emerges, the behavioural stlye of the person in that role has important consequences for group performance. Leadership style affects task performance, morale and the cohesiveness of the group.

Hemphill (1950) conducted a large-scale study in which subjects rated leaders' behaviour on over 1000 different aspects. Two important behavioural dimensions emerged: *group-centred* and *directive* behaviours. Group-centred or 'consideration' behaviours included warmth of personal relationships, mutual trust, willingness to listen to followers' suggestions and a democratic approach allowing all members to participate in decision making. Directive behaviours, called 'initiating structure', included maintenance of standards and performance, assigning tasks to members, ensuring individuals followed rules and conformed to norms and making sure the members understood the leader's role. Consideration behaviours bear a similarity to the behaviours of the socio-emotional leader and initiating structure behaviours to the task-oriented leader found by Bales with the IPA.

A classic experiment by Lewin, Lippett and White (1939) demonstrated how leadership style affects group performance. Groups of 10- and 11-year-old boys working in groups where they had to carve models from bars of soap were exposed to three different leadership styles: authoritarian, democratic and *laissez-faire*. Authoritarian leaders made all the decisions for the group, did not participate in group activities, assigned boys to tasks without saying why and made changes without consultation. Democratic leaders made decisions only after consultation with the group, were friendly to group members, participated in group activities, gave reasons for praise and criticism, and offered help when required. *Laissez-faire* leaders played a passive role, did not attempt to direct or coordinate the group and made neither positive or negative evaluations of the group.

The democratic style of leadership was found to produce highest morale in the group and greatest friendliness and cooperation; however, groups with this style of leadership produced fewer models than those under authoritarian leadership though the models were of higher quality. The boys also kept working in the absence of the leader. The authoritarian style resulted in more models being made but misbehaviour occurred when the leader was absent. Poorest performance was under the *laissez-faire* style of leadership, here fewest models were produced and misbehaviour occurred all the time, however the boys were friendly towards the leader. After the boys had experienced each type of leadership style they were found to prefer the democratic approach most. In summary, group performance in terms of quality of models made and group cohesiveness was highest with the democratic style of leadership.

Subsequent research has offered mixed support for these early findings: Hare (1962) found productivity to be higher with an authoritarian style, but Kahn and Katz (1953) found the democratic style to result in highest productivity. Groups with an authoritarian leader (a higher score on the F-scale, see Chapter 5) were less likely to show dissent or express criticism and leaders had less influence over the group than non-authoritarian leaders (low F-scale score). Leaders with a high F-scale score were less sensitive to the needs of the group and less concerned with receiving approval from other group members.

### 11.6.3 Fiedler's contingency theory

A highly influential theory of leadership *effectiveness* has been proposed by Fielder (1971), this takes both leadership style *and* situational factors into account. There are three situational factors: (a) leader–follower relations: if the leader is accepted, trusted and respected relations are good, if not relations are bad; (b) task structure: high task structure is where the task set the group is well-defined, low is where it is vague; and (c) power of the leader: the leader has strong position of power if the leader's power is both legitimate and can draw on resources to impose rewards and sanctions on members of the group as a whole; position of power is weak if both these are absent. These three situational factors, since they can each take on one of two values, yield eight different combinations or *octants* as Fiedler (1971) calls them. For each octant the *overall* favourableness of the situation can be assessed, favourableness ranges from extremely high to extremely low. Figure 11.4 depicts the eight octants and the overall favourableness rating of each. For example, one favourable situation (octant I) is where leader–follower

| | OCTANTS | | | | | | | |
|---|---|---|---|---|---|---|---|---|
| | I | II | III | IV | V | VI | VII | VIII |
| Leader – follower relations | Good | Good | Good | Poor | Poor | Poor | Poor | Poor |
| Task structure | High | High | Low | Low | High | High | Low | Low |
| Leader position power | Strong | Weak | Strong | Weak | Strong | Weak | Strong | Weak |
| Overall situational favourableness | Extra high | High | High | Mod. high | Mod. high | Low | Low | Extra low |

**Figure 11.4** Fiedler's typology of leadership situations and situational favourableness. Adapted from Fiedler (1971).

relations are good, task structure is high and the leader's position or power is strong.

In order to predict effective leadership in each of these octants Fielder says we need to know the *leadership style* of the person. This is measured by asking leaders, or anybody for that matter, to cast their mind over all the people they have worked with in the past and think about the person they least liked – the *least preferred co-worker* or LPC. With this person in mind subjects are asked to fill in a set of semantic differential scales (see Chapter 4) containing such items as 'friendly – unfriendly', 'cooperative – uncooperative', etc. A favourable attitude towards the LPC would attract a high score (high LPC) and an unfavourable attitude a low score (low LPC). For Fiedler a *high* LPC score indicates a *relations-oriented* (socio-emotional) leader and a *low* LPC a *task-oriented* leader.

Task-oriented leaders will be most effective in either very favourable or very unfavourable situations; relations-oriented leaders will be most effective where the situation is moderately favourable, this is shown in Figure 11.5. The most important situational factor is leader–follower relations, when this is good (or bad) only one other situational factor needs to be good (or bad) for the overall situation to be favourable (or unfavourable). Accordingly, octants I, II and III in Figure 11.4 represent the highly favourable conditions in Figure 11.5; octants VI, VII and VIII represent the highly unfavourable

| | SITUATIONAL FACTORS | | |
|---|---|---|---|
| LEADERSHIP STYLE | *Highly favourable* | *Moderately favourable* | *Highly favourable* |
| *Relationship oriented leader (High LPC)* | Ineffective | Effective | Ineffective |
| *Task oriented leader (Low LPC)* | Effective | Ineffective | Effective |

**Figure 11.5** Effectiveness or ineffectiveness of different types of leaders according to situational favourableness. Adapted from Fiedler (1971).

conditions. In both cases groups would be effectively led by a task-oriented leader. Octants IV and V are moderately favourable and a relations-oriented leader would be most effective here.

Why should such leadership styles be most effective in these different situations? Fiedler argues that when conditions are unfavourable the group would be willing to overlook interpersonal conflicts and tensions in order to get on with the task: hence the appropriateness of a task-oriented leader. In favourable conditions the leader can get on with the task in hand since the situation is a positive one with little interpersonal conflict, again a task-oriented leader is most appropriate. Where the situation is only moderately favourable conflict and tension within the group may be the biggest problem: the socio-emotional or relations-oriented leader is needed to sort this out before the group can get on with their task.

Fiedler (1964) conducted a series of studies which gave support to his contingency theory: American Airforce bomber crews were found to be more effective when led by low LPC (task-oriented) rather than high LPC (relations-oriented) leaders. However, when leader–follower relations were poor, high LPC leaders produced the most effective crews. Low LPC board chairmen of small companies produced better group performence when the situation was very unfavourable (octant VIII), and high LPC board chairmen produced higher group performance when leader–follower relations were poor.

The contingency theory of leadership effectiveness has been used to train leaders: the basic idea is to sensitize leaders to the demands of the group at any one time so that a leader can adapt his style according to the situation. Leaders who are primarily task-oriented need to be sensitized to perceiving and dealing with conflict and tension in the group. Relations-oriented leaders are trained to become more task-oriented in very favourable or unfavourable situations.

In summary, Fiedler has produced a theory *not* along the lines of good and bad leaders, but proposing 'there are leaders who perform well in one situation but not in another' (Fiedler, 1973, p. 26). The theory is a complex one which characterizes the complexity inherent in the study of leadership – both leadership style and situational factors are integrated to predict when and what sort of leaders will be *effective*.

### 11.6.4 Leadership skills

Morley and Hosking (1984) argue that leadership is best conceptualized by regarding it as a *skill*. A skilful leader is one 'who is able to create and maintain a social order based on systems of power and systems of value' (Hosking and Morley, 1985, p. 18). The skills of leadership they are concerned with are not those of 'micro' communication social skills (described in Chapter 9), the leader is assumed to possess these, but 'macro' social skills. Macro skills involve the leader being extremely knowledgable about the environment in which he or she works. At the heart of this model are the basic skills of interpretation, the ability to influence people when in possession of sufficient information, and the ability to make decisions based on this information.

Skilful, as opposed to unskilful, leaders are people who secure the best possible outcome for the group given the circumstances. This approach differs from others on leadership in three main ways: (a) it focuses on the ability of leaders to process information. Such an emphasis on cognition assumes people are limited processors of information – a person highly knowledgable about the work environment will be overloaded at a higher point than a person new to the environment. This means leadership skill takes time to develop as it takes time to understand an organization. (b) Skilled leaders, in order to secure the best outcome, must be good at bargaining and negotiation – perhaps the 'micro' social skills are important here. (c) Leadership is a process – leaders learn from other leaders. Social influence at this level is not to do with the way people behave but the way people think about and represent the environment in which they work.

This approach offers a new direction for leadership research as it is less concerned with style and situational factors but more concerned with how leaders process information, understand the environment in which they work and use this knowledge in bargaining and negotiation.

## 11.7  Decision making

Decision making is a common feature of our lives both domestically and at work. Day-to-day routine decisions are usually made individually. However, when facing more important decisions which may have far-reaching effects on our lives, such as whether to accept a job in another part of the country, move house, etc., we often discuss the problem with significant others in order to arrive at the best choice from among the alternatives. Likewise at work routine decisions we usually make on our own, for more important decisions, such as ones of policy, formal decision-making groups are either constituted or already exist. Industrial organizations have board and committee meetings, schools and colleges have staff meetings and governments have cabinet meetings or their equivalent. At every layer in our society and other societies, people come together to make decisions – it is assumed that the collective wisdom of a body of people produces a more informed and a higher quality decision than could be achieved by a single person working alone. Much research, as we shall see, has addressed itself to testing the validity of these and related assumptions.

In what follows the questions of whether groups make better decisions will first be addressed, this is followed by consideration of factors affecting the *quality* of group decisions. Finally, poor or defective decision making will be analysed using Janis's notion of *Groupthink*, this will allow further suggestions for improving the quality of decision making by groups.

### 11.7.1  Individuals versus groups

Assessing whether groups make better decisions than individuals is dependent on how the word 'better' is interpreted and used. If there is an objective standard to compare individual and group decisions with then performance judgements can easily be made. However, most decisions, both domestically and at work, cannot be easily compared to an objective standard. For example, was the decision to make the wearing of seat belts compulsory by law a good or bad one? Research had supported the view that wearing seat belts saved lives, but it may be that the wearing of seat belts causes more accidents, resulting in more non-fatal injuries, since people may feel safer with a seat belt on and be prepared to take greater risks than when they did not wear them.

Comparing individual and group performance on problem solving tasks, as we saw earlier in this chapter, showed groups solved more problems correctly than individuals working alone, but were less efficient in terms of man-hours per problem. However, whilst the quality of group problem solving is higher than that of the average individual it is rarely better than that of the most able group member (Shaw, 1971). An extremely capable individual is best left to work alone rather than in a group.

Many techniques have been developed by social scientists (economists, psychologists, etc.) to assess the quality of decisions in relation to their consequences. One such technique is cost-benefit analysis in which the perceived costs are weighed against the perceived benefits in order to arrive at (or evaluate) the choice which embodies the least cost for the most benefit. The problem for this approach is to arrive at an adequate means of assessing costs and benefits; different people may have different perceptions.

A strategy for assessing whether individuals or groups make higher quality decisions is to compare their performance on a task with expert opinion. Such a strategy was employed in the 'moon' problem of Hall and Watson (1970) who were interested in two things: whether (a) groups made higher quality decisions than individuals; and (b) instructions on how to reach a group decision would result in a higher quality group decision. In the first stage of the experiment individuals were given the following task:

You are a member of a space crew originally scheduled to rendezvous with a mother ship on the lighted surface of the moon. Due to mechanical difficulties, however, your ship was forced to land at a spot some 200 miles from the rendezvous point. During the crash landing much of the equipment aboard was damaged and since survival depends on reaching the mother ship the most critical items available must be chosen for the 200 mile trip. Below are listed the 15 items left intact and undamaged after landing. Your task is to rank order them in terms of their importance in allowing your crew to reach the rendezvous point. Place the number 1 by the most important item, the number 2 by the second most important item, and so on. Place the number 15 by the least important item.

Individual Ranking

Box of matches . . . . . . . . . . . . . . . . . . . . . . . . . . . . . . . . . . . . . . . . . . . . . . . . .

Food concentrate . . . . . . . . . . . . . . . . . . . . . . . . . . . . . . . . . . . . . . . . . . . . . . .

50 feet of nylon ropes . . . . . . . . . . . . . . . . . . . . . . . . . . . . . . . . . . . . . . .

Parachute silk . . . . . . . . . . . . . . . . . . . . . . . . . . . . . . . . . . . . . . . . . . . . . . . . . .

Portable heating unit . . . . . . . . . . . . . . . . . . . . . . . . . . . . . . . . . . . . . . . . . . . .

Two .45 calibre pistols . . . . . . . . . . . . . . . . . . . . . . . . . . . . . . . . . . . . . . . . . .

1 case dehydrated milk . . . . . . . . . . . . . . . . . . . . . . . . . . . . . . . . . . . . . . . . . .

2 hundred-pound tanks of oxygen . . . . . . . . . . . . . . . . . . . . . . . . . . . . . . . . .

Stellar map (of the moon's constellation) . . . . . . . . . . . . . . . . . . . . . . . . . . . .

Life raft . . . . . . . . . . . . . . . . . . . . . . . . . . . . . . . . . . . . . . . . . . . . . . . . . . . . . . . .

Magnetic compass . . . . . . . . . . . . . . . . . . . . . . . . . . . . . . . . . . . . . . . . . . . . . . .

5 gallons of water . . . . . . . . . . . . . . . . . . . . . . . . . . . . . . . . . . . . . . . . . . . . . . .

Signal flares . . . . . . . . . . . . . . . . . . . . . . . . . . . . . . . . . . . . . . . . . . . . . . . . . . . .

First Aid kit containing injection needles . . . . . . . . . . . . . . . . . . . . . . . . . . .
Solar powered FM receiver-transmitter . . . . . . . . . . . . . . . . . . . . . . . . . . .

Subjects were given 10 minutes to do the ranking task, then put in groups of four to six and instructed to reach a group consensus on the rankings of each of the 15 items. Group consensus is where each member of the group agrees upon the ranking decision for each item. Half the groups then proceeded with this task, the other half were given the following guidelines for reaching consensus:

1. Avoid arguing for your own individual judgements. Approach the task on the basis of logic.
2. Avoid changing your mind only in order to reach agreement and avoid conflict. Support only solutions with which you are at least able to agree partially.
3. Avoid conflict-reducing techniques such as majority vote, averaging, or trading, in reaching your decisions.
4. View differences of opinion as helpful rather than a hindrance in decision-making.

Groups in both conditions were allowed 45 minutes to reach consensus on each of the items. Individual and group rankings for each item were then compared with the rankings given by experts* (in this case NASA). For both individuals and groups a *total difference* score is worked out by calculating the deviation of each item ranked from the rank given that item by the NASA experts, these are then added together. The higher the score the greater the disagreement with NASA rankings and hence the poorer quality of decision making.

Hall and Watson found groups to perform better than individuals, although, as previously, the best individual usually produced an overall higher quality decision than the group. It was also found that groups given instructions on how to reach consensus produced better quality decisions, but this was not a very pronounced finding. On the whole, then, both this and other research we have looked at validates the claim that groups produce better quality decisions than the average individual.

## 11.7.2 Group decision making

In the previous chapter we saw how groups polarize individual opinion and produce more risky or cautious decisions according to the nature of the problem. Here aspects of group structure and composition influencing the quality of decision making will be considered.

For any group to function there must be a degree of cohesiveness; in newly formed groups though, cohesiveness may be a desired goal yet to be achieved. Maier and Solem (1952) showed how the desire for cohesiveness may stifle valid and important minority opinions. In this experiment individual subjects were given the following problem:

*the NASA rankings were as follows: Box of matches – 15; food concentrate – 4; 50 feet of nylon rope – 6; parachute silk – 8; portable heating unit – 13; two .45 calibre pistols – 11; 1 case of dehydrated milk – 12; 2 hundred-pound tanks of oxygen – 1; stellar map – 3; life raft – 9; magnetic compass – 14; 5 gallons of water – 2; signal flares – 10; first aid kit – 7; solar powered FM receiver-transmitter – 5.

A man bought a horse for £60 and sold it for £70. Then he bought it back for £80 and sold it again for £90. How much money did he make in the horse business?

After giving their individual answers subjects were put into groups of five or six and asked to arrive at an answer unanimously agreed upon by the group. Maier and Solem found majority group views to dominate even when the minority had the correct answer.

Torrance (1954) showed status to inhibit the quality of group decisions, he gave the above horse-selling problem to three-man US Airforce bomber crews. The crews were made up of a pilot (high status), a navigator (middle status) and a gunner (low status). Before group discussion the correct answer was given most often by navigators (50 per cent) and less often, but roughly equally, by pilots and gunners (around 30 per cent). Group decisions did not reflect this: over 90 per cent of pilots who had the right answer convinced their group they were correct, but only just over 60 per cent of gunners and 80 per cent of navigators managed to persuade their group to their correct view.

If the task facing the group can be broken down into sub-tasks and so allow sub-committees to be formed the end result is likely to be of higher quality then if the group tackles the task as a whole (Steiner, 1972). Creating sub-groups to deal with the different components of the task facilitates each member's participation and allows an individual's skills and expertise to be utilized more fully.

Group composition in terms of group size, as we saw earlier in this chapter, has an important influence on performance: larger groups (of say 20 or more) are likely to produce poorer quality decisions than smaller groups. Researchers have not been able to specify an optimum size for decision-making groups, however, Slater (1958) found group members preferred groups of five or six even though such groups tended to be more tense, tactful and constrained than larger groups where competitiveness and aggression were more in evidence. Groups composed of individuals differing in expertise, social background and personality characteristics have been found to be more effective than more homogeneous groups (Hoffman, 1966). Generally, heterogeneity provides for a range of skills and viewpoints which should result in a more informed decision being made, but there may be a cost in terms of time since more material will be thrown up for group discussion.

In summary, group decision making may be of higher quality if the group is small, the task can be broken down into smaller distinct components, status is not allowed to interfere with open discussion and the composition is heterogeneous.

### 11.7.3 When decision go wrong – groupthink

On 17 April, 1961 a brigade of 1400 Cuban exiles invaded a swampy part of the coast of Cuba known as the Bay of Pigs. The ultimate aim of this invasion was the overthrow of Fidel Castro's government. However, nothing went as planned: by the first day two of the supply ships had been sunk by Castro's Air Force and the remaining two supply ships had fled. By the second day the brigade of exiles was surrounded at the Bay of Pigs by Castro's Army, and by the end of the third day it was all over: what was left of the invasion force was captured and imprisoned. The Bay of Pigs fiasco, as it came to be called, was approved by President Kennedy and his small group of highly experienced policy and military advisers. Shortly afterwards Kennedy admitted making a dreadful decision and asked 'how could I have been so stupid as to let them go ahead'. Consequences of the fiasco were far-reaching: less than a year later Russia was installing nuclear weapons and a large military force in Cuba. This led to the Cuban missile crisis of October, 1962 which posed the greatest threat of nuclear war in the world's history. This crisis, fortunately, was effectively dealt with by the Kennedy administration.

Irving Janis (1972) was interested to discover how such a highly experienced group of men could make such a defective decision. The group, composed of such people as Dean Rusk (the Secretary of State), Robert McNamara (the Secretary of Defense), Arthur Schlesinger and other leading figures, were, Janis observed, 'shrewd thinkers, capable of objective rational analysis and accustomed to speaking their minds' (p. 19). Why, then, did they fail to detect the serious flaws in the decision to invade Cuba?

Janis proposed that the members of this group, including President Kennedy himself, were victims of *groupthink*, which occurs in a highly cohesive group striving for unanimity of opinion rather than a realistic appraisal of the situation. Groupthink is 'a deterioration of mental efficiency, reality testing and moral judgement that results from ingroup pressures' (Janis, 1972, p. 9). Janis has analysed other 'fiascos' in international decision-making such as Pearl Harbor, the escalation of the war in Vietnam and the Watergate affair, and produced evidence of groupthink operating there as well.

When is groupthink likely to occur, how can it be identified and how does it produce defective decision making? Figure 11.6 shown how the concurrence-seeking tendency or striving for unanimity results from five antecedent conditions. The first, high cohesiveness is, perhaps, the most important; isolation of the group from outside criticism and the lack of procedures in the group for evaluating properly different alternatives are also very important.

The eight symptoms of groupthink, shown in Figure 11.6, can be illustrated by reference to the six major assumptions, all proved to be wrong, made when deciding to go ahead with the invasion of the Bay of Pigs. An illusion of invulnerability led to excessive optimism and risk taking – the group was unrealistic about the cover story holding up, unrealistic in assessing the Cuban Air Force and Army to be ineffective and unrealistic about the morale and willingness of the Cuban exiles to carry out the invasion on their own. Belief in the inherent morality of the group led members to think that what they were doing was right and that because of this it was bound to succeed. Direct pressures on dissenters within the group prevented critical evaluation of the six assumptions. An illusion of unanimity in the group led to 'silences' in group discussion to be interpreted as agreement. Finally, and most sinister of all the symptoms of groupthink, is the emergence of self-appointed '*mindguards*'. These were members of the group who took it upon themselves to protect the group from criticism and dissent and so fostered a false feeling of unanimity.

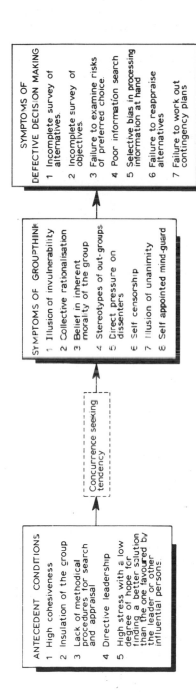

**ANTECEDENT CONDITIONS**

1 High cohesiveness
2 Insulation of the group
3 Lack of methodical procedures for search and appraisal
4 Directive leadership
5 High stress with a low degree of hope for finding a better solution than the one favoured by the leader or other influential persons.

→ Concurrence seeking tendency →

**SYMPTOMS OF GROUPTHINK**

1 Illusion of invulnerability
2 Collective rationalisation
3 Belief in inherent morality of the group
4 Stereotypes of out-groups
5 Direct pressure on dissenters
6 Self censorship
7 Illusion of unanimity
8 Self appointed mind-guard

→

**SYMPTOMS OF DEFECTIVE DECISION MAKING**

1 Incomplete survey of alternatives.
2 Incomplete survey of objectives.
3 Failure to examine risks of preferred choice.
4 Poor information search
5 Selective bias in processing information at hand
6 Failure to reappraise alternatives
7 Failure to work out contingency plans

**Figure 11.6** The antecedent conditions prevailing in a group which lead to concurrence seeking tendencies. Such tendencies result in the eight symptoms of groupthink, groupthink results in decision making being defective in seven major ways. From Janis and Mann (1977).

**Table 11.2** The six assumptions Janis claims President Kennedy and his group of advisers made when approving the invasion of the Bay of Pigs. All six assumptions proved wrong. Adapted from Janis (1972).

ASSUMPTION 1: No one will know that the United States was responsible for the invasion of Cuba. Most people will believe the CIA cover story, and sceptics can easily be refuted.

ASSUMPTION 2: The Cuban air force is so ineffectual that it can be knocked out completely just before the invasion begins.

ASSUMPTION 3: The 1400 men in the brigade of Cuban exiles have high morale and are willing to carry out the invasion without any support from United States ground troops.

ASSUMPTION 4: Castro's army is so weak that the small Cuban brigade will be able to establish a well-protected beachhead.

ASSUMPTION 5: The invasion by the exile brigade will touch off sabotage by the Cuban underground and armed uprisings behind the lines that will effectively support the invasion and probably lead to the toppling of the Castro regime.

ASSUMPTION 6: If the Cuban brigade does not succeed in its prime military objective, the men can retreat to the Escambray Mountains and reinforce the guerrilla units holding out against the Castro regime.

These eight symptoms of groupthink produce the seven aspects of defective decision-making shown in Figure 11.6. For example, poor information search resulted in the group not looking properly at a map of Cuba – if they had done so they would have realized the Escambray mountains lay 80 miles away through impenetrable swamp. This realization would quickly have shown assumption 6 to be false. Any group showing symptoms of groupthink and showing most of the antecedent conditions is highly likely to produce defective decisions.

### 11.7.4 Countering groupthink

The Cuban missile crisis, less than a year after the Bay of Pigs, was dealt with by the same group of people but, according to Janis, was characterized by high quality decision making. The symptoms of groupthink, given in Figure 11.6, tell us which group properties are undesirable and should suggest ways of avoiding them. For example, group members should not suppress their doubts (self-censorship); dissent from group opinions should be encouraged rather than suppressed. If the group appears unanimous it would be important to ascertain that this is actually the case rather than assume it to be so. Of course, these and others you may be able to think of introduce conflict and tension into a group and so *reduce* cohesiveness.

Janis (1972) offers numerous prescriptions for avoiding groupthink: three of the more important ones will be given. First, the leader or chairperson of the group should encourage each group member to express doubts and objections to a proposed course of action. Second, the leader of the group should attempt to be impartial rather than state his or her preferences at the outset, this avoids concurrence tendencies from other members. Third, the group should, if possible, set up other independent groups to work on the same problem and make their own recommendations, the products of the two groups could then be evaluated and the most soundly reasoned decision taken. Costs are incurred for adopting such procedures – it will take longer to reach a decision, conflict within the group and between individual members will increase, and group cohesiveness will decrease.

As you can see, there is no easy, foolproof way of avoiding groupthink, but if decision making groups are more concerned with the quality of decision than satisfaction with their being members of the group such costs will be accepted. In the end, it must be just as, if not more, satisfying to be a member of a decision making group producing high quality rather than defective decisions, even if more argument and greater time is spent reaching a decision.

## 11.8 Summary

○ Small groups may be understood in terms of group composition, group structure and group processes. These affect the task performance of the group and individual change and group development.

○ Social facilitation occurs when a task is familiar or well learned, inhibition occurs with new or complex tasks. Groups solve more problems and produce more correct solutions than the average individual, but take more time and rarely perform as well as the most able group member.

○ Group composition has been researched in reference to group size, and homogeneity or heterogeneity of membership. As group size increases member satisfaction decreases, contribution is more variable and leadership style changes.

○ Group structure influences individual members' behaviour; group cohesiveness, roles and status, and communication structure are the important variables. Cohesive groups provide greater member satisfaction and usually result in better productivity. Roles exert normative influences, a distinction is made between expected, perceived and enacted roles. Communication networks affect performance and satisfaction, the more centralized network produces better performance but lower member satisfaction.

○ Individual behaviour in groups is analysed using Bales's Interaction Process Analysis. Behaviour, both verbal and non-verbal is divided into four main areas: positive and negative socio-emotional, questions and attempted answers about the task. Three roles are found to differentiate over time in unstructured groups – task leader, socio-emotional leader and high participator.

○ Early leadership research failed to find personality differences between leaders and non-leaders; situational factors may account for the emergence of leaders. Leader behaviour has been analysed into two main components – group centred and directive behaviours. Authoritarian, democratic and *laissez-faire* leadership styles produce important differences in group behaviour and productivity

○ The most influential theory of leadership has been Fiedler's contingency theory. This takes both leadership style (task-oriented or relations-oriented) and situational factors (leader–follower relations, task structure and leader power) into account to predict leadership effectiveness. Task leaders are more effective when the overall favourableness of the situation is either high or low.

○ Decision making by groups is generally of higher quality than by individuals, except when group performance is compared with that of the most able individual. The quality of group decisions is affected by cohesiveness, task structure and group composition.

○ Janis attributed defective group decision making to *groupthink*, this occurs in high cohesive groups striving for unanimity of opinion rather than a realistic appraisal of decision alternatives. Symptoms of groupthink include an illusion of invulnerability, belief in the inherent morality of the group and the emergence of 'mindguards'. Groupthink may be countered by encouraging members to be more critical, express doubts and have others work on the problem.

## 11.9 Suggestions for further reading

Davis, J.H. *Group Performance* (Reading, Mass., Addison-Wesley, 1969).
Concise introduction to selected areas covered in this chapter, good for more detail on individual and group performance, and the ways in which group size, composition and cohesiveness affect performance.

Janis, I. *Victims of Groupthink: A Psychological Study of Foreign-Policy Decisions and Fiascos* (Boston, Houghton Mifflin, 1972) 2nd edn.
Excellent book giving numerous case studies of poor quality and high quality decision making at high governmental levels. The cases are analysed from the groupthink perspective, which Janis gives a full account of and offers suggestions for ways of preventing it occurring.

Shaw, M.E. *Group Dynamics: The Psychology of Small Group Behaviour* (New York, McGraw Hill, 1971).
Comprehensive text covering the many aspects of group dynamics, a bit dry in places, but worth consulting for finding out more detail about all the issues covered in this chapter.

# References

Abramson, L.Y. and Martin, D.J. 1981: Depression and the causal inference process. In J.M. Harvey, W. Ickes and R.F. Kidd (eds.), *New Directions in Attribution Research* (Hillsdale, NJ: Erlbaum), vol. 3.

Abramson, L.Y., Seligman, M.E.P. and Teasdale, J.D. 1978: Learned helplessness in humans: critique and reformulation. *Journal of Abnormal Psychology* **87**, 49–74.

Adorno, T.W., Frenkel-Brunswick, E., Levinson, D.J. and Sanford, R.N. 1950: *The Authoritarian Personality*. New York: Harper.

Ainsworth, M.D. 1973: The development of infant–mother attachment. In B.M. Caldwell and H.N. Ricciati (eds.), *Review of Child Development Research* (Chicago: University of Chicago Press).

Ainsworth, M.D.S., Bell, S.M.V. and Stayton, D.J. 1971: Individual differences in strange-situation behaviour of one-year olds. In H.R. Schaffer (ed.), *The Origins of Human Social Relations* (New York: Academic Press).

—— 1974: Infant–mother attachment and social development. In M.P.M. Richards (ed.), *The Integration of the Child into the Social World* (Cambridge: Cambridge University Press).

Ainsworth, M.D. and Wittig, B.A. 1969: Attachment and exploratory behaviour of one year olds in a strange situation. In B.M. Foss (ed.), *Determinants of Infant Behaviour* (London: Methuen).

Ajzen, I. and Fishbein, M. 1977: Attitude-behaviour relations: a theoretical analysis and review of empirical research. *Psychological Bulletin* **84**, 888–918.

Allen, V.L. and Levine, J.M. 1971: Social pressure and personal influence. *Journal of Experimental Social Psychology* **7**, 122–4.

Allport, F.H. 1924: *Social Psychology*. Boston: Houghton Mifflin.

Allport, G.W. 1954: *The Nature of Prejudice*. Reading, Mass: Addison-Wesley.

Alper T. 1952: Memory for socially relevant material. *Journal of Abnormal and Social Psychology* **47**, 25–37.

Altmann, I. and Taylor, D.A. 1973: *Social Penetration: The Development of Interpersonal Relationships*. New York: Holt, Rinehart & Winston.

Apsler, R. 1975: Effects of embarrassment on behaviour towards others. *Journal of Personality and Social Psychology* **32**, 145–53.

Argyle, M. 1983: *The Psychology of Interpersonal Behaviour*. Harmondsworth: Penguin, 4th edn.

Argyle, M. and Cook, M. 1976: *Gaze and Mutual Gaze*. London: Cambridge University Press.

Argyle, M. and Dean, J. 1965: Eye-contact, distance and affiliation. *Semiotica* **6**, 32–49.

Argyle, M. and Ingham, R. 1972: Gaze, mutual gaze and proximity. *Semiotica* **6**, 32–49.

Aronson, E. 1969: The theory of cognitive dissonance: a current perspective. In L. Berkowltz (ed.), *Advances in Experimental Social Psychology* (New York: Academic Press), vol. 4.

Aronson, E. and Mills, J. 1959: The effect of severity of initiation on liking for a group. *Journal of Abnormal and Social Psychology* **59**, 177–81.

Asch, S. 1946: Forming impressions of personality. *Journal of Abnormal and Social Psychology* **41**, 258–90.

—— 1955: Opinions and social pressure. *Scientific American* **193 (5)**, 31–5.

Back, K.W., Festinger, L., Hymovitch, B., Kelley, H.H., Schachter, S. and Thibaut, J.W. 1950: The methodology of studying rumour transmission. *Human Relations* **3**, 307–12.

Backman, C.W. and Secord, P.F. 1959: The effect of perceived liking on inter-personal attraction. *Human Relations* **12**, 379–84.

Bales, R.F. 1950: *Interaction Process Analysis: A Method for the Study of Small Groups*. Reading, Mass: Addison-Wesley.

Bales, R.F. and Borgatta, E.F. 1956: Size of groups as a factor in the interaction profile. In A.P. Hare, E.F. Borgatta and R.F. Bales (eds.), *Small Groups* (New York: Knopf).

Bales, R.F. and Slater, P. 1955: Role-differentiation in small decision-making groups. In T. Parsons (ed.), *Family, Socialization and Interaction Processes* (New York: Free Press).

Bales, R.F. and Strodtbeck, F.L. 1951: Phases in group problem solving. *Journal of Abnormal and Social Psychology* **46**, 485–95.

Bales, R.F., Strodtbeck, F.L., Mills, T.M. and Roseborough, M.E. 1951: Channels of communication in small groups. *American Sociological Review* **16**, 461–8.

Bandura, A. 1965: Influence of model's reinforcement contingencies on the acquisition of initiative responses. *Journal of Personality and Social Psychology* **1**, 589–95.

—— 1977: *Social Learning Theory*. Englewood Cliffs, NJ: Prentice Hall.

Bandura, A and McDonald, F.J. 1963: The influence of social reinforcement and the behaviour of models in shaping children's moral judgements. *Journal of Abnormal and Social Psychology* **67**, 274–81.

Bandura, A., Ross, D. and Ross, S.A. 1961: Transmission of aggression through imitation of aggressive models. *Journal of Abnormal and Social Psychology* **63**, 575–82.

—— 1963: Imitation of film-mediated aggressive models. *Journal of Abnormal and Social Psychology* **66**, 3–11.

Baron, R.A. and Byrne, D. 1977: *Social Psychology: Understanding Human Inter-action*, 3rd edn. Boston: Allyn & Bacon.

Bateson, G., Jackson, D., Haley, J. and Weakland, J. 1956: Towards a theory of schizophrenia. *Behavioural Science* **1**, 251–64.

Bavelas, A. 1950: Communication patterns in task-oriented groups. *Journal of the Acoustic Society of America* **22**, 725–30.

Beattie, G. 1983: *Talk: An Analysis of Speech and Non-Verbal Behaviour in Conversation*. Milton Keynes: Open University Press.

Beattie, G.W. and Bradbury, R.J. 1979: An experimental investigation of the modifi-ability of the temporal structure of spontaneous speech. *Journal of Psycho-linguistic Research* **8**, 225–48.

Bell, G. and French, R. 1950: Consistency of individual leadership position in small groups of varying membership. *Journal of Abnormal and Social Psychology* **45**, 764–5.

Bem, D.J. 1967: Self-perception: an alternative interpretation of cognitive dissonance phenomena. *Psychological Review* **74**, 183–200.

Bergin, A.E. 1962: The effects of dissonant persuasive communications upon changes in self-referring attitudes. *Journal of Personality* **30**, 423–38.

Berkowitz, L. 1969: The frustration – aggression hypothesis revisited. In L. Berkowitz (ed.), *Roots of Aggression: A Re-examination of the Frustration Aggression Hypothesis* (New York: Atherton Press).

Berscheid, E., Boye, D. and Darley, J.M. 1968: Effect of forced association upon voluntary choice to associate: *Journal of Personality and Social Psychology* 33, 709–18.

Berscheid, E., Dion, K., Walster, E. & Walster, G.W. 1971: Physical attractiveness and dating choice: A test of the matching hypothesis. *Journal of Experimental Social Psychology* 7, 173–89.

Berscheid, E., Stephan, W. and Walster, E. 1971: Sexual arousal and heterosexual perception. *Journal of Personality and Social Psychology* 20, 93–101.

Berscheid, E. and Walster, E.M. 1974: A little bit of love. In T.L. Huston (ed.), *Foundations of Interpersonal Attraction* (New York: Academic Press).

—— 1978: *Interpersonal Attraction*. Reading, Mass: Addison-Wesley, 2nd edn.

Bexton, W.H., Heron, W. and Scott, T.H. 1954: Effects of decreased variation in the sensory environment. *Canadian Journal of Psychology* 8, 70–6.

Bierbrauer, G. 1979: Why did he do it? Attribution of obedience and the phenomenon of dispositional bias. *European Journal of Social Psychology* 9, 67–84.

Boden, M. 1979: *Piaget*. London: Fontana.

Bower, T.G.R. 1977: *Development in infancy*. San Francisco: W.H. Freeman, 2nd edn.

Bowlby, J 1951: *Maternal Care and Mental Health*. Geneva: World Health Organization.

Brehm, J.W. 1956: Post-decision changes in the desirability of alternatives. *Journal of Abnormal and Social Psychology* 52, 384–9.

Brehm, J.W. and Cohen, A.R. 1962: *Explorations in Cognitive Dissonance*. New York: John Wiley & Sons.

Bronfenbrenner, U. 1970: *Two Worlds of Childhood: US and USSR*. New York: Pocket Books.

Bruner, J.S. and Goodman, C.C. 1947: Value and needs as organising factors in perception. *Journal of Abnormal and Social Psychology* 42, 33–44.

Bruner, J.S. and Tagiuri, R. 1954: Person perception. In G. Lindzey (ed.), *Handbook of Social Psychology* (Reading, Mass: Addison-Wesley). vol. 2.

Bryan, J.H. and Test, M.A. 1967: Models and helping: naturalistic studies in helping behaviour. *Journal of Personality and Social Psychology* 6, 400–7.

Bull, R. 1983: *Body Movement and Interpersonal Communication*. New York: John Wiley & Sons.

Byrne, D. 1961: The influence of propinquity and opportunities for interaction in classroom relationships. *Human Relations* 14, 63–9.

—— 1966: *An Introduction to Personality*. Englewood Cliffs, NJ: Prentice-Hall.

—— 1971: *The Attraction Paradigm*. New York: Academic Press.

Byrne, D. and Clore, G.L. 1970: A reinforcement model of evaluative responses. *Personality: An International Journal* 1, 103–8.

Byrne, D., Ervin, C.R. and Lamberth, J. 1970: Continuity between the experimental study of attraction and real-life computer dating. *Journal of Personality and Social Psychology* 16, 157–65.

Byrne D. and Nelson, D. 1965: Attraction as a linear function of proportion of positive reinforcement. *Journal of Personality and Social Psychology* 1, 659–63.

Byrne, D. and Wong, T.J. 1962: Racial prejudice, interpersonal attraction and assumed similarity of attitudes. *Journal of Abnormal and Social Psychology* 65, 246–53.

Campbell, A.A. 1971: *White Attitudes Towards Black People*. Ann Arbor, Mich: Institute for Social Research.

Campbell, D.T. 1967: Stereotypes and the perception of group differences. *American Psychologist* 22, 817–29.

Campbell, D.T. and Stanley, J.C. 1966: *Experimental and Quasi-experimental Designs for Research*. Chicago: Rand McNally.

250   *References*

Candee, D. 1976: Structure and choice in moral reasoning. *Journal of Personality and Social Psychology* **34**, 1293–301.

Cann, A., Sherman, S.J. and Elkes, R. 1978: Effects of initial request size and timing of a second request on compliance. *Journal of Personality and Social Psychology*.

Capra, F. 1975: *The Tao of Physics*. London: Fontana.

Cartwright, D. and Zander, A. 1968: *Group Dynamics: Research and Theory*. New York: Harper & Row.

Cattell, R.B. and Nesselrode, J.R. 1967: Likeness and completeness theories examined by 16 personality factor measures on stable and unstable married couples. *Journal of Personality and Social Psychology* **7**, 351–61.

Chalmers, A.F. 1978: *What is this Thing Called Science?* Milton Keynes: Open University Press.

Christie, R. and Cook, P. 1958: A guide to the published literature relating to the authoritarian personality. *Journal of Psychology* **45**, 171–99.

Cialdini, R.B. *et al.* 1975: Reciprocal concessions procedure for inducing compliance: The door-in-the-face technique. *Journal of Personality and Social Psychology* **31**, 206–15.

Clark, K. and Clark, M. 1947: Racial identification and preference in Negro children. In T.M. Newcomb and E.L. Hartley (eds.), *Readings in Social Psychology*. (New York: Holt).

Clarke, A.C. 1952: An examination of the operation of residual propinquity as a factor in mate selection. *American Sociological Review* **27**, 17–22.

Clarke, A.M. and Clarke. A.D.B. 1976: *Early Experience: Myth and Evidence*. London: Open Books.

Cline, V.B., Croft, R.G. and Corrier, S. 1972: The desensitization of children to television violence. *Proceedings of the American Psychological Association* **80**, 99–100.

Clore, G.L., Wiggins, N.H. and Itkin, S. 1975: Gain and loss in attraction: attributions from non-verbal behaviour. *Journal of Personality and Social Psychology* **31**, 706–12.

Collis, G.M. and Schaffer, H.R. 1975: Synchronisation of visual attention in mother–infant pairs. *Journal of Child Psychology and Psychiatry* **16**, 315–20.

Coombs, B. and Slovic, P. 1978: *Causes of death: Biased newspaper coverage and biased judgements*. Eugene, Oregon: Decision Research.

Coopersmith, S. 1967: *the Antecedents of Self-Esteem*. San Francisco: Freeman.

Cronbach, L.H. 1955: Processes affecting scores on 'understanding others' and 'assumed identity'. *Psychological Bulletin* **52**, 177–93.

Crutchfield, R.S. 1955: Conformity and character. *American Psychologist* **10**, 191–8.

Culbert, S.A. 1967: *Interpersonal processes of self-disclosure*. Washington, DC: NTL Institute for Applied Behavioural Science.

Curtiss, S. 1977: *Genie: A Psycholinguistic Study of a Modern Day 'Wild Child'*. New York: Academic Press.

Davitz, J.R. 1964: *The Communication of Emotional Meaning*. New York: McGraw-Hill.

DeFleur, M.A. and Westie, F.R. 1958: Verbal attitudes and overt acts: an experiment on the salience of attitudes. *American Sociological Review* **23**, 667–73.

Deutsch, M. and Collins, M.E. 1951: *Interracial Housing: A Psychological Evaluation of a Social Experiment*. Minneapolis: University of Minneapolis Press.

Deutsch, M. and Gerard, H.B. 1955: A study of the normative and informational social influence on individual judgement. *Journal of Abnormal and Social Psychology* **51**, 629–36.

Deutsch, M. and Solomon, L. 1959: Reaction to evaluation by others as influenced by self-evaluations. *Sociometry* **22**, 93–112.

Dollard, J., Doob, L.W. Miller, N.E., Mowrer, O.H. and Sears, R.R. 1939:

*Frustration and Aggression*. New Haven: Yale University Press.

Doms, M. and Avermaet, E. Van. 1981: The conformity effect: A timeless phenomenon?. *Bulletin of the British Psychological Society* **34**, 383–5.

Doster, J.A. and Strickland, B.R. 1969: Perceived child-rearing practices and self-disclosure patterns. *Journal of Counselling and Clinical Psychology* 33, 382.

Driscoll, R., Davis, K.E. and Lipitz, M.E. 1972: Parental interference and romantic love: the Romeo & Juliet effect. *Journal of Personality and Social Psychology* **24**, 1–10.

Duncan, B.L. 1976: Differential social perception and attribution of intergroup violence: testing the lower limit of stereotyping blacks. *Journal of Personality and Social Psychology* **34**, 590–8.

Duncan, S. 1972: Some signals and rules for taking speaker turns in conversations. *Journal of Personality and Social Psychology* **23**, 283–92.

Dutton, D.G. 1972: Effect of feedback parameters on congruency versus positivity effects in reactions to personal evaluations. *Journal of Personality and Social Psychology* **24**, 510–17.

Dutton, D.G. and Aron, A.P. 1974: Some evidence for heightened sexual attraction under condition of high anxiety. *Journal of Personality and Social Psychology* **30**, 510–17.

Duval, S. 1972: Conformity as a function of perceived level of uniqueness and being reminded of the object status of self. Unpublished doctoral dissertation, University of Texas at Austin.

Duval, S. and Wicklund, R.A. 1972: *A Theory of Objective Self-Awareness*. New York: Academic Press.

Eibl-Eibesfeldt, I. 1970: The expressive behaviour of the deaf and blind born. In M. von Cronach (ed.), *Non-verbal Behaviour and Expressive Movement* (London: Academic Press).

—— 1972: Similarities and differences between cultures in expressive movements. In R.A. Hinde (ed.), *Nonverbal Communication* (Cambridge: Cambridge University Press).

Ekman, P. 1972: Universal and cultural differences in facial expressions of emotion. In J. Cole (ed.), *Nebraska Symposium on Motivation* (Lincoln: University of Nebraska Press), vol. 19.

Ekman, P. and Friesen, W.V. 1971: Constants across cultures in the face and emotion. *Journal of Personality and Social Psychology* **29**, 288–98.

—— 1975: *Unmasking the face: A guide to recognising emotions from facial cues*. Englewood Cliffs, NJ: Prentice Hall.

Ekman, P. 1982: *Emotion in the Human Face*, 2nd edn. Cambridge: Cambridge University Press.

Ekman, P. Friesen, W.V. and Ellsworth, P. 1972: *Emotion in the Human Face*. Elmsford NY: Pergamon Press.

Ekman, P., Sorenson, E.R. and Friesen, W.V. 1969: Pan cultural elements in the facial displays of emotion. *Science* **164**, 86–8.

Ehrlich, D., Guttman, I., Schonback, P. and Mills, J. 1957: Post-decision exposure to relevant information. *Journal of Abnormal and Social Psychology* **54**, 98–102.

Ellis, G.T. and Sekgra, F. 1972: The effect of aggressive cartoons on the behaviour of first-grade children. *Journal of Psychology* **81**, 37–43.

Ellsworth, P. and Carlsmith, J.M. 1973: Eye-contact and gaze aversion in an aggressive encounter. *Journal of Personality and Social Psychology* **29**, 280–92.

Elms, A.C. and Milgram, S. 1966: Personality characteristics associated with obedience and defiance toward authoritative command. *Journal of Experimental Research in Personality* **1**, 282–9.

Emler, N., Renwick, S. and Malone, B. 1983: The relationship between moral reasoning and political orientation. *Journal of Personality and Social Psychology* **45**, 1073–80.

Endler, N.S. 1966: Conformity as a function of different reinforcement schedules. *Journal of Personality and Social Psychology* **4**, 175–80.

Endler, N.S. and Magnusson, D. 1976: *Interaction, Psychology and Personality*. Washington, DC: Hemisphere.

Erikson, E. 1950: *Childhood and Society*. London: Triad/Paladin.

—— 1968: *Identity: Youth and Crisis*. London: Faber.

Exline, R.V. 1972: Visual interaction: the glances of power and preference. In J.K. Cole (ed.), *Nebraska Symposium on Motivation* (Lincoln: University of Nebraska Press), vol. 9.

Eysenck, H.J. 1954: *The Psychology of Politics*. London: Routledge & Kegan Paul.

Eysenck, H.J. and Kamin, L. 1981: *Intelligence: The Battle for the Mind*. London: Pan.

Feather, N.T. 1969: Attribution of responsibility and valence of success and failure in relation to initial confidence and task performance. *Journal of Personality and Social Psychology* **13**, 129–44.

Felipe, N.J. and Sommer, R. 1966: Invasions of personal space. *Social Problems* **14**, 206–14.

Fenigstein, A., Scheier, M.F. and Buss, A.H. 1975: Public and private self-consciousness: assessment and theory. *Journal of Consulting and Clinical Psychology* **43**, 522–7.

Ferguson, N. 1977: Simultaneous speech, interruptions and dominance. *British Journal of Social and Clinical Psychology* **16**, 295–302.

Festinger, L. 1954: A theory of social comparison processes. *Human Relations* **7**, 117–40.

—— 1957: *A Theory of Cognitive Dissonance*. Stanford, Cal.: Stanford University Press.

Festinger, L. and Carlsmith, J.M. 1959: Cognitive consequences of forced compliance. *Journal of Abnormal and Social Psychology* **58**, 203–10.

Festinger, L., Riecken, H.W. and Schachter, S. 1956: *When Prophecy Fails*. Minneapolis: University of Minnesota.

Festinger, L., Schachter, S. and Back, K. 1950: *Social Pressures in Informal Groups: A Study of Human Factors in Housing*. Stanford, Cal.: Stanford University Press.

Fiedler, F.E. 1964: A contingency model of leadership effectiveness. In L. Berkowitz (ed.), *Advances in Experimental Social Psychology*. (New York: Academic Press), vol. 1.

—— 1971: Validation and extension of the contingency model of leadership effectiveness: a review of empirical findings. *Psychological Bulletin* **76**, 128–48.

—— 1973: The trouble with leadership training is that it doesn't train leaders. *Psychology Today* **92**, 23–9.

Fishbein, M. and Ajzen, I. 1975: *Belief, Attitude, Intention and Behaviour*. Reading, Mass: Addison-Wesley.

Fishkin, J. Keniston, K. and Mackinnon, C. 1973: Moral reasoning and political ideology. *Journal of Personality and Social Psychology* **27**, 109–19.

Fiske, S.T. and Cox, M.G. 1979: The effects of target familiarity and descriptive purpose on the process of describing others. *Journal of Personality and Social Psychology* **47**, 136–61.

Fitts, W.H. 1964: *Tennessee Self Concept Scale*. (Nashville: Counselor Recodings and Tests.

Fraser, C. 1978: Small groups I & II. In H. Tajfel and C. Fraser (eds), *Introducing Social Psychology* (Harmondsworth: Penguin).

—— 1984: Social groups, nonsense groups and group polarization. In H. Tajfel (ed.), *The Social Dimension* (Cambridge: Cambridge University Press), vol. 2.

Fraser, C., Gouge, C. and Billig, M. 1971: Risky shifts, cautious shifts and group polarisation. *European Journal of Social Psychology* 1, 7–29.

Freedman, J.L. and Fraser, S.C. 1966: Compliance without pressure: The foot-in-the-door technique. *Journal of Personality and Social Psychology* 7, 117–24.

Freud, A. and Dann, S. 1951: An experiment in group upbringing. *Psychoanalytical Studies of the Child* 6, 127–68.

Freud, S. 1914: *The Psychopathology of Everyday Life*. London: Unwin.

Frisch, K. von, 1954: *The Dancing Bees*. London: Methuen.

Furnham, A. 1979: Assertiveness in three cultures: Multidimensionality and cultural differences. *Journal of Clinical Psychology* 35, 522–7.

Gale, A. and Chapman, J. 1984: *Psychology and Social Problems*. New York: John Wiley & Sons.

Garfinkel, H. 1964: Studies of the routine grounds of everyday activities. *Social Problems* ii, 225–50.

Garland, H.A., Hardy, A. and Stephenson, L. 1975: Information search as affected by attribution type and response category. *Personality and Social Psychology Bulletin* 1, 612–15.

Gellner, E. 1985: *The Psychoanalytic Movement: The Cunning of Unreason*. London: Paladin.

Gergen, K.H. 1965: The effects of interaction goals and personalistic feedback on the presentation of self. *Journal of Personality and Social Psychology* 1, 413–24.

Gibb, J.R. 1951: The effects of group size and of threat reduction upon creativity in a problem-solving situation. *American Psychologist* 6, 324.

Gilchrist, J.C., Shaw, M.E. and Walker, L.C. 1954: Some effects of unequal distribution of information in a wheel structure group. *Journal of Abnormal and Social Psychology* 49, 554–6.

Goffman, E. 1959: *The Presentation of Self in Everyday Life*. Harmondsworth: Penguin.

—— 1963: *Behaviour in Public Places*. Glencoe, Ill: Free Press.

Goldman-Eisler, F. 1968: Pauses, clauses and sentences. *Language and Speech* 15, 103–13.

Gould, S.J. 1985: *The Mismeasure of Man*. Harmondsworth: Penguin.

Gruder, C.L. 1971: Determinant of social comparison choices. *Journal of Experimental Social Psychology* 7, 473–89.

Guetzkow, H. and Simon, H.A. 1955: The impact of certain communication nets upon organization and performance in task-oriented groups. *Management Science* 1, 233–50.

Guiton, P. 1959: Socialisation and imprinting in brown leghorn chicks. *Animal Behaviour* 7, 26–34.

Habra, J. and Grant, G. 1970: Black is beautiful: A re-examination of racial preference and identification. *Journal of Personality and Social Psychology* 16, 398–402.

Hall, E.T. 1968: Proxemics. *Current Anthropology* 9, 83–108.

Hall, I. and Watson, W.H. 1970: Individual and group decision-making. *Human Relations* 23, 299–317.

Hamblin, R.L. 1958: Leadership and crisis. *Sociometry* 21, 322–35.

Hamilton, D.L. 1981: *Cognitive Processes in Stereotyping and Intergroup Behaviour*. Hillsdale, NJ: Erlbaum.

Haney, C., Banks, W.C. and Zimbardo, P.G. 1973: Interpersonal dynamics in a simulated prison. *International Journal of Criminology and Penology* 1, 69–79.

Hare, A.P. 1962: *Handbook of Small Group Research*. Glencoe, New York: Free Press.

Harlow, H.F. and Harlow, M.K. 1959: Love in infant monkeys. *Scientific American*, June, 100–107.

Harvey, O.J. and Consalvi, C. 1960: Status and conformity to pressure in informal groups. *Journal of Abnormal and Social Psychology* **60**, 182–7.

Harvey, J.H., Town, J.P. and Yarkin, K.L. 1981: How fundamental is 'The Fundamental Attribution Error'? *Journal of Personality and Social Psychology* **40**, 346–9.

Harvey, J.H., Yarkin, K.L., Lightner, J.M. and Town, J.P. 1980: Unsolicited interpretation and recall of personal events. *Journal of Personality and Social Psychology* **38**, 551–68.

Hastorf, A.H. and Cantril, H. 1954: They saw a game: a case study. *Journal of Abnormal and Social Psychology* **49**, 129–34.

Heider, F., 1944: Social perception and phenomenal causality. *Psychological Review* **51**, 358–74.

—— 1958: *The Psychology of Interpersonal Relations*. New York: John Wiley & Sons.

Hemphill, J.K. 1950: Relations between the size of a group and the behaviour of 'superior leaders'. *Journal of Social Psychology* **32**, 11–22.

Hess, E.H. 1959: Imprinting. *Science* **130**, 133–41.

—— 1965: Attitude and pupil size. *Scientific American* **212**, 46–54.

Hetherington, E.M., Cox, M. and Cox, R. 1979: Play and social interaction in children following divorce. *Journal of Social Issues* **35**, 26–49.

Hewstone, M. and Jaspers, J. 1984 Social dimensions of attribution. In H. Tajfel (ed.), *The Social Dimension* (Cambridge: Cambridge University Press), vol. 2.

—— 1982: Explanations for racial discrimination: the effect of group discussion on intergroup attribution. *European Journal of Social Psychology* **12**, 1–16.

Hinde, R.A. 1970: *Animal Behaviour*. New York: McGraw-Hill, 2nd edn.

Hockett, C.F. 1960: The origin of speech. *Scientific American* **203**, 89–96.

Hoffeditz, E.L. 1934: Family resemblances in personality traits. *Journal of Social Psychology* **5**, 214–27.

Hoffman, R.L. 1966: Group problem solving. In L. Berkowitz (ed.), *Advances in Experimental Social Psychology* (New York: Academic Press), vol. 2.

Hollander, E.P. 1964: *Leaders, Groups and Influence*. New York: Oxford University Press.

Homans, G.C. 1961: *Social Behaviour: Its Elementary Forms*. New York: Harcourt, Brace & World.

Hooff, J. van 1967: The facial displays of the catarrhine monkeys and apes. In D. Morris (ed.), *Primate Ethology* (London: Weidenfeld & Nicolson).

Hosking, D.M. and Morley, I.E. 1985: The skills of leadership. Paper presented at the Eighth Biennial Leadership Symposium, Texas Tech. University, Lubbock, Texas, USA, July 1985.

Hovland, C.I., Janis, I.L. and Kelley, H.H. 1953: *Communication and Persuasion*. New Haven, Conn: Yale University Press.

Hyman, H.H. and Sheatsley, P.B. 1954: The authoritarian personality – a methodological critique. In R. Christie and M. Jakoda (eds.), *Studies in the Scope of the Authoritarian Personality* (New York: Free Press).

Izard, C.E. 1972: *The Face of Emotion*. New York: Appleton-Century-Crofts.

Janis, I. 1972: *Victims of Groupthink*. Boston: Houghton-Mifflin, 2nd edn.

Janis, I.L. and Hovland, C.I. 1959: An overview of persuasibility research. In C.I. Hovland and I.L. Janis (eds.), *Personality and Persuasibility* (New Haven: Yale University Press).

Janis, I.L. and Mann, L. 1977: *Decision Making: A Psychological Analysis of Conflict, Choice and Commitment*. New York: Free Press.

Johnson, T.J., Feigenbaum, R. and Weibey, M. 1964: Some determinants and consequences of the teacher's perception of causality. *Journal of Educational Psychology* **55**, 237–46.

Jones, E.E. 1965: Conformity as a tactic of ingratiation. *Science* **149**, 144–50.

Jones, E.E. and Davis, K.E. 1965: From acts to dispositions: the attribution process in person perception. In L. Berkowitz (ed.), *Advances in Experimental Social Psychology*. (New York: Academic Press), vol. 2.

Jones, J.M. 1972: *Prejudice and Racism*. Reading Mass: Addison-Wesley.

Jourard, S. 1971: *Self-disclosure: An Experimental Analysis of the Transparent Self*. New York: John Wiley & Sons.

Jung, J. 1971: *The Experimenter's Dilemma*. New York: Harper & Row.

Kagan, J. 1976: Emergent themes in child development. *American Scientist* **64**, 186-96.

Kahn, R. and Katz, D. 1953: leadership practices in relation to productivity and morale. In D. Cartwright and A. Zander (eds.), *Group Dynamics: Research and Theory* (Evanston, Ill: Row, Peterson).

Kahneman, D. and Tversky, A. 1982: The simulation heuristic. In D. Kahneman, P. Slovic and A. Tversky (eds.), *Judgement Under Uncertainty: Heuristics and Biases* (Cambridge: Cambridge University Press).

Karlins, M., Coffman, T.L. and Walters, G. 1969: On the fading of social stereotypes: studies in three generations of college students. *Journal of Personality and Social Psychology* **13**, 1-16.

Katz, D. 1960: The functional approach to the measurement of attitudes. *Public Opinion Quarterly* **24**, 163-204.

Kauffman, I.C. and Rosenblum, L.A. 1969: Effects of separation from mother on the emotional behaviour of infant monkeys. *Annual of the New York Academy of Science* **159**, 681-95.

Kelley, H.H. 1950: The warm-cold variable in first impressions of persons. *Journal of Personality and Social Psychology* **18**, 431-9.

—— 1951: Communication in experimentally created hierarchies. *Human Relations* **4**, 39-56.

—— 1967: Attribution theory in social psychology. In *Nebraska Symposium on Motivation* (Lincoln: University of Nebraska Press).

—— 1972: Causal schemata and the attribution process. In E.E. Jones *et al.* (eds.), *Attribution: Perceiving the Causes of Behaviour* (Morristown, NJ: General Learning Press).

Kelley, H.H. and Thibaut, J.W. 1969: Group problem solving. In G. Lindzey and E. Aronson (eds.), *Handbook of Social Psychology*, vol. 4. (Reading, Mass: Addison-Wesley.)

Kelman, H.C. 1958: Compliance, identification and internalization: three processes of attitude change. *Journal of Conflict Resolution* **2**, 51-60.

—— 1967: Human use of human subjects: The problem of deception in social psychological experiments. *Psychological Bulletin* **67**, 1-11.

Kendon, A. 1967: Some functions of gaze direction in social interaction. *Acta Psychologica* **26**, 1-47.

Kennedy, G. 1983: *Invitation to Statistics*. Oxford: Martin Robinson.

Kerr, W.A. Koppelmeier, G. and Sullivan, J.J. 1951: Absenteeism, turnover and morale in a metals fabrication factory. *Occupational Psychology* **25**, 50-5.

Kiesler, S.B. and Baral, R.L. 1970: The search for a romantic partner: the effects of self-esteem and physical attractiveness on romantic behaviour. In K. Gergen and D. Marlow (eds.), *Personality and Social Behaviour* (Reading, Mass: Addison Wesley).

Kiseler, C.A. and Keisler, S.B. 1969: *Conformity*. Reading, Mass: Addison Wesley.

Killian, M.N. 1952: The significance of multiple-group membership in disaster. *American Journal of Sociology* **57**, 309-13.

Kilman, W. and Mann, L. 1974: Level of destructive obedience as a function of transmitter and executant roles in the Milgram obedience paradigm. *Journal of Personality and Social Psychology* **29**, 696-702.

Kogan, N. and Wallach, M.A. 1967: the risky-shift phenomenon in small decision-making groups: a test of the information exchange hypothesis. *Journal of Experimental Social Psychology* 3, 75–85.

Kohlberg, L. 1976: Moral stages and moralisation: a cognitive-developmental approach. In T. Lickona (ed.), *Moral Development and Behaviour* (New York: Holt, Rinehart & Winston).

Kohlberg, L. and Kramer, R.B. 1969: Continuities and discontinuities in childhood and adult moral development. *Human Development* 12, 93–120.

La Piere, R.T. 1934: Attitudes versus actions. *Social Forces* 13, 230–7.

Leavitt, H.J. 1951: Some effects of certain patterns on group performance. *Journal of Abnormal and Social Psychology* 46, 38–50.

Leeper, R. 1935: A study of a neglected portion of the field of learning – the development of sensory organisation. *Journal of Genetic Psychology* 46, 41–75.

Lefkowitz, M.M., Eron, L.D., Walder, L.O. and Heusmann, L.R. 1972: Television violence and child aggression: a follow-up study. In G.A. Cornstock and E.A. Rubinstein (eds.), *Television and Society* (Washington: US Government Printing Office).

Leon, M. 1977: Pheremonal mediation of maternal behaviour. In T. Alloway, P. Pliner and L. Krames (eds.), *Attachment Behaviour* (New York: Plenum), vol. 3.

Leventhal, H. 1970: Findings and theory in the study of fear communications. In L. Berkowitz (ed.), *Advances in Experimental Social Psychology* (New York: Academic Press), vol. 5.

Levine, M.H. and Sutton-Smith, B. 1973: Effects of age, sex, and task on visual behaviour. *Developmental Psychology* 9, 400–5.

Levinger, G. 1974: A three-level view on attraction: toward an understanding of pair relatedness. In T.L. Huston (ed.), *Foundations of Interpersonal Attraction* (New York: Academic Press).

Lewin, K., Lippett, R. and White, P.K. 1939: Patterns of aggressive behaviour in experimentally created 'social climates'. *Journal of Social Psychology* 10, 271–99.

Lieberman, S. 1956: The effects of changes in roles on the attitudes of role occupants. *Human Relations* 9, 385–402.

Likert, R. 1932: A technique for the measurement of attitudes. *Archives of Psychology* 22, 140.

Locke, D. and Pennington, D.C. 1982: Reasons and other causes: their role in attribution processes. *Journal of Personality and Social Psychology* 42, 212–23.

Lorenz, K. 1957: *On Aggression*. New York: Bantam.

Luchins, A.S. 1957: Primacy–recency in impression formation. In C. Hovland (ed.), *The Order of Presentation in Persuasion* (New Haven, Conn: Yale University Press).

McArthur, L.Z. 1972: The how and why of what: some determinants and consequences of causal attribution. *Journal of Personality and Social Psychology* 22, 171–93.

McDougall, W. 1908: *Introduction to Social Psychology*. London: Methuen.

McGinnies, E. 1949: Emotionality and perceptual defense. *Psychological Review* 56, 244–51.

McGrath, J.E. 1964: *Social Psychology: A Brief Introduction*. (New York: Holt, Rinehart & Winston).

McGuire, W.J. 1969: The nature of attitudes and attitude change. In G. Lindzey and E. Aronson (eds.), *Handbook of Social Psychology* (Reading, Mass: Addison-Wesley), vol. 3.

Maccoby, E. 1980: *Social Development: Psychological Growth and Parent–Child Relationship*. New York: Harcourt Brace Jovanovich.

Maier, N.R.F. 1955: *Psychology in Industry*. New York: McGraw Hill.

Maier, N.R.F. and Solem. A.R. 1952: the contribution of a discussion leader to the quality of group thinking: the effective use of minority opinion. *Human*

*Relations* 5, 277–88.

Mann, R.D. 1959: A review of the relationships between personality and performance in small groups. *Psychological Bulletin* 56, 241–70.

Marler, P. 1970: A comparative approach to verbal learning: song development in white-crowned sparrows. *Journal of Comparative Physiological Psychology* 71, 1–25.

Maslow, A.M. 1954: *Motivation and Personality*. New York: Harper & Row.

Middlemast, R.D. Knowles, E.S. and Matter, C.F. 1976: Personal space invasions in the lavatory: suggestive evidence for arousal. *Journal of Personality and Social Psychology* 33, 541–6.

Milgram, S. 1963: Behavioural study of obedience. *Journal of Abnormal and Social Psychology* 67, 371–8.

—— 1965: Some conditions of obedience and obedience to authority. *Human Relations* 18, 57–76.

—— 1974: *Obedience to Authority*. Tavistock: London.

Miller, N.E. and Bugelski, R. 1948: Minor studies in aggression: the influence of frustration imposed by the ingroup in attitudes expressed towards the outgroups. *Journal of Psychology* 25, 437–42.

Milmoe, S., Rosenthal, R., Blane, H., Chafetz, M. and Wolf, I. 1967: The doctor's voice: postdictor of successful referral of alcoholic patients. *Journal of Abnormal Psychology* 72, 78–84.

Minard, R.D. 1952: Race relations in the Pocahontas coalfield. *Journal of Social Issues* 8, 29–44.

Mischel, W. 1968: *Personality and Assessment*. New York: John Wiley & Sons.

Mischel, W. and Mischel, H.N. 1976: A cognitive social learning approach to morality and self-regulation. In T. Lickona (ed.), *Moral Development and Moral Behaviour* (New York: Holt, Rinehart & Winston).

Mixon, D. 1972: Instead of deception. *Journal for the Theory of Social Behaviour* 2, 145–78.

Moeller, G.H. and Applezweig, M.H. 1957: A motivational factor in conformity. *Journal of Abnormal and Social Psychology* 55, 116–20.

Morley, I. and Hosking, D. 1984: Decision making and negotiation: leadership and social skills. In M. Gruneberg and T. Wall (eds.), *Social Psychology and Organizational Behaviour* (New York: John Wiley & Sons).

Morley, I.E. and Stephenson, G.M. 1969: Interpersonal and interparty exchange: a laboratory simulation of an industrial negotiation at plant level. *British Journal of Psychology* 60, 543–5.

Morley, I.E. and Stephenson, G.M. 1970: Formality in experimental negotiations: a validation study. *British Journal of Psychology* 61, 383–4.

Morris, W.N. and Miller, R.S. 1975: The effects of consensus-breaking and consensus-preempting partners on reduction of conformity. *Journal of Experimental Social Psychology* 11, 215–23.

Morse, S.J. and Gergen, K.H. 1970: Social comparison, self-consistency and the concept of self. *Journal of Personality and Social Psychology* 16, 148–56.

Morton, T. 1978: Intimacy and reciprocity of exchange: a comparison of spouses and strangers. *Journal of Personality and Social Psychology* 36, 72–81.

Moscovici, S. 1976: *Social Influence and Social Change*, European Monographs in Social Psychology, vol. 10. London: Academic Press.

Moscovici, S. and Faucheux, C. 1972: Social influence, conformity bias and the study of active minorities. In L. Berkowitz (ed.), *Advances in Experimental Social Psychology* (New York: Academic Press), vol. 6.

Moscovici, S., Lage, E. and Naffrechoux, M. 1969: Influence of a consistent minority on the response of a majority in a colour perception task. *Sociometry* 32, 365–79.

Moscovici, S. and Nemeth, C. 1974: Social influence II: minority influence. In

C. Nemeth (ed.), *Social Psychology: Classic and Contemporary Integrations* (Chicago: Rand McNally).

Moscovici, S. and Zavalloni, M. 1969: The group as a polarizer of attitudes. *Journal of Personality and Social Psychology* **12**, 125–35.

Mugny, G. 1984: The influence of minorities. In H. Tajfel (ed.), *The Social Dimension* (Cambridge: Cambridge University Press), vol. 2.

Myers, D.G. and Lamm, H. 1976: The group polarization phenomenon. *Psychological Bulletin* **83**, 602–27.

Natale, M., Entin, E. and Jaffe, J. 1979: Vocal interruptions in dyadic communication as a function of speech and social anxiety. *Journal of Personality and Social Psychology* **37**, 865–78.

Nemeth, C. and Wachtler, J. 1973: Consistency and modification of judgement. *Journal of Experimental Social Psychology* **9**, 65–79.

Newcomb, T.M. 1943: *Personality and Social Change: Attitude Formation in a Student Community*. New York: Dryden.

—— 1950: *Social Psychology*. New York: Dryden.

—— 1961: *The Acquaintance Process*. New York: Holt, Rinehart & Winston.

—— 1971: Dyadic balance as a source of clues about interpersonal attraction. In B.I. Murstein (ed.), *Theories of Attraction and Love* (New York: Springer).

Nisbett, R.E., Caputo, C., Legant, P. and Marecek, J. 1973: Behaviour as seen by the actor and as seen by the observer. *Journal of Personality and Social Psychology* **27**, 154–64.

Nisbett, R.E. and Schachter, S. 1966: Cognitive manipulations of pain. *Journal of Experimental Social Psychology* **2**, 227–36.

Novak, D.W. and Lerner, M.J. 1968: Rejection as a function of perceived similarity. *Journal of Personality and Social Psychology* **9**, 147–52.

Oppenheim, A.N. 1966: *Questionnaire Design and Attitude Measurement*. London: Heinemann.

Orlofsky, J.C., Marcia, J.E. and Lesser, I.M. 1973: Ego identity status and the intimacy versus isolation crisis of young adulthood. *Journal of Personality and Social Psychology* **2**, 211–19.

Orne, M.T. 1962: On the social psychology of the psychology experiment: with particular reference to demand characteristics and their implications. *American Psychologist* **17**, 776–83.

Osborn, A.F. 1957: *Applied Imagination*. New York: Scribners.

Osgood, C.E., Suci, G.J. and Tannenbaum, P.H. 1957: *The Measurement of Meaning*. Urbana: University of Illinois Press.

Osgood, C.E. and Tannenbaum, P.H. 1955: The principle of congruity in the prediction of attitude change. *Psychological Review* **62**, 42–55.

Patterson, M.L. 1977: Interpersonal distance, affect and equilibrium theory. *Journal of Social Psychology* **101**, 205–14.

Parkinson, B. and Manstead, A.S.R. 1981: An examination of the roles played by meaning of feedback and attention to feedback in the Valin's effect. *Journal of Personality and Social Psychology* **38**, 725–43.

Pennington, D.C. 1981: The Yorkshire Ripper police enquiry: hindsight and social cognition. *British Journal of Social Psychology* **20**, 225–7.

—— 1982: Witnesses and their testimony: effects of ordering on juror verdicts. *Journal of Applied Social Psychology* **12**, 318–33.

Pennington, D.C. and Rutter, D.R. 1981: Information or affiliation: effects on visual interaction. *Semiotica* **35**, 29–39.

Pepitone, A. 1949: Motivational effects in social perception. *Human Relations* **3**, 57–76.

Perlmutter, J.V. and Montmollin, G. 1952: Group learning of nonsense syllables. *Journal of Abnormal and Social Psychology* **47**, 762–9.

Perrin, S. and Spencer, C. 1980: The Asch-effect: a child of its times? *Bulletin of the British Psychological Society* 32, 405–6.

Pessin, J. 1933: The comparative effects of social and mechanical stimulation on memorising. *American Journal of Psychology* 45, 263–70.

Pettigrew, T. 1958: Personality and sociocultural factors in intergroup attitudes: a cross-national comparison. *Journal of Conflict Resolution* 2, 29–42.

—— 1959: Regional differences in anti-negro prejudice. *Journal of Abnormal and Social Psychology* 59, 28–56.

Phares, E.J. and Wilson, D.G. 1972: Responsibility attribution: role of outcome severity, situational ambiguity and internal–external control. *Journal of Personality and Social Psychology* 40, 392–406.

Phares, E.J. Wilson, K.G. and Klyver, N.W. 1971: Internal–external control and attribution of blame under neutral and distracting conditions. *Journal of Personality and Social Psychology* 18, 285–8.

Proust, M. 1983: *Remembrance of Things Past*, vol. 1. Harmondsworth: Penguin.

Reader, N. and English, H.B. 1947: Personality factors in adolescent female friend-ships. *Journal of Consulting Psychology* 11, 212–20.

Regan, D.T. 1971: The effects of a favour and liking on compliance. *Journal of Experimental Social Psychology* 7, 627–39.

Regan, D.T. and Totten, J. 1975: Empathy and attribution: turning observers into actors. *Journal of Personality and Social Psychology* 32, 850–6.

Rim, Y. 1977: Personality variables and interruptions in small group discussions. *European Journal of Social Psychology* 7, 247–51.

Rivenbark, W.H. 1971: Self-disclosure patterns among adolescents. *Psychological Reports* 38, 35–42.

Robertson, J. and Robertson, J. 1971: Young children in brief separation: a fresh look. *Psychoanalytic Study of the Child* 26, 264–315.

Rokeach, M. 1960: *The Open and Closed Mind*. New York: Basic books.

—— 1968: *Beliefs, Attitudes and Values*. San Francisco: Jossey-Bass.

Rokeach, M., Smith, P.W. and Evans, R.I. 1960: Two kinds of prejudice or one? In M. Rokeach (ed.), *The Open and Closed Mind* (New York: Basic Books).

Rose, E.J. 1969: *Colour And Citizenship: A report on British Race Relations*. Oxford: Oxford University Press.

Rosenberg, L.A. 1963: Conformity as a function of confidence in self and confidence in partner. *Human Relations* 16, 131–41.

Rosenberg, M.J. and Abelson, R.P. 1960: An analysis of cognitive balancing. In M.J. Rosenberg, C.I. Hovland, W.J. McGuire, R.P. Abelson and J.W. Brehm (eds.), *Attitude Organisation and Change* (New Haven, Conn: Yale University Press).

Rosenberg, M.J. Nelson, C. and Vivekanathan, P.S. 1968: A multidimensional approach to the structure of personality impression. *Journal of Personality and Social Psychology* 9, 283–94.

Rosenberg, S. and Sedlak, A. 1972: Structural representation of implicit personality theory. In L. Berkowitz (ed.), *Advances in Experimental Social Psychology* (New York: Academic Press), vol. 6.

Rosenthal, R. 1969: Interpersonal expectations: effects of experimenter's hypothesis. In R. Rosenthal and R.L. Rosnow (eds.), *Artifacts in Behavioural Research* (New York: Academic Press).

Rosenthal, R. and Fode, K.L. 1963: The effect of experimenter bias on the perfor-mance of the albino rat. *Behavioural Science* 8, 183–9.

Rosenthal, R. and Jacobson, L. 1968: *Pygmalion in the Classroom: Teacher Expecta-tions and Pupil Intellectual Development*. New York: Holt, Rinehart & Winston.

Ross, L. 1977: The intuitive psychologist and his shortcomings. In L. Berkowitz (ed.), *Advances in Experimental Social Psychology* (New York: Academic Press), vol. 10.

Ross, L.D., Amabile, T.M. and Steinmetz, J.L. 1977: Social roles, social control and biases in social-perception processes. *Journal of Personality and Social Psychology* **35**, 485–94.

Ross, L., Bierbrauer, G. and Polly, S. 1974: Attribution of educational outcomes by professional and nonprofessional instructors. *Journal of Experimental Social Psychology* **29**, 609–18.

Ross, L.D., Greene, D. and House, P. 1977: The 'false consensus' effect: an egocentric bias in social perception and attribution processes. *Journal of Experimental Social Psychology* **13**, 279–301.

Ross, L., Lepper, M.R. and Hubbard, M. 1975: Perseverence in self-perception and social perception: biased attribution processes in the debriefing paradigm. *Journal of Personality and Social Psychology* **32**, 880–92.

Rotter, J.B. 1966: Generalised expectancies for internal versus external control of reinforcements. *Psychological Monographs* **80**, (whole no. 609).

Rubin, Z. 1970: Measurement of romantic love. *Journal of Personality and Social Psychology* **16**, 265–73.

Rubin, Z. and Shenker, S. 1978: Friendship, proximity and self-disclosure. *Journal of Personality and Social Psychology* **46**, 1–23.

Ruse, M. 1979: *Sociobiology: Sense or Nonsense?* Dordrecht: Reidel Publishers.

Rutter, D. R. 1984: *Looking and Seeing: The Role of Visual Communication in Social Interaction*. New York: John Wiley & Sons.

Rutter, D.R. and Durkin, K. 1982: The development of turn-taking in mother–infant interaction. *International Journal of Psycholinguistics* **19**, 111.

Rutter, D.R., Morley, I.E. and Graham, J.C. 1972: Visual interaction in a group of introverts and extroverts. *European Journal of Social Psychology* **2**, 371–84.

Rutter, D.R. and Robinson, B. 1981: An experimental analysis of teaching by telephone: theoretical and practical implications for social psychology. *Progress in Applied Social Psychology*, (Chichester: John Wiley & Sons), vol. 1.

Rutter, D.R. and Stephenson, G. 1979: The functions of looking: effects of friendship on gaze. *British Journal of Social and Clinical Psychology* **18**, 203–5.

Rutter, D.R., Stephenson, G. Ayling, K. and White, P.A. 1978: The timing of looks in dyadic conversation. *British Journal of Social and Clinical Psychology* **17**, 17–21.

Rutter, D.R., Stephenson, G.M., Lazzerini, A.J., Ayling, K. and White, P.A. 1977: Eye-contact: a chance product of individual looking? *British Journal of Social and Clinical Psychology* **16**, 191–92.

Rutter, M., 1971: Parent–child separation: psychological effects on children. *Journal of Child Psychology and Psychiatry* **12**, 233–60.

—— 1981: *Maternal Deprivation Reassessed*. Harmondsworth: Penguin, 2nd edn.

Saegert, S., Swap, W. and Zajonc, R.B. 1973: Exposure, context, and interpersonal attraction. *Journal of Personality and Social Psychology* **25**, 234–42.

Sanford, N. 1956: The approach of the authoritarian personality. In J.L. McCary (ed.), *Psychology of Personality* (New York: Grove Press).

Sarnoff, I. and Zimbardo, P.G. 1961: Anxiety, fear and social affiliation. *Journal of Abnormal and Social Psychology* **62**, 356–63.

Scarman, Lord 1982: *The Scarman Report: the Brixton Disorders 10–12th April, 1981*. Harmondsworth: Penguin.

Schachter, S. 1951: Deviation, rejection and communication. *Journal of Abnormal Social Psychology* **46**, 190–207.

—— 1959: *The Psychology of Affiliation*. Stanford, Cal.: Stanford University Press.

—— 1964: The interaction of cognitive and physiological determinants of emotional state. In L. Berkowitz (ed.), *Advances in Experimental Social Psychology* (New York: Academic Press), vol. 1.

Schachter, S. and Singer, J.E. 1962: Cognitive, social and physiological determinants of emotional state. *Psychological Review* **69**, 379–99.

Schaffer, H.R. 1971: *The Growth of Sociability*. Harmondsworth: Penguin.

Schaffer, H.R. and Emerson, P.E. 1964: The development of social attachments in infancy. *Monographs of Social Research in Child Development*, vol. 29, 4.

Scheier, M.F. 1980: The effects of public and private self-consciousness on the public expression of personal beliefs. *Journal of Personality and Social Psychology* **39**, 514–21.

Schlenker, B.R. 1980: *Impression Management: The Self-Concept, Social Identity and Interpersonal Relations*. Monterey, Cal.: Brooks/Cole.

Schutz, W.C. 1958: The interpersonal underworld. *Harvard Business Review* **36**, 123–35.

Secord, P.F. and Backman, C.W. 1974: *Social Psychology*. Tokyo: McGraw-Hill, 2nd edn.

Segal, M.W. 1974: Alphabet and attraction: a unobtrusive measure of the effect of propinquity in a field setting. *Journal of Personality and Social Psychology* **30**, 654–7.

Segall, M.H., Campbell, D.T. and Herskovits, M.J. 1966: *The Influence of Culture on Visual Perception*. Indianapolis: Bobbs Merrill.

Seligman, M.E.P. 1975: *Helplessness*. San Francisco: Freeman.

Seligman, M.E.P., Abramson, L.Y. Semmel, A. and Von Baeyer, C. 1979: Depressive attributional style. *Journal of Abnormal Psychology* **88**, 242–7.

Shaw M.E. 1932: Comparison of individuals and small groups in the rational solution of complex problems. *American Journal of Psychology* **44**, 491–504.

—— 1964: Communication networks. In L. Berkowitz (ed.), *Advances in Experimental Social Psychology* (New York: Academic Press).

—— 1971: *Group Dynamics: The Psychology of Small Group Behaviour*. New York: McGraw-Hill.

Sherif, M. 1936: *The Psychology of Social Norms*. New York: Harper & Row.

—— 1966: *Group Conflict and Cooperation: Their Social Psychology*. London: Routledge & Kegan Paul.

Sigall, M and Aronson, S. 1969: Liking for an evaluator as a function of her physical attractiveness and nature of the evaluations. *Journal of Experimental Social Psychology* **5**, 93–100.

Silverman, B.I. 1974: Consequences, racial discrimination and the principle of belief congruence. *Journal of Personality and Social Psychology* **29**, 497–508.

Sistrunk, F. and McDavid, J.W. 1971: Sex variable in conforming behaviour. *Journal of Personality and Social Psychology* **17**, 200–7.

Skeels, H.M. and Dye, H. 1939: The study of the effects of differential stimulation on mentally retarded children. *Proceedings of the American Association of Mental Deficiency* **44**, 114–36.

Slater, P.E. 1958: Contrasting correlates of a group size. *Sociometry* **21**, 129–39.

Smith, M.B., Bruner, J.S. and White, R.W. 1956: *Opinions and Personality*. New York: John Wiley & Sons.

Snyder, M. 1978: Seek, and ye shall find: testing hypotheses about other people. In E.T. Higgins, C.P. Herman and M.P. Zanna (eds.), *Social Cognition: The Ontario Symposium on Personality and Social Psychology* (Hillsdale. NJ: Erlbaum).

—— 1979: Self-monitoring processes. In L. Berkowitz (ed.), *Advances in Experimental Social Psychology* (New York: Academic Press), vol. 12.

Sommer, R. 1965: Further studies of small group ecology. *Sociometry* **28**, 337–48.

—— 1969: *Personal Space*. Englewood Cliffs, NJ: Prentice-Hall.

Spence, S.H. 1981: Validation of social skills of adolescent males in an interview conversation with a previously unknown adult. *Journal of Applied Behaviour Analysis* **14**, 159–68.

Spence, S.H. and Marzillier, J.S. 1979: Social skills training with adolescent male offenders: Short-term effects. *Behaviour Research and Therapy* **17**, 7–16.

Spitz, R.A. and Wolf, K.M. 1946: The smiling response: a contribution to the ontogenesis of social relationships. *Genetic Psychological Monographs* **34**, 57–125.

Sroufe, L.A. and Waters, E. 1977: Attachment as an organisational construct. *Child Development* **48**, 1184–99.

Stang, D.J. 1973: Effects of interaction rate on ratings of leadership and liking. *Journal of Personality and Social Psychology* **27**, 405–8.

Stark, P.A. and Traxler, A.J. 1974: An empirical validation of Erikson's theory of identity crisis in late adolescence. *The Journal of Psychology* **86**, 25–33.

Stein, A.H. 1972: Mass media and young children's development. *71st Yearbook of the National Society for the Study of Education*, 191–202.

Steiner, I.D. 1972: *Group Processes and Productivity*. New York: Academic Press.

Stephan, W.G. 1978: School desegregation: an evaluation of predictions made in Brown v Board of Education. *Psychological Bulletin* **85**, 217–38.

Stephenson, G. and Rutter, D. 1970: Eye-contact, distance and affiliation: a re-evaluation. *British Journal of Psychology* **61**, 385–93.

Stern, D. 1974: Mother and infant at play: the dyadic ineraction involving facial, vocal and gaze behaviours. In M.Lewis and L. Rosenblum (eds.), *The Effects of the Infant on the Caregiver* (New York: John Wiley & Sons).

Steuer, F.B., Applefield, J.M. and Smith, R. 1971: Televised aggression and interpersonal aggression of preschool children. *Journal of Experimental Child Psychology* **11**, 442–7.

Stoner, J.A.F. 1961: *A Comparison of Individual and Group Decisions Involving Risk*. Cambridge Mass: Massachussetts Institute of Technology.

Storms, M.D. 1973: Videotape and the attribution process: reversing actors' and observers' points of view. *Journal of Personality and Social Psychology* **27**, 165–75.

Strack, F., Erber, R. and Wicklund, R.A. 1982: Effects of salience and time pressure on ratings of social causality. *Journal of Experimental Social Psychology* **18**, 581–94.

Strodtbeck, F.L. 1957: Social status in jury deliberations. *American Sociological Review* **22**, 713–19.

Strongman, K.T. and Champness, B.G. 1968: Dominance hierarchies and conflict in eye-contact. *Acta Psychologica* **28**, 376–86.

Taguiri, R. 1958: Social preference and its perception. In R. Taguiri and L. Petrullo (eds.), *Person, Perception and Interpersonal Behaviour* (Stanford, Cal.: Stanford University press).

Tajfel, H. 1970: Experiments in intergroup discrimination. *Scientific American* **223**, 96–102.

Tajfel, H. and Billig, M. 1974: Familiarity and categorisation in intergroup behaviour. *Journal of Experimental Social Psychology* **10**, 150–70.

Tajfel, H. and Wilkes, A.L. 1963: Classification and quantitative judgement. *British Journal of Psychology* **54**, 101–14.

Taylor, D.W., Berry, P.C. and Block, C.H. 1958: Does group participation when using brainstorming facilitate or inhibit creative thinking? *Administrative Science Quarterly* **3**, 23–47.

Taylor, D.W. and Faust, W.L. 1952: Twenty questions: efficiency in problem solving as a function of group size. *Journal of Experimental Social Psychology* **44**, 360–8.

Taylor, S.E. and Fiske, S.T. 1975: Point-of-view and perceptions of causality. *Journal of Personality and Social Psychology* **32**, 439–45.

Taylor, S.E., Fiske, S.T. Etcoff, N.L. and Ruderman, A.J. 1978: Categorical bases of person memory and stereotyping. *Journal of Personality and Social Psychology* **36**, 778–93.

Taylor, D.M. and Jaggi, V. 1974: Ethnocentrism and causal attribution in a South

Indian context. *Journal of Cross Cultural Psychology* **5**, 162–71.

Tedeschi, J.T. and Lindskold, S. 1976: *Social Psychology: Interdependence, Interaction and Influence*. New York: John Wiley & Sons.

Tedeschi, J.T. Schlenker, B.R. and Bonoma, T.V. 1971: Cognitive dissonance: private ratiocination or public spectacle. *American Psychologist* **26**, 685–95.

Tesser, A. 1978: Self-generated attitude change. In L. Berkowitz (ed.), *Advances in Experimental Social Psychology* (New York: Academic Press), vol. 11.

Tesser, A and Conlee, M.C. 1975: Some effects of time and thought on attitude polarisation. *Journal of Personality and Social Psychology* **31**, 262–70.

Thayer, S. and Schiff, W. 1969: Stimulus factors in observer judgement of social interaction: facial expression and motion patterns. *American Journal of Psychology* **82**, 73–85.

Thibaut, J.W. and Kelley, H.H. 1959: *The Social Psychology of Groups*. New York: John Wiley & Sons.

Thomas, A., Chess, S. and Birch, H. 1970: The origin of personality. *Scientific American*, August, 11–13.

Tinbergen, N. 1951: *The Study of Instinct*. London: Oxford University Press.

Tizard, B. and Hodges, J. 1978: The effect of early institutional rearing on the development of eight-year-old children. *Journal of Child Psychology and Psychiatry* **19**, 99–118.

Tizard, B. and Joseph, A. 1970: Cognitive development of young children in residential care: a study of children aged 24 months. *Child Development* **11**, 177–86.

Tizard, B. and Rees, J. 1974: A comparison of the effects of adoption, restoration to the natural mother, and continued institutionalisation on the cognitive development of four-year-old children. *Child Development* **45**, 92–9.

Torrance, E.P 1954: Some consequences of power differences on decision making in permanent and temporary three-man groups. *Research Studies* (State College of Washington) **20**, 130–40.

Travis, L.E. 1925: The effect of a small audience upon eye-hand coordination. *Journal of Abnormal and Social Psychology* **20**, 142–6.

Triandis, H.C. 1961: A note on Rokeach's theory of prejudice. *Journal of Abnormal and Social Psychology* **62**, 184–6.

—— 1971: *Attitudes and Attitude Change*. New York: John Wiley & Sons.

Triandis, H.C. and Davis, E. 1965: Race and belief as determinants of behavioural intentions. *Journal of Personality and Social Psychology* **2**, 715–22.

Turner, J.C. 1981: The experimental social psychology of intergroup behaviour. In J.C. Turner and H. Giles (eds.), *Intergroup Behaviour* (Oxford: Basil Blackwell).

Tversky, A. and Kahneman, D. 1974: Judgement under uncertainty: heuristics and biases. *Science* **185**, 1124–31.

Valins, S. 1966: Cognitive effects of false heart-rate feedback. *Journal of Personality and Social Psychology* **4**, 400–8.

Vernon, P.E. 1933: Some characteristics of the good judge of personality. *Journal of Social Psychology* **4**, 42–58.

Vinokur, A. 1971: Cognitive and affective processes influencing risk-taking in group: an expected utility approach. *Journal of Personality and Social Psychology* **20**, 472–86.

Veitch, R. and Griffith, W. 1976: Good news, bad news: affective and interpersonal effects. *Journal of Applied Social Psychology* **6**, 69–75.

Wallace, J. and Sadalla, E. 1966: Behavioural consequences of transgression: I. The effects of social recognition. *Journal of Experimental Research and Personality* **1**, 187–94.

Wallston, B.S. and Wallston, K.A. 1978: Locus of control and health: a review of the literature. *Health Education Monographs* **6**, 107–11.

Walster, E. Aronson, E. and Abrahams, D. 1966: On increasing the persuasiveness of a low prestige communicator. *Journal of Experimental Social Psychology* **2**, 235–42.

Walster, E. Aronson, V., Abrahams, D. and Rottman, L. 1966: Importance of physical attractiveness in dating behaviour. *Journal of Personality and Social Psychology* **4**, 508–16.

Walster, E., Berscheid, E. and Walster, G.W. 1976: New directions in equity research. In L. Berkowitz (ed.), Advances in Experimental Social Psychology (New York: Academic Press), vol. 9.

Walster, E. and Walster, G.W. 1976: Interpersonal attraction. In B. Seidenberg and A. Snadoursky (eds.), *Social Psychology: An Introduction* (New York: Free Press).

Walster, E., Walster, G.W. and Berscheid, E. 1977: *Equity Theory and Research*. Boston: Allyn & Bacon.

Waterman, A.S. and Waterman, C.K. 1971: A longitudinal study of changes in ego identity during the freshman year at college. *Developmental Psychology* **5**, 167–73.

Weatherley, D. 1961: Anti-Semitism and the expression of fantasy aggression. *Journal of Abnormal and Social Psychology* **62**, 454–7.

Weiner, B. 1979: A theory in motivation for some classroom experiences. *Journal of Educational Psychology* **71**, 3–25.

Weiner, M., Devoe, S., Rubinow, S. and Geller, J. 1972: Non-verbal behaviour and non-verbal communication. *Psychological Review* **79**, 185–214.

Whiting, B.B. and Whiting, J.W.M. 1975: *Children of Six Cultures: A Psycho-cultural Analysis*. Cambridge, Mass: Harvard University Press.

Wicker, A.W. 1969a: Attitudes v actions: the relationship of verbal and overt responses to attitude objects. *Journal of Social Issues* **25**, 41–78.

—— 1969b: Size of church membership and members' support of church behaviour settings. *Journal of Personality and Social Psychology* **13**, 278–88.

Wiesenthal, D.L., Endler, N.S., Coward, T.R. and Edwards, J. 1976: Reversability of relative competence as a determinant of conformity across different perceptual tasks. *Representative Research in Social Psychology* **7**, 35–43.

Wiggins, J.A. Dili, F. and Schwartz, R.D. 1967: On 'status ability'. *Sociometry* **28**, 197–209.

Wilson, E.O. 1975: *Sociobiology*. Cambridge, Mass: Harvard University Press.

Winch, R. F. 1958: *Mate-Selections: A Study of Complementary Needs*. New York: Harper.

—— 1965: Another look at the theory of complementary needs in mate selection. *Journal of Marriage and the Family* **29**, 756–62.

Wishner, J. 1960: Reanalysis of 'Impressions of Personality'. *Psychological Review* **67**, 96–112.

Witkin, H.A., Dyk, R.B., Fasterson, H.F., Goodenough, D. and Karp, S.A. 1962: *Psychological Differentiation: Studies of Development*. New York: John Wiley & Sons.

Wolff, P.H. 1969: The natural history of crying and other vocalisations in infancy. In B.M. Foss (ed.), *Determinants of Infant Behaviour* (London: Methuen).

Worchel, S., Andreoli, V.A. and Folger, R. 1977: Intergroup cooperation and intergroup attraction: the effect of previous interaction and outcome of combined effort. *Journal of Experimental Social Psychology* **13**, 131–40.

Zajonc, R.B. 1965: Social facilitation. *Science* **149**, 269–74.

Zimbardo, P.G. 1969: The human choice: Individuation, reason and order versus deindividuation, impulse and chaos. In W.J. Arnold and D. Levine (eds.), *Nebraska Symposium on Motivation* (Lincoln: University of Nebraska Press).

Zimmerman, D.H. and West, C. 1975: Sex roles, interruptions and silences in conversation. In B. Thorne and N. Henley (eds.), *Language and Sex* (Rowley, Mass: Newbury House).

# Index

# Index

Abelson, R.P. 68, 160
Abrahams, D. 70-1
Abramson, L.Y. 142, 143, 144
'acquiescent response set' 84, 85
actor/observer differences 136-8
Adorno, T.W. 83-5
affectionless psychopathy 34
aggression 54-5, 56-7, 87
Ainsworth, M.D. 27, 28-30
Ajzen, I. 62, 78
Allen, V.L. 203
Allport, G.W. 59
Alper, T. 222
Amabile, T.M. 134-5
American Psychological Association 13
antisemitism 84, 87
Applezweig, M.H. 215
Apsler, R. 197
Argyle, M. 183, 184, 192-3
Aron, A.P. 167-8
Aronson, E. 70-1, 74-5
Aronson, S. 156
Asch, Solomon 111-13, 199-200, 202, 204
Asch paradigm 199-202
assumptions about human behaviour 3-4
attachment
    differences in 28-30
    in animals 24-5
    in early childhood 25-30
    phases in 26-7
attention 120-1
attitudes 59-79
    and behaviour 75-6, 77-9
    and cognitive dissonance 71-5
    and decision making 72-3
    and effort 74-5
    and forced-compliance behaviour 73-4
    and impression management 76
    and interpersonal relationships 156-7
    and personality 79

balance theory of 67-9
congruity principle 69-71
definition of 60-3
direct measures of 65-6
functional approach to 62-3
indirect measures of 64-5
organization of/change in 66-79
self-generated change in 76-7
self-perception theory of 75-6
structural approach to 61-2
attraction, interpersonal see interpersonal relationships
attribution 126-45
    actor/observer differences in 136-8
    and personality 139-40
    and social context 141-2
    attributional style 143-5
    biases in 134-9
    causal schemata model of 130-1
    correspondent inference model of 133-4
    covariation model of 131-3
    fundamental error in 134-6
    internal/external 129-30, 131-3, 136-9
    of depression 142-5
    self-serving bias in 138-9
authoritarian personality 83-5, 98, 213, 235
authority, obedience to see obedience to authority
autokinetic effect 198-9
Avermaet, E. Van 205

Back, K. 154
Backman, C.W. 80, 82
balance theory 67-9, 159-61
Bales, R.F. 223, 230, 231, 232
Bandura, A. 52-3, 54-5, 56
Baron, R.A. 197
Bateson, G. 67
Bavelas, A. 228-9
Bay of Pigs fiasco 241-2, 244

Beattie, G. 189, 190-1
behaviour
  and attitudes 75-6, 77-9
  causes of *see* attribution
  moral *see* moral behaviour
behavioural intention 78
behavioural style 216-18
behaviourism 3, 20, 139-40, 158-9
beliefs 60
Bell, G. 233
Bell, S.M.V. 28-30
Bem, D.J. 75-6
Berkowitz, L. 87
Berry, P.C. 223
Berscheid, E. 99, 153, 163-6, 167
Bexton, W.H. 150
Bierbrauer, G. 135
Billig, M. 94
Birch, H. 20-1, 28
birds 173
Block, C.H. 223
body language 178-9
body orientation 178
'bolstering' 72
Bonoma, T.V. 76
Borgatta, E.F. 232
Bowlby, J. 23, 24, 35
Boye, D. 99
Bradbury, R.J. 190
brainstorming 223
Brehm, J.W. 73, 74
British Psychological Society 13, 14
Brixton riots 97
Bronfenbrenner, U. 22
Bruner, J.S. 106, 114
Bugelski, R. 87
Buss, A.H. 121
Byrne, D. 149, 156-7, 158-9, 197
Byrne-Clore Reinforcement-Affect
  Model 158-9
Byrne's Interpersonal Judgement Scale
  157

Callaghan, James 191
Campbell, A.A. 98
Campbell, D.T. 90-1
Candee, D. 50, 51
Cantril, H. 107
Carlsmith, J.M. 73-4
Cartwright, D. 225
Cattell, R.B. 157
causal schemata model 130-1
causes of behaviour *see* attribution

Chess, S. 20-1, 28
childhood 18-36
  attachment in 25-30
  conceptions of 19-20
choice dilemma questionnaires 206-7
Churchill, Winston 232
Cialdini, R.B. 197-8
Clark, K. 90
Clark, M. 90
Clarke, A.C. 154
Clarke, A.D.B. 32
Clarke, A.M. 32
Clore, G.L. 158-9
coaction effects 222
Coffman, T.L. 90
cognitive consistency 66-7
cognitive dissonance 71-5
cognitive structure 67
Cohen, A.R. 74
Collins, M.E. 154
communication
  networks 228-9
  types of 170-1
  *see also* non-verbal communication
communication theory of attachment
  27-8
companionate love 164-6
'comparison level' 161-2
competition 93-4, 95-6
'complementary needs' 164
compliance 197-8
conflict 93-4
  avoidance 204
conformity 198-205, 216-17
  and Asch paradigm 199-202
  and autokinetic effect 198-9
  and group cohesiveness 225-6
  and 'groupthink' 241-4
  and personality 214-15
  and resisting group pressure 202-3
  criticism of research on 205
  explanations of 204
  factors affecting 202
  moral 46-7, 50-1
  to values 91-2
congruity principle 69-71
Conlee, M.C. 76-7
consensus-reaching 240-1
contact between groups 98-9
conversation 188-92
  hesitations in 189-90
  interruptions in 190-2
Coombs, B. 123

cooperation 99–100
Coopersmith, S. 23
correlational research 7–8
correspondent inference model 133–4
covariation model 131–3
Cox, M. 33
Cox, R. 33
Cronbach, L.H. 125
Crutchfield, R.S. 198, 200–1
Cuban missile crisis 242, 244
cuelessness 187–8
Culbert, S.A. 162
culture 21–3, 96–7, 174–6
Curtiss, S. 32
Cyril Burt scandal 12

Dann, S. 32
Darley, J.M. 99
Darwin, Charles 20, 124, 174
Davis, E. 90
Davis, K.E. 166
De Fleur, M.A. 78
Dean, J. 183, 184
deception of subjects of research 14–15
decision making 72–3, 238–45
    and 'groupthink' 241–5
    group characteristics in 240–1
    individuals v. groups 238–40
decoding 181
Defoe, Daniel 150
deindividuation 213
demand characteristics 12
depression 142–5
Deutsch, M. 154, 155, 202
development, moral *see* moral development
development, psychosocial, stages in 18–19, 39–41
discounting principle 130
distress 33
dogmatism 85
Dollard, J. 87
dominance 174, 184
Doms, M. 205
Driscoll, R. 166
Duncan, B.L. 141–2
Duncan, S. 189
Dutton, D.G. 156, 167–8
Duval, S. 120–1, 204

effort 74–5
ego
    defence of 63

development of 39–41
Ehrlich, D. 72–3
Eibl-Eibesfeldt, I. 175–6
Ekman, P. 124, 174–5, 177, 178
Ellis, G.T. 56
Elms, A.C. 214
Emerson, P.E. 26, 28
Emler, N. 51, 52
emotion 116–18
empirical method 2
encoding 181
Endler, N.S. 202
English, H.B. 157
equity theory 164–6
Erber, R. 120
Erikson, Eric 36, 38–45
Ervin, C.R. 149
'eternal triangle' 68–9
ethical considerations in research 13–15, 211
ethnocentrism 84
evaluation 155–6
evaluation apprehension 13
Evans, R.I. 88
Exline, R.V. 174, 181, 184
experimenter effects 12–13
eye-contact 27, 177, 183, 184–5, 187
Eysenck, H.J. 85–6

facial expression 124, 174–6, 177–8
facism 84–5
family influence 22
Felipe, N.J. 179
Fenigstein, A. 121
Frenkel-Brunswick, E. 83–5
Festinger, L. 10, 71, 73–4, 154, 204
Fiedler, F.E. 235–7
Fiedler's contingency theory 235–7
field studies 9–11, 15, 181
field-dependent/field-independent 109–10
Fishbein, M. 62, 78
Fishkin, J. 50–2
Fiske, S.T. 120
'floor changes' 185–7, 188–9, 190–2
Fode, K.L 13
'foot-in-the-door' technique 197
forced-compliance behaviour 73–4
foreclosure 42–3
Fraser, S.C. 197
Freedman, J.L. 197
French, R. 233
Freud, A. 32

Freud, Sigmund  166, 216
friendship choices  88-9
Friesen, W.V.  124, 174-5, 178
frustration  87
F-scale  7-8, 84-5, 214
functional approach  62-3
fundamental attribution error  134-6
Furnham, A.  194

Garland, H.A.  132-3
Gerard, H.B.  202
Gergen, K.H.  119
Gestalt psychologists  105, 111
Gibb, J.R.  224
Goldman-Eisler, F.  189
Goodman, C.C.  106
Graham, J.C.  184
'great man' theory  233-4
Griffith, W.  159
group comparisons  20
group polarization  205-8
   explanations of  208
groups  220-45
   and communication structure  228-30
   and consensus reaching  240-1
   and decision making  238-45
   and leadership  232-8
   and roles  226-7, 231-2
   and social influence  224-30
   and status  227, 241
   aspects of  220-1
   cohesiveness of  225-6
   homogeneity of  224
   processes of  230-2
   size of  223-4, 241
   structure of  224-30
   v. individuals  221-3, 238-40
'groupthink'  241-5
Guetzkow, H.  229

Haley, Alec  97
Hall, E.T.  179
Hall, J.  239-40
Hamblin, R.L.  234
hand gestures  179
Hare, A.P.  235
Harlow, H.F.  30-2, 151
Harlow, M.K.  30-2, 151
Harvey, J.H.  122, 135-6
Hastorf, A.H.  107
head nods  179
Heatherington, E.M.  33
Heider, F.  67, 128-9, 159

'Heinz dilemma'  48-9
Hemphill, J.K.  224, 234
Heron, W.  150
hesitations  189-90
heuristics  122-3
Hewstone, M.  142
Hinde, R.A.  175
Hodges, J.  33, 34-5
Hoffeditz, E.L.  157
Hollander, E.P.  215
Homans, G.C.  216
honey-bees  172-3
Hooff, J. Van  173
Hosking, D.  237
Hovland, C.I.  69-70
Hubbard, M.  119
Hyman, H.H.  85

identity  41-5
   crisis  41-3
   status of  42-5
ideology  50-1
   and personality  84-6
'idiosyncracy credits'  215-16, 227
implicit personality theory  114-15
impression management  76
impressions
   and central/peripheral traits  111-12
   and implicit personality theory
      114-15
   and stereotypes  115-16
   first  112-14
imprinting  24-5
informational pressure  201, 208
Ingham, R.  183
'ingroup'/'outgroup'  92, 141
instinct  3
institutional environments  33-4
intelligence  3, 97
Interaction Process Analysis  230-2
interpersonal relationships  147-68
   and attitudes  156-7
   and evaluation  155-6
   and fear  151-2
   and personality  157
   and physical attractiveness  153
   and proximity  153-5
   and reciprocity  155-6
   and self-disclosure  162-3
   and similarity  156-8
   balance theory of  159-61
   Byrne-Clore Reinforcement-Affect
      Model of  158-9

companionate 164–6
development of 158–63
intimate 163–8
need for other people 149–52
romantic 166–8
social exchange theory of 161–2
interruptions 190–2
intimacy
and self-disclosure 162–3
companionate love 164–6
romantic love 166–8
status of 44–5
intimacy model for eye-contact 184–5
introversion/extroversion 113
isolation 150–1

Jaggi, V. 141
Janis, I.L. 69–70, 242–3
Jaspers, J. 142
Johnson, T.J. 138
Jones, J.M. 98
Joseph, A. 33
Jourard, S. 162
jurors 113–14, 227
justice 45
system 97

Kagan, J. 27
Kahn, R. 235
Kahneman, D. 122, 123
Karlins, M. 90
Katz, D. 235
Kauffman, I.C. 32
Keech, Mrs 10
Kelley, H.H. 70, 112, 130, 131–2, 161, 222, 227
Kelman, H.C. 15, 201
Kendon, A. 182, 183, 185
Kennedy, John F. 242
Kerr, W.A. 225
Kiesler, C.A. 198
Kiesler, S.B. 198
Killian, M.N. 227
Knowles, E.S. 179–80
Kohlberg, L. 36, 45–53
Kramer, K.B. 50
Kuhn, Thomas 6

La Piere, R.T. 77–8
laboratory experiments 8–9, 181
Lage, E. 216–17
Lamberth, J. 149
Lamm, H. 207–8

laughter 173
leadership 232–8
Fiedler's contingency theory of 235–7
'great man' theory of 233–4
skills 237–8
style 234–5, 236–7
'learned helplessness' model 142–3
least preferred co-worker (LPC) 236–7
Leavitt, H.J. 229, 233
Leeper, R. 105–6
Lefkowitz, M.M. 56
Leon, M. 24
Lepper, M.R. 119
Lerner, M.J. 157
Lesser, I.M. 44
Leventhal, H. 71
Levine, J.M. 203
Levine, M.H. 183
Levinger, G. 147–9
Levinson, D.J. 83–5
Lewin, K. 234–5
Lieberman, S. 92
Likert, R. 65
Likert scale 65–6, 207
Lindskold, S. 220
Lipitz, M.E. 166
Lippett, R. 234–5
Locke, John 19
'locus of control' 139–40
longitudinal studies 20, 56
looking 27–8, 177
and 'floor changes' 185–7
and mental illness 184
and seeing 187–8
functional aspects of 184–7
intimacy model of 184–5
structural aspects of 183–4
Lorenz, K. 24
Luchins, A.S. 113

McArthur, L.Z. 132
Maccoby, E. 24
McDonald, F.J. 52–3
McDavid, J.W. 203
McDougall, W. 4
McGinnies, E. 106–7
McGrath, J.E. 224, 233
Maier, N.R.F. 112, 240
Mann, R.D. 233
Marcia, J.E. 44
Marler, P. 173
Martin, D.J. 143, 144
Marzillier, J.S. 193

Maslow, A.M. 166-7
matching hypothesis 153
maternal deprivation 30-5
   consequences of 32-5
   in animals 30-2
Matter, C.F. 179-80
memory 122-3
mental illness 184, 194
methodological issues 181-3
Middlemast, R.D. 179-80
Milgram, Stanley 13-14, 209-13, 214
Milgram's experiments 13-14, 135, 209-13
Miller, N.E. 87
Miller, R.S. 202-3
Mills, J. 74-5
Milmoe, S. 180-1
'minimum effort' principle 68, 160
minority influence 215-18
   and behavioural style 216-18
   and status/power 215-16
   in groups 226-7
Mixon, D. 211
modelling 54-7, 193
Moeller, G.H. 215
Montmollin, G. de 223
moral behaviour 51-7
   and television 56-7
   social learning theory of 53-5
moral development 45-53
   and ideology 50-1
   measuring 48-50
moral reasoning 45-8
   and moral behaviour 51-3
   levels of 46-8
moratorium 42
Morley, I. 187-8, 237
Morley, I.E. 184
Morris, W.N. 202-3
Morse, S.J. 119
Moscovici, S. 207, 216-17
Mueller-Lyer illusion 109
Mugny, G. 216, 217-18
Myers, D.G. 207-8

Naffrechoux, M. 216-17
natural experiments 10
naturalistic observation 10
nature/nurture issue 3-4
need for other people 149-52
negotiation 187-8
Nelson, D. 156-7
Nemeth, C. 217

Nesselrode, J.R. 157
Newcomb, T.M. 159-61
Nisbett, R.E. 118
non-common effects of behaviour 133
non-verbal communication 26-8, 170-94
   and conversation 188-92
   and social skills 192-4
   cross-cultural consistencies in 174-6
   in animals 172-4
   innate 174-6
   looking 177, 183-8
   methodological issues in 181-3
   signals of 176-81
normative pressure 201, 208
Novak, D.W. 157

obedience to authority 209-13
   and defiance 212-13
   and legitimacy of authority 211-12
   and willingness to perform torture 209-11
observations 6
Orlofsky, J.C. 44
Orne, M.T. 12
Osborn, A.F. 223
Osgood, C.E. 66, 69

paralanguage 180-1
Pennington, D.C. 113-14, 185
Pepitone, A. 107-8
perception 103-26
   accuracy in 124-6
   and attention 120-1
   and inferences 122-3
   and personality 108-10, 124-5
   and self-concept 118-20
   forming impressions 110-16
   of emotion 116-18
   of objects 105-7
   of similarity/difference 95
   person memory 121-2
   processes of 120-3
   self-perception 116-20
   social 107-8
perceptual accentuation 106
perceptual sensitivity 193
Perlmutter, J.V. 223
Perrin, S. 205
perseverance effect 119
person memory 121-2
personal space *see* space, personal

personality
  and attitudes 79
  and attribution 139–40
  and conformity 214–15
  and ideology 84–6
  and interpersonal relationships 157
  and perception 108–10, 124–5
  and prejudice 83–6
  and self-consciousness 121
  authoritarian *see* authoritarian
    personality
  central/peripheral traits 111–12
  implicit theory of 114–15
  warm/cold 111–12, 114–15
  *see also under individual head-
    ings, e.g.* 'tough-minded'/'tender-
    minded'; introversion/extroversion
persuasive communications 69–71
Pessin, J. 222
Pettigrew, T. 91–2
Phares, E.J. 140
physical attractiveness 153
physiological arousal 116–18, 167–8
Piaget, Jean 46
pictographic system 182
police harassment 97
Popper, Karl 5
posture 178
prejudice 5, 6, 7–9, 78, 81–101, 141–2
  and competition 93–4
  and conformity 91–2
  and contact 98–9
  and cooperation 99–100
  and culture 96–7
  and frustration 87
  and personality 83–6
  and shared beliefs 88–9
  and shared identities 89–90
  and social categorization 94–6
  and social context 96–8
  and stereotypes 90–1
  individual approach to 82–7
  institutional 97–8
  intergroup approach to 83, 92–6
  interpersonal approach to 83, 87–92
  reducing 98–101
primacy/recency effects 112–14
primates, non-human 173–4
principled reasoning 47–8
proximity 153–5

race 88–90, 96–8, 141–2
Reader, N. 157

Rees, J. 33
Regan, D.T. 137, 197
relationships *see* interpersonal relation-
  ships
research 5–15
resisting authority 212–13
resisting group pressure 202–3
Riecken, H.W. 10
risk-taking 205–7
'risky shift' 206, 208
Robertson, J. 33
Robinson, B. 188
Rokeach, M. 85, 86, 88–9
roles 226–7, 231–2
  influence of 213–14
romantic love 166–8
Rose, E.J. 98
Rosenberg, L.A. 215
Rosenberg, M.J. 68, 160
Rosenblum, L.A. 32
Rosenthal, R. 12–13
Ross, D. 54, 56
Ross, L. 119, 129, 134–5, 138
Ross, S.A. 54, 56
Rotter, J.B. 139
Rousseau, Jean Jacques 19–20
Rutter, D.R. 27, 183, 184, 185–7, 188
Rutter, M. 33, 34, 35

Sadalla, E. 197
Saegert, S. 154
Sanford, N. 84
Sanford, R.N. 83–5
Sarnoff, I. 152
scapegoating 87
Scarman Report (1982) 97
Schachter, S. 10, 116–18, 150–2, 154,
  167, 225, 226
Schaffer, H.R. 26, 28
Scheier, M.F. 121
Schiff, W. 177
Schlenker, B.R. 76
school desegregation 99
Schutz, W.C. 224
scientific method 4–5
Scott, T.H. 150
Secord, P.F. 80, 82
Segal, M.W. 154
Sekgra, F. 56
self-awareness 120, 204
self-concept 118–20
self-disclosure 162–3
self-esteem 23, 119–20, 215

self-monitoring 79
self-perception theory 75–6
self-presentation 180
self-serving bias 138–9
Seligman, M.E.P. 142, 143–5
Semantic Differential 66
shared beliefs 88–9
shared identities 89–90
Shaw, M.E. 222, 226, 229
Sheatsley, P.B. 85
Sherif, M. 93–4, 99–100, 198
Sigall, M. 156
Silverman, B.I. 153
similarity 156–8
Simon, H.A. 229
Singer, J.E. 116–18, 167
Sistrunk, F. 203
Slater, P. 223, 231, 232, 241
Slovic, P. 123
smiling 173
Smith, P.W. 88
social categorization 94–6
social cognition
    and attribution 126–45
    and perception 103–26
social comparison 204
social context 141–2
    and prejudice 96–8
social desirability of behaviour 133–4
'social distance scale' 89–90
social exchange theory 161–2
social facilitation 221–2
social identity theory 95
social inference 122–3
social influence 196–218
    and groups 224–30
    and influence of roles 213–14
    compliance of roles 197–8
    conformity 198–205
    group polarization 205–8
    minority influence 215–18
    obedience to authority 209–13
    on development 22
social learning theory 53–5
social norms 78, 92
social penetration theory 163
social psychology of experiments 12–13
social skills 192–4
social skills training 192, 193, 194
socialization
    in adulthood 38–57
    in childhood 18–36
sociobiology 4

Solem, A.R. 240
Solomon, L. 155
Sommer, R. 178, 179, 234
space, personal 179–80, 184–5
Spence, S.H. 193–4
Spencer, C. 205
Sptiz, R.A. 33
Sroufe, L.A. 28
Stanford prison experiment 213–14, 215
Stang, D.J. 202
Stark, P.A. 43
status 215–16, 227, 241
Stayton, D.J. 28, 29
Stein, A.H. 56
Steinmetz, J.L 134–5
Stephan, W. 90, 167
Stephenson, G. 183, 185, 187–8
stereotypes 90–1, 115–16
Stern, D. 27
Stoner, J.A.F. 205–7
Storms, M.D. 136
Strack, F. 120
Strodtbeck, F.L. 227, 231
structural approach 61–2
subject effects 13
Suci, G.J. 66
Sutton-Smith, B. 183
Swap, W. 154

theories 5
Tagiuri, R. 114
Tajfel, H. 94, 95
Tannenbaum, P.H. 66, 69
Taylor, D.M. 141
Taylor, D.W. 223
Taylor, S.E. 120
Tedeschi, J.T. 76, 220
television 56–7
temperament, biological differences in
    20–1
Tesser, A. 76–7
Thatcher, Margaret 191–2
Thayer, S. 177
theories 6; *see also under individual
    headings, e.g.* 'two-component'
    theory
Thibaut, J.W. 161, 222
Thomas, A. 20–1, 28
Tizard, B. 33, 34–5
Torrance, E.P. 241
torture/ill-treatment, willingness to per-
    form 209–11, 213–14
Totten, J. 137

touch 178
'tough-minded'/'tender-minded' 85–6
Town, J.P. 135–6
Travis, L.E. 221–2
Traxler, A.J. 43
Triandis, H.C. 89–90
Turner, J.C. 94–5
Tversky, A. 122, 123
'two-component' theory 167–8

validity of experiments 11–12
Valins, S. 118
Valins effect 118
values 60, 91–2
variables in research 8–9
Veitch, R. 159
Vernon, P.E. 124–5
vicarious reinforcement 54–5

Wallace, J. 197
Wallston, B.S. 140
Wallston, K.A. 140
Walster, E. 70–1, 163–6, 167
Walster, E.M. 153
Walster, G.W. 164–6
Walters, G. 90
Waterman, A.S. 43, 44
Waterman, C.K. 43, 44
Waters, E. 28
Watson, W.H. 239–40

Weiner, B. 142–3
Weiner, M. 171
Weisenthal, D.L. 202
West, C. 190
Westie, F.R. 78
White, P.K. 234–5
Whiting, B.B. 22
Whiting, J.W.M. 22
Wicker, A.W. 78
Wicklund, R.A. 120–1
Wilberforce, William 96
Wilkes, A.L. 95
Wilson, D.G. 140
Winch, R.F. 164
Wishner, J. 114
Witkin, H.A. 109
Wittig, B.A. 28
Wolf, K.M. 33
Wong, T.J. 156
Worchel, S. 99

Yarkin, K.I. 135–6

Zajonc, R.B. 154, 222
Zander, A. 225
Zavalloni, M. 207
Zimbardo, P.G. 152, 213–14, 215, 226
Zimmerman, D.H. 190